ELECTORAL MOBILIZATION
AND PUBLIC OPINION

ELECTORAL MOBILIZATION AND PUBLIC OPINION

The Venezuelan Campaign of 1973

by JOHN D. MARTZ
and ENRIQUE A. BALOYRA

The University of North Carolina Press
Chapel Hill

Copyright © 1976 by
The University of North Carolina Press
All rights reserved
Manufactured in the United States of America
ISBN 0-8078-1268-4
Library of Congress Catalog Card Number 75-34257

Library of Congress Cataloging in Publication Data

Martz, John D
   Electoral mobilization and public opinion.

   Bibliography: p.
   Includes index.
   1. Electioneering—Venezuela. 2. Elections—
Venezuela. I. Baloyra, Enrique A., 1942—   joint
JL3892.M37   329'.00987   75-34257
ISBN0-8078-1268-4

CONTENTS

TABLES

FIGURES

FOREWORD

The genesis of our study of politicization and participation in Venezuela, of which this is the first volume, dates from preliminary discussions in 1971. It built upon an earlier foundation of research and study in Venezuela that Martz began in 1962 and Baloyra in 1965, to which repeated investigation and writing accrued during the intervening years. Venezuelan democratic political campaigning was observed by Martz in 1968 and on subsequent visits in 1969 and 1972. Baloyra visited the country on three separate occasions in 1973, the last of these covering the three final months of the year, and Martz was in residence for a full year beginning in May 1973.

We must preface our writing with the expression, however inadequate, of personal and professional indebtedness to many persons and institutions, for during the years of visiting and living in Venezuela both of us have accumulated countless obligations. We must first acknowledge the unfailingly kind, sympathetic, and courteous assistance of the political leaders themselves. It has been Martz's good fortune to have known, observed, and interviewed each president of the Republic since 1958: Rómulo Betancourt, Raúl Leoni, Rafael Caldera, and Carlos Andrés Pérez. All but Leoni have been accompanied during political campaigns. During a brief visit in late 1968 Martz toured with the campaigns of Gonzalo Barrios, Rafael Caldera, and Luis B. Prieto; the pressure of time regrettably made it impossible to accompany Miguel Angel Burelli Rivas as well. In 1973 Martz spent the final six months of that campaign traveling with the entourages of presidential candidates Jesús Angel Paz Galarraga, Carlos Andrés Pérez, and José Vicente Rangel. Baloyra also traveled with Paz, and one or both of us observed and attended meetings and campaign activities of Germán Borregales, Lorenzo Fernández, Pedro Tinoco, Pedro Segnini La Cruz, and Jóvito Villalba.

During the course of campaign travels, we visited all but one state in the Republic and have been in most of them numerous times. We can only issue a blanket statement of deep appreciation to presidents and presidential candidates, and to their staffs.

Gratitude is also expressed to the many Venezuelan political activists who have so generously and warmly shared their time and consideration through the years. Besides those previously mentioned, we are especially indebted to (in alphabetical order): Fernando Alvarez Paz, Diego Arria, Antonio Casas González, Oscar Carvallo, Luis Augusto Dubuc, Mercedes **Fermín**, Eduardo Fernández, Guillermo Feo Calcaño, Leomagno Flores, Germán Lairet, Rigoberto Lanz, Rádames Larrazábal, Octavio Lepage, Esperanza Lucena, Said Moanack, David Morales Bello, Ismael Ordaz, Luis Manuel Peñalver, José Lorenzo Pérez, Juvencio Pulgar, José Elías Rivera Oviedo, José Rodríguez Iturbe, Narciso Romero, José Agustín Silva Michelena, and Enrique Tejera París.

Our gratitude is also due the faculty and staff of the Instituto de Estudios Superiores de Administración (IESA). Thanks to the kindness of Dr. Henry Gómez, Academic Director of IESA, we were able to enjoy important logistical support during our research. Even more important was the unfailing personal friendship and intellectual stimulation provided by everyone at IESA. Special mention must also be made of Gene Bigler, whose friendship, enthusiasm, and advice was of great value. The VENEVOTE political survey which provides the major source of data for this and the following volume was made possible through the professional skill of DATOS, C.A. We are appreciative to its director, Andrew F. Templeton, and to Nelson Villasmil, Domingo Acevedo, Ivar Stabilito, Pedro Rodríguez, José Vicente Alemán, and the DATOS interviewers who energetically and conscientiously labored on our behalf.

None of the study could have been undertaken without support from the National Science Foundation, which is warmly thanked. Institutional backing was also provided from the University of North Carolina, Chapel Hill, through the supplemental support of a Kenan research award for Martz. The professional skills and facilities of the UNC Institute for Research in Social Science, under the vigorous leadership of its directors, James W. Prothro during the early stages of the project and Frank Munger during the latter, have been of inestimable assistance. The aid and encouragement of our friend and colleague, Dr. Federico G. Gil, Director of the Institute of Latin American Studies at UNC, has been constant and unwavering. Martz must also express appreciation to the colleagues and staff members who made it possible for him to set aside the duties of departmental chairman during a year's absence abroad.

Indeed, we would be remiss were we not to issue a collective expression of gratitude to our many **colleagues** and associates at Chapel Hill, both political scientists and those in other disciplines with Latin American interests. The Comparative Politics discussion group in particular provided collective encouragement, criticism, and advice at several junctures of our enterprise. We are reassured by the certainty that this will continue as we move further with our project. None of this is to say, obviously, that what follows is free from errors of omission and commission, nor that any one who has helped us shares in our own shortcomings. Our own close collaboration has permitted a mutual improvement and reinforcement of our research and its reporting. Be that as it may, we willingly share responsibility for errors and flaws; they are ours, all ours.

John D. Martz
Enrique A. Baloyra
Chapel Hill, North Carolina

INTRODUCTION
Studying Political Campaigns

In 1967 Richard Rose offered the following commentary on
analyses of political campaigns: "The study of voting behavior
and the study of the behavior of campaigners are both important in
understanding politics. To date, social scientists have
concentrated much more sophisticated attention upon the systematic
study of voters. In the past quarter-century, students of voting
in America, Britain and other countries have developed rigorous and
elaborate techniques for analyzing influences upon voting behavior.
Unfortunately, we do not have a similar sophisticated conceptual
framework for studying the behavior of campaigners...."[1]
The construction of a conceptual framework, the positing of
generalizations, and the articulation and testing of empirical
hypotheses concerning political campaigning require both
cross-national comparisons and longitudinal studies of individual
politics. The paucity of theoretical formulations in the literature
forces the student of political campaigns to start from the
beginning. One could borrow a line from Duverger's now-familiar
introduction to his classic discussion of parties: a general theory
of campaigns will eventually be constructed, but only upon the
preliminary work of many profound studies; however, these studies
cannot be truly profound as long as there exists no general theory
of campaigns.[2]
The student of Latin American campaigns must first examine the
available bibliography on parties and elections. As was suggested
a decade ago--and is still largely accurate--the results of this

1. Richard Rose, Influencing Voters, p. 23. For an earlier
statement that parallels the first section of this introduction,
see John D. Martz, "Democratic Campaigning in Latin America: A
Typological Approach to Cross-National Research," Journal of
Politics 33, no. 2 (May 1971): 370-99.

2. For his original statement see Maurice Duverger, Political
Parties, p. xiii.

search are less than encouraging.[3] Any review of contemporary
political history in the region reveals elections bearing the musty
whiff of the museum-piece or of government manipulation--showpieces
of "democracy" that insult the intelligence of the people. But at
the same time, campaigns and elections have more than symbolic
meaning in some parts of Latin America. Costa Rica has held regular
elections since 1953--most recently in 1974--and its electorate has
frequently turned the governing party out of office. In Colombia
the conclusion of the sixteen-year constitutional experiment for
equal division of offices between the two traditional parties
permitted an active and vigorous campaign for national office in
1974. The peculiarities of the Mexican "single-party dominant
system"[4] raise both practical and theoretical problems that divide
scholarly opinion.[5]

This variety serves to emphasize that parties, elections, and
political campaigning are not irrelevant to the politics of the
region, suggesting rather the importance of analyzing critically
the nature of the political environment in which partisan politics
and campaigns take place. Obviously, this critical analysis would
determine the applicability of our typological approach to political
campaigns and the ultimate possibility of studying a democratic
political campaign in such a manner. In the case which we propose
to study, the initial assumption about the relevance of parties

3. John D. Martz, "Dilemmas in the Study of Latin American
Political Parties," Journal of Politics 26, no. 3 (August 1964):
509-32.

4. For a precise definition of the term, see Ronald H.
McDonald, Party Systems and Elections in Latin America, pp. 15-18.

5. Karl Schmitt reminds us that Mexican campaigns do indeed
provide a meaningful systemic function. See his "Congressional
Campaiging in Mexico," Journal of Inter-American Studies 11, no. 1
(January 1969): 93-111. A similar interpretation is endorsed by
Barry Ames in "Bases of Support for Mexico's Dominant Party,"
American Political Science Review 64, no. 1 (March 1970): 153-67.
See also W. V. Antonio and Richard Suter, "Elecciones preliminares
en un municipio mexicano: nuevas tendencias en la lucha de México
hacia la democracia," Revista Mexicana de Sociología 29 (January-
March 1967): 93-108. A different interpretation of elections and
campaigns in Mexico is proffered, among others, by Roger D. Hansen,
The Politics of Mexican Development, and Kenneth Johnson, Mexican
Democracy, A Critical View. More recently, Kenneth Coleman and
John Wanat added a new dimension to this debate in showing that
federal budgetary allocations to the Mexican states follow a
schedule of rewards and sanctions that closely follows the division
of the vote in federal elections. See their "Models of Political
Influence on Federal Budgetary Allocations to Mexican States"
(Paper delivered at the 1973 annual meeting of the American
Political Science Association in New Orleans). A revised version
appeared in Latin American Research Review 10, no. 1 (Spring 1975).

and elections is borne out by our analysis of the 1968 and the 1973 electoral campaigns for the presidency. We do not reject Myers observation that campaigns are not exclusively the preserve of democratic systems.[6] Our focus, however, is centered on conditions and circumstances that accrue within a democratic setting. If Venezuela is by no means the only such example, it qualifies by its scope, vigor, and intensity as a prototype for democratic political campaigning in Latin America.

Finally, our selection of the Venezuelan case allows us to seek a solution to Duverger's riddle. By studying two successive campaigns we are able to generate an analytical framework from the first that we may develop, refine, and expand in its application to the second. Although this in itself constitutes no guarantee of a profound understanding of political campaigning it undoubtedly provides a useful point of departure.[7]

6. David J. Myers, Democratic Campaigning in Venezuela, pp. 24-31.

7. The methodologies and research strategies of the two analyses vary somewhat. First of all, Martz followed the 1968 campaign with very limited resources and time, therefore necessarily confining his data-gathering techniques to personal interviews with candidates and staff, participant-observations of campaign trips, and archival research. This research effort produced the theoretical piece on campaigns already mentioned--see John D. Martz, "Democratic Political Campaigning in Latin America: A Typological Approach to Cross-Cultural Research," Journal of Politics 33, no. 2 (May 1971)--plus an aggregate analysis of urban voting behavior in metropolitan Caracas. See John D. Martz and Peter B. Harkins, "Urban Electoral Behavior in Latin America: The Case of Metropolitan Caracas, 1958-1968," Comparative Politics 5, no. 2 (July 1973): 523-49.

Our collaborative effort, departing from the theoretical bases laid out in the first study, properly starts with the 1973 campaign. Our research strategy was essentially twofold: first, to replicate the 1968 study and, second, to try to link the behavior of campaign actors to their evaluation by the mass public, and to link the functional consequences of campaign tactics and strategies to the behavior of the mass public.

It is also important to stress the fact that this volume primarily represents an attempt to expand and build upon the previous formulation rather than being an exercise in model-building as far as voting behavior is concerned. We plan to deal with this and related issues in a companion volume--Enrique Baloyra and John D. Martz, Political Attitudes and Political Culture in Venezuela, in preparation--and in a series of articles.

Our utilization of a national sample survey greatly adds to our inference-making capabilities and constitutes an essential component of the methodology of the second study. The survey was completed on 4 November 1973, more than a month before the election and consequently cannot be utilized as an instrument of electoral

THE LITERATURE

In considering the intellectual ancestry of our research, it is appropriate to review both the Latin American literature and the comparative writings on parties, party systems, voting, and campaigns. The Latin American studies are not numerous. For more than a decade there have been periodic pleas that political science research include more intensive investigation of political parties. One authority commended the field "to a whole generation of prospective graduate students in political science";[8] another commented bluntly that "Latin American political parties are outstanding in that very little research has been done on them."[9] Yet a full thirteen years passed between the first and second full-length studies of a Latin American political party,[10] and more recent scholarship has altered the pattern only slightly.[11] At this writing only two books exist that deal with parties on a hemispheric basis.[12]

The anticipated upsurge of Latin American "stasiology," in Duverger's terminology, evolved instead with agonizing slowness. Testimony to the continuing inattention came in disciplinary assessments of Latin American-related research appearing within the last decade.[13] The studies that do exist concentrate on parties at

---

prediction. All the batteries and questions that bear upon the subject matter that occupies us at present are discussed throughout the text. For the sake of simplicity we refer to these data as VENEVOTE.

8. Russell H. Fitzgibbon, "The Party Potpourri in Latin America," Western Political Quarterly 10, no. 1 (March 1957): 22.

9. George I. Blanksten, "The Politics of Latin America," in Gabriel Almond and James S. Coleman, eds., The Politics of the Developing Areas (Princeton: Princeton University Press, 1960), p. 479.

10. Harry Kantor, The Ideology and Program of the Peruvian Aprista Movement; John D. Martz, Acción Democrática.

11. Burt H. English, Liberación Nacional in Costa Rica; Grant Hilliker, The Politics of Reform in Peru; Franz A. von Sauer, The Alienated "Loyal" Opposition.

12. McDonald, Party Systems; and Robert J. Alexander, Latin American Political Parties.

13. See the comments of Merle Kling, "The State of Research on Latin America: Political Science," in Charles Wagley, ed., Social Science Research on Latin America (New York: Columbia University Press, 1964), pp. 168-214; Kalman H. Silvert, "An Essay on Interdisciplinary and International Collaboration in Social Science Research in Latin America," in Stanley Ross, ed., Latin America in Transition: Problems in Training and Research (Albany: State University of New York Press, 1970), pp. 105-19; and John D. Martz, "Political Science and Latin American Studies: A Discipline in Search of a Region," Latin American Research Review 6, no. 1 (Spring 1971): 73-99.

the macro level and have been more descriptive and narrative than analytical or conceptual. Little progress has been made in building theory or accumulating comparable investigation. The literature has been largely bereft of concern with party origins and the creation of loyalties. Fresh and new empirical data have rarely been generated, and the collection or utilization of existing data has been nearly as infrequent. To the extent that serious investigation has been undertaken, it has customarily been confined to examination and perusal of party doctrinal statements and effusive speeches delivered at assemblies and conventions. There has been less concern with organizational structures, systemic functions, and inputs into the policy process than with doctrine and ideology.[14]

Voting studies and electoral analyses have also been relatively slight, although attracting more scholarly attention than research on parties. The series of election factbooks and monographs[15] published by the Institute for the Comparative Study of Political Systems (ICOPS) was sometimes useful, but the data were often either unreliable or inadequate for all but the crudest secondary analysis. Perhaps unsurprisingly, the relatively long tradition of competitive party politics in Chile prior to the brutal uprooting in 1973 encouraged a disparate degree of research interest.[16]

14. For example, Edward J. Williams, Latin American Christian Democratic Parties; Miguel Jorrín and John D. Martz, Latin American Political Thought and Ideology; and Harold E. Davis, Latin American Thought.

15. Representative of the ICOPS monographs are Federico G. Gil and Charles J. Parrish, The Chilean Presidential Election of September 4, 1964, An Analysis, published in 1965, and Kenneth F. Johnson, The Guatemalan Election of March 6, 1966, which appeared in 1967.

16. Glaucio Soares and Robert L. Hamblin, "Socio-Economic Variables and Voting for the Radical Left: Chile 1952," American Political Science Review 61, no. 4 (December 1967): 1053-66; Ronald H. McDonald, "Apportionment and Party Politics in Santiago, Chile," Midwest Journal of Political Science 13, no. 3 (August 1969): 455-71; Alejandro Portes, "Leftist Radicalism in Chile: A Test of Three Hypotheses," Comparative Politics 20, no. 2 (June 1970): 251-75; Sandra Powell,""Political Change in the Chilean Electorate, 1952-1964," Western Political Quarterly 23, no. 2, (June 1970): 374-84; Arturo Valenzuela, "The Scope of the Chilean Party System," Comparative Politics 4, no. 1 (March 1972): 179-99; Steven H. Sinding, "The Evolution of Chilean Voting Patterns; A Reexamination of Some Old Assumptions," Journal of Politics 34, no. 3 (August 1972): 774-97; Robert N. Ayres, "Political History, Institutional Structure, and Prospects for Socialism in Chile," Comparative Politics 5, no. 4 (July 1973): 497-523; James W. Prothro and Patricio E. Chaparro, "Public Opinion and the Movement of Chilean Government to the Left, 1952-1972," Journal of Politics 36, no. 1 (February 1974): 2-44.

Urban studies, which have enjoyed popularity, have occasionally dwelt on electoral activities and party roles in different countries,[17] although only a few have made direct use of electoral and demographic data.[18]

Campaigns have received little attention in more general works on political parties and elections; they have even less frequently been the subjects of whole books. These are predominantly unscientific and atheoretical in the extreme; their attention to the politics of a given policy far outstrips any devoted to the theory of campaigns. Thus Kantor's work,[19] for one, is an unstructured account that includes extensive background on Costa Rican parties and electoral laws, but it is totally devoid of any theoretical framework. A more systematic analysis in the same country over a decade later provided a discussion of the 1966 contest which included strategy and tactics, the performance of party leaders, propaganda, and organization, but the essential thrust was to provide a chronological narrative, and there is little concern with conceptualization.[20] For Mexico, Schmitt has examined a provincial congressional campaign in Yucatán, stressing candidate recruitment and system-building functions of the contest. Scott's broader work on Mexican politics[21] includes an informative narrative of the 1958 presidential campaign which incorporates analyses of strategical and tactical questions, as well as what he terms "campaign devices." There are also a few scattered passages

17. Irving Louis Horowitz, "Electoral Politics, Urbanization, and Social Development in Latin America," in Glenn H. Beyer, ed., The Urban Explosion in Latin America; Wayne A. Cornelius, Jr., "Urbanization as an Agent of Latin American Political Instability: The Case of Mexico," American Political Science Review 63, no. 3 (September 1969): 833-58; Clifford Kaufman, "Urbanization, Material Satisfaction, and Mass Political Involvement: The Poor in Mexico City," Comparative Political Studies 4, no. 3 (October 1971): 295-321; William L. Furlong, "Peruvian and Northern Mexican Municipalities: A Comparative Analysis of Two Political Subsystems," Comparative Political Studies 5, no. 1 (April 1972): 59-83.

18. John D. Martz, "Costa Rican Electoral Trends, 1953-1966," Western Political Quarterly 20, no. 4 (December 1967): 888-909; Ronald H. McDonald, "Electoral Behavior and Political Development in El Salvador," Journal of Politics 31, no. 2 (May 1969): 397-419; Sandra Powell, "Political Participation in the Barriadas," Comparative Political Studies 2, no. 2 (July 1969): 195-216; also Martz and Harkins, "Urban Electoral Behavior in Latin America."

19. Harry Kantor, The Costa Rican Election of 1953.

20. John Yochelson, "What Price Political Stability? The 1966 Presidential Campaign in Costa Rica," Public and International Affairs 5, no. 1 (Spring 1967): 270-307. A more recent study, also sound in scholarship but lacking in theoretical rigor, is Michael J. Francis, The Allende Victory.

21. Robert E. Scott, Mexican Government in Transition, pp. 229-30.

elsewhere in the country-oriented literature which give some flavor of the external dynamics of campaigning.[22]   In the realm of Latin American political campaigning, the only work given to serious analysis and theory construction is David Myers's on the 1968 Venezuelan race, which built on Martz's previously cited typological approach.[23]   A fine treatment of the 1970 Colombian race employs survey data in its analysis.[24]

For the scholar in search of intellectual inspiration from previous investigations, in short, the literature is anything but rich, and the risks of pioneering largely virgin territory must be accepted. This necessary journey, moreover, can rely little on studies of systems outside Latin America. The bibliography derived from the United States and elsewhere is nearly as impoverished as the Latin American. A British scholar put it well in remarking that the task is one of developing "a conceptual framework that satisfactorily identified and relates the basic structure and processes of campaigning...."[25] The great bulk of the literature outside Latin America consists of narrow case studies.[26]

Even the classic works on political parties, including more recent writings on political development, provide little of a heuristic nature. Perhaps Bryce summarized it for generations when, after some three hundred pages dealing with parties in the United States, he lamented not knowing of any author "who has set himself

22. For example, Philip B. Taylor, Jr., Government and Politics in Uruguay, pp. 44-45; and Federico G. Gil, The Political System of Chile, p. 230.

23. Myers, Democratic Campaigning in Venezuela. The authors wish to acknowledge with pleasure the many stimulating and mutually rewarding exchanges of recent years with Professor Myers on these and related problems.

24. Judith Talbot Campos and John F. McCamant, Cleavage Shift in Colombia.

25. Rose, Influencing Voters, p. 24.

26. A much more detailed and lengthy perusal of the literature, especially as it regards Europe, the Commonwealth, and the non-Western areas, appears in Martz, Democratic Campaigning, pp. 377-81. Appreciation must be reiterated to our colleague Jeffrey Obler, who was an invaluable guide through the literature of European campaigns and elections. One work deserving citation here is Roger-Gérard Schwartzenberg, La campagne presidentielle de 1965 (Paris: Presses Universitaires de France, 1967). Schwartzenberg takes particular interest in the effect of candidate personality; he also posits thoughtful insights into the blend of "classic" and "modern" elements of campaign activity. Students of campaigns are also directed to a meticulous study of a different cultural setting in Gerald L. Curtis, Election Campaigning Japanese Style (New York: Columbia University Press, 1971).

to describe impartially the actual daily working of that part of
the vast and intricate political machine which lies outside the
Constitution...."[27] In contemporary times, the redoubtable Duverger
has a surprisingly brief discussion of campaigns, examining the
bases for financing and drawing a distinction between party and
electoral propaganda. He is content with the comment that
"elections themselves ill interpret the true state of opinion as
much as they represent it; they form it by propaganda; they impose
a prefabricated mould upon it; the party system is not only the
reflection of public opinion but also the result of external
technical factors (like ballot procedures) which are imposed upon
opinion."[28] Neumann has little to say on campaigns, although he
seems to imply that a meaningful electoral campaign would serve
certain party functions, notably the political education of the
private citizen, the channeling of communications between government
and public opinion, and the selection of leaders.[29]

In summary, the Latin American literature has largely ignored
political campaigning, with the few exceptions being strongly
nontheoretical in orientation; moreover, the major theoretical and
conceptual treatments of parties also reflect little interest in
campaigns. To this must be added the absence of relevant works by
Venezuelans. Writings on parties and related subjects are skimpy,
and political campaigning has been for the most part ignored. The
national literature can be classified under three headings:
(1) political surveys of broad historical scope;[30] (2) works
inclined toward ideological exposition;[31] and (3) partisan
narratives of party history by actual participants.[32] Similarly,

27. James Bryce, The American Commonwealth, 1: 637.

28. Duverger, Political Parties, p. 422.

29. Sigmund Neumann, ed., Modern Political Parties.

30. More notable of these include Rafael Gallegos Ortiz, La
historia política de Venezuela; Luis Troconis Guerrero, La cuestión
agraria en la historia nacional; Rodolfo Luzardo, Notas
histórico-económicas; Juan Bautista Fuenmayor, 1928-1948, Veinte
años de política; Manuel Vicente Magallanes, Partidos políticos
venezolanos; Magallanes' Los partidos políticos en la evolución
histórica venezolana; and Humberto Njaim et al., El sistema político
venezolano.

31. Readers are directed to Guillermo Feo Calcaño, Democracia
vs. dictadura; Iván Claudio, Breve historia de URD; José Rivas
Rivas, Las tres divisiones de Acción Democrática; and the several
works of Domingo Alberto Rangel, with particular reference to Los
andinos en el poder and also Los mercaderes del voto.

32. Of particular interest are Gonzalo Barrios, Los días y la
política; Rómulo Betancourt, Venezuela, política y petróleo; Rodolfo
José Cárdenas, El combate político; José Elias Rivera Oviedo, Los
social cristianos en Venezuela; and Juan Bautista Rojas, Los adecos.

writings by North Americans, whatever their merits, devote little
if any attention to political campaigns.[33] The wealth of data and
richness of analytical insight in the massive collaborative work
of Bonilla, Silva Michelena, and associates proved to be valuable
in the development of our survey instrument.[34] Unfortunately, the
scope of their work was outside our subject. The aggregate
analysis by Bunimov Parra runs only through the 1963 elections and
is limited to descriptive reviews of the percentages of the vote
by state.[35] A more recent analysis published in Venezuela is
restricted to the parroquias of Caracas, and although inferences
are made on the basis of survey data, the sample size is small and
the author was not concerned with the question of campaigning; far
more insightful are the 1974 electoral analyses of a host of
leftist leaders.[36]
      We are led, then, to three conclusions concerning writings on
campaign behavior: (1) to date students of comparative politics
have rarely gone beyond individual, discrete case studies which,
whatever their merits, have consisted of predominantly chronological
threads woven into the cultural and political fabric of the society
in question; (2) methods have not been sophisticated, failing to
articulate a general theory of campaigns and--more realistically
and less ambitiously--even to classify data and research findings;
(3) given the evident shortcomings, students who turn their

      33. Works with some degree of attention to political parties
not previously cited include Robert J. Alexander, The Venezuelan
Democratic Revolution; also The Communist Party of Venezuela; John
Duncoan Powell, Political Mobilization of the Venezuelan Peasant;
Leo B. Lott, Venezuela and Paraguay; and David E. Blank, Politics
in Venezuela.

      34. The three-volume series is composed of Frank Bonilla and
José A. Silva Michelena, eds., A Strategy for Research on Social
Policy; Bonilla, The Failure of Elites; Silva Michelena, The
Illusion of Democracy in Dependent Nations. The overall title is
The Politics of Change in Venezuela. Professors Alejandro Grajal
and Pedro Pablo Yáñez, of the Centro de Estudios del Futuro and
CENDES, thoroughly reviewed and criticized our research design as
well as our survey instrument and we are extremely grateful to them.
Professor Silva Michelena received a copy of our instrument and our
pledge of a copy of our complete data set for permanent possession
and use by CENDES. At the time of this writing, the technical
details involved in the generation of a tape copy--the
characteristics of which match the hardware available to the CENDES
staff--are being worked out.

      35. Boris Bunimov Parra, Introducción a la sociología
electoral venezolana.

      36. These later essays appear in Federico Alvarez, et al., La
izquierda venezolana y las elecciones del 73 (Caracas: Síntesis
Dosmil, 1974); for the Caracas survey, see Santiago Alejandro
Bonomo, Sociología electoral en Venezuela; Un estudio sobre Caracas
(Buenos Aires: Editorial Paidos, 1973).

attention to the study of campaigns find themselves embarking onto unchartered seas. Investigation of the politics of Western Europe has outstripped that in the less developed areas, yet there has been a cavalier neglect of campaigns. Political scientists specializing in the Latin American area have little justification for chauvinistically pointing to deficiencies of research on other parts of the globe.

DIMENSIONS OF DEMOCRATIC CAMPAIGNING: AN ANALYTICAL FRAMEWORK
     Elaboration of a scientific framework of political campaigns can benefit substantially from case studies, despite the fact that concentrating on the details of single examples precludes the testing of generalizations. Undeniably, the proliferation of such studies will eventually provide cumulative data for more systematic empirical study. Rose put it well: "The development of a conceptual framework that satisfactorily identifies and relates the basic structure and processes of campaigning is thus a matter of some academic and practical importance. Only if such a framework is developed can we begin to analyze and compare campaigns in ways leading to a more adequate explanation of the things that campaigners do and do not."[37]
     A modest but attainable preliminary objective is the articulation of an analytic typology. Ideally this may achieve both greater understanding of a particular campaign and, more importantly, suggest a means of ordering relevant data to clarify and identify the basic structure and processes of campaigning. To adopt this dual objective is to tread a middle path between presumably premature efforts at large-scale theory formulation and a more microcosmic concentration on one particular aspect of campaigning, such as electoral propaganda, finances, or television style.
     Our present effort, to repeat, grows out of previous inquiry at the time of the 1968 Venezuelan campaign, subsequently enhanced by Myers's work. At the outset, the primary direction was far more classificatory than theoretical. Granted minimal previous research on the subject, even a preliminary typological approach represented necessary spadework before more significant analysis might be undertaken. If indeed a theory of political campaigning could eventually be articulated--and that remains an open proposition-- the ordering of available information through a modest categorization of the elements of campaigns should precede such theory construction. While political science is sometimes too enamored of typologizing for its own sake, there is value in ordering pertinent components, especially where so little prior work exists. Therefore, we have begun by focusing on the classification of factors in political campaigning. There was no assumption that such activites were universally or independently decisive to a given electoral outcome. Rather, there was the belief that a systematic and concise ordering of concepts and propositions might bring deeper meaning to the data, assisting in the formulation of questions and ultimately in the

37. Rose, Influencing Voters.

positing of generalizations with potential validity beyond the discrete case study.[38]

It is precisely the possibility that campaigns may make the difference in certain kinds of electoral contests that provides us with the intellectual motivation to try to specify the conditions under which campaigns do influence electoral outcomes. Because of their transient nature campaigns help bring about not only the far too obvious "mobilization of biases" but also the creation of causal linkages between the more volatile elements of the political process: they provoke and make explicit societal cleavages, crystallize public opinion about issues and policies, adjust the differences between the perceived and the real strength of the parties, and may even help to redistribute some income. In brief, the functional consequences of campaigning may represent idoneous vehicles for political change.[39]

Following this rationale we utilize three broad rubrics in our conceptualization: (1) the political and institutional environment, (2) the mobilization of forces, and (3) the processes of implementation. Together they constitute a campaign system, in which a finite number of functional and causal relationships between

38. We are aware of the plethora of available and complementary conceptualizations that strengthen our analysis. Game theory, decision-making theory, and coalition analysis seem to be the more obvious. Yet at this early stage in our inquiry we will content ourselves with a partial formalization of our framework. That is to say, we will attempt to state our assumptions, hypotheses, and propositions in a language that is consonant with them.

39. Clearly, democratic campaigning is compatible with certain kinds of political regimes. However, the possibility of conducting limited campaigning in authoritarian regimes may create or exacerbate crises of legitimacy for these regimes. The Venezuelan experience of the years between 1936 and 1958 clearly indicates this concrete possibility--more on this in ch. 1. Conversely, the Chilean tragedy suggests that democratic campaigning may help to precipitate the demise of democratic regimes. Along similar lines, Guillermo O'Donnell's analysis of the Argentine campaigns which excluded the Peronists suggests that we have a considerable distance to travel in order to determine the boundaries of inquiry. See O'Donnell, Modernization and Bureaucratic Authoritarianism. Finally, to keep the list of possible combination of factors short, Giovanni Sartori's concept of "polarized pluralism" provides a case in which democratic campaigning would be feasible but not very helpful--given the low probability of turnover as a result of centrifugal cleavages and the proliferation of minor parties. See "European Political Parties: The Case of Polarized Pluralism," in Joseph LaPalombara and Myron Weiner, eds., Political Parties and Political Development, pp. 137-76.

its constituent elements creates a transient arena of political activity. Structural differentiation and role specialization are clearly discernible in this arena, providing a functional boundary between it and other aspects of the political process.[40]

THE POLITICAL AND INSTITUTIONAL ENVIRONMENT

Clearly, campaigns do not take place in a vacuum and cannot be extricated from the body politic. An examination of the political and institutional environments becomes a logical and inevitable starting point for analysis because these environments are the most important factors in the crystallization of a democratic campaign system. Two environmental agents seem to have particular importance: the party system and the ground rules affecting electoral competition. By "party system" we do not merely mean the number and nature of the parties and the degree of competition, but also the relationships between the distribution of partisan loyalties and the patterns of political cleavage,[41] the distribution of opinion about relevant issues and policies,[42] and the nature of

40. The notion of "system" may introduce more problems than it solves, but we would advance two considerations concerning our tentative use: first, we believe that all three dimensions are related and we expect to bear this out in our analysis. Furthermore, we are prepared to describe the "functionally related" parts included in each dimension, and--in subsequent chapters--the relationships between these dimensions. The notion of system seems appropriate although we recognize the transient nature of this "unit in an environment." Second, we want to dramatize and to underline the fact that campaigning not only concerns the activities that will identify as contained in "processes of implementation" but also includes a set of more stable components of the political process. Thus, we are trying to achieve a theoretical closure involving the activities traditionally identified as "campaigning," and the institutional, political, and electoral factors that impinge on campaigning.

41. There are many different ways to state the question of the nature of the relationship between socioeconomic and cultural cleavages and partisan loyalties. Following the comments of Lipset and Rokkan we could write: "In this volume the emphasis (concerning this question) will be on conflicts and their translation into party systems....Our concern in this introductory discussion...is with parties as alliances in conflicts over policies and value commitments within the larger body politic...." Seymour Martin Lipset and Stein Rokkan, eds., Party Systems and Voter Allignments, p. 5.

42. Independent of the arguments about "voter rationality," "modal opinion," and "issue convergence between candidates and voters," we would simply put forward the proposition that parties try to develop satisfactory responses to the public's preferences regarding salient issues and policies. In more established party systems parties probably are identified with issues more readily.

the belief systems of the mass public.   We adopt this very broad
notion of party system for two reasons: first, party competition
may tell us if democratic campaigning is possible or not, while
other features may have their own, indirect influence on
campaigning. Second, to limit the notion of electoral competition
to that of party competition is tautological and simplistic.[43]
    In short, a first wave of analysis must concern itself with
the nature of party competition and a description of the other
features of the party system that are relevant to campaigning.
These dimensions are very much a part of the campaign system in that
they act as structural constraints to the changes in beliefs,
attitudes, partisan loyalties, and other aspects which may be
"produced" through campaigns.[44] However, we do not cover all
dimensions of competitiveness with our preliminary analysis.   A
second step is necessary, relating to a factor that both reflects
and reinforces party competition: the operational ground rules
within which the campaign competitors function. Two types of rules
may be distinguished: the constitutional and the electoral.

The important point for us is that this is another dimension of the
party system that becomes salient through campaigning.

    43. For the moment, we are content to adopt tentatively
McDonald's classification of party systems--including the
single-party dominant, the two-party competitive, the multiparty
dominant, and the multiparty loose--as sufficiently heuristic for
our purposes. McDonald, Party Systems, p. 17. Obviously, the
concern is with the ability to differentiate between hegemonic and
turnover situations.

    44. In part, elections and electoral campaigns are necessary
because parties and party systems are not totally efficient in their
integrative and representative functions. It is axiomatic that the
distribution of partisan loyalties and the distribution of the
vote are never the same. Otherwise, a census of party affiliates
would do the job. Moreover, we know that partisan loyalties change
over time, and that there are shifts in the distribution of party
loyalties that follow much slower changes in the socioeconomic
structure. Campaigners try to work on those elements of the makeup
of the electorate that can be more easily changed. Thus, one
cannot try to change demographic characteristics of the electorate,
but one can try to erode whatever identifications exist between
certain parties and minorities. This is, in part, why the scrutiny
of electoral trends--both secular and recent--is a necessary
companion of this first wave of analysis. Customarily, trend data
of electoral statistics are used to make inferences about
competitiveness and/or to classify a particular election, placing
it in a larger context. See the classic studies by V. O. Key,
"A Theory of Critical Elections," Journal of Politics 17, no. 1
(February 1955): 3-18 and "Secular Realignment and the Party
System," Journal of Politics 21, no. 2 (May 1959): 198-210.

Constitutional norms sometimes describe the conditions and
limitations under which the campaign may take place,[45] while
electoral rules provide more specific meaning to the skeletal
constitutional rules.

Among the latter, some "technical" details may be amenable to
manipulation for partisan advantage.[46]   For instance, the form of
the ballotingusually receives considerable attention in Latin
America.   Furthermore, in systems of proportional representation,
the question of electoral quotients is central to the thinking of
the minor candidates.   In Venezuela, for instance, the adoption of
an electoral quotient in addition to more orthodox application of
proportional representation has contributed directly to the
proliferation of presidential candidates.[47]   Both types of rules

45. The type of issues that constitutional ground rules deal
with include questions like: Is the national system presidential
or parliamentary? Are elections fused or staggered? What is the
prevailing basis of representation? What are the participatory
regulations for the exercise of the suffrage? Criteria for voter
elegibility have been usually elaborated around one or more of the
following: age, sex, literacy, income, place of birth, and
civilian or military status. Constitutional rules also engage in
the regulation of the electoral process itself, creating independent
electoral commissions and/or utilizing the military in order to
supervise the voting process and the counting of ballots.

46. Electoral rules concern themselves with more pedestrian
but no less significant aspects. In Latin America, these rules are
often intricately complex, and they were frequently the basic
motivation for palace revolts in the nineteenth century. In many
cases, manipulation of these rules served to deliver the election
to the actors doing the manipulation.

In actual practice, the scrupulous observance of these rules
may do more to stimulate public support for the institution of
elections than the quality of the candidates and the parties
themselves. In a thoughtful study, Jack Dennis tried to
differentiate between "the perceived efficacy of one particular
election" and the level of public support for the electoral process
itself. See "Support for the Institution of Elections by the Mass
Public," American Political Science Review 64, no. 3 (September
1970): 819-35. Following the division we have tried to introduce
between the more permanent and the more transient elements of the
party system, we turn to a distinction between these two types of
opinion regarding elections by the mass public. In Latin America,
electoral rules also concern electoral census, party registration,
audits, rules concerning "null voting"--the casting of blank
ballots--and the form in which the actual voting act will take
place.

47. As described later in full, a marginal presidential
candidate in Venezuela may, through application of the electoral
quotient, gain a congressional seat, thus, the phenomenon of
"presidential" candidates running for a congressional seat!

normally discriminate against some type of fringe or radical, minor participant such that we can rarely talk about a completely competitive, truly unrestricted electoral process.   In Latin America and elsewhere total governmental control of campaigning and balloting shuts the door to democratic campaigning.   However, attempts by the government party to manipulate procedural rules and utilize the resources of the state for its own ends are not confined to authoritarian regimes.   Party competition, then, creates and fosters the environment of democratic campaigning; operational rules help institutionalize the political environment of democratic campaigning.

MOBILIZATION OF FORCES
     Having thus defined the political and institutional environment and identified campaign boundaries and constraints, we turn to a more readily identifiable area: the mobilization of forces.   Here our concerns are four: candidate selection, campaign organization, strategies and tactics, and ideologies and programs. The choice of the campaign leader, the organization of his advisers and supporters, the elaboration of strategy, and the ideological and value premises for their choices are all integral components of the process.   Nominating a candidate is a reasonable and important starting point.   Pre-convention forces and pre-candidacies within a party (if its choice is made by means of a nominating convention) must be studied.   The existence of rival factions, with or without doctrinal differences, may well influence subsequent campaign decisions, orientations, and the degree of organizational strength and flexibility.   Venezuela offers conclusive evidence that party divisions, sown by struggles for the nomination, can change the entire course of the electoral process--thus creating, through feedback, the conditions for changes in the "environment" and in the policy itself.   Moreover, the fact that the process through which a party or coalition selects its candidate is frequently ad hoc, lacking the patina of institutionalization, creates the strong possibility that the candidate's legitimacy will be in question from the very beginning.   Presidential intervention, manipulation by party notables, and unwillingness to accept the results of the selection process are a few of the weapons that can destroy their users.
     It may be as the result of frustrated ambitions that additional, "independent" candidates emerge.   In addition, self-declared candidates may avoid party nomination struggles and seek instead an alliance of disparate forces.   Their initial campaigning may be intended primarily as a means of demonstrating popularity, thus persuading uncommitted forces to join their ranks. The eventual emergence of a major electoral contender may thereby take shape without the prior convening of a convention.   A variation of the same theme may ensue if a significant sector of the electorate is deprived of its favorite candidate through illness, absence, or constitutional disqualification.   The process of candidate selection therefore extends beyond the orthodox

nominating procedures of large parties, including the formation of electoral coalitions and alliances.

One pattern involves a coalition of two actors: one major, one minor. The scale of incentives would not be the same for both because their expectations would differ: the major partner would try to win the election with the extra votes of the minor; the goals of the minor become incremental, hoping to gain in strength and prestige through a share in patronage. This we term a <u>coalition of unequal partners</u>, while a second type is a <u>coalition between equal partners</u>. This latter type brings together two or more parties that are incapable of winning by themselves. Such a coalition is relatively unstable in that the nomination of a candidate is accomplished by two methods: the selection of an independent, nonparty notable or by the election of a leader of one of the partners through <u>ad hoc</u> procedures. A third type brings together a series of actors who may or may not differ in their relative strength, but who find it expedient to form a common front. More homogeneous than the other two types, this <u>sectoral coalition</u> is the type of phenomenon associated with the formation of "popular fronts" in Latin America and is predicated on a similarity of interest and ideological goals. The three types do not fulfill the criteria of exclusiveness and exhaustiveness but seem to be the more frequent. In our subsequent dissection of the Venezuelan case, we will classify not only the coalitions but also their members, identified as either "major" or "minor" by placing in the second category those parties or coalitions unlikely to attract more than 10 **percent** of the total vote.[48]

Attention will then shift to campaign organization. General characteristics of the parties act as environmental **determinants of** the type of campaign organization their candidates could have. Consistent with other relationships between campaign features and campaign environment, the organization of a candidate's campaign may reproduce some of the structural features of the party; however, we must always be aware that the candidate may choose to run his own

48. Such determinations are clearly subject to criticism: in a two-party system, for example, or even in what McDonald terms "multiparty dominant"--one in which the "winner" receives between 40 and 60 percent of the vote--the terminology would simply have to be altered. See McDonald, <u>Party Systems</u>, p. 17. A viable option for Venezuela was proposed by Myers for the 1968 race in the form of a trichotomy embracing major, minor, and marginal. Those under 5 **percent** **would** be marginal; from 5 to 20 percent, minor; and over 20 percent, major. Myers, <u>Democratic Campaigning in Venezuela</u>, p. 31. This is a fully defensible position, but we believe that the continuing proliferation of Venezuelan parties and candidates, with the concomitant fragmentation of the electorate, mitigates against meaningful distinctions of the "minor-marginal" type. The high fluidity of the party scene further suggests the inadvisability, by 1973, of employing other than a dichotomous schema.

show. In any event, having specified the backdrop of party
organization[49] in the preliminary description of the party system,
we turn to the structure of campaign organizations. Five
dichotomies are offered for this analytical task: centralization
versus decentralization, fusion versus diffusion, regularization
versus specialization, institutionalization versus personalization,
and endogenous versus exogenous financing. These are set forth as
ideal types, and each of the five deserves further exposition.[50]

It must be said by way of introduction that the organizational
structure of the campaign may have as many as five bodies or groups
through which the campaign activities may be devised, channeled,
and implemented: national party headquarters, a special electoral
commission, the candidate(s) and personal staff (notably in
presidential campaigns), regional and local party, and independent
groups representing the interests of various private sectors. In
a given campaign we may be able to observe some or all of these
formulations. The relationships among and between them may assume
various permutations. A simplified representation of these
relations is suggested in figure 1. Our examination of Venezuelan
campaign organizations will show several forms. In the event of
a multiparty alliance, of course, the overall structure will
necessarily become more complex, given the inclusion of organs from
more than one party. The basic structural patterns, however, will
remain within these five sets of characteristics.

The centralization-decentralization dimension relates
fundamentally to vertical organizational control, centering on
relations between national and regional or local headquarters.
National leadership may exercise tight control over the campaign
at lower levels or it may permit a substantial degree of local
autonomy. A centralized structure need not ignore or overlook its
local leadership, but in the final analysis overall supervision and
control will be exerted from above, with directives passing from the
top to lower echelons. We hypothesize that the probability of

49. Organizational features of the parties refer to whether
they are weakly articulated or rigidly structured, prone to local
influence and decentralized control or to democratic centralism.
The assumption holds that prevailing tendencies are expected to
carry into the campaign apparatus.

50. Since campaigning is usually conceptualized as a process,
and because of the notion of a transitory campaign system being
utilized, we prefer to state the polar types of each dichotomy in
dynamic rather than static terms. This will not prevent us from
saying that someone's campaign was "fused" or "decentralized" in
order to shed some light on the particular campaign being described.
However, it would be an exercise in futility to assign static
characteristics to short-lived phenomena.
While speaking about ideal types we clearly anticipate a blend
of traits, although we would not be startled by the occasional
appearance in reality of ideal types in relatively pure form.

FIGURE 1. The Structure of Campaign Organization. Solid lines
represent the anticipated direction of relationships between
different groups; broken lines indicate further possible
relationships that may appear. Although a direct relationship
between national and local headquarters is both conceptually and
practically possible, no arrows have been drawn in to represent
these relationships.

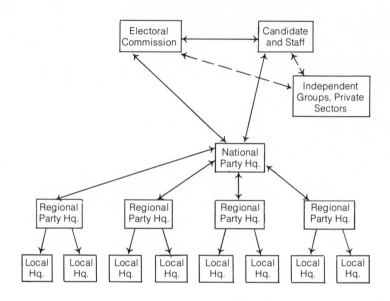

centralization is greatest in a presidential campaign, whereas
congressional or local elections, when not held concurrently with a
presidential race, will more likely be decentralized. In the latter
case, congressional or municipal candidates may well prefer, indeed
request, that national leaders not participate in the campaign; on
the other hand, the visits by such leaders may be perceived as
important for the achievement of victory. Where a presidential
contest is held simultaneously with congressional or local elections,
it is our working hypothesis that centralization and strong vertical
organizational control is the more effective form.

The fusion-diffusion dimension, in contrast, describes the
nature of horizontal control and is most pertinent in the analysis
of coalition campaigns. Presuming reasonably similar party
organizations for the partners, fusion is accomplished by effective
communications back and forth between the component members,
including at the apex a unified body that can assure the authority
of the campaign and enforce smooth horizontal transmission of
information and effective control. The fused model therefore
insures an association and sharing of privilege, authority, and

overall campaign activities. Fusion is most effective if centered
in a single body including representatives of all members of the
coalition and the presidential candidate himself. In the absence
of any such organ, even the most forceful candidate is unlikely to
enjoy effective authority; horizontal communications will be
incomplete and distorted, and the resulting form will be diffused.
Effective fusion, we hypothesize, will be more difficult in a
coalition of more than two members. The fusion-diffusion dimension
may operate in parallel fashion where independent, nonparty entities
are incorporated into the campaign, and relations between the party,
candidate, and affiliated independent sectors may be delicate in
the extreme.

Regularization-specialization is an axis that pertains to the
national level of organization. In organizations clustered around
the regularization pole we find that the quest for support is
primarily conducted within the existing party framework.
Specialization is the result of the decision by the leadership or
the candidate to establish a separate structure--frequently an ad
hoc electoral commission. The relationship between national party
headquarters and the electoral commission can vary but must be
close if the latter is to serve as a positive instrument for the
party. The electoral organ, customarily smaller in size than the
national party directorate, will be composed of a few ranking party
leaders with overlapping membership in the directorate, a team of
advisers and experts with specialized talents in campaigning, and,
obviously, the candidate himself. Composition of the ad hoc unit
may also be flexible, with its normal membership expanded or opened
to representatives of independent sectors in the case of a fused
system of horizontal control.

It is important to distinguish the functions of policymaking
and implementation in the specialized form. The electoral
commission may be central to the planning and operation of a
national campaign, strongly influencing the candidate himself;
however, its major contribution may well be almost purely technical,
while the candidate makes his strategic and tactical choices apart
from the commission. Where a staff of workers, technicians, and
advisers is drawn from within and without the regular party
structure, a candidate may be reluctant to go beyond the use of its
expertise. Similarly, the degree of autonomy exercised by the
electoral commission may be substantial. We will look at the
Venezuelan case for possible confirmation of our belief that
creation of a specialized campaign structure has become the
prevalent pattern. Moreover, with the multiplication of
increasingly complex problems of propaganda, voter mobilization, and
media salesmanship, we will advance the hypothesis that the
successful campaign must be specialized rather than regularized.

Another important organizational facet is the presidential
candidate and his staff. In some cases it is little more than an
accompanying entourage that makes travel arrangements, facilitates
liaison on minor matters, and frees the candidate from routine
personal concerns; thus it will consist in large part of travel
organizers, chauffeurs, luggage carriers, bodyguards, photographers,

and the like. Other times, however, a personal staff may provide
significant advice and counsel to the candidate, apart from the rest
of the campaign structure; this presents us with the
personalization-institutionalization dimension. The relationships
among the candidate's staff, the party directorate, and the
electoral commission may not necessarily be smooth, and considerable
friction may develop.

A candidate chosen from the ranks of independents may rely
heavily upon a nonparty personal staff. If the candidate of a
multimember coalition, he may feel particularly attracted to a body
of advisers with differing party loyalties and commitments. This
personalization will lead the candidate to include relatives,
friends, former business associates, and others who have not been
among the party faithful over the years. Similarly, such a
candidate may insist that this personalization extend to the
electoral commission. Personalization is also probable in new
nations, where the parties themselves are newly founded and seeking
recognition through identification with outstanding nominees.
Another form of personalization concerns the candidate who has
emerged as the perennial nominee of his party after years of
partisan labor. Such a candidate may limit his personal staff to
the role of a traveling entourage, in which case the arrangement is
clearly institutionalized. Where a personal staff does play a
politically relevant part, it will customarily be smaller than the
electoral commission, just as the latter in turn is more limited in
membership than the party directorate.

Finally, consideration of campaign organization must deal with
the question of campaign finances. Many students of parties and
elections have commented on the difficulty, if not the impossibility,
of collecting data on campaign finances.[51] As an initial step, one
can suggest that endogenous versus exogenous sources of campaign
finances are a relevant subject to be explored. By endogenous
financing we mean a situation in which the campaigners rely very
heavily on membership contributions; exogenous financing implies
that the campaign cost is mainly underwritten by actors outside
the party. An important hybrid of the two types occurs when a
government party makes covert use of the financial resources of the
state. Myers describes this situation well: "Here the party in
power uses the personnel, institutions and resources of the
bureaucracy to enhance its image and chances for reelection. Since
propaganda emanating from bureaucracies can be duplicated by other
parties only at great expense, the government itself becomes an
important source of campaign financing."[52] Campaigners try to
combine all possible sources of financing. In monetary terms we can

51. An initial effort in the analysis of the American case has
been made by Delmer D. Dunn, Financing Presidential Campaigns.
Dunn builds on the pioneering efforts of Alexander Heard in his The
Costs of Democracy.

52. Myers, Democratic Campaigning in Venezuela, p. 34.

also speculate that loans, securities, bonds, and even personal
estates and inheritances are not beyond the reach of avid
campaigners. Also, the utilization of party members or volunteer
workers helps cut down campaign costs.

A study of strategies and tactics is no less deserving of
careful scrutiny. At the outset, attention must be directed to the
fundamental objectives of the campaigners; once again we stress the
assumption that the scale of inducements is not the same for all
campaigners although we will concern ourselves with two types of
campaign goals: the electoral and the institutional. In the first
case, the goal is the immediate achievement of political power, the
basic concern is the achievement of national office, gaining the
maximum in political power and influence, and, in the case of fused
elections, seeking the largest possible congressional representation.
But Duverger is quite correct in calling for a distinction "between
true electoral propaganda, carried out by the candidate in his
attempt to secure election, and party propaganda at election time,
which aims at spreading party doctrine, extending its influence and
increasing its membership."[53] Whether the objective is immediate
success at the ballot box or a strengthening of party organization
and doctrine for the long haul is an empirical question.
Institutional objectives exist where the contender is not
anticipating victory, but rather is campaigning to enhance prospects
for a future contest. Emphasis may therefore be placed on clear
educational appeals directed toward the strengthening of party
doctrine, organization, candidate visibility, and a broadened
electoral base.

Turning explicitly to strategies and tactics, we treat the
former as more general, overarching electoral plans, and the latter
as manipulative efforts to implement strategies. Strategies fall
into two broad types: consensual and conflictual. Each in turn
has two subtypes. The consensual may be oriented toward
reinforcement and recruitment, both essentially positive in nature.
The reinforcement strategy places a premium on the retention of
existing supporters and followers. Most efficacious where a
well-established political party enjoys strong voter identification,
this strategy maximizes the salience of existing loyalties; in
baldest terms, it responds to the well-known imperative to "get out
the vote" on election day. The recruitment strategy, which is
complementary of the reinforcement strategy but not uniquely
associated with it, seeks the support of nonmembers, whether
independent, previously indifferent, or new voters about to cast

53. Duverger, Political Parties, p. 366. A note of caution is
in order concerning the use of content analysis in an attempt to
identify the "real" goals of campaigners. It is an arduous and
difficult task, if approached in this manner, because most
campaigners try to convince the public that they can "win" and, to
that effect, try to disguise their true objectives as best they can.
Obviously, financial sources of support may dry up very quickly for
those who admit that they are not in the contest to win.

their first ballot. Whatever the exact proportion of unaffiliated
voters in a political system, it will customarily be sufficiently
large to have a potentially decisive impact in all but the more
one-sided contests. We believe that this is a universal feature of
most contemporary competitive systems. To summarize, a
well-established party utilizes a consensual strategy to achieve
two basic intermediate objectives: expansion of its hard-core
support and an increase in the number of its marginal supporters.

   Distinguished from such consensual strategies are those we
call conflictual. Essentially negative in tone and cast,
conflictual strategies include two subtypes: realigning and
discrediting. The realigning strategy attempts to win away
supporters from rival candidacies. Opponents' alleged weaknesses,
failures to comply with earlier political promises, and inability to
fulfil present commitments are outlined. Their supporters are
encouraged to believe that grievances can be rectified and resolved
only by a switch in loyalty. The most negative and potentially
destructive of strategies is discrediting. Here the opponent is
attacked frontally, with the ultimate aim nothing less than the
obliteration of credibility. Assaulting the opponent, attempting
to weaken and divide his support and contribute to his removal from
serious contention, the discrediting strategy is especially
advantageous when directed against an electoral alliance or
coalition. Discrediting strategies are also well suited to those
parties and coalitions that are trying to undermine "the system."
They are, consequently, an apt weapon for those campaign
participants trying to introduce drastic modifications in the party
system. In figure 2, we provide a summary of our discussion.

FIGURE 2. Campaign Policies

Type of Strategy	Goal	Instrument	Criteria
Consensual	Maximization of own votes	Reinforcement, recruitment	Consensus
Conflicting	Minimization of others' votes	Realignment, discrediting	Conflict

   As "maneuvers for the implementation of strategies," tactics
may be classified as those of inducement and disinducement, in both
cases relying upon a blend of material and symbolic arguments.
Both can be utilized as instruments for the factorization of the
goals of consensual and conflictual strategies. Material
inducements go well with consensual strategies since they include a
broad repertoire of commitments to jobs, services, desired policies
and, fundamentally, a promise of rewards in exchange for votes. The
voter may be reminded of past achievements and commitments, or
receive promises for the future. The incumbent party will
predictably stress the achievements of the outgoing administration

while pledging its continuation and extension for the new
constitutional period. A former government party, campaigning in
the role of opposition, will remind the voter of its past
accomplishments, suggesting greater and more glorious times if only
restored to office. Symbolic inducements are oriented toward
identification with objects and values of which the voters approve.
This can suggest the strength of symbolic association with the
party, its present and past leaders, or the legitimacy of the
system. Certain appeals to nationalism and to pride in great
historical figures may also be employed. Very bluntly, the
question here is who can wave the flag hardest.

When material and symbolic inducements are combined with the
goals of conflictual strategies, the opposite side of the coin
turns up. Material disinducements are then utilized to instil
fears concerning the possible loss of present standards of living,
income, purchasing power, and the like for the electorate at large.
A similar scenario is unveiled for the benefit of the party
faithful concerning the material consequences of an electoral
defeat in terms of the loss of rewards, patronage, and power.
Symbolic disinducements come readily to the architect of a
conflictual strategy in that it allows the articulation of threats
concerning the probable ascension of unpopular values and or
orientations, deviant conceptions of the dominant culture, and
foreign-oriented beliefs that threaten to inflict blows to the
national prestige.

The final aspect of the mobilization of forces concerns the
role of ideologies and programs in the campaign. Analysis of the
former deals with campaign competitors' fundamental orientation
and with systems of beliefs and values. It underlines the salience
of what, for lack of a better term, can be construed as "party
doctrine." Party doctrine is articulated within the context of a
cataloguing of national socioeconomic and political conditions,
accompanied by explanations of their desirability and the party's
position with respect to them. The literature suggests that
feedback loops operate to adjust discrepancies between party
doctrine and clientele interests, but the issue is still far from
settled as to how this really operates and which of the two
flows--party to clientele or the reverse--is stronger. In any
event, party doctrine is malleable and can always be subordinated
to the candidate's platform, with the party program inevitably
legitimized as congruent with party doctrine. What platforms and
programs usually reflect, at a less global and more mundane level,
are prevalent national issues and the candidates' responses to
them.

PROCESSES OF IMPLEMENTATION
The third major dimension brings us to the public activities
of the campaign. This is what has traditionally been called "the
campaign," but must bring into the picture both environment and
mobilization. This is the area of the public electoral crucible
in which all the preparations and struggles--from candidate
selection and organizational inventiveness to the design of

strategies and tactics, with or without a doctrinal framework--
remain to be tested. With the candidates themselves providing the
main axes of activity, it seems appropriate to begin with <u>candidate</u>
<u>style</u>.

A major determinant of public campaign activities is the
candidate himself. This factor is always included as a major one
in the explanation of voting decisions; candidates attract attention
to individual abilities and, for many voters, the image projected
during the campaign will be their most important, if not decisive,
perception. No presidential contest can be devoid of personality
issues, and never within the cultural milieu of Latin America. The
daily appearances of the candidate, his image both on the campaign
trail and through the media, and the projection of his capacity
before the issues and needs of the day--all go into the personal
style of the candidate and blend into questions of information and
political communications. Whatever the style, whatever the
programmatic message and the organizational structure, effective
and unremitting political communications carry the burden of
reaching the electorate. While forms of communication are varied
and their configuration unending, for analytic purposes they may
be compressed into a pair of ideal types. A French scholar has
argued persuasively that such communication can be identified as
either "modern" or "classic."[54] The former is oriented toward the
mechanisms of the mass media and contemporary public relations,
while the latter involves traditional and time-honored techniques
of extensive candidate appearances at rallies and mass demonstrations
throughout the country.

In the present study, activities typifying modern and classic
forms are distinguished as either presentational or participatory,
with the role of the audience--here the electorate--being the
decisive variable. A study of <u>presentational techniques</u> focuses
largely on the activites of the mass media. Political preferences
and affiliations of the press are of great importance to campaign
contenders. Radio and television are also ready sources of
communication; the Venezuelan case will show heavy emphasis on both,
with a high degree of professional expertise. The appeals and
appearances of a candidate and his campaign will be reaching voters
who may or may not constitute an interested and responsive audience.
Whatever the effectiveness or **sophistication** of the techniques
employed, then, there is an inevitable depersonalization with
presentational techniques. Thus the role of the audience is one of
passivity rather than involvement.

Indeed, one of the fundamental distinctions between
presentational and participatory techniques is that the former
relies on a mechanical process that intervenes between the candidate
and the mass audience.[55] In figure 3, which simplistically depicts

54. Schwartzenberg, <u>La campagne presidentielle de 1965</u>, pp.
67 ff.

55. We realize that one could, at this point, produce a
fourfold table yielding the combination of (1) projection of
candidate style--modern or classic--by (2) communication technique--

FIGURE 3. Campaign Communications

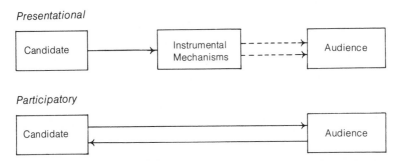

the candidate-audience communication, we see that presentational
methods introduce a filtering process that may distort or dilute
the candidate's message; furthermore, there is little responsive
feedback from the audience. This is not the case with the
participatory methods. Presentational communications also fail to
reach the voter who is without access to printed news, is
uninterested, or is functionally illiterate. The listener and the
viewer may also be beyond the reach of radio and television. And
of course, in the horrified nightmares of candidates' media experts,
he may become bored or irritated and simply turn the knob on the
set. A candidate who relies on the mass media, in short, benefits
greatly from the potential size of the audience but suffers from
the countervailing problems of media filtering, audience passivity
and disengagement, and depersonalization of his campaign message.
    Participatory techniques have quite different strengths and
weaknesses. Extensive campaign tours by party leaders and by the
candidate himself inject a strong dose of personality, strengthening
the public perception of the candidate and his style. The immediacy
of personal appearances and of direct contact convey a sense of
humanity and involvement that presentational techniques cannot hope
to equal. When a candidate or other political leader appears at a
mass rally in a small rural town, the personal exchange with that
small segment of the electorate, often on a one-to-one basis, has
an immediate impact. The permanence of the impact is an uncertain
if important variable, and virtually impossible to measure.
Personal appearances, thus, may more effectively mobilize voters
than a radio speech or television interview. Participatory
activities also meet the important function of providing the
candidate with a feel for grass-roots sentiment on important issues.
Extensive personal tours permit the exchange of views with local
party leaders, who can acquaint the candidate with dominant voter
concerns.
    An important corollary is the strengthening of local leadership

_____

presentational or participatory. We could then proceed to insert
relevant examples in each cell but, as we said above, these are not
clear-cut dichotomies.

growing out of even the briefest candidate visit. There is also
an opportunity for individual voters to enter into a dialogue with
party leaders, and this too is of consequence in discussions between
national and local campaign officials. In any campaign, the
leadership must take a host of hard decisions in weighing the
relative value and potential payoff of participatory and
presentational techniques, as well as of the many forms that these
may take. Given a particular environment, the effectiveness of such
techniques may vary widely. Reliance on mass media can be efficient
in swiftly reaching a large audience but, among other things, is
financially costly. More personalized techniques, however, are
expensive in terms of time and energy, which may be as precious as
the money in party coffers.

Whether communications are of a presentational or participatory
style, we are brought back to candidate style and identification.
Given the absence of survey research and public opinion polling in
many countries, the effect of communications and of a candidate's
personality is difficult to assess. Our VENEVOTE data for Venezuela
will hopefully provide enlightment. Obviously, the personality and
style of the candidate, whatever its characteristics, will exert a
pervasive influence on all aspects of a campaign. The candidate's
role is central in the realm of communications and political
appeals. His effectiveness on television, whether delivering a
prepared statement or responding extemporaneously to interviewers'
questioning, may win or lose votes. Appearances on the campaign
trail are no less important, whether he discusses party matters
with local officials, speaks individually with voters as he walks
from home to home, or unleashes oratorical rhetoric at a mass
meeting in the town plaza. Participatory techniques stress personal
identification with the candidate, and these will draw upon his own
style, individual idiosyncracies, past political career and image,
private habits, and family life.

In summary, our entire discussion has attempted to isolate and
to order those aspects of political campaigning that should have
fairly universal and generalizable application. If this framework
is more taxonomic than theoretical, it at least suggests a research
agenda for future case studies which can produce cumulative
knowledge through repeated testing of relevance propositions.

THE RESEARCH AGENDA: AN INVENTORY

The research inventory implied by our statement of the
dimensions of democratic political campaigns can be summarized in
propositional form. This will permit the articulation of tentative
hypotheses, the analysis of which may enrich our understanding of
the entire phenomenon of campaigning. We begin at the broadest
level of generality with definitions of the more stable environmental
features of the campaign system.

Definition: Democratic political campaigning is a transitory
             political system that intermittently appears in
             competitive party systems.

In Latin America, this phenomenon is characteristic of two-party
competitive, multiparty dominant, and multiparty loose systems.

Moreover, the efficacy of democratic campaigning is related to the probability of turnover as a result of campaigning. This probability is a function of three sets of campaign variables: environmental, mobilizational, and implementational. Of these, the environmental have the greatest impact on the potential efficacy of campaigning; conversely, the effect of campaigning on environmental variables is marginal.

    Definition: Environmental variables include the distribution of partisan loyalties; the relationship between party loyalties and politically relevant cleavages; the nature of the beliefs of the mass public; the public's attitudes about elections in general and its perceived efficacy for each particular election; and the electoral strength of each party as demonstrated by secular electoral trends.

    Definition: Campaign efficacy refers to the probability that the outcome of an electoral contest is changed as the result of a political campaign.

Changes in the distribution of voting intention and related attitudes of the mass public, although not indicative of the magnitude of campaign efficacy, suggest the operation of a campaign effect on the electorate.

    Bearing in mind these elements of the campaign system, we will proceed to specify our assumptions about the nature of the relationships between campaign efficacy and the other two dimensions of the system.

Mobilization

A. Candidate Selection

    Hypothesis 1: Campaign efficacy is diminished by candidate selection that results from one or more of the following: (a) manipulation of the nominating process by party notables; (b) formation of splinter candidacies as a result of conflicts over nomination; and (c) protracted conflict over the rules of nomination. The legitimacy of the nominee will be damaged, thereby creating a loss of campaign efficacy.

    Hypothesis 2: The nominees of unequal coalitions have a comparative advantage in campaign efficacy over the nominees of equal coalitions.

B. Campaign Organization

    Proposition: Campaign efficacy and efficiency are relevant only to the calculus of major campaigners, whereas minor candidates must follow criteria of efficiency to maximize their goals.

    Hypothesis 1: Campaign efficacy is increased by centralized and by fused organizations.

    Hypothesis 2: Campaign efficiency is increased by specialized organizations, but only if this specialization entails close collaboration between permanent party organs and electoral commissions.

      Hypothesis 3: Campaign efficacy is not necessarily increased
         by adoption of either an institutionalized or personalized
         campaign.

      Hypothesis 4: Maximization of financial support and
         diversification of its sources are a necessary but not a
         sufficient condition for increased campaign efficacy.

C. Strategies and Tactics

      Proposition: All campaigners combine electoral strategies and
         tactics. However, they may emphasize a particular one,
         either throughout the entire campaign or at certain
         critical junctures.

      Hypothesis 1: Consensual strategies increase the campaign
         efficacy of major campaigners.

      Hypothesis 2: Conflictual strategies increase the campaign
         efficacy of minor campaigners.

      Hypothesis 3: Campaign efficacy increases with a blend of
         reinforcement and recruitment strategies.

      Hypothesis 4: Inducement tactics most increase efficacy when
         combined with consensual strategies, and disinducement
         with conflictual. In either case, efficacy is enhanced by
         a blend of material and symbolic subtypes.

D. Ideologies and Programs

      Proposition: Programmatic electoral appeals are enhanced if
         based on ideological premises, but the latter element is
         secondary in importance.

      Hypothesis: Programmatic appeals increase campaign efficacy
         more than ideological appeals.

Implementation

A. Candidate Style

      Proposition: Presentation of a clear and recognizable
         candidate style, whatever its content, is more important
         than ideological or programmatic appeals. Styles are
         strongly influenced by the political and institutional
         environment.

      Hypothesis 1: Candidate style is the single most important
         factor in mobilizing an effective campaign.

      Hypothesis 2: No single candidate style necessarily increases
         campaign efficacy more than others.

B. Communications

      Proposition: Presentational and participatory techniques have
         distinctive advantages and disadvantages. Relative
         efficacy is determined by the environment and is increased
         by combining techniques.

      Hypothesis 1: The optimal combination of presentational and
         participatory techniques is determined by the environment.

      Hypothesis 2: The greater the institutionalization of the
         party system, the greater the increase of campaign
         efficacy produced by predominantly presentational methods.

    We would emphasize that the preceding is no more than what it
has been labeled—a research agenda. By no means all of the above
will prove susceptible to measurement or quantification in the
Venezuelan case. Assessment of campaign impact at the mass level is

especially problematic. In spite of our VENEVOTE data--the first such empirical evidence to be collected for Latin America--several campaign dimensions require qualitative rather than quantitative analysis. At a minimum, our commitment to this inventory buttresses the proposed taxonomy whereby relevant elements of a campaign system are identified. Despite problems of operationalization, and even granting the tautological quality of some hypotheses, however, it should carry us a modest step beyond sheer description and classification. In conjunction with similar studies of other campaign systems, our inquiry may help to link concern over campaigning in Latin America with the broader field of comparative politics.

The nature of our enterprise, then, is to bring a logical framework to the study of political campaigning, to raise and consider pertinent research questions, and to provide an unpretentious base from which further study of theoretical relationships can proceed. It also presents a detailed view of a decisive electoral contest in a nation rapidly assuming a position of leadership in Latin America.

ABBREVIATIONS

AD	Acción Democrática
AD-ARS	Acción Democrática Arsistas
AD-OP	Acción Democrática en Oposición
AEI	Agrupación Electoral Independiente
AIR	Acción Independiente Revolucionaria
ANAPRO	Acción Nacional Progresista
API	Alianza Popular Independiente
ARPA	Alianza Revolucionaria Patriótica
ARVI	Acción Revolucionaria Vencedora Independiente
AVI	Asociación Venezolana de Independientes
AVM	Automatic Voting Machine Corporation
BIN	Bloque Independiente Nacionalista
CCN	Cruzada Cívica Nacionalista
CECLA	Comisión Especial de Coordinación Latinoamericana
CEN	Comité Ejecutivo Nacional
CENDES	Centro de Estudios del Desarrollo
CES	Comités Ejecutivo Seccional
CIPES	Comité de Independientes por el Socialismo
CONACIL	Comisión Nacional Coordinadora de Independientes (of COPEI)
COPEI	Comité de Organización Política Electoral Independiente
CORA	Coordinadores Regionales Adjuntos
COZ	Coordinador Zonal
COZA	Coordinadores Zonales Adjuntos
CSE	Consejo Supremo Electoral
CSJ	Corte Suprema de Justicia
CTV	Confederación de Trabajadores de Venezuela
CUR	Comité de Unidad Revolucionaria
CUTV	Confederación Unica de Trabajadores Venezolanos
CVP	Corporación Venezolana de Petróleo
DesCom	Desarrollo de la Comunidad
DP	Democracia Popular
DPV	Democracia Popular Venezolana
FALN	Fuerzas Armadas de Liberación Nacional
FDP	Fuerza Democrática Popular

FE	Fuerza Emancipadora
FEV	Federación Estudiantil Venezolana
FEVO	Federación Venezolana de Obreros
FIPO	Frente Independiente Popular
FND	Frente Nacional Democrático
FUN	Frente Unido Nacionalista
ICOPS	Institute for the Comparative Study of Political Systems
IESA	Instituto de Estudios Superiores de Administración
INCIBA	Instituto de Cultura y Bellas Artes
INRA	International Research Associates
IP	Independientes Progresistas
IPFN	Independientes Pro-Frente Nacional
JRC	Juventud Revolucionaria Copeyana
MAI	Management Assistance Incorporated
MAN	Movimiento de Acción Nacional
MAS	Movimiento al Socialismo
MD	Movimiento Desarrollista
MDI	Movimiento Democrático Independiente
MEP	Movimiento Electoral del Pueblo
MIA	Movimiento Independiente Apureño
MIR	Movimiento de Izquierda Revolucionaria
ML	Movimiento Libertador
MPJ	Movimiento Popular Justicialista
MPL	Movimiento Prensa Libre
NIN	Nuevo Ideal Nacional
ODCA	Organización Demócrata Cristiana de América Latina
OPINA	Opinión Nacional
OPIR	Organización Popular Independiente Revolucionaria
OR	Organización de Revolucionarios
PCV	Partido Comunista de Venezuela
PDN	Partido Democrático Nacional
PDV	Partido Democrático Venezolano
PL	Partido Liberal
PNI	Partido Nacional Integracionalista
PRIN	Partido Revolucionario de Integración Nacional
PRIVO	Profesionales Independientes del Volante
PRN	Partido Revolucionario Nacionalista
PSD	Partido Socialista Democrático
UMS	Unión de Mujeres Socialistas
UNE	Unión Nacional Estudiantil
UPA	Unión para Avanzar
UPI	Unión Popular de Izquierda
UPV	Unión del Pueblo Venezolano
URD	Unión Republicana Democrática
URI	Unión de Revolucionarios Independientes
VENEVOTE	Martz and Baloyra statistical data, Venezuelan Campaign 1973
VJU	Vanguardia Juvenil Urredista
VPN	Vanguardia Popular Nacionalista

PART I
THE POLITICAL SETTING

1. PARTIES, ELECTIONS, AND PATTERNS OF CAMPAIGNING

Even in a hemisphere of pronounced contrast and diversity, Venezuela stands out as a strikingly singular land. By the final third of the twentieth century it had assumed a position of leadership within the Latin American bloc; its natural resources provided the bases for notable economic growth and expansion; and despite appallingly gross inequities and social imbalances, its population was among the most mobile, vital, and optimistic on the continent. Moreover, the country had evolved a political system which, despite many flaws, stood among the most representative and participatory in a region more noted for the absence of liberties and citizen involvement. A series of elections commencing in 1958 demonstrated a public vigor and vibrancy in political affairs which by the 1970s was a rarity in Latin America. Perhaps most extraordinarily, these characteristics were of recent date, for the Venezuelan heritage had been quite different. Homeland of the legendary Liberator Simón Bólivar and seedbed of the revolutionary wars for independence in the early nineteenth century, Venezuela experienced over a century of impoverishment and backwardness before the discovery of massive petroleum deposits propelled the country into the dizzying social and economic transformations that followed.

Mainland Venezuela, first discovered on Columbus's third voyage in 1498, passed through three centuries of Spanish colonial rule as a relative backwater of the empire. Apparently lacking in the mineral wealth and resources sought by the conquerors, the land on the Caribbean shore of South America was relegated to a secondary position. A rural, agricultural region, it finally became a captaincy-general of the empire in 1777, existing largely as a group of heterogenous and loosely linked provinces. Only with a sharp rise of cacao production in the second half of the eighteenth century did its economic activity begin to draw slightly greater attention from Spanish officials. Overall, however, the colonial experience "was one of administrative confusion, regional jealousies, official indifference, and a very modest measure of self-government."[1] By the close of this period, the existing social order was on the point of collapse; the independence wars

were not merely a conflict between native born <u>criollos</u> and Spanish
<u>peninsulares</u>, but at the same time a struggle among slaves, <u>pardos</u>,
and <u>criollos</u>. Not only were the dominant <u>criollos</u> operating at
cross-purposes with the masses, but regional interests were also in
conflict. With the disintegration of Bolívar's ambitious Gran
Colombian federation[2] in 1830 and the proclamation of Venezuelan
independence, the task of defining a national consciousness loomed
large on the political horizon.

For the better part of a century regional <u>caudillos</u> competed for
wealth and power "within a network of personal alliances cemented
together by community of interest, by force of personality, by ties
of friendship and even of family."[3] National authority was fragmented rather than institutionalized, with the capital city of
Caracas little more than one of many provincial market centers.
Antonio Arraiz has calculated that from 1830 to 1900, there were
"39 significant revolutions and 127 minor revolts; in total, 166
revolts, which together lasted 8,847 days."[4] In a phrase from one
of Venezuela's major nineteenth-century rulers, Antonio Guzmán
Blanco, Venezuela was "like a dry hide; you step on it on one end
and it pops up on the other."[5] National power passed through the
years from the hands of <u>llaneros</u> ("plainsmen") to men from the
east, later to the west and, by the turn of the century, to the
Andes. Economically the country remained preponderantly agricultural, with the decline of cacao giving way to a boom in coffee production by the 1880s. By the early years of the twentieth century,
Venezuela possessed a one-product economy with a stagnant per
capita rate of growth, accompanied by a political system that was
fragmented, primitive, and violent. In the words of a noted
Venezuelan sociologist, the sole route to upward social mobility
was "through participation in armed bands or political revolts,
for education continued to be the privilege of a very small elite."[6]
Such was the setting when General Juan Vicente Gómez seized power
in 1908, to be followed in a few years by the beginnings of the
oil bonanza that has so dominated Venezuelan life and society for
the past half-century.

The first great oil strike was brought in late in 1922, and
from that time forward the entire fabric of Venezuelan life was
subjected to its impact. Vast reserves in the Maracaibo Basin
attracted international corporations to the country, agricultural
products went into sharp decline, and the national transformation
began to take shape.[7] An additional catalyst was provided by the
twenty-seven-year rule of Gómez, the storied "Tyrant of the Andes."[8]
A shrewd, cunning, and unprincipled authoritarian, Gómez provided
Venezuela with a concentration of political power previously unknown.
Relying heavily on fellow <u>andinos</u>, he encouraged conditions from
which a powerful bourgeois capitalist system developed.[9] The armed
forces as well as national government were centralized, a
bureaucratic structure was elaborated, the internal market was
integrated, and traditional patterns of <u>latifundista</u> power were
shattered. Commercial activities were reoriented from domestic
agricultural production to world trade, with a nascent national
industry eventually blooming under the paternalistic patronage of

international economic interests. The latter led to the growth and
flourishing of what has become known in pejorative terms as the
"criollo oligarchy," enriching the vocabulary of Marxists and
non-Marxists alike. For the Venezuelan masses, political activity
was rigidly circumscribed, a circumstance that led to abortive
rebellion against the dictator, most notably in 1928.[10] However,
it was not until the peaceful death of Juan Vicente Gómez from
old age in 1935 that modern political life in Venezuela, as we
know it, was introduced to its people.

PARTIES AND PARTICIPATION
    The year 1935 proved a landmark in national political history.
Not only had nearly three decades of harsh personal absolutism
been ended, but an energized and newly mobile populace was approaching an era of activity and vitality that still endures. The
populace was to wait yet another decade before truly representative
party leaders came to power. However, the body of Gómez had
scarcely been entombed when the nascent elite issued its challenge
to traditional authority. The result was a gradual if grudging
relaxation of government repression under General Eleazar López
Contreras (1935-1941), and then fuller liberalization with General
Isaías Medina Angarita (1941-1945), both andinos. Members of the
original Generation of '28 by 1937 had divided into Marxist and
non-Marxist wings with the latter becoming known as the Partido
Democrático Nacional (PDN). Under López Contreras there were
official restrictions on political activity, although lacking the
harshness of the gomecista era. Elections were annulled, opposition
leaders exiled, and censorship imposed. Yet important organizational groundwork was laid--especially for the PDN, which was permitted
to organize legally under the name of Acción Democrática (AD) on
29 July 1941.[11] The Partido Comunista de Venezuela (PCV), whose
leadership included members of the 1928 student movement,[12] also
gained legal recognition from the Medina government.[12] By 1945,
the newly emerging elite was prepared for the assumption of national
power.[13]
    Amidst a crisis over presidential succession that aggravated
the rivalry between Generals Medina and López Contreras, an armed
uprising in October 1945 brought to power a provisional government
headed by Rómulo Betancourt. Supported by junior military officers,
the AD led the country through a three-year period, known as the
trienio, which was both productive and turbulent. AD undertook
the sweeping national change, bent upon a veritable revolution in
both political and socioeconomic dimensions. A Constituent
Assembly, chosen in Venezuela's first direct elections, returned
the party with 78.8 percent of the vote, and the resulting
Constitution of 1947 was largely the party's handiwork. New
elections were convened and the internationally renowned author
Rómulo Gallegos, the AD candidate, won the presidency with 74.4
percent. He was inaugurated early in 1948, and in May municipal
elections--destined to be the last free vote for ten years-AD again
won easily, although its total dropped to 70.1 percent.[14]
    The party system took on greater diversity with the creation

of two new organizations. The Unión Republicana Democrática (URD)
was legally recognized on 14 December 1945 and soon fell under the
personal dominion of Jóvito Villalba, erstwhile leader of the 1928
student rebellion.[15] Composed largely of former members of the
Partido Democrático Venezolano (PDV) which President Medina had
attempted to organize, the URD offered outspoken opposition to the
government. Although plagued by difficulties in defining a clear
ideological position—a problem the URD would never adequately
resolve—it provided vocal criticism and fiery rhetoric in the
declarations of Villalba. The URD ran third in each of the trienio
elections, never reaching 5 percent of the vote. During the same
period, former leaders of the Catholic student movement founded the
Comité de Organización Política Electoral Independiente, later
known officially as the Partido Social Cristiano COPEI.[16] Having
originated as the Unión Nacional Estudiantil (UNE) in opposition to
the national student organization in 1936, it was directed from
the outset by Rafael Caldera. Converted in part to an electoral
movement in Caracas in 1938 under the name Acción Electoral, it
underwent additional changes in nomenclature and structure before
the official creation of COPEI on 13 January 1946. Following brief
service as procurador general under the Betancourt government,
Caldera resigned in April 1946 and led COPEI into angry and intransi-
gent opposition. Emerging as Venezuela's second electoral force,
it polled roughly one-fifth of the vote during the trienio.[17]

    During its first stewardship in power, the AD attempted to
introduce massive changes. In addition to seeking direct political
democracy, the AD undertook drastic social and economic reforms,
ranging from health, education, and housing through oil policy,
state industrialization, and agrarian reform. Despite broad
popular support, important forces were thoroughly alienated. The
Church was repelled by the anticlericalism of educational reforms;[18]
landowners opposed agrarian reform; the business sector feared adeco
radicalism; international oil interests fought government reforms;
the military mistrusted the AD attitude toward the role of the armed
forces; and opposition political parties were harassed by the
sectarian self-righteousness of the AD. The dominant party,
convinced of its omniscience and impatient to transform the country
after years of study and preparation—much of it while in exile or
clandestine activity—brooked little opposition. The result was
perhaps inevitable. In November 1948, rebuffed in a series of self-
serving demands on President Gallegos, the military deposed the
elected government and assumed power. The subsequent decade of
dictatorship, dominated by the person of then-Colonel Marcos Pérez
Jiménez, proved among the darker pages of Venezuelan history.

    Political persecution, street assassination, and concentration
camps for critics and opponents were pronounced, with civil liberties and public freedoms grossly abused. At first, the adecos were
the major target, but after 1952 the URD and COPEI also fell
victims. An attempt by Pérez Jiménez to legitimize his rule through
elections in 1952 failed abysmally. With members of the outlawed
AD voting for Jóvito Villalba, the URD candidate raced to an early
lead. Suddenly all electoral bulletins were suspended,

Pérez Jiménez declared himself president, and Villalba was sent winging his way into exile.[19] Urredistas felt the wrath of the regime, and COPEI suspended all activities.[20] In lieu of the emphasis on social welfare and human development that had character- ized the AD government and even that of General Medina to a degree,[21] the military regime focused on public works of massive proportions. With government revenue doubling between 1951 and 1956 as oil pro- duction boomed under the impetus of the Korean fighting, precedence was given to flashily expensive construction.

The world's most luxurious officers' club was built in Caracas; a chain of uneconomical luxury hotels was begun, including the Humboldt atop Mount Avila overlooking the valley of Caracas. The latter proved a massive white elephant, while yet greater irrational- ity was demonstrated by the futuristic helicoide commercial center in Caracas. Never completed, its shell stands today as further testimony to the grandiose pretensions of that government. As economic mismanagement and sagging oil prices began to bedevil the regime, clandestine opposition spread. A fraudulent plebiscite in December 1957, intended to solidify its position, instead undermined the regime. A nationwide general strike and uprising on 23 January 1958, supported by the military, drove Pérez Jiménez into exile and led to the restoration of elected, constitutional government.[22] A caretaker regime under Vice Admiral Wolfgang Larrazábal ruled until December elections. With the inauguration of an elected president in March of 1959, Venezuela passed another historic milestone and entered an era of popular, representative government. The roots were to sink deeply into national soil by the time of the 1973 campaign.

Venezuelan politics during the intervening fifteen years have for better or worse been dominated by the parties, to an extent uncommon for Latin America and without precedent in Venezuela. Despite a progressive fragmentation of parties and the proliferation of "micro-parties" after 1958, national policy largely emanated from party leaders. At the same time, economic and commercial elites were drawn into collaboration with elected officials, either through co-optation or sheer necessity. In the terminology of one scholar, "the modernizing establishment and middle-class counterelite [represented by the party leadership] moved toward reconciliation."[23] The AD, badly seared by the results of its trienio experience, renounced its past narrow sectarianism and moderated the leftist doctrinal stance of earlier years. As it moved toward the center, COPEI in turn gravitated from its earlier conservatism toward a similar position on the political spectrum, while the URD wavered from one side to the other, its evident doctrinal opportunism and inconsistency too clever by half. In time a new political "establishment" emerged, to the dismay of the Venezuelan left, which was soon describing the dominant parties as the "status" and charging the AD and COPEI with being opposite sides of the same coin. As the system of centrist party domination and moderate reformism in government took hold, both domestic and foreign economic interests increasingly collaborated in policy formulation.

With business and commerce supporting mass-based popular

democracy in exchange for consultation and cooperation from the
government in the articulation of policies, divisiveness and rancor
were increasingly moderated. This was not achieved without difficulty and, indeed, bloodshed. The overthrow of Marcos Pérez
Jiménez and the subsequent election of Rómulo Betancourt were
roughly paralleled by the collapse of Fulgencio Batista in Cuba
and the emergence of Fidel Castro as the hemisphere's great
revolutionary leader. The early impact of Castro was nowhere
stronger than in Venezuela, and by 1960 young leftists rose in
rebellion against the government. Young adecos angrily left the
party that year, denouncing President Betancourt for betraying his
principles and delivering the country to Yankee imperialism.
Organizing the Movimiento de Izquierda Revolucionaria (MIR), they
soon embarked on a campaign to topple the government by force. The
experience proved highly instructive in understanding revolutionary
strategy and tactics in contemporary Latin America.[24] First
determined to win power by duplicating the Cuban experience, the
miristas, with somewhat reluctant support from the PCV, initiated
guerrilla fighting in the countryside. Ignoring the fact that the
AD had founded and built the peasant movement,[25] as well as
Betancourt's vast popularity with the campesinos, the revolutionaries found their efforts frustrated, their intended clientele
hostile. Eventually reorienting their strategy toward urban centers,
the self-styled Fuerzas Armadas de Liberación Nacional (FALN)
launched a campaign of widespread terrorism.

Hoping to so undermine public order that the government would
eventually collapse, the urban guerrillas robbed banks, burned
foreign-owned enterprises, and fell increasingly to indiscriminate
violence. The Betancourt administration, wholeheartedly supported
by copeyano members of the government coalition, responded harshly.
Constitutional guarantees were suspended frequently, policy counter-
measures were firm, and leftist congressmen were arrested in
violation of parliamentary immunity. Revolutionary unity of purpose
and action dissolved following the psychologically shattering
failure to block 1963 elections.[26] Violence gradually declined,
leaders withdrew or defected, and by 1968 the communists were
permitted to run for office, although under the name of Unión para
Avanzar (UPA). Conciliatory government attitudes turned to
full-fledged amnesty under the Caldera government, and by 1973
the left had fully returned to legitimacy and electoral competition.
The experience of the early 1960s, however, had left a strong
imprint on public attitudes and was to plague the left upon its
reincorporation to electoral activity.

In the meantime, both personalistic ambitions and doctrinal
disagreements were fueling a progressive dispersion of parties.
While characteristic of the entire system, the force of the
dissension and fragmentation was nowhere more evident than within
the AD. It led first to the loss of a legislative majority and,
ultimately, to a fall from power. The separation of the MIR in
1960 was followed by another division two years later in which a
number of prominent second-generation leaders, thwarted in an
attempt to seize control of the party organization, departed to

organize the Partido Revolucionaria Nacionalista (PRN). Even more
damaging was the 1967 division which led to the founding of the
Movimiento Electoral del Pueblo (MEP) under Luis B. Prieto Figueroa
and Jesús Angel Paz Galarraga. The URD also suffered losses, first
from its left wing in 1964 and two years later from its right.[27]
Only COPEI escaped serious dissension. As suggested in figure 4,
fragmentation had multiplicative effect. From four parties and
three presidential candidates in 1958, divisions and personalistic
regroupings led to seven nominees in 1963. By 1968 there were,

FIGURE 4. Party Fragmentation and Major Presidential Candidates,
1958–1968.

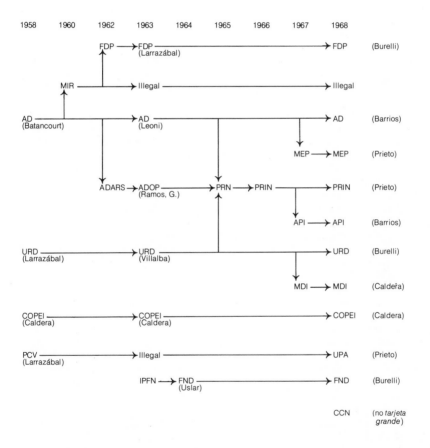

in addition to six presidential contenders, a total of sixteen
separate presidential ballots, while another seventeen parties
competed in congressional and municipal races. The zenith was to
be reached in 1973, with no fewer than a dozen presidential

candidates and more than twice as many national or regional parties competing for legislative and municipal positions.[28]

Although congressional and municipal seats were distributed over an increasingly wide array of political organizations, national authority remained with the major parties. In the 1958 elections Rómulo Betancourt polled 49.2 percent of the vote in defeating Wolfgang Larrazábal, running with URD and PCV backing (34.6 percent) and COPEI's Rafael Caldera (16.2 percent). A tripartite coalition, negotiated in the days after the ouster of Pérez Jiménez, was broken in 1960 by URD withdrawal, but COPEI remained in close alliance with the AD throughout the Betancourt administration.[29] In 1963 the adeco vote, although dropping to 32.7 percent, still assured easy victory for Raúl Leoni, and Rafael Caldera ran second with 20.2 percent.[30] Jóvito Villalba was third with his URD and Arturo Uslar Pietri, representing a business-oriented "anti-party" group of independents, followed with 16.1 percent. Larrazábal, without URD backing, polled 9.4 percent, and former adeco Raúl Ramos Giménez for the PRN received 2.3 percent. Contrary to the strong desires of retiring President Betancourt, the AD and COPEI failed to reach agreement on terms for a renewal of the coalition. The Social Christians thus spent the next five years in opposition, under the slogan of Autonomy of Action. Leoni, another member of the Generation of '28 and a senior leader of the AD, consolidated policies initiated by his predecessor while pursuing reconciliation for a populace sorely tested by the domestic turmoil of the early 1960s.[31] The new president negotiated the Amplia Base coalition with the URD and the Frente Nacional Democrático (FND), the latter having grown out of Uslar's 1963 candidacy.

While the rightist orientation of the FND made the coalition a somewhat unwieldy instrument, Leoni was skillful in manipulating it. The FND withdrew in 1966, but the URD remained until the approach of 1968 elections drove Villalba away from the government. Just as the aggressive and combative pugnacity of Betancourt had well served the regime during his administration, Leoni's phlegmatic serenity and modest reserve were appropriate for his years in office. It also contributed to stabilizing what proved in 1968 the most intense and intensive campaign struggle the country had yet known. By that year, Venezuela's exceptional rate of population growth had brought the population from 6,785,680 in 1958 to 9,832,998. Registered voters during the decade had increased from 2,913,801 to 4,068,481. With over 90 percent of registered voters exercising their rights, it was estimated that a total of 3.7 million valid votes would be cast in 1968, an increase of 1.1 million over 1958 and 800,000 above 1963.[32] The electoral rules of the game were consistent with legal prescriptions adopted in 1958, in many cases derived from the democratizing reforms instituted by the AD during 1945-1948. Elections were fused, with all offices being chosen simultaneously at five-year intervals, by direct vote. Universal suffrage was adopted from the age of eighteen, without restrictions as to literacy, sex, or property ownership. Each voter cast two electoral tarjetas or cards--one for the presidency and one for party-selected candidates to all legislative and municipal offices.[33]

1968 ELECTIONS AND THE MOBILIZATION OF FORCES
The alignment of political forces began long before elections, eventually developing into a contest in which four major nominees vied for the presidency with serious expectations of victory. By following the analytic paths mapped out in the Introduction, the reader can see the campaign patterns that preceded the 1973 competition more clearly, as well as the political elements that would assert themselves during the five intervening years. A summary of organizational characteristics is presented in figure 5. Our attention will be directed first toward dimensions of campaign mobilization, then to issues and the media.

FIGURE 5. Summary of Organizational Characteristics of the Four Main Actors--The Presidential Campaign of 1968

	COPEI	AD	MEP	Frente
Candidate Selection	By consensus	By referendum, division, and consensus	By consensus	Ad hoc, by party notables
Campaign Structure	Centralized, fused	Centralized, fused	Loosely centralized, diffused	Loosely centralized diffused
Electoral Structure	Highly specialized	Specialized	Specialized	Specialized
Candidate Role	Institutionalized and personalized	Institutionalized	Institutionalized	Personalized
Financing	External, internal	External, internal	Internal	External
Campaign Efficiency	High	Moderate, high	Moderate	Low

Candidate Selection
The selection of candidates for the 1968 elections began with the entry of Rafael Caldera, for the fourth time carrying the banner of the Social Christian party COPEI.[34] The undisputed leader of the party since the 1936 founding of the Catholic student movement, he was its guiding political genius while serving as party secretary general. Yet even Caldera's stature was not sufficient to prevent internal problems prior to his nomination. The conflict revolved about differences between leftist views of the party youth-Juventud Revolucionaria Copeyana (JRC)--and the moderate leadership of the secretar general and his close associates. The JRC itself was divided, with its factions popularly known as the astronautas, avanzados, and araguatos.[35] Although the latter group remained

slavishly loyal to the party leadership, such brilliant student
leaders as Joaquín Marta Sosa and Abdón Vivas Terán shredded the
unity of the party's youth movement. Disciplinary measures against
the most outspoken student leaders eventually upheld Caldera's power,
and elements that favored a shift to a new and fresh candidate were
outmaneuvered by the orthodox leadership, guided by Lorenzo
Fernández. By March of 1967, firmly in control of COPEI and
enthusiastically backed by its rank and file, Rafael Caldera
undertook a campaign in which the party future as well as his own
was at stake. Optimism was high, with the party well prepared to
launch a determined, unified, and cohesive campaign under the
banner of its most distinguished leader. The victory of Chile's
Christian Democrats in 1964 further spurred COPEI with the thought
that the hemispheric configuration of political forces was moving
inexorably in its favor. Moreover, prospects for victory soon
gleamed even more brightly as internal conflict within AD
threatened to leave it in a shambles after ten years in power.[36]
     The adeco struggle was without parallel in the annals of
Venezuelan party history. Only the barest outlines of the controversy can be sketched here.[37] Following the 1963 election of Leoni,
growing doctrinal and policy differences began to polarize around
the so-called pacistas and betancuristas. The former, standing
on the party left, were dominated by AD Secretary General Jesús
Angel Paz Galarraga. The latter represented the opposing loyalists
of the former president, then living in self-imposed European exile.
Animosity between Paz and Betancourt had quietly grown when the
latter was in office and the former ran party affairs; the
independent posture of Paz was but one of the factors contributing
to the rift. Policy differences during the Leoni administration
further exacerbated the internal situation. Paz himself seemed
to be driving toward a presidential candidacy, a prospect totally
unacceptable to betancuristas. At the start of 1967 Paz seemingly
played a masterful card by throwing his support to Luis B. Prieto
Figueroa, president of Congress and one of the last remaining
members of the AD's senior leadership. In reaction, the opponents
banded together behind Gonzalo Barrios, also an eminent party
founder.
     From mid-1967 the struggle escalated dramatically, with internal
party functions complicated by Prieto's position as AD president
and that of Barrios as recently elected secretary general. In an
effort to unravel the tangled skein of rivalry and hostility, the
AD conducted an unprecedented party primary in September of 1967.
The outburst of violence between followers of the two pre-candidates
in Cumaná prevented a final tally of the vote, although Prieto was
the clear winner with a majority in at least fifteen of the party's
twenty-five regional organizations. Balanced against Prieto's
greater popularity with adeco rank and file was Barrios's firm
control of a majority on both the National Executive Committee and
the National Directive Council. The strong influence of Rómulo
Betancourt was also injected into an already embittered and
rancorous struggle.[38] The conflict extended as well into the AD-
dominated labor federation and the national peasant organization.[39]

The climactic dispute--revolving around the secondary issue of the
primary vote in Cumaná--culminated in the withdrawal of prietistas
from party executive bodies and their expulsion by the betancuristas.
Leaving with Prieto were Paz Galarraga, numerous other national
leaders, and a large body of middle-level regional leaders. The
result was the proclamation in February 1968 of the rival
candidacies of Barrios and Prieto, the latter with the newly formed
MEP.

The division assured a clear path to nomination for both men.
In the AD, the choice of Barrios was inevitable. For the MEP, there
could be no candidate other than Prieto. However, the inability of
the AD to resolve its internal differences had decimated the
organization even before the holding of a nominating convention.
In a sense, the eventual Barrios nomination represented the
determination of a majority of senior leaders to impose him in
contradiction to grass-roots sentiment. Thus the role of party
notables blocked nomination of the party's most popular pre-
candidate. Prieto and the MEP, in contrast, could boast of a
nomination legitimized by the obvious wishes of its membership.
In both cases, however, the process of candidate selection had
been grievously injurious.

Still to be heard from were the URD, FND, and Fuerza Democrática
Popular (FDP). With none of the three matching the popular support
of COPEI and the AD, each was nonetheless dominated by a
personalistic leader. For the URD, the caudillistic Jóvito Villalba,
whose 1963 candidacy had failed, determined to play a major role
in the coming campaign. In January of 1968 he began serious
discussions with the FND and FDP, headed respectively by Arturo
Uslar Pietri and Wolfgang Larrazábal. Personalistic domination
over party apparatus on the part of all three left the final
decision in the hands of a few dominant personalities. Jóvito
Villalba ignored arguments of several prominent urredistas that
the party had little in common with either the FND or FDP, and that
alliance with the AD was wiser. Agreeing with Uslar Pietri and
Larrazábal in a mutual sacrifice of ambitions, Villalba played the
central role in considering potential independent candidates.
Agreement was eventually reached on the politically unknown Miguel
Angel Burelli Rivas, President Leoni's ambassador to Great Britain.
Burelli later received the questionable legitimization provided by
rubber-stamp party conventions.

Beyond the tripartite Frente de la Victoria supporting Burelli,
there were several minor electoral arrangements. A coalition of
the unequal type affiliated the Partido Revolucionario de Integración
Nacional (PRIN)--remnants of the 1962 adeco defection--with the MEP.
While running its own candidates for congressional and local offices,
the PRIN supported Prieto for the presidency. The perezjimenista
Cruzada Cívica Nacionalista (CCN) officially ignored the
presidential race to concentrate on congress. The communists,
legalized as the UPA, concentrated on the small tarjetas while
maintaining a flirtation with Prieto. The Partido Socialista
Democrático (PSD) presented the noted industrialist Alejandro
Hernández, and the folkloric figure of Germán Borregales, a

copeyano militant who had left it for alleged betrayal of traditional
interests and values, represented his own Movimiento de Acción
Nacional (MAN).

Campaign Organization

For COPEI a prime organizational task was the effort to build
a truly national structure, extending from its traditional Andean
base. Supervision of regional and local organs was close, and of
a centralized type. In addition to strong vertical controls, the
copeyano organization was fused through its horizontal relationships
with assorted independent and ad hoc associations. The best
example was that of the so-called desarrollistas, professionals and
business entrepreneurs who joined in support of Caldera in 1968, as
did those commercial interests represented in the Movimiento
Democrático Independiente (MDI). The miniscule Partido Liberal (PL)
also allied with the Social Christians. Thus the structure was both
centralized and fused. It was the specialized quality, however,
that was most striking. Following the 1963 elections Rafael Caldera
and his colleagues had drastically revised the party apparatus,
including the adoption of a highly centralized electoral organization.
Four new sub-secretary generals were placed directly under Caldera's
personal command, most importantly the Electoral Sub-Secretariat
and the Operational Sub-Secretariat. The former was placed under
the direction of José Curiel, a young engineer with expertise in
organizational techniques.

Breaking from traditional emphases on geographical and political
jurisdictions, the party defined series of zonal, regional, and
local organs for electoral purposes; Curiel as sub-secretary general
had the authority to appoint or to remove their respective heads.
In lending the specialized characteristic to the copeyano campaign
effort, this structure also maximized firm centralized control by
Curiel, and therefore by the candidate, who remained in close
touch with all aspects of the campaign. Caldera's role was both
institutionalized and personalized, for the organization had been
personally molded through the years. His own staff was not ignored,
however, and he particularly valued the views of the youthful
Eduardo Fernández, a former JRC leader who accompanied him
throughout the lengthy campaign.

Support from important elements of the business community
included financial assistance. While the disciplined party
membership certainly contributed its share, the most important
funding came from external sources. Private interests sympathetic
to the Caldera candidacy included large landowners as well as
affluent businessmen. International ties with the Christian
Democratic movement undoubtedly opened doors to additional sources.
Just as Chileans generally believed that money from West Germany
aided the Christian Democrats in the 1964 campaign of Eduardo Frei,[40]
so did Venezuelans accept similar conclusions with regard to COPEI.
Contributions also came to COPEI from international petroleum
interests, as with the AD. In sum, COPEI tapped all available
sources, both internal and external; a concentrated and massive
campaign expenditure was therefore possible.

The impact of its division on the AD was initially devastating.
The loss of key party organizers to the MEP, notably in Caracas
and Maracaibo, largely neutralized several years' painfully
developed party infrastructure. The AD faced the problem of
rebuilding its apparatus in conjunction with a national campaign,
relying frequently on junior party bureaucrats or untried newcomers.
A few of their more capable leaders were also serving in the Leoni
administration and thus unable to devote full energies to the
party cause. Because of the havoc created by the party conflict,
the AD adopted a highly centralized stance--more so than might
otherwise have been the case. In its earlier years local activity
and relative autonomy had been encouraged, although the reins
from Caracas were tightened somewhat for a campaign. That was
not a realistic course in the wake of the division. While the
Organization Secretariat labored to rebuild a national structure
out of the existing rubble, a special Electoral Commission was
created under Octavio Lepage. It swiftly assumed major
responsibilities in the campaign and created a number of ad hoc,
specialized suborganizations: Women for Gonzalo, Doctors for
Gonzalo, and others.

Even after the hasty restaffing of regular party organs,
the AD continued to lean heavily on the Electoral Commission.
The campaign structure, in addition to its centralized and
specialized traits, was also directed toward effective fusion with
related sectors. Gonzalo Barrios frequently understated his party
affiliation, seeking the uncommitted vote and appealing to
independent sectors. Thus an array of "independent journalists for
Barrios," "independent doctors for Barrios," and similar groups
were laboring on his behalf. It was the task of the Electoral
Commission to maintain communications and horizontal control over
these bodies. The candidate's staff was quite small, and in this
sense the adeco structure was institutionalized rather than
personalized. As a member of the party's old guard, Barrios had
been less the leader of anti-Prieto forces than a figure about
whom they could coalesce, and he leaned heavily upon party
institutions and bureaucrats. The candidate's personal trust,
especially his reliance on such men as Lepage and Carlos Andrés
Pérez, the latter a confidante of Betancourt, further underlined
campaign institutionalization.

Finances were derived from both internal and external sources.
Once again the recent party division complicated the task. When
Prieto and his followers departed, control over some of the party
bank accounts remained in their hands, and as much as $7 million
may have moved to the MEP.[41] This estimate appears exaggerated,
but certainly substantial funds were lost. The party continued to
receive pay in the form of monthly dues, but this had been designed
more for the promotion of party identification and a sense of
participation.[42] As Venezuela's government party the AD , despite
ritualistic proclamations of neutrality, enjoyed substantial
benefits. In addition to administration propaganda boasting of
the accomplishments of the AD government, official printing presses
were available. Private financing was also substantial. For the

first time the Venezuela business community was sympathetic to an
adeco campaign, and many economic interests, including the petroleum
companies, contributed to Barrios as well as to Caldera. With the
AD as with COPEI, the financing was adequate for a costly campaign.
The organization of the MEP campaign presented its own
particular characteristics. Prieto was faced with the task of
simultaneously organizing a party and a national campaign; this
presented serious difficulties throughout 1968. Given the
precipitous rush of events into which the MEP was hurled, campaign
organization was more informal and less tightly controlled than
in COPEI and the AD. The MEP did undertake as systematic and
rational an organization as was possible, benefiting from the
presence of many long-time colleagues of Prieto from the AD,[43] all
under the experienced Jesús Angel Paz Galarraga. A party structure
and electoral machine were both articulated at the national level,
and a concerted effort was made to gain control of former AD
regional and local organs. Although the basic characteristic was
centralization, considerable autonomy was permitted state and local
leaders. National leadership devoted more time to those geographic
areas in which the AD was strongest, attempting to create effective
mepista organs in competition with those loyal to Barrios. The
relationship between the MEP and the PRIN was never firm in
organizational terms, thus being diffused rather than fused.
   Creation of a National Electoral Commission under Luis Lander,
who had played a similar role for the AD in 1958 and 1963, provided
the specialized character of the campaign. The commission
possessed wide political experience but lacked the extensive staffs
enjoyed by Caldera and Barrios. The National Electoral Commission
worked closely with the Organization Secretariat, headed by Adelso
González. Part-time volunteer workers were relied upon heavily,
including many who could devote only partial attention to the
campaign. Supportive work was thus of an uneven quality. Although
the primacy of Prieto and his personal magnetism was an overriding
characteristic of the mepista campaign, it was institutionalized
rather than personalized. The interrelationship between Prieto,
the campaign commission under Lander, and the party leadership was
tightly knit. Lines of authority and control were not always
carefully or fully articulated, however. Again, the individual
style of Prieto and the close personal ties among the party leaders
contributed to a cooperative informality at some variance with that
of the other campaign organizations.
   As the one serious contender whose election was both feared and
opposed by major business and economic sectors,[44] Luis B. Prieto
confronted serious financial difficulties. His campaign was the
most poorly funded of the four and was thus handicapped in competing
with the expensively high-powered public relations of his opponents.
The only nonparty sector with an affinity for Prieto's programs was
the labor movement, but its division at the time of the AD conflict
minimized its capacity to provide meaningful financing. Financing
was therefore almost entirely membership-based, the other major
source being the funds that had been taken from the AD at the time
of the split.[45] Given the extravagance of the 1968 campaign,[46] the

MEP was at a severe disadvantage imposed by its financial
constraints.

The Frente de la Victoria campaign necessarily reflected those
characteristics necessitated by the very nature of the three-party
coalition. Organizational problems were severe. The existence of
an overarching Policy Committee with representatives of the three
parties proved inefficient in the extreme. Deadlock was frequent
and the three separate party organizations relentlessly went their
individual ways. By July 1973, Burelli and his personal advisers
were forced to take matters into their own hands. Although a
political novice, Burelli Rivas was unable to count on the
organizations supporting him. The problem was compounded by the
personalistic nature of all three parties. The URD, the only
alliance member with vestiges of a national structure, nonetheless
reflected Villalba's own qualities of rhetorical brilliance, erratic
political opportunism, and organizational ineptitude. For the FDP,
the admitted political talents of ex-adeco Jorge Dáger were
dependent upon the personal appeal of Wolfgang Larrazábal. FDP
organizational strength was limited to the poorer barrios of
metropolitan Caracas. In the FND, Uslar had never established a
viable structure outside the Caracas area, and the bulk of his
support in 1963 had been based upon explicit appeal as an
"anti-party" candidate.[47]

The Burelli-created organization therefore was centered upon
his own personal staff, and coordination with the three member
parties was ineffective. In that the campaign was directed from
Caracas, the structure was essentially centralized, but the lack
of meaningful authority over the parties from the candidate himself
rendered it virtually fictitious much of the time. The degree of
specialization and personalization was therefore pronounced;
meantime the staffs of the URD, FND, and FDP frequently operated
at cross-purposes. When Jóvito Villalba joined Burelli Rivas on
a campaign swing, he would stress the importance of casting the
small tarjeta for the URD slate, in addition to voting for Burelli.
Uslar Pietri, Dáger, and Larrazábal did much the same.

Organizational obstacles, then, forced Burelli in the direction
of an increasingly personalized campaign. Given the necessity of
presenting a new political face to the electorate, the greatest
possible exposure was necessary in a short period of time. It was
also important that Burelli identify himself with the three party
leaders of the coalition, recognizing the extent to which past
electoral support had derived more from personalities than from
party loyalties. He made joint public appearances with these men,
but he toured the country alone with his staff for the bulk of
his campaign. The fates of the parties of Villalba, Larrazábal,
and Uslar rested on the outcomes of the small tarjeta vote, and
Burelli's campaign was damaged in the process. By the close of
the contest, he had in effect developed a separate campaign of
his own, one that was not coordinated closely with those of the
three individual parties.

The candidate enjoyed financial support from business and
commercial interests, although apparently much less than either

Caldera or Barrios. The endorsement of the Association of the
Middle Class and of the National Electoral Movement of Independents
represented business support, and influential members of Fedecámaras
also backed him. The financing of his campaign rested on external
bases, for the funds received from the coalition parties were
minimal. Furthermore, the bulk of available party funds was
channeled into the competition for party representation on
congressional and municipal bodies. A further obstacle to major
financing from private sources was the tendency of Venezuelan
entrepreneurs to doubt, until the final stages of the race, that
the Burelli candidacy represented a serious option for victory.

Strategies and Tactics
      For COPEI and Rafael Caldera, the basic outlines were sharp
and clear-cut. Campaign objectives were electoral; the strategy
was consensual, blending both reinforcement and recruitment;
tactics of inducement were employed, stressing material more than
symbolic elements. Whereas the basic objective through 1958 had
been instrumental, by 1963 the shift was toward the electoral,
and it was fully completed in 1968. The party had but a single
goal--victory and the achievement of national power. For Caldera
himself, the campaign was his best and last opportunity to realize
his dream of becoming president. Devising a strategy that was
consensual, the copeyanos chose an equal emphasis on reinforcement
and recruitment. With the former, they exerted maximum effort in
turning out the party faithful. With party membership placed
between 700,000 and 800,000, the task of getting out the copeyano
voters was crucial. Simultaneously, COPEI sought to reach
independent and unaligned voters, especially in the urban sector.
The result was the tailoring of special appeals to disparate
groups, including campaign appeals directed specifically at
attracting such uncommitted voters. Tactically, COPEI emphasized
material inducements. With party loyalists these included
discussion groups, open forums, and a host of other participatory
devices. The promise of government jobs and material improvement
were also offered. For independents, incentives were related to
specialized interests. Artists, students, professionals, and
women were all extended specific promises. Women in particular
were actively proselytized. Although Sra Caldera was relatively
inactive, many other wives took a large part, and there were
innumerable "Coffees with Caldera" at which the candidate presented
himself.
      Symbolic tactics were not ignored, but were less widely employed.
Association with the Church, especially in the Andes, provided ties
with an important legitimizing symbol. In addition, voters were
reminded that COPEI, as a partner in the Betancourt administration,
had loyally stood fast in opposing urban terrorism and guerrilla
revolutionaries. The responsibility of its stance during the five
years of opposition to Raúl Leoni was also emphasized. Nonpartisan
tactics were implemented in appeals to independents, as COPEI
recognized the legitimizing role of all loyal Venezuelans, not
simply party members alone. Both material and symbolic inducements

were provided by programmatic references to many existing government
activities, as these were often praised in general terms before
promising to provide more effective implementation if Caldera were
elected. The party slogan of Cambio ("change") was constantly
reiterated. For both the AD and the MEP, campaign strategies and
tactics were less precisely defined. With the AD, although the
electoral victory of Gonzalo Barrios was obviously paramount,
accompanying this was the instrumental objective of party
reorganization. Both consensual and conflictual strategies were
adopted as a means of compensating for the recent schism.
Reinforcement strategy sought to demonstrate that Barrios, rather
than Prieto, was the true AD candidate; loyal adecos, stunned and
confused over the course of events, were to be convinced that
Barrios was the representative of party ideals and Prieto an
opportunistic traitor. Widespread use of party tradition was
employed in the rural areas. For the urban centers, in contrast,
recruitment efforts were directed toward independents; in Caracas
itself, which had been strongly anti-AD in both 1958 and 1963, the
candidate was presented as a statesmanlike figure standing above
petty partisan interests, disassociated from party signs and
symbols. Conflictual strategy was also viewed as necessary to
blunt the opposition from both COPEI and the MEP. COPEI, as the
AD's most serious opponent in recent years, represented a serious
challenge that deeply worried party strategists. The situation
with MEP was of course quite distinctive. The necessity of
presenting Barrios as the legitimate AD standardbearer also implied
the need to question Prieto's credentials; thus a discrediting
strategy was adopted to confront the mepista candidate.
     The tactics adopted to implement the AD's multipronged
strategies were similarly varied. Reinforcement was sought through
both material and symbolic inducements. The achievements of ten
years' government were heralded, with the party faithful assured
that Gonzalo Barrios was indeed the legitimate AD candidate. His
election would assure a continuation and expansion of established
policies and programs. Familiar party slogans, symbols, and banners
were heavily employed with appeals also based upon past adeco
presidents: Rómulo Gallegos, Rómulo Betancourt, and Raúl Leoni.
A different set of appeals were employed in seeking the urban and
previously anti-AD vote through reliance on other organizations.[48]
Recruitment campaigns in the cities used such slogans as Gonzalo--
A Great President, or With Gonzalo--Five Years of Confidence,
explicitly omitting party identification. The tactic of
disinducement was directed toward Rafael Caldera and COPEI, but
especially against Luis B. Prieto. Vivid illustration of AD tactics
came from the appearances and declarations of ex-President
Betancourt upon his return to Venezuela for the closing weeks of
the campaign.
     Betancourt devoted his time to appearances outside the largest
urban centers. Traveling the interior in the company of Barrios,
he would typically remind his audience of his visits there when
president of the Republic; there would be references to public works
of the Leoni administration and Barrios was proclaimed as the

natural leader of five more years of AD government. Thus he
employed both material and symbolic inducements on behalf of the
party. Disinducements were directed toward Prieto and Caldera.
Although explicitly refusing to attack "a close colleague of
thirty-five years," he emphasized that Prieto's candidacy had
grown out of unwillingness to accept majority decision within
the party. Prieto was further discredited by strong insinuations
that although he was an anti-communist, there were elements within
the MEP that were dangerously sympathetic to the PCV. As for
COPEI, Betancourt stressed its character as being aligned with the
presumably international nature of Christian Democracy. A bleak
picture of Chilean conditions under Christian Democracy was painted.
When late in the campaign a cabinet crisis and related strikes in
Italy made headlines, Betancourt was swift to incorporate references
to the Italian crisis into his speeches, concluding that
internationally the record of Christian Democracy was poor.

        Barrios himself, while emphasizing party allegiance in the
countryside, appealed to urban voters as if entirely above party
and partisanship. Stressing past government accomplishments and
promising to move ahead along similar lines, he struck the pose
of a serenely progressive, eminently rational candidate whose
concerns were national rather than partisan. The timing of his
campaign saw months of early effort to attract independent voters
and placate business and economic sectors. With the return of
Betancourt in September, he devoted later efforts to a wooing of
the party rank and file in the interior. By the conclusion of the
campaign, it was apparent that Barrios had been highly successful
in devising and implementing an intricately complex mixture of
diverse strategies and tactics. Post-election analyses subsequently
agreed that, although starting in difficult circumstances, Barrios
had put together and led a politically shrewd and highly effective
campaign.

        For Luis B. Prieto the campaign situation was also complex.
The initial need was to direct attention to the many adecos who
had supported him in the AD primary and subsequent struggle for
party control. The task was complicated by adeco efforts to
portray him as having deserted the party for reasons of personal
ambition. An obvious response was to claim that he himself was
the victim of betrayal and that party oligarchs, in rejecting his
candidacy, had denied the popular will of the rank and file. The
MEP was therefore presented as the true "party of the people."
Prieto argued that the schism had been founded on programmatic and
doctrinal rather than personal bases. The previous decade of AD
government policies was strongly criticized. It was further stated
that Prieto and his close colleagues, after years of frustration in
the effort to modernize and to reorient AD policy, had no choice
but to strike out on their own. The MEP was forced further onto
the defensive with sardonic AD ripostes that it had taken the
prietistas ten years to reach their decision and that the
precipitous departure of Prieto after more than three decades in
the movement was assuredly due solely to personal ambitions.

The effort to represent the true aspirations of adeco grass-
roots therefore followed the consensual strategy of reinforcement.
Conflictual patterns centered on anti-Barrios attacks but also
included strong criticism of COPEI. Prieto's own anticlericalism
led naturally to tactics intended to weaken the Caldera candidacy.
This, however, helped to strengthen the common perception of the
MEP as representing the sectarian and leftist element of the AD and
sapped mepista efforts to attract independents. The bid for
nonaligned voters was pitched on an effort to stress Prieto's
grass-roots strength and legitimacy as the representative of the
poor. As a non-Marxist who nonetheless stood to the left of his
major competitors, Prieto was also forced to defend himself against
charges that the MEP was seriously compromised by Venezuelan
communists. When the UPA in mid-summer publicly urged its
membership to cast the communist presidential tarjeta in favor of
Prieto, he was immediately subjected to inevitable attack. The
subsequent return of Rómulo Betancourt to the campaign trail further
forced the MEP onto the defensive.[49] Despite herculean efforts, the
campaign was never fully able to resume the initiative on a
sustained basis.
    The Frente de la Victoria never fully articulated its campaign
appeals. Its very objectives were somewhat amorphous, with the
URD, FDP, and FND each pursuing primarily recruitment policies in
the quest for party supporters, while the presidential candidate
emphasized independence and disassociation from the existing
political elite. The conflicting appeals were not channeled or
localized, as was the case with the AD. Credibility was therefore
strained, and Burelli was never able to cope with the problem
adequately. Conflictual strategies were also applied in somewhat
contradictory fashion. The stress upon Burelli's independence and
nonpartisanship led to attacks, both direct and indirect, upon the
existing parties. This of course clashed directly with the need
to attract sympathizers of the three Frente parties. A discrediting
strategy was also applied against COPEI, based on charges that its
program was essentially fascist in nature. COPEI never fully
eliminated the issue from the minds of voters.
    The conflicting interests of Burelli and the three parties of
the Frente were never fully resolved. The candidate's campaign
confronted the necessity of acquainting the electorate with the
unfamiliar name and face. Burelli with increasing ease played the
role of the new leader who, through a combination of youthful vigor
and innovative policy approaches, could bring fresh attitudes and
approaches to the operation of Venezuelan government. Yet the
party support that he required inevitably muddied the image
presented to the public. The candidate's insistence that he was
free of political ties, unshackled by past commitments and
obligations, struck many as both unconvincing and improbable. In
short, the nature of the Frente coalition created strategic and
tactical incompatibilities, along with the organizational
difficulties already outlined.

Ideologies and Programs
      Examination of these questions for the 1973 campaign allows a
cursory statement here. Rafael Caldera and COPEI sought a position
between what it viewed as the AD status quo and the leftist stance
of Prieto and the MEP. Free enterprise was praised, while
Venezuela's large array of state entitites were also viewed
sympathetically. The existing balance between the private and
public sectors was to remain intact, although new government
programs were projected as extending somewhat the scope of state
enterprise. Copeyano technicians labored for months to produce the
near-encyclopedic Programa de Gobierno, which was presented in
August of 1968.[50] In a serious effort to identify national problems
and to propose solutions,[51] the party also argued the necessity of
reorganizing and reinvigorating existing programs. Predictable
references to the family and hearth, to morality and decency,
added a veneer of Christian democratic ideology to the program.
      The AD program advocated an extension and continuation of
ten years' government policies. The party was fully committed to
the existing balance between the public and private sectors.
Priorities were viewed as sound, with Barrios and his colleagues
willing for a large sector of the economy to remain untouched by
state intervention. It was held that the Betancourt and Leoni
administration had developed new programs where necessary, and that
the task for the coming constitutional period was essentially that
of improving the quality of already-existing government services.
The emphasis on industrialization during the preceding decade was
defended in fulsome terms, and by 1968 the AD was arguing that the
takeoff point had been reached in such areas as steel, electricity,
aluminum processing, and petrochemicals. The industrial park
established by the Leoni administration in Valencia was cited as an
imaginative and collaborative example of public-private cooperation
in the interests of national development and economic
diversification.
      The MEP, symbolizing as it did the self-proclaimed "democratic
left" in Venezuela, advocated an increase of state activities in
areas previously occupied exclusively by the private sector. Yet
there was a marked reluctance to specify these areas, owing largely
to uneasiness over the evident hostility of the nation's
entrepreneurs. Programmatic proposals devoted greater attention to
social welfare measures: educational reforms, a restructuring of
agrarian reform, and an improvement in the delivery of health and
housing facilities. Criticism was directed at the AD for its
alleged delivery of important economic activities into the hands
of foreign interests. Industrialization was characterized as
dominated from abroad, and the MEP pledged—again in vague
generalities—to undertake a "Venezuelanization" of the economy and
means of production.
      Although the stance of the Frente de la Victoria was often
ambiguous, it seemed to suggest a position at least marginally to
the right of the AD. Burelli did not advocate a rejection of state
activities but preferred a more active role for the private sector.

Discussions of existing social legislation were muted; to have
criticized them would have alienated both the URD and FDP, although
delighting the FND. Burelli's programmatic declarations were
couched in more general terms than those of his three major
competitors. Stress was therefore placed upon charges of government
inefficiency, with many of its programs characterized as well-
intentioned but bungling. It was contended that greater productivity
could be achieved through a close working relationship between
private enterprise and the state, with entrepreneurial experience
and insight being brought to bear on future development of
Venezuelan industry.

   A crude index of the overall conflictual strategies of the
four major actors of the 1968 presidential campaign is suggested
in figure 6. The lines in the figure represent the flow of negative
messages between campaigners. There is an implicit assumption that
each campaigner "targeted" its negative messages in order to (1)
maximize its own gains and (2) maximize the losses of its main
contender(s). We obviously lack the data to support any
generalizations concerning the volume and symmetry of these 1968

FIGURE 6. Primary Dimensions of Conflict between Campaign Actors
in the 1968 Presidential Election

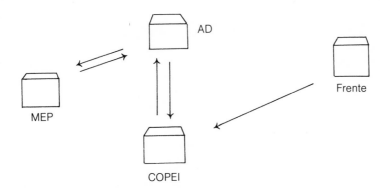

exchanges, but in terms of the observations conducted by Martz and
the descriptions by Myers, the following propositions are plausible.
First, the AD was clearly in the most difficult position, having to
counteract the conflictual strategies of MEP and COPEI, both of
which were primarily targeted against the AD. Second, MEP and
COPEI minimized their negative exchanges since each would profit

from losses inflicted upon the AD by the other. Finally, the Frente concentrated its attacks on COPEI, which studiously chose to underplay them. The operationalization of these propositions would require the collection of campaign messages between each pair of actors in order to measure their frequency and intensity. This would involve a very laborious task which lies beyond the space limitations of this work, but this graphic representation provides further clarification of the main lines of conflict in the 1968 campaign, with the caveat that this type of model can be formalized where data are available.

CAMPAIGN CRUCIBLE 1968

Candidate Styles

Each of the candidates projected a distinctive image. For COPEI, Rafael Caldera epitomized the image of a handsome, stylish, statesmanlike figure, somewhat aloof and paternalistic in manner, but eminently presidenciable. Caldera more than any of his opponents stood as unchallenged leader and spokesman for his party. A man of culture and wide international experience, he was a fastidious dresser who was rarely seen with a hair out of place, even amid the enthusiastic throng of partisans.[52] Although preferring more formal speechmaking to mingling in the crowds, years of experience had taught him the techniques of pressing the flesh with the most ill-clad campesino. A vigorous speaker with the capacity to build and sustain the involvement of his listeners, he was eloquent in his cataloguing of national problems and proposals for change and reform. A man of commanding presence, Rafael Caldera looked every inch a president.

Gonzalo Barrios, trained in the law but a lifelong public servant and political activist, was particularly noted as a polished, skillful negotiator. In style and manner a diplomat, he had been personally close to ex-President Rómulo Gallegos and had contributed to the smoothing of relationships between the intellectual writer and more politically oriented men like Betancourt and Leoni. A major parliamentary figure in the AD-COPEI alliance during the Betancourt government, he had later held the key Interior ministry under Raúl Leoni. A bachelor known for continental tastes and an interest in fine foods, wines, and literature, Barrios was relatively unimpressive as a public speaker. Consistently giving a rumpled impression on the campaign trail, he was more effective in small informal discussions than in campaign oratory. The Barrios image, nonetheless, was one of political stature and, despite a lifetime in politics, as a unifier appealing to all sectors of the population.

No other candidate was endowed with the distinctive qualities and charisma of Luis Beltrán Prieto Figueroa, at age sixty-six the oldest of the candidates. Regarded by some as a political anachronism in the Venezuela of 1968, he was nonetheless well equipped to be presented as the man of the people. Known to friends and followers as "El Maestro," he was founder of the national teachers' federation and had achieved wide recognition as an educator. His long political career included service as the

president of the Senate and, of course, as president of the AD prior
to the 1967 division. Although a man of erudition who had pioneered
educational reforms and authored more than two dozen books, Prieto
possessed the common touch that his opponents sometimes lacked. An
imposingly tall and large man with prominent ears which were adopted
by the MEP as the symbol of the party, Prieto spoke with ease in
the vernacular of lower-class Venezuelans. A sharp and penetrating
wit, combined with his references to the traits of the town or
region in which he appeared, contributed to the effectiveness of
his public appearances. Mepista campaign rallies, more than those
of his rivals, radiated a festive air; spontaneity and gaiety
seemed to typify the atmosphere as Prieto mingled with the crowds.
     Miguel Angel Burelli Rivas thrived under the glare of the
political spotlight. Vigorous, active, younger looking than his
forty-six years, he swiftly overcame an initial stiffness to develop
a style of his own. As a public speaker his more positive traits
were earnestness and candor. Jut-jawed and handsome, he left many
voters with a belief in the integrity and seriousness of the man.
His growing effectiveness and popularity as the campaign progressed
was recognized by the increasingly sharp attacks he drew from his
opponents. The projection of a new and youthful political
personality was greatly enhanced by the extensive campaigning of
his wife María, whose charm and good looks represented important
political capital. Appearing more frequently than the wives of
Caldera or Prieto, she was seen alongside her husband on campaign
posters urging the voter to choose "the presidential couple." This
also served to stress the fact of Gonzalo Barrios's bachelorhood,
which was a handicap for the adeco candidate.
     A word is also necessary for a few other major figures whose
public appearances were important. For the AD, the appearance of
Rómulo Betancourt was a strong asset. After five years' absence
from Venezuela, his arrival at a campaign meeting invariably had
an electric quality, and his first appearance on the speakers'
stand inevitably triggered elated waving of white handkerchiefs[53]
and a wave of chants, "Rómulo, Rómulo." When his distinctively
rasping voice began with the phrase he had used for years,
"Conciudadanos... compañeros y compañeras...," the roars were
deafening. He tended to overshadow Barrios, but Betancourt generally
kept his remarks brief, then stepping aside and leaving the major
address to the candidate. There was unanimity in post-electoral
analyses as to the tangible assistance Betancourt lent the adeco
cause. Mepista leaders angrily estimated that he had cost them
at least 100,000 votes. It should not be forgotten that the AD's
Raúl Leoni, as president of the Republic, did his bit for the
party cause by increasing his public appearances at dedications of
public works and similar occasions. A reserved man whose presidency
was surprisingly nonpartisan and national in character, Leoni as
chief executive was inevitably an obvious reminder of the AD.
     The participation of the three party leaders supporting Burelli
Rivas was of variable quality, and the impact is difficult to judge.
Least effective of the three was Arturo Uslar Pietri. His relative
electoral success in 1963 had been largely the result of an

effective media campaign--the first in Venezuelan history to make prominent use of television. Appearances with Burelli Rivas were not frequent and had pro forma quality to them. For the FDP, Wolfgang Larrázabal was not an accomplished speaker, but in house-to-house campaigning he was invariably well-received. The admiral's personal appeal, especially in slum areas, was later believed to have contributed to Burelli's respectable showing in Caracas and environs. Jóvito Villalba remained the stem-winding, fiery orator of the 1920s, whose own style and rhetoric was increasingly dated by 1968. His public appearances did have the value of rallying the urredista faithful, who remained dedicated to "El Maestro."

Communications and the Media

Presentational techniques were much more widely used in 1968 than ever before.[54] Press, radio, and television all inundated the Venezuelan voter with political messages. With the former, the greatest controversy arose over COPEI's mid-1968 agreement with Miguel Angel Capriles, whose chain of newspapers and magazines was currently the most extensive in the country. Although the notoriety of the Capariles chain caused grave reservations within COPEI over the pact, Rafael Caldera concluded that his campaign demanded more favorable and extensive coverage than could otherwise be expected. Once the bargain was struck, the Capriles publications launched a major publicity effort in Caldera's behalf, with effusive praise of his campaign and venomous attacks on the opposition. In exchange Capriles and his associates were placed on certain party slates.[55] El Nacional, Caracas's most prestigious daily, responded by barring its editorial pages to the Social Christians, as did Maracaibo's Panorama. Burelli received sympathetic treatment in El Nacional, and its editorial pages were also open to both the AD and MEP, despite lack of sympathy for the latter. La República, which had been founded by the AD in 1961 and was headed by a party member, obviously provided an outlet for Barrios.

The radio listener was deafened with paid political messages, but the television viewer was even more saturated. Presidential and congressional candidates paraded across the screen in an incessant stream of paid appearances. Such interview programs as the popular "Buenos Días" permitted the candidates to expound their ideas at length; this was of particular value for Prieto and Burelli, who had less ample financing than Caldera and Barrios. Unlike the campaign of 1963, there were no major direct debates between the presidential candidates, although various of their more prominent supporters confronted one another on live telecasts. Despite such major usage of presentational methods, however, much of the real action remained on the campaign trail, where traditional participatory techniques continued to receive emphasis.

Each of the four candidates traveled the length and breadth of Venezuela for many months, returning to all of the states and visiting most of the 642 municipalities. Caldera initiated the electoral touring in the first half of 1967. Prieto and Barrios had undergone months of travel during the nomination struggle with

the AD and continued after their February 1968 nominations.   Burelli
was the last to begin.   All means of transportation were used, from
private plane to extended automobile caravans.   Typically, the
morning and afternoon hours were filled with small meetings,
door-to-door campaigning in selected neighborhoods, and breakfasts
or lunches with local leaders.   A "major" speech would be delivered
each night as a conclusion to day-long appearances and conversations.
There local leaders would whip up crowd enthusiasm with harangues,
often interspersed with music, entertainment, and intermittent
cheers.

Eventually the candidate himself fought his way through the
throngs, delivered a speech normally no longer than a half-hour,
and then repaired to a local club, restaurant, or home of a local
supporter.   Amid greater informality, both local party leaders
and independents would seize the opportunity to shake the candidate's
hand, exchange pleasantries, and perhaps ask for autographs.   It
was rigorously demanding, yet none of the candidates, ranging in age
from Prieto (sixty-six) and Barrios (sixty-five) to Caldera
(fifty-two) and Burelli (forty-six), showed signs of more than
normal fatigue.   Although campaign managers made much of the size
and enthusiasm of crowds, they privately admitted that logistical
skill in bussing supporters to meetings often had much to do with
crowd size.   In smaller towns, the arrival of a candidate
represented a break in daily routine, and many citizens would
successively attend each of the candidates' rallies.   Even
recognizing such facts, campaign organizers would not infrequently
base intuitive calculations of local electoral strength on such
mass concentrations.

Although in retrospect many politicians questioned the
effectiveness of mass rallies, they remained convinced that rallies
retained important, even unique functions.   They viewed involvement
of large numbers of people as significant, encouraging a sense of
participation and commitment.   Furthermore, the exchange of views
between local and regional leaders and candidates on the spot,
rather than in Caracas headquarters, was regarded as positive.   The
very appearance of a national candidate also provided identification
and renewed energy for local leaders in the effort to mobilize
the electorate.   Finally, the candidates themselves retained an
almost mystical belief in the importance of meeting and greeting
individual voters face-to-face.   Direct personal contact, they all
argued, had no real substitute and provided the most basic electoral
tool of the campaign.

Political symbols were used extensively.   For COPEI, the party
symbol of a vertical point of a lance and its traditional green
color was widely used.   A popular device was the pre-rally
distribution of green plastic maracas, which would be shaken at
appropriate moments during a meeting; the volume of several
thousand, rattled simultaneously, was startling.   The most widely
used slogan throughout the copeyano campaign was el cambio va
("change is coming").   The party placed large calendars in public
squares throughout Venezuela with the message el cambio va, adding
the number of days until elections.   One of Caracas's major

intersections, at the Plaza Venezuela, was the site of the largest copeyano calendar in the country; nightly music, songs, and proselytizing of passing pedestrians and motorists also enlivened the proceedings. A huge rectangular green block was also suspended from a skyscraper fronting on the Plaza Venezuela—appropriately enough, hung from the new Capriles Building.

The AD distributed tens of thousands of small rubber pipes, representing the familiar personal symbol of Rómulo Betancourt. "Gonzalo Presidente" was taped on the bowl, and blowing into the rubber stem produced a cacophony of loud quacking sounds. The AD made wide use of its traditional white color throughout the campaign. At party rallies, especially during the final weeks, Barrios and Betancourt would mount the podium and wave white handkerchiefs to the crowd while loudspeakers played the national anthem and the audience cheered. However, campaign banners and signs in Caracas consistently omitted either the familiar AD symbol or any explicit references to the party. The symbolism was entirely that of Gonzalo Barrios, un gran presidente, un presidente de confianza, above the partisanship of petty politics and sectarian interests.

The most striking use of emblems and slogans was that of Prieto. The official symbol of the MEP was la oreja ("the ear") which appeared on party advertisements and even on the ballot itself. Party headquarters at the Edificio Restrepo in downtown Caracas even boasted on its side a two-story-high effigy of the candidate, juxtaposed with a huge ear and the initials of the MEP. Slogans and commercials urged the electorate to "put the ear in the presidential palace," "the ear will hear the voice of the people," and so on. Prietista supporters wore lapel buttons in the shape of an ear, and cab drivers would have small ears hanging from the sun visors. For Burelli, largely lacking in familiar party symbols from his coalition, advertisements and posters tended to focus on him and his wife, advocating the cause of "the presidential pair."

Political communications relied far more heavily upon presentational techniques than in earlier years. This was especially true of Caldera and Barrios, who enjoyed the financing necessary for wide use of the communications media. Burelli and Prieto were less able to afford such expensive techniques, and Prieto himself, reflecting his long experience of politics in pre-media days, preferred the participatory approach. There was a general recognition, however, that press, radio, and television were fundamentally important to a winning campaign. The immense expenditure of time and physical energy on personal tours, moreover, was becoming ever more difficult in the light of Venezuela's rapidly expanding population. Post-election interviews with the principals verified a general consensus that (1) campaigning had become far too long and expensive; (2) that the continuing evolution of campaign techniques would necessitate a growing reliance on the mass media; and (3) although personal appearances would continue to be important, their drain on time and energy was not commensurate with the value as measured by the mobilization of popular support.

Campaign Issues

With the major contours of the campaign already described, only
a few specific issues arising during the course of the contest
deserve mention. The two most salient revolved about the question
of safety and personal security. Increasing rates of common crime
led the opposition parties to attack the AD. COPEI in particular
focused on the problem, charging the government with a breakdown of
law and order while pledging less permissive security policies and
greater efficiency in fighting crime. Burelli gave less emphasis
to the issue whereas Prieto, as an ex-AD leader, felt constrained
to skirt the problem. Wide attention was also directed toward
anti-guerrilla policies. The AD claimed success for its posture,
noting the virtual defeat of revolutionary violence and the sharp
reduction in numbers of unreconstructed guerrillas.[56] The
legalization of the communists under the UPA banner was hailed as
further evidence of adeco successes in reincorporating former
activists into the political system. Caldera contended that the
harshness of methods under AD governments had been unwise and
counterproductive. Prieto firmly advocated a greater openness
toward former insurgents, while Burelli remarked that his absence
from domestic politics for much of the past decade left him uniquely
qualified to proceed with total pacification and reconciliation.

The debate over foreign domination of the economy was conducted
largely by the MEP, and its emphasis on redistribution politics
provoked relatively little response from the opposition. A variety
of perspectives of the desired forms of future industrialization
were presented as well as the means of achieving effective
modernization and diversification of the economy. Government
inefficiency or corruption inevitably were cited by Barrios's
opponents, with predictable claims that a new administration could
"clean up the mess." Perhaps the only unexpected controversy
came with the denunciation of copeyano "fascism," which resulted
from its August release of Caldera's government program.[57] The
September return of Rómulo Betancourt stimulated an expectation
that campaign appearances by the "greatest adeco of all" would
provoke a rise in the intensity of propaganda and verbal exchanges,
but this proved not to be the case. It was generally true, however,
that the campaign climate was more heated and tense than in either
1958 or 1963. The common interest in defending the democratic
system against the revolutionary left in 1963 had faded during the
intervening five years. The change of political environment
between 1963 and 1968 rendered unnecessary the earlier camaraderie
of all democratic forces in defense of the system; by 1968, "little
camaraderie remained."[58]

Election Results and Conclusions

The 1968 race proved the closest in national history. After
a nerve-wracking week during which the count mounted with agonizing
slowness as the result of malfunctions in a newly installed computer
system,[59] Rafael Caldera was proclaimed the victor by a margin of

31,000 in an electorate of 3.7 million. His 29 percent of the vote
was 0.8 percent ahead of Barrios, while Burelli polled 22 percent
and Prieto 19 percent. The AD won congressional elections with
COPEI second, followed by the MEP. The coalition backing Burelli
fared poorly, with both the FND and FDP devastated. The great
surprise was the strong showing by the perezjimenista CCN, which
ran first in the Federal District, thereby placing Pérez Jiménez
in the Senate and 11 of 37 candidates in the Chamber of Deputies.[60]
The composition of the new Senate, totaling 52 members, included 19
for Acción Democrática, 16 for COPEI, 5 for the MEP, 4 from the CCN,
3 from the URD, and 2 from the FDP. In the 213-person lower house,
the AD also led with 63 deputies, followed by 50 for COPEI, 25 from
the MEP, and 21 from the CCN. URD representation was 20, the FDP
10, and FND 4. The communists, standing as the UPA, elected 1
senator and 5 deputies.

Examination of regional returns indicated that COPEI's victory
was based on an incremental growth of support throughout the
country. Only in the Andes was its percentage lower than in 1963,
and it still stood at an impressive 49.5 percent. The weakest area
remained the East, where Caldera was fourth with less than 15
percent of the popular vote. The AD remained strong in the East
but lost ground from 1963 as a result of mepista incursions. Its
loss was directly traceable to an abysmal showing in the states of
Zulia and Lara, notably the cities of Maracaibo and Barquisimeto.
The mepista division had virtually destroyed AD leadership and
organization in Zulia, while weakening it significantly in Lara.
A deficit of 40,000 votes in the former and 24,000 in the latter as
compared with Caldera's totals more than balanced AD strength
elsewhere. For Prieto there were several disappointments. The
expected power in Zulia failed to offset his showing elsewhere in
the West; despite Eastern gains at the expense of the AD, these
could not compensate for weakness in the core cities of Caracas,
Maracay, and Valencia. Burelli Rivas carried metropolitan Caracas
and environs but was surprisingly weak in the East despite past
urredista popularity in the region. He ran poorly in both the
Andes and in Zulia.

Characteristics of the four major campaigns can be summarized
succinctly. That of Rafael Caldera and the Social Christians was
in many ways superior, even had the outcome been different. A
well-organized party, supplemented by an efficient campaign team,
COPEI was centralized, fused, and specialized. Enjoying ample
financing, skilled use of the media, and the advantages of opposing
a party regime bearing the burdens of a decade, it stood well
prepared for the competition. Central to the entire effort, of
course, was Rafael Caldera himself, the imprint of whose brilliant
party leadership was indelibly stamped upon the party organization,
ideology, program, and campaign techniques. For AD, the weight of
the 1967 division was simply too great to bear; the narrowness of
the margin by which Gonzalo Barrios lost the election was remarkable
given the impact of the schism. Clearly the activities of the Leoni
administration, the availability of government resources, and the
long tradition of adeco loyalties were crucial to the strength that

Barrios did display. Given the organizational debris that existed
less than a year before elections, it was remarkable that so much
was nonetheless accomplished in a short time. The impact of
Betancourt on behalf of the AD campaign must also be noted.

With the benefit of hindsight, the Burelli and Prieto
candidacies can be seen as less promising than they appeared at
the time. The myriad problems confronted by the former in the
ill-fitting and awkward Frente de la Victoria was insuperable. With
a longer time to campaign, Burelli might have raised his vote
somewhat, although scarcely enough to reach Miraflores. It was
only when he abandoned the respective party organizations and struck
out on his own that momentum was built up. Fourth, the campaign of
Luis B. Prieto had seemingly promised greater returns than were
achieved. Early in 1968 he was viewed as the front-runner; unless
that perception was vastly distorted, his position deteriorated
during the campaign. However, he was faced with imposing challenges;
the government lent its weight to the AD effort, damaging the MEP
in the process; months of attacks from the AD, most tellingly those
by Betancourt, led many adecos to view Prieto as having deserted
the cause for personalistic reasons; and the task of building both
a national party and a campaign team simultaneously was well-nigh
impossible under the circumstances. The clear positioning of the
MEP to the left of its three rivals may also have been, for 1968,
a serious electoral disadvantage. Notwithstanding its disappointment,
the MEP could take some pride in having emerged in no more than
twelve months as Venezuela's third-most-powerful political party.

The intensity of the 1968 campaign, underlined by the pronounced
degree of competition, had proven the first in which the outcome
had been in doubt. The importance of organization, strategy,
communications, and the myriad related elements was central to the
electoral process. For the political leadership of the nation, the
experience inevitably assured further development and refinement
for the next contest, five years hence. As a subject for study
and investigation--notwithstanding the limits of our research, as
explained earlier--the campaign suggested the broad applicability
of our model. Although it would be inappropriate to go beyond this
taxonomic narrative of 1968 phenomena, there seemed a heuristic
validity in applying the analytic model closely to the 1973
campaign.

2. THE POLITICO-INSTITUTIONAL
ENVIRONMENT

The patterns of population and electoral regionalism in
Venezuela had become well established by 1973. Regulatory
mechanisms--both constitutional and organic in nature--had been
elaborated extensively during the previous fifteen years.
Furthermore, a growing public understanding of the party system and
of national political dynamics helped to produce a greater awareness
of public issues. The identification and handling of salient
problems therefore acquired greater relevance for the campaign
competitors. Both environmental political conditions and public
opinion would contribute importantly to the milieu within which the
rivals competed for support on 9 December 1973.

THE ELECTORAL SYSTEM
The fundamental contours of existing constitutional and
electoral guidelines were introduced during the trienio.
Emendations since 1958 have produced changes in degree rather than
kind, while the Consejo Supremo Electoral (CSE) has come to occupy
a vital role in supervising the process. The CSE has achieved
increasing legitimacy in recent elections, although it is by no
means free from political controversy. The 1961 Constitution, now
the second most durable in national history,[1] drew extensively on
the 1947 charter,[2] including its pre-eminently presidential
character. Contrary to past tradition, however, the 1961 document
called for direct and fused rather than staggered elections, to
be convened at five-year intervals. Thus the Venezuelan electorate
is called upon to choose simultaneously five different categories
of officeholders: the president, all national senators,
representatives to the national Chamber of Deputies, members of
the twenty state legislative assemblies, and all municipal councilmen.
As had first been prescribed during the 1945-48 period, universal
suffrage by secret ballot from age eighteen was provided. There
were no restrictions in terms of sex,[3] literacy, or property
ownership; only members of the armed forces and citizens under
judicial sentence for the commission of crimes were ineligible to
vote. The act was described as an obligation of the citizen and

hence mandatory.[4] A variety of penalties was described for those
failing to exercise the vote.[5]
    The presidency is decided by simple plurality. Former
presidents become lifetime members of the Senate.[6] Representation
to the Senate is set constitutionally at two from the Federal
District and each of the twenty states, while the two federal
territories are without senators. Thus forty-two are chosen by
direct vote, in addition to a handful of others selected by indirect
methods, to be explained shortly. The 1961 Constitution allocated
national deputies per state on the basis of population, assigning
one per 50,000 inhabitants or a fraction over 25,000. Regardless
of population, no state was to have fewer than two deputies. The
two federal territories were automatically awarded one each. The
number of state legislators was established in proportion to the sum
of districts or municipalities within a state; the municipal councils
were composed of seven members, excepting the Federal District.

TABLE 1. Quotas for Deputies, 1973

Entities	National Population	National Deputies	State Deputies
Distrito Federal	2,381,423	37	
Anzoátegui	557,971	10	15
Apure	177,267	3	11
Aragua	482,122	7	13
Barinas	219,409	3	11
Bolívar	464,889	7	13
Carabobo	572,972	9	15
Cojedes	104,116	2	11
Falcón	443,451	7	13
Guárico	369,864	6	13
Lara	669,142	10	15
Mérida	364,716	6	13
Miranda	805,464	12	17
Monagas	346,992	5	13
Nueva Esparta	127,470	2	11
Portuguesa	324,748	5	13
Sucre	532,193	8	15
Táchira	584,241	9	15
Trujillo	406,813	7	13
Yaracuy	241,982	2	11
Zulia	1,547,632	24	23
Terr. Amazonas	13,331	1	
T. Delta Amacuro	34,714	1	
Venezuela	11,772,922	183	274

Note: Census estimates for 8 December 1973 were provided the CSE
       by the Ministerio de Fomento.

However, revision of the Suffrage Law in 1973 changed certain
representational bases. For the Chamber of Deputies--unwieldy in
number and growing every five years--the population base was set
at 0.55 percent of the total Venezuelan population (for 1973, using
an estimated population of 11,772,922, the base was therefore
64,751). The number of deputies per state was then determined by
dividing the state population by that predetermined national base
(if the remainder was over half of 64,751, an additional seat was
assigned to the state). Again, each state was guaranteed a minimum
of two deputies whatever its population, while the two sparsely
inhabited territories were assured one each. The addition of
deputies chosen indirectly through an electoral quotient was
maintained. A new base was also legislated for the legislative
assemblies. States with 300,000 inhabitants or fewer were allocated
eleven state deputies; from 300,001 to 500,000 received thirteen
deputies. Similar increases continued, reaching a maximum of
twenty-three deputies for any state with a population of 1,300,001
or above.[7] The specific allocations for 1973 appear in table 1.

Proportional representation, used in only a few other Latin
American republics at the time, was introduced to Venezuela in
1947, then re-established in the 1961 document. Appearing in
Article 113 of the Constitution and Chapter IV of the Suffrage Law,
the system adopted was that of Victor d'Hondt.[8] As modified by
the Venezuelans, each party list of candidates, chosen by the
casting of the small tarjeta or electoral card, is divided
successively by 1, 2, 3, 4, 5, and so on, until all seats have
been assigned. Luis B. Prieto illustrates its application with a
hypothetical example which assumes a state that is electing six
representatives.[9]

party list A	50,000	votes
party list B	25,000	votes
party list C	15,000	votes
state totals	90,000	votes

Setting up an electoral table by successive division produces:

party list A	party list B	party list C
50,000	25,000	15,000
25,000	12,500	7,500
16,666	8,333	5,000
12,500	6,250	3,750
10,000	5,000	3,000
8,333	4,166	2,500

The six positions will therefore be determined in descending order:
A, 50,000; A, 25,000; B, 25,000; A, 16,666; C, 15,000; A, 12,500.
Party line A is allocated four seats, with one each for B and C.
Distortion would still exist of course. Party A with 55 percent
of the vote would have 66 percent of the seats; and B, although
polling 10,000 more votes than C, would have the same representation.

Patterns can fluctuate substantially, rarely approximating fully the precise division of the vote. All of the familiar arguments about the salutary and unhealthy elements of proportional representation can be brought to bear by both supporters and critics of the system.[10] The fundamental objective remains the most perfect possible equality of franchise and representation. The classic statement remains that of John Stuart Mill.

> The pure idea of democracy, according to its definition, is the government of the whole people, by the whole people, equally represented. Democracy, as commonly conceived and hitherto practiced, is the government of the whole people by a mere majority of the people exclusively represented. The former is synonymous with equality of all citizens; the latter, strangely confounded with it, is a government of privilege in favor of the numerical majority, who alone possess practically any voice in the state. This is the inevitable consequence of the manner in which the votes are now taken, to the complete disenfranchisement of minorities.[11]

Venezuelans, in an effort to make the system as truly representative as possible, have introduced an electoral quotient in addition to the d'Hondt mechanism. The result is an effective bonus to some parties, derived from their national vote totals. The quotient is calculated by dividing the total number of seats in a congressional body into the total number of small card votes cast. The fixed number of forty-two Senate seats is applied there, while for the Chamber of Deputies, as we have seen, the number is established by 0.55 percent of the national population. The resulting cuociente is in turn divided into the small tarjeta vote total of 3,646,610, producing a quotient of 18,797. Applied to the small PRIN, the quotient was divided into the PRIN vote total of 85,694. This process awarded the PRIN four seats in the lower house. The PRIN had not won a single seat by direct means, so all four of its 1969–74 deputies enjoyed their position through application of the quotient. Similarly, the stronger URD won fourteen seats directly but according to the quotient had earned seventeen; an additional three were assigned to the party. The Suffrage Law limits a party to a maximum of two additional Senate seats and four in the Chamber of Deputies. Use of the quotient in conjunction with the d'Hondt system perhaps illustrates the striking comment by Milnor: "While it is probably the fate of man forever to pursue the better gadget, the power of man as an inventor seems to have found its real focus in the electoral system, where his passion for politics is wed to his passion for gadgetry."[12] For Venezuela, utilization of the quotient, although valid for all parties, in practice best serves the interests of the small parties. It also offers at least slight encouragement to the proliferation of small parties and presidential candidates.[13]

At least two other characteristics of the representational system are relevant to the rules of the game: the centralized control by party elites over congressional candidacy and membership,

and the virtual irrelevance of local interests for national
legislators. Given the use of so-called complete lists, each party
bears the responsibility for drawing up the planchas or slates of
its candidates for all offices. Not only does the party name its
nominees but also the order in which they appear. A party unlikely
to win more than three deputies in a given state will be doing an
aspiring party member little favor in placing him fifth or sixth;
his only possibility of reaching office would be as a suplente
replacing a person higher on the list who, although elected,
resigned or vacated the position. The role of the party leadership
in such matters is patently of immense importance. On election day
the voter chooses the list of a party, thereby being forced to
accept the candidates and the order in which they are placed. The
loyalties of legislative candidates are consequently to the party
and its central directorate, rather than to local voters. It is
not uncommon to place a candidate on the planchas of a state in
which he is not a resident, therefore weakening further the quality
of representation that local interests may expect. Moreover, an
individual may also appear on more than one plancha at the same
time. The local constituency suffers from an absence of leverage or
bargaining power with both the party and congress. Efforts by
party leaders to consult with local and regional figures are erratic
and often unproductive.

The nature and quality of representation is a distinctive one,
and clearly at variance with some political systems, especially
those with a single-member single-district pattern. Constituencies
are essentially without direct representation; to the extent that
local issues and problems are articulated, they must be communicated
primarily through resident party functionaries for transmission to
Caracas. The links between grass-roots sentiment and congressional
officeholders are therefore tenuous. The centralization of the
party system minimizes the direct impact of local sentiment. A
civic-minded person anxious to work on behalf of his town or
community is virtually prohibited from electoral office unless
he affiliates politically and puts himself under the discipline of
national party authority. Levine calls this operative norm the
"concentration rule" of the Venezuelan party system, to wit, "the
monopolization of political action by political parties."[14] An
operational corollary to this norm is provided by the operation of
the cuociente guaranteeing the representation of minority parties.

THE REGULATION OF ELECTORAL CONFLICT
Central to the entire process is the CSE, with authority
assigned by the Constitution and specific duties outlined in the
Suffrage Law. Its nine members are elected by Congress for five
years, coinciding approximately with the period of national
government. Law specifies that five will be chosen from the five
parties polling the largest vote in the previous election; in
practice they are put forward by their respective organizations.
The remaining four CSE members are independents, prohibited from
having political affiliation; one is designated as representing
the smaller parties. For parties not finishing among the top five

but having polled at least 3 percent of the last vote, representation with voice but not vote is provided. The council chooses its president and two vice-presidents from among its membership, with all three customarily being among the independents. The administrative structure for the handling of electoral functions also embraces Juntas Electorales Principales, Distritales, Municipales, and Mesas Electorales, in descending order of authority. The principales are seven-member bodies located in each state, the Federal District, and both territories. The lesser entities operate at district and municipal levels; some fifteen thousand mesas conduct the actual voting on election day.[15]

The magnitude of CSE duties is imposing.[16] They include the creation and maintenance of a Permanent Electoral Registration; the organizing, administering, and overseeing of all electoral bodies; application of proportional representation and the electoral quotient to determine the composition of legislative and municipal bodies; the tabulation, verification, and proclamation of the vote; and the judging of charges of irregularities or fraud. Moreover, by 1973 the council, with a large permanent staff, had become an increasingly important agency to which parties and candidates directed their complaints and requests. The CSE in the final months of the 1973 campaign was confronted with a wide array of subjects on which swift response was necessary, as described later.

The first amendment to the 1961 Constitution must also be mentioned. Presented to Congress in October 1972 and approved by the necessary two-thirds of state legislatures in early 1973, it effectively disqualified the candidacy of General Marcos Pérez Jiménez. The amendment provided a new requirement of constitutional eligibility for president, in addition to those already appearing in articles 149, 152, 182, and 213. The crucial passage read as follows: "Those who have been judged guilty by means of a definitive sentence dictated by Ordinary Tribunals, with a prison sentence greater than three years, for crimes committed in the management of public functions...cannot be elected President of the Republic, Senator or Deputy to Congress, or Magistrate of the Supreme Court of Justice."[17] The only means of appeal was directly to the Corte Suprema de Justicia (CSJ) itself. A subsequent plea to the court by followers of Pérez Jiménez was unsuccessful, leading to the progressive electoral disarray of perezjimenista forces analyzed elsewhere. Be that as it may, Venezuelan constitutional prescriptions essentially established a presidential, fused system, with highly centralized administrative control of elections by an independent body. Alterations in the institutional rules of the game will require constitutional amendment.

Specific electoral mechanisms set forth in ordinary legislation are more susceptible to revision, however. Indeed, important changes were twice introduced between 1968 and 1973 balloting, casting a pall of scandal over representatives of several political parties. In the three elections from 1958 through 1968, the basic system utilized a pair of separate tarjetas or cards, with the large one cast for the presidency and the small one for all other offices. Originally designed to facilitate accurate voting by

illiterates, the system was highly visual. Each party had its own
distinguishing colors, emblems, and insignias on its card, sometimes
including a picture of the presidential candidate. The colors of
the older parties were nationally known--**green for COPEI, white for
the AD**, and yellow for the URD. Distinctive symbols included a
ship's helm for the candidacy of Admiral Larrazábal, the effigy of
an ear for Luis B. Prieto, an orange horse for the PRIN, a red
rooster for the communists, a bell for the FND, and so on.[18]
Geometric figures were employed for the use of the blind. On
election day the voter would be given a copy of each large and each
small tarjeta. Stepping into privacy, he would choose one of each,
place the two in a sealed envelope and, after discarding the unused
tarjetas, would slip it into the ballot box.[19]

By 1968, with the proliferation of parties and candidates, the
process had become exceedingly awkward. Great care by officials
at the individual voting mesa or table was necessary to assure that
all cards were present and that the piles were not mixed with one
another. The voter who arrived at the mesa found himself confronted
with piles of tarjetas--**more than a dozen for national parties and**
up to fourteen more in the case of certain regional or state parties.
It was a slow and painstaking task for each voter to pick up so
many cards individually. The entire process had become confusing,
cumbersome, and unwieldy in the extreme. Following 1968 elections,
the cry for reform was widespread. In time it led to a proposal
that the nation adopt voting machines, and in due course this led
to a scandal of major proportions.

Initial discussion took place in Congress, which bore the
responsibility for introducing any changes in the system.
Preliminary contacts were established with several manufacturers
in the United States, mock models of voting machines were studied,
the act of voting was simulated, and prices were quoted. COPEI,
the government party at the time, was among those opposing a change
of system, arguing that the expense was too great and that it was
unwise of Venezuela to invest so heavily in voting machines which
would be used but once every five years. Others, led by the AD,
regarded the introduction of a modern and presumably fool-proof
voting system as deserving high priority. Nationalistic pride was
fanned by the information that Venezuela would become the first
country in Latin America to employ an automatic voting system. The
AD was not without its partisan interests in advocating the purchase
of machines: never entirely convinced that the party had indeed
truly lost the 1968 contest, it also believed that the best
insurance against official fraud by the copeyano government in 1973
would be a system of machines. It was ultimately decided to
purchase 10,000 electronic machines from the Automatic Voting
Machine Corporation (AVM), at a cost of $1,100 each, thus totaling
$11 million. The first machines began to be shipped to Venezuela,
while two down payments totaling nearly $3 million were paid in
September and November of 1972.

There were rumors that irregularities were involved in the
decision to favor AVM rather than accepting the bids of Litton
Corporation or of others. Not unil March of 1973, however, did

scandal suddenly blossom as the result of revelations in a Miami
courtroom. During proceedings involving an internal fight among
AVM officers and shareholders, it was charged that Hans Mangin,
a key figure in the negotiations with Venezuela, had surreptitiously
offered commissions to certain congressmen. Allegedly, Omar Rumbos
of the URD and Antonio Espinoza Prieto were to be paid $10 per unit,
while an additional $40 per unit was destined for the URD and
MEP, and $47 to the AD. Mangin himself had denied the charge,
while the AVM vice-president refused to answer on the grounds of
self-incrimination under the Fifth Amendment. The Venezuelans
named in the charge denied all complicity, as did the respective
political parties. However, cries to annul the contract were
immediately raised in Caracas.

Virtually all the parties demanded the contract with AVM be
rescinded, with the exception of the AD. The latter, while
reiterating its innocence, insisted that the advantages of the
machines over the tarjeta system were sufficient to justify the
honoring of the contract. Angry polemics were exchanged between
copeyano Secretary-General Pedro Pablo Aguilar and his adeco
counterpart Octavio Lepage, whose duelling on behalf of their
parties continued to enliven the campaign to its conclusion. The
office of the comptroller general launched an investigation that
concluded in June 1973 with the recommendation that the contract
be canceled. Its final report and accompanying documents to the
courts suggested irregularities by both Espinoza Prieto and Rumbos.
A special committee in the Chamber of Deputies, chaired by José
Rodríguez Iturbe of COPEI, concluded its own inquiry with a report
also recommending concellation. The CSE initiated an investigation
by a commission of jurists, which reported in May with the
conclusion that the terms of the contract concerning payment of
commissions had been violated. The CSE, according to the jurists,
had full authority to cancel the contract.

The climax was reached when on 7 June 1973 the CSE by a vote
of 6-2, with one abstention, rescinded the original contract
signed 31 July of the previous year.[20] Representatives of the MEP
and AD opposed the action. The AD maintained its contention that
the only defense against possible fraud by COPEI was the use of
the electronic machines. As a consequence of the vote, the CSE
wrote to AVM on 11 June officially demanding recovery of the
down payment. AVM's representatives returned to Venezuela a check
for 12,517,179,83 bolívares ($2,854,545) on 23 August 1972.
Official inquiries into the alleged offers of illegal commissions
continued in the next few months, but attention then turned to
other campaign matters.[21]

For the CSE, months of preparation for the introduction and
installation of the machines, as well as the training of technicians
and the educating of the public on their use, were rendered
meaningless. With election day only a few months ahead, a new
system had to be adopted and implemented. Even this could not
begin until Congress, already impatient for its recess and eager
to hit the campaign trail, decided on another method of voting.
The AD provided the major stimulus. A five-man commission headed

by the AD's Carlos Canache Mata presented a report to Congress at
the beginning of July. It recommended a system different from
either of the others, although based on the notion of large and
small cards. The new system, referred to as the boleta única
(literally, the "single ticket"), called for the voter to receive
but one card. Approximately the size of a full newspaper page,
it would have two squares per party, one large and the other small.
Each square would resemble the separate tarjetas of past elections,
with the usual party colors and symbols. All parties legally
registered with the CSE would have their two squares placed side
by side. The voter would mark one large and one small card each
with a seal bearing the initials CSE, then fold the sheet several
times and deposit the wad of paper in the ballot box.

The boleta that faced the voters on election day 1973 was a
rainbow of colors and symbols, party initials, and candidate
pictures. The respective set of large and accompanying small-card
squares were arrayed in three vertical columns, offering the
selection of forty-eight alternatives for national, state, or local
office. Zoological suggestions came with the inclusion of a
rooster, horse, lion, and tiger; other symbols included an ear, bow
and arrow, bell, plumed Indian, point of a lance, nautical wheel,
harp, dove, clenched fist, and mountain sunrise. The parties had
chosen their positions on the boleta in the order of their
legislative finish in 1968; lots were drawn for new parties.
Despite the imposing appearance of the boleta--presumably no more
intimidating to the voter than the several dozen piles of cards he
would have been confronted with under the 1968 system--at least
three major advantages resulted. First, with the boleta única,
there was no danger of a voter's receiving an incomplete set of
cards. Second, it would no longer be theoretically possible to
control the voter by demanding that he later return those cards he
did not case. And finally, the cumbersome physical problems of the
multiple card system, with candidates and parties multiplying at
a rapid pace, would be avoided.

Despite the pressures of time in replacing the voting machines,
adoption of this new system was not without its political dimensions.
The proposed revision was reported to Congress only four months
prior to elections and was soon caught up in the campaign struggle.
COPEI prevented a legislative quorum for some ten days and two
extensions of the legislative session were required; rumors
suggested that the AD-led opposition might apply pressure by
denying President Caldera the necessary permission to leave the
country for a projected visit to the United Nations. Cooler heads
eventually prevailed, but the reform legislation was not completed
and signed by the president until a bare three months before
election day. The limited time thereby available to the CSE for
implementation of the new system was to prove a serious problem,
as described in chapter 8. In addition to the boleta única,
several other changes were included in the bill, which eventually
comprised twenty-six separate articles. Perhaps the most pertinent
was the provision that on election day, once individual mesas had
completed the voting and tallied the results, one copy would be

sent directly to the CSE in Caracas, in addition to those provided
the local electoral entity. Thus the official vote tabulation
would begin more rapidly than in past elections, when all totals
had first been compiled at local and then at regional levels before
being forwarded to Caracas.

Late in November Dr. Luis A. Pietri, president of the CSE,
announced to the press that following the elections the CSE would
formulate recommendations for further reform. The new Congress in
1974 would be asked to consider remedies for the remaining
"deficiencies" of the system. Dr. Pietri cited five specific areas
of concern.[22] Several of his proposals resulted directly from
broader criticisms generated during the 1973 campaign. Details
were to be elaborated by the CSE prior to submission to the new
Congress. Whatever the final outcome, it seemed likely that the
rules of the game in future contests would differ somewhat from
those presently in effect. Be that as it may, September revisions
of the Suffrage Law solidified the regulatory mechanisms employed
for 1973 elections.[23]

ELECTORAL DEMOGRAPHY

With some 352,000 square miles, Venezuela is roughly comparable
in size to Texas and Oklahoma combined. For political and electoral
purposes it may be divided into five principal areas: the Andes,
the West, the llanos or plains, the Center, and the East.[24] Each
is composed of several states possessing at least a modicum of
ecological similarities, although the classification is admittedly
arbitrary and flawed. The Andean highlands, embracing the states
of Táchira, Mérida, and Trujillo, by 1973 included 11.5 percent of
the national population, with the largest cities San Cristóbal,
Valera, and Mérida. An agricultural region in which coffee is the
predominant commercial crop, the Andes is in many ways the most
distinctive region of the country. Traditionally isolated from
the rest of Venezuela, insular and provincial in outlook, the
andino population has been regarded as the bastion of conservatism.
At one time strongly influenced by neighboring Colombia, it has
remained orthodox in its Catholicism and resistent to change. The
Social Christians dominated the region since their founding in
1946. The three Andean states cast 11.4 percent of the total
presidential vote in 1968. With the completion of the 1973
electoral registration, however, its portion of inscribed voters
stood at 10.4 percent.

The West has more than twice the population of the Andes, with
24.7 percent of all Venezuelans. It includes the states of Zulia,
Lara, Yaracuy, and Falcón, with the Maracaibo Basin in Zulia the
center of petroleum production. The city of Maracaibo itself is
second only to Caracas in population and importance. In Lara,
Barquisimeto has become a major marketing and commercial center,
with industrial development also notable in recent years. The
region also includes productive agricultural areas, although much
of the lower-lying land is subject to periodic droughts as well
as floods. Maracaibo is known for the distinctive characteristics
of its inhabitants—the maracuchos—with strongly Caribbean traits

intermingled with strains of the Guajiro Indians who inhabit the westernmost reaches of Zulia. The producer of vast petroleum wealth, Zulia and particularly the city of **Maracaibo** have become of utmost electoral importance. According the 1973 data, 23.9 percent of all registered voters were in the West. Until 1968 a bastion for the AD, the region later became a major battleground of the campaign.

FIGURE 7. Regional Distribution of Population, 1973

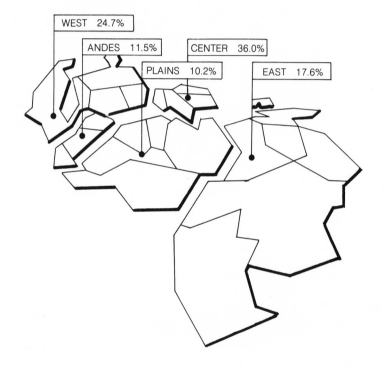

Note: Adapted from are illustration in David J. Myers,   <u>Democratic Campaigning in Venezuela</u> (Caracas: Fundación La **Salle** de **Ciencias** Naturales, 1973), p. 28.

The llanos to the south constitute a sparsely populated rural
expanse which contains the states of Apure, Barinas, Portuguesa,
Cojedes, and Guárico. Only 10.2 percent of the population inhabits
the plains region, and the state capitals are among the smallest
in Venezuela. Featuring a flat, sprawling landscape with annual
flooding, much of the llanos extends along the Orinoco River,
which runs over six hundred miles from the foothills of the Andes
to the Atlantic. Cattle raising, traditionally the main economic
activity, continues to dominate much of the region today. Residents
are descendants of the original llaneros, including the first
president of Venezuela and former lieutenant of Bolívar, José
Antonio Páez. Roughhewn and nomadic cattlemen fearing neither God
nor their fellow man, the llaneros have contributed heroic pages
to national history. Today their independence and individualism
is reflected in sharp electoral differences of opinion. The AD
enjoyed strength in the region for some years, having been the
first to organize there extensively. This gradually shifted,
however, with COPEI making inroads in Barinas, Apure, and Portuguesa.
For the 1973 elections, 9.8 percent of registered voters were found
in the plains states.
    The Center represents the core of the Venezuelan populace and
the major locus of national politics. Lying between the llanos
and the Caribbean, it encompasses the Federal District plus the
states of Miranda, Aragua, and Carabobo. Venezuela's smallest
region in territory, it contains 36.0 percent of the population,
centered predominantly in the urban centers of Caracas, Maracay,
and Valencia. The natural center for impassioned political
competition, it has long been of key importance to electoral
contests. Metropolitan Caracas in particular has been a political
maverick, much to the despair and frustration of two generations
of party leaders. The Caracas vote went to the 1958 "phenomenon"
of Wolfgang Larrazábal; five years later the choice of that
electorate was Arturo Uslar Pietri; and in 1968 the four
presidential contenders labored mightily only to split the vote
indecisively, while the perezjimenista CCN startled the political
world by sweeping the legislative contest. In 1973, 38.6 percent
of registered voters was located in the Center.
    Lastly is the oriente or East, a rather heterogeneous region
composed of Nueva Esparta, Sucre, Anzoátegui, Monagas, and Bolívar,
along with the federal territories of Delta Amacuro and Amazonas.
With 17.6 percent of the population, these states are a diverse
lot, ranging from the fishermen on the islands of Nueva Esparta
and the shores of Sucre to commercial centers in Anzoátegui and
Bolívar, from the cattlemen of Monagas to the industrial workers
of the iron ore region. Although population growth has decelerated
markedly in Nueva Esparta and Sucre as the result of economic
hardship, urban slums have proliferated in the cities of Bolívar
with immigration attracted by massive industrialization spurred by
the presence of vast natural resources in the region. Bolívar,
a particular focus for future national development, occupies a
leading position in all projections of economic and demographic
growth. The oriente began politically as an adeco area in which

the URD made substantial inroads. The 1968 AD division resulted in
sizable votes for Prieto and the MEP. Villalba and Prieto, both
natives of Margarita, also vied for dominations in Nueva Esparta.
For the 1973 elections, 17.1 percent of the voters were inscribed
in the region.

TABLE 2. Venezuelan Population and Growth by States, 1950-1973

Entities	Years				Growth
	1950	1961	1968	1973	1950-73
Distrito Federal	709,602	1,257,515	1,855,386	2,381,423	235.60%
Anzoátegui	242,058	382,002	478,200	557,971	130.51
Apure	88,939	117,577	150,511	177,267	99.31
Aragua	189,891	313,274	406,960	482,122	153.89
Barinas	79,944	139,271	183,211	219,409	174.45
Bolívar	127,436	213,543	349,424	464,889	264.80
Carabobo	242,923	381,636	487,860	572,972	135.87
Cojedes	52,111	72,652	91,119	104,116	99.80
Falcón	258,759	340,450	393,796	443,451	71.38
Guárico	159,523	244,966	313,504	369,864	131.86
Lara	368,169	489,140	587,543	669,142	81.75
Mérida	211,110	270,641	323,212	364,716	72.76
Miranda	276,273	492,349	661,155	805,464	191.55
Monagas	175,560	246,349	303,751	346,992	97.65
Nueva Esparta	75,899	89,492	107,144	127,470	67.94
Portuguesa	122,153	302,707	268,316	324,748	165.85
Sucre	333,607	391,992	477,303	532,193	59.53
Táchira	304,181	402,472	501,567	584,241	92.07
Trujillo	162,759	316,634	372,235	406,813	149.95
Yaracuy	132,436	175,291	213,446	241,982	82.72
Zulia	560,336	919,863	1,259,479	1,547,632	176.20
Amazonas	10,582	11,757	12,649	13,331	25.98
Delta Amacuro	33,648	33,979	34,227	34,714	3.17
	4,917,899	7,605,552	9,831,998	11,772,922	139.64%

Taking national population figures as a whole, the 1973
estimate of 11,772,922 dramatized the rapidity of increase in
Venezuela. The briefest inspection of data reveals at least three
major patterns: (1) national growth (2) increase of the urban
population and (3) the growing concentration of the population in
nine major urban centers. Of particular relevance is the expansion
of metropolitan Caracas itself. Table 2 provides testimony to the
national increase of 139.6 percent from 1950 to 1973, as well as
the pronounced growth in all but a few states and regions. Of the
twenty states, ten have more than doubled during the twenty-three-
year period, while the Federal District--most of which is a part of
metropolitan Caracas--has grown by 239.5 percent. There was naturally
a concomitant expansion in the electorate (see table 3). The final
registration figure for 1973 elections--4,661,252--was some 600,000
higher than for the elections five years earlier. With completion

of the electoral registration, the CSE announced a total of 4,916,812
voters. Using Ministerio de Fomento estimates of 5,103,748 voters,
this meant that 96.33 percent had been reached in the process, an
uncommonly high figure.

TABLE 3. Electoral Population and Registration, 1973

Entity	Estimated Electoral Population	Registered	National Percentage	Number of Mesas
Distrito Federal	933,926	863,179	18.51	2,393
Anzoátegui	231,056	213,873	4.58	676
Apure	71,407	63,039	1.35	242
Aragua	274,773	238,080	5.10	702
Barinas	104,763	89,325	1.91	359
Bolívar	184,204	169,570	3.63	559
Carabobo	330,973	294,441	6.31	908
Cojedes	42,997	41,881	0.89	169
Falcón	190,152	177,814	3.81	662
Guárico	143,715	131,306	2.81	448
Lara	322,491	297,869	6.38	937
Mérida	166,089	145,680	3.12	539
Miranda	424,838	402,449	8.63	1,227
Monagas	128,845	130,952	2.37	422
Nueva Esparta	62,722	57,558	1.10	181
Portuguesa	134,291	134,844	2.80	432
Sucre	209,525	197,838	4.24	703
Táchira	206,878	177,230	3.80	621
Trujillo	181,608	163,532	3.50	664
Yaracuy	102,896	97,208	2.08	392
Zulia	623,114	544,092	11.67	1,657
Terr. Amazonas	10,212	10,092	0.21	37
T. Delta Amacuro	22,273	19,463	0.41	81
	5,103,748	4,661,315	100.00	15,011

Compared with the 3,720,660 valid votes cast in 1968, and
assuming some 10 percent of abstentions or null votes, this led to
the estimate that approximately 780,000 Venezuelans would be voting
in 1973 for the first time. However, the initial announcement from
the CSE preceded the necessary purification to eliminate errors,
double registrations, ineligible voters, and other irregularities.
Not until 23 November, less than three weeks before elections, was
the process finally completed and official totals released.
According to the CSE, 4,661,252 citizens were registered and eligible
to vote on the 9 December.[25] Comparison with 1968 data thus showed
a total of 526,324 new voters--11.29 percent of the electorate. The
bulk of the registered voters was located in the Federal District
and four states--Zulia, Miranda, Lara, and Carabobo. Together they
constituted 51.5 percent of the entire voting population. Estimates
on the age of the electorate, drawn from the Ministry of Development

and the CSE, showed that over one-third of the voters were under
the age of twenty-five (1.5 million), and that fully one-half were
between the ages of thirteen and thirty-two (2.4 million). The
mean age of the entire Venezuelan population was twenty-one.

TABLE 4. Electoral Participation, 1958-1968

| | Presidential Election Years | | |
	1958	1963	1968
Eligible voters	3,335,460	4,072,292	4,240,000
Registered voters	2,913,801	3,369,968	4,134,928
% registered	(87.36)	(82.75)	(97.52)
Abstentions	191,748	262,405	135,311
Total vote	2,722,053	3,107,563	3,999,617
Voting turnout (%):			
effective	(81.61)	(76.31)	(94.33)
electoral	(93.42)	(92.21)	(96.73)
Null votes	111,220	188,650	278,957
Valid votes	2,610,833	2,918,913	3,720,660
% valid votes:			
effective	(78.28)	(71.68)	(87.75)
electoral	(95.91)	(93.93)	(93.03)

Sources: Consejo Supremo Electoral, Datos estadísticos del registro
electoral de 1968 (Caracas, 1968), pp.88-89, and
Escrutinios de las elecciones desde 1946 hasta 1968
(Caracas, n.d.), pp. 20,31,42.

Note: Effective percentages computed as a fraction of eligible
voters; electoral percentages computed as a fraction of
registered voters.

SYSTEM LEGITIMACY AND POPULAR PARTICIPATION IN ELECTIONS
     The intensity with which candidates and parties participate in
elections in Venezuela and the degree to which the rules of
electoral competition have been institutionalized would mean little
if popular interest in elections was very low. The case is quite
the opposite, however; what justifies such intensity and the complex
set of institutional norms is the tremendously high level of popular

participation in Venezuelan elections. Without attempting to theorize here, we offer the reader the statistics of table 4. These data indicate that elections are very salient for the overwhelming majority of the public, as further demonstrated by high levels of registration, turnout, and valid votes in the presidential contests of 1958, 1963, and 1968. Only in 1963 was there some slackening in what could otherwise be characterized as a growth curve. Yet it should not be forgotten that in 1963, the FALN conducted a series of terrorist attempts on election day to impose a boycott on the electorate, an effort that failed. The more rigorous measurement of popular participation is represented by the effective percentages presented in the table. These percentages indicate the level of participation relative to all possible participants. The other measure, electoral percentages, follows standard criteria. In both cases, the levels are very high, far above such figures for the United States and comparable to Western European values. Tentatively, we could say that there is a very high level of support for the institution of elections. Happily, this need not be left to conjecture since results of our VENEVOTE survey--conducted in the early fall of 1973--elucidate the point. Six questions in the survey offer relevant data on attitudes toward elections.

First of all, it should be observed that the compulsory nature of the vote affects the quality of popular support. We found Venezuelans to be equally divided when asked if they would continue to vote should the compulsory requirement be dropped; 48.2 percent said "yes" and 48.4 percent said "no"; 3.5 percent were undecided. Venezuelans vote, in part, because they have to. Second, accepting the fact that they have to vote, a full 73.3 percent say that they would never invalidate their vote; that is, they would never vote "null." The remaining 27 percent of the voters said they would vote null if they disliked or disagreed with all available candidates (18.5 percent), or in order to "protest the system" (a remarkably low 2.2 percent, given the importance that the protest vote allegedly has in Latin America); only 1.5 percent said they would always vote null; the remaining 4.8 percent offered a host of reasons, or simply no reason at all for voting null.

The other four survey questions were standard ones for the topic: "Voting is a very important factor in politics"; "in order to have democracy there must be elections"; "a candidate-elect worries about the problems of the people who elected him"; and "elections force the government to worry about the problems of the people." Analysis of the responses showed they were distributed cumulatively, enabling us to locate the majority of our respondents in a very favorable disposition toward elections: 1,467 out of 1,521 were grouped into the "favorable" and "very favorable" categories when the six items were combined.[26] This distribution of opinion neither necessarily reflects nor results from a high level of system legitimacy. Rather, it indicates that the majority of Venezuelans believe that elections provide a practical instrument to select and constrain political leaders.

If Venezuelans think highly of the institution of elections, they do not extend an equally positive evaluation to their parties, politicians, and government officials. Indeed, the level of cynicism and exasperation for Venezuelans is similar to that of citizens in other democratic countries. In order to explore these dimensions of popular support for relevant political objects we utilized batteries of questions similar to those of Michigan's Survey Research Center. In dealing with opinion about government and politics in general, we modified the questions to reflect opinion about Venezuelan political regimes of the last fifteen years. Seven questions were posed. Three nonscalable items concerned the appropriateness of these regimes' policies, the capacity of their officials, and the personal benefits bestowed upon the respondent by actions of the regimes. Most responses were moderately positive, following an intermediate, noncommital category in two of the items. In contrast, the public seems impressed by the qualifications of government officials (see table 5).

TABLE 5.   Evaluation of Regime Outputs

	Favorable	Neutral or Intermediate	Unfavorable	Don't Know
Appropriateness of Gov't Action	25.1%	41.2%	28.0%	5.8%
Capacity of Gov't Officials	57.9	11.4	26.6	4.1
Benefit of Gov't Action	8.1	73.8	16.6	1.5

A more adverse trend is uncovered by the distribution of the Guttman scale scores derived from our four remaining items. These deal with opinions concerning the manner in which democratic regimes have spent government resources, about whether they have mainly served the citizenry or special interests, about the honesty of officials serving these regimes, and the regimes' impact on the nation. Most Venezuelans would give their democratic regimes failing grades on these criteria. As shown in table 6, less than 20 percent of our respondents evaluate the regimes in a positive or very positive fashion. By contrast, although only 10 percent have a very negative evaluation of the democratic regimes, nearly half our respondents proffered a negative evaluation. This in no way implies that they would prefer more authoritarian alternatives—as suggested by the results of the 1973 elections—but it indicates an unmistakably negative evaluation of the national government during the last fifteen years.

TABLE 6.   Regime Evaluation Scale

Evaluation of the Regime	Scale Score	Frequency	Percent
Positive	1	80	5.3
	2	199	13.1
	3	385	25.3
	4	697	45.8
Negative	5	160	10.5

Coefficient of Reproducibility=0.90
Coefficient of Scalability=0.65

Similar results were found in the public's evaluation of the role of the professional politicians (see table 7). There were two reasons to tap this vein. First, Venezuelans tend to identify their present system with the major national parties, which are directed by career politicians. Second, the most common alternative to liberal or social democracy in contemporary Latin America is bureaucratic authoritarianism. An important element of such authoritarian regimes implies the elimination of political parties and the role of party politicians, with government technicians assuming much of the policymaking function. This allegedly curtails political corruption and the "inefficiency" of partisan politics.

TABLE 7.   Evaluation of Politician's Role Scale

Evaluation of Politicians	Scale Score	Frequency	Percent
Positive	1	78	5.1
	2	252	16.6
	3	322	21.2
	4	359	23.6
Negative	5	510	33.5

In gauging the public's evaluation of the performance of party politicians in Venezuela, we again drew inspiration from mainstream North American political polling, therefore utilizing reductionist techniques to develop more reliable profiles of our respondents. We employed a battery of six questions and produced a four-item Guttman scale. The reproducibility of the scale was 0.90 and its scalability 0.68. The distribution of scale scores is very similar to that for regime evaluation, indicating similarly negative attitudes by the majority of the public. Two-thirds of our respondents thought of Venezuelan politicians in very negative terms.

"politicians talk much and do nothing," and disagreement with such statements as "politicians care about people's problems," "politicians care about national problems," and "politicians help the community." The two items that could not be scaled together with the others failed to show greater appreciation or affection for politicians among the mass public. An overwhelming 81.1 percent agreed with the statement that "politicians always lie," and a more modest but still decisive 56.5 percent agreed with the statement that "government would be better without politicians."[27]

TABLE 8. Attitudes About Political Parties

	Yes	Depends	No	Don't Know
Best for One Party to Rule	22.3%	10.8%	64.7%	2.1%
Opposition Critique Useful	75.3	2.8	19.9	2.1
Parties Controlled by Minorities	74.3	5.5	12.0	8.2
Parties Care Only About Elections	69.0	7.6	20.6	2.7

One final area related to "objects of political support" concerns public opinion about parties in general and about Venezuelan parties in particular (see table 8). The public's tendency to identify the present democratic regime with the main Venezuelan parties again compelled us to probe this dimension. We found on the one hand a majority favoring the exercise of partisan opposition and the desirability of different parties' coming to power, and on the other negative sanction of the internal characteristics of parties. Our data show almost two-thirds of the public opposed to the idea of one-party rule; three-fourths have a favorable evaluation of the role of the opposition. The data show similar proportions believing the parties to be controlled by self-seeking minorities, interested only in winning elections. Thus our preliminary assessment depicts an ambivalent situation: support for a competitive party system and agreement with the desirability of political opposition, accompanied by dissatisfaction with the organizational deficiencies of political parties.

We also gathered evidence concerning opinion about Venezuelan parties. We are not referring to partisanship as currently understood in our second volume but to popular feelings about Venezuelan parties. Our respondents were asked a series of questions along the following lines. First, we wanted to determine how important the public thought parties were in Venezuela. Precisely 69.0 percent said they played a very important part in national life. Second, we asked our respondents their opinions about the number of parties in Venezuela. An overwhelming 95.5 percent said there were too many parties in the country. We probed further and invited them to mention the number that they believed optimal. We received the following responses:

none	2.8%	three	23.1%
one	6.5%	four or	
two	40.6%	more	26.9%

In essence, the Venezuelan electorate was demanding a reduction in
the number of parties to a more manageable set of alternatives.
This may have been a reflection of arguments about "polarization"--
holding that the main cleavage in Venezuelan politics was between
the AD and COPEI--and about the "economy of the vote"-which held
that a vote for any minor contender was wasted. Both of these
arguments were advanced by the adecos and copeyanos; whatever their
empirical adequacy, the Venezuelan electorate was advocating a
political system with a reduced number of parties.

A more subtle line of inquiry concerned the issue of the
strength of existing sympathies and loyalties for different
Venezuelan parties. We wanted to ascertain the proportion of the
electorate that could be swayed as a result of the 1973 campaign.
In V. O. Key's terminology,[28] we wanted an idea of the potential
number of "switchers" that could be produced. We departed from the
assumption that party loyalties are challenged by campaign stimuli.
The longer these loyalties have had to mature the more difficult it
is to displace them, and the lower the probability that a campaign
can change them. With most of the Venezuelan electorate developing
and strengthening these loyalties during a period of only fifteen
years, we believed that the 1973 campaign had a good probability
of influencing the loyalties of this electorate. In short, we
believed that the overall efficacy of the Venezuelan campaign of
1973 would be high. Following this rationale we approached the
measurement of this portion of the electorate from several
perspectives. Three have an immediate bearing on this discussion.

Our first estimate of the potential impact of the 1973
electoral campaign is given by the responses to two questions. The
first involved a "soft" estimate of the potential impact provided
by those respondents who were members of any political party in
the fall of 1973. Almost three-fourths of our respondents--74.1
percent--told us that they were not, at the time of the interview,
members of any political party. The 25.9 percent who said they
were members of a political party should not be considered switchers
in terms of this question. A second, "harder" estimate of the
number of switchers may be derived from the responses to a question
involving respondent sympathy toward a political party; 34.8 percent
said they did not sympathize with any political party while 65.2
percent expressed sympathy for one of the parties--of these 22.3
percent and 26.8 percent identified respectively with the AD and
COPEI. The probability function associated with the process of
producing a switch, or at least the crystallization of a preference
for a particular candidate, oscillated from a low of 34.8 percent
measured in terms of sympathy--to a high of 74.1 percent--measured
in terms of party membership--among the mass public. We tried a
final approach to the potential impact of the campaign, without
getting directly into the question of partisanship or voting

intention, by offering our respondents a choice between the
following alternatives: "Today, in Venezuelan politics, do you
consider yourself an _independent_, a _sympathizer_ of a political
party, or a person who is not interested in politics?" We obtained
the results shown in table 9.

TABLE 9. Degree of Partisanship

	Frequency	%
Sympathizers	677	44.6
Independent	291	19.2
Not Interested	487	32.0
Other*	62	4.1

*Includes "members" and "militants" of
a party who identified themselves in
terms of these labels.

We need not take any of these different criteria as the most
reliable; in fact, we never selected one while in the field.
Furthermore, we have said nothing about voting intention and
partisanship, which were measured separately and are probably as
good, if not better, estimates. What we would stress here is that
although there were a series of mistakes and miscalculations on
the part of campaigners, their effort was relevant because of a
sufficiently high number of undecided voters, weak partisans,
uncommitted independents, and unconcerned electors. The fluidity
of the loyalties of a substantial proportion of the electorate
justified a vigorous campaign effort. In short, campaigning was
eminently important in the Venezuelan **election** of 1973.
    To summarize, there is in Venezuela a high level of popular
support for the institution of elections, substantial agreement
on the need for a competitive party system and political opposition,
but fairly widespread disenchantment with the performance of the
system and negative evaluations of the roles played by political
parties and politicians. Venezuelans want the advantages of
democratic procedures but also desire the full benefits to be
derived therefrom; having agreed on the procedural norms, they
are now concerned with substantive results. This leads to
consideration of 1973 campaign issues.

THE ISSUES OF THE CAMPAIGN
    The policies and practices of the Caldera administration were
obviously relevant; public perceptions of government performance,
of major issues, and of policy preferences were also crucial to
the campaign. Moreover, it was the popular attitude toward
political leadership and institutions that framed the response
to electoral appeals and techniques. Our concern is not an
evaluation of the Social Christian government but a review of
issues on which the campaign was fought. Our findings demonstrate
that the 1973 campaign was fought primarily over bread-and-butter

issues. In assessing issues of **greatest salience to the public, we**
can employ results of a summer pre-test[29] as well as the VENEVOTE
findings. These appear in table 10.

TABLE 10. Campaign Issues

Summer of 1973			Fall of 1973
	%	%	
Cost of living	30.0	37.4	Cost of living
Unemployment	23.2	21.3	Unemployment
Crime, delinquency	8.8	7.8	Education
Education	7.6	7.2	Crime
Drought, lack of water	4.0	5.1	Food scarcity, hoarding
Youth, student unrest	3.6	3.4	Agriculture
Hunger, poverty	3.2	2.6	Housing
Housing	2.8	2.3	Poverty
All other	16.8	13.0	All other

Note: These frequencies are the results of a probe. The question
was "What are, in your opinion, the most important national
problems of the moment?" Having annotated all the problems
mentioned by the respondent, the interviewer then asked,
"And which of these is the most important national problem?"

The only notable variation came from termination of a drought
that was of major concern, especially to our rural respondents,
during the summer. The two issues of **greatest concern showed** a
combined increase as the election approached; the cost of living
and unemployment clearly preoccupied the citizenry. It is noteworthy
that housing did not rank high, and that crime and personal security
also received limited mention. The data are also interesting in
what they omit. The virtual absence of any mention of oil indicates
the extent to which it was not seen as germane to the electoral
debate. When asked of the most important national problem, only
1.5 percent cited oil, reflecting the nonpartisanship with which
the subject is customarily treated. Another significant omission
is the absence of any reference to foreign affairs, with all issues
of concern domestic in nature. The Venezuelans were essentially
preoccupied with fundamental economic issues and problems of daily
life. Tying these responses to the conditions prevailing in the
Venezuela of 1973, it seemed at best questionable whether attitudes
toward the government would prove helpful to the COPEI campaign,
while opposition attacks on real or alleged shortcomings might well
tap a responsive current. We will see in part two how competing
forces themselves viewed such matters and incorporated them into
the campaign, but it is clear that the economy was the issue of the
1973 Venezuelan campaign.

We followed up issue questions with a logical probe,[30] expecting
the public to demand solutions from the public **sector.** Our

expectations were confirmed, as reported in table 11.

TABLE 11. Agents of Issue Resolution

Summer of 1973	%	Fall of 1973	%
President	66.4	Government	49.6
Private initiative	10.0	Government agency	15.0
Government	6.8	President	12.5
Candidates	2.4	Congress	4.3
Congress	1.6	Candidates	3.5
Nobody	5.2	Private initiative	3.3
Don't know	4.4	Nobody	3.5
All other	3.2	All other	8.3

The implications of these results were twofold. First, the
incumbent administration could not divest itself of responsibility
for the solution of these problems in the eyes of the public.
Conversely, no serious opposition campaigner could fail to address
these basic issues. We were therefore led to explore the public
evaluation of the Caldera administration's performance. As of
summer 1973, we found 45.2 percent of our respondents dissatisfied
with the manner in which the government had confronted the national
issues. During the fall of 1973, opinion on the subject was as
follows:

Q. "How would you evaluate the job that the government of
President Caldera has been doing solving the national
problems during the last five years?"

	Frequency	%
Excellent	188	12.5
Good	375	24.7
So-so	685	45.5
Bad	153	10.1
Very Bad	105	6.9
Don't know	15	1.0

Obviously, Caldera received positive evaluations from roughly
37 percent of our respondents. We proceeded with a question
concerning popular expectations about the performance of a
government formed by a different party. The responses suggested
that the copeyanos had reason to worry about the likelihood of
their staying in power.

Q. "Do you believe that if a different party came to power
that party would do a better job than the Caldera
government in solving national problems?"

	Frequency	%
Yes, better	504	33.1
Depends	485	31.9
No	358	23.5
Don't know	173	11.5

Thus, only 23.5 percent of the public did not believe that another party could outperform the Caldera administration. Moreover, when we asked about changes that had occurred to the standard of living of respondents' families during the Caldera administration, only 17.7 percent reported an improvement. Almost a majority--48.9 percent--failed to cite any changes, while 33.3 percent said that family living standards definitely deteriorated. In short, public evaluation of the administration's performance was less than enthusiastic. And as the campaign progressed, a variety of socioeconomic problems were available to generate debate and discourse among the competitors.

Despite the measurable increase of both income and expenditure during the 1969-1974 period, economic and social imbalances remained grave. While partisanship colored many electoral claims and counterclaims, it could be said without serious contradiction that the income gap remained large and that the nation's agricultural sector was in dire straits. Suffering from years of inadequate investment, flawed policy, and general negligence, agriculture was further plagued in 1973 by serious droughts, especially in Guárico, Anzoátegui, and Monagas. Despite inherent agricultural wealth, Venezuela by 1973 was importing most food products--the only major exceptions were chickens, eggs, and rice. Even the famous caraotas--black beans long a staple of the diet--were being imported. The Banco Central reported toward the close of the campaign that during the first seven months of 1973 agricultural prices rose more than three times as much as in the preceding four years. After an increase of only 4.9 percent during 1968-72, agricultural wholesale prices were up 15 percent.

The stagnancy of agriculture became an important focus for campaign debate. With production down, poor harvests for two years running, and the 1973 drought in the oriente further aggravating conditions, cattle production dipped severely and pig raisers were forced to import food. The government, determined to hold prices in line during an election year, set price ceilings on many items, leaving the producers to absorb the largest costs. This in turn further discouraged production, and inevitable rises in the price of many foodstuffs were passed along in part to the consumer. As with agricultural prices, 1973 brought an increase in living costs. After an accumulated price rise of only 10.8 percent from 1968-72, the rate of inflation in 1973 pushed up toward 15 percent over a period of months, while unofficial sources claimed that it was actually greater. Given Venezuelan dependence on the industrialized countries and the grave blows under which the world economy was reeling, much of the problem was beyond the control of the Caldera administration. With over 20 percent of the gross national product consisting of imports, the impact from increasing foreign prices was unavoidable. Yet the relative failure of ameliorative measures further fanned opposition charges of economic mismanagement.

Furthermore, many of the economic accomplishments of the Social Christian government possessed long-term importance but limited immediate impact on the electorate. The movement toward industrialization, spurred by the AD government of Raúl Leoni, was extended and amplified under Rafael Caldera. Unlike his predecessor, Caldera gave particular emphasis to the elaboration of regional "poles of development," most notably, the metallurgical complex at Ciudad Guayana, which drew upon Bolívar's enormous wealth of hydroelectric power, bauxite, high-quality iron ore, and gas. A steel plant and aluminum industry, both state-owned, were tied to the burgeoning industrial center around the confluence of the Orinoco and Caroní rivers. Production of iron also rose, although in 1973 representing but 3 percent of Venezuela's dollar earnings. Of considerable additional importance was the petrochemical complex El Tablazo near Zulia's petroleum and natural gas fields. With construction nearing completion by 1974, El Tablazo would produce large quantities of ammonia and urea for fertilizer, with exports valued at nearly $50 million anticipated within a year's time.

The overall economic picture was generally promising, then, with the important exception of agriculture. The fact remained, however, that too little was being delivered to the Venezuelan masses. A crisis of distribution--to use the terminology of developmental theorists[31]--was an unresolved problem of epic proportions. Despite fifteen years of generally progressive, reformist governments, Venezuelans of 1973 were still subjected to the onslaught of poverty, disease, and malnutrition amidst a society and environment of superficial affluence. Pressures of the population explosion also pressed implacably upon both rural and urban Venezuela. One thousand Venezuelans were being born daily by 1973, with the population doubling every two decades; the growth rate in metropolitan Caracas, swollen by migration from the countryside, climbed to 4 percent. As the flood of people from the campo continued, it was projected that in less than fifteen years the caraqueño population would have doubled to some 4.5 million inhabitants.[32]

Estimates varied widely, but at least a quarter of all Caracas residents were living in substandard conditions, their ranchos clinging stubbornly if precariously to hillsides throughout the city. Massive government programs of low-cost housing failed to keep pace. As one wag remarked with unhappy accuracy, the housing program no more solved the problem of ranchos than the construction of freeways in Los Angeles alleviated that city's traffic congestion. The national birth rate was 43 per thousand per annum, nearly double that of other countries at a similar economic level ($1,000 per capita annually). The average Venezuelan girl of age fifteen could expect to have six children by age forty-nine. Medical facilities and disease control had cut the annual death rate to 5,000--lower than in the United States. However, one-quarter of the deaths were of infants under the age of one year, whereas the comparable figure for the United States was 4 percent.[33] The social costs were devastating. Abortions, although illegal, are estimated at 100,000 per year, and 60 percent of all children are illegitimate. Caracas alone has an estimated 280,000 abandoned children. And finally, more than 90 percent of the population earns less than 1,500 bolívares monthly (slightly over $300).

The presence of such social problems, set within an economy that despite agricultural malaise was among the hemisphere's most dynamic, reflected failures of the political system over the entire preceding fifteen years. In 1973, however, it was inevitable that the electorate would largely hold the existing government responsible for unresolved problems. Given the magnitude of national problems, one might ask, "In the light of all the problems that must still be solved in Venezuela, isn't campaigning frivolous?" "Isn't it immoral to waste so much money in an effort when all of that money could be put to better use?" Clearly, as a way of capturing power within a democratic framework, campaigning is no more or less immoral than any other device to acquire the necessary support, constituting a fully justifiable activity on both moral and strategic grounds. The contests, conception, procedures, and goals of a Venezuelan campaign, as well as its very magnitude, might become in themselves immoral and grotesque. But if one could design a scenario in which party competition is possible but party loyalties are not secular, and in which the campaign environment does not predetermine the electoral outcome, no better example could be found than the Venezuelan general election of 1973.

PART II
THE MOBILIZATION OF FORCES

3. CANDIDATE SELECTION

The results of the 1968 presidential race did not eliminate any of the three major defeated candidates from future consideration. In addition, there were a number of other potential aspirants to the 1973 nomination. It was a situation susceptible to profoundly partisan manipulation, open to the maneuvers of would-be contenders. There were fewer "natural" or automatic candidates on the scene; thus the aspirations of individual politicians were legion. For the newly governing Social Christians, the victory of their perennial candidate and strongest leader left the question of his succession unsettled. Lorenzo Fernández, Edecio La Riva, Luis Herrera Campins, and José Antonio Pérez Díaz were the most presidenciable of the senior leadership, and Rodolfo José Cárdenas, Pedro Pablo Aguilar, and Arístides Beaujon were among the more important rising figures in the hierarchy. AD had the option of renominating Gonzalo Barrios, while Carlos Andrés Pérez and Reinaldo Leandro Mora were possibilities from the next generation of party leadership. And overriding all other AD possibilities was the eligibility of Rómulo Betancourt to seek another term if he chose.

The MEP also had the option of running its 1968 candidate. Like Barrios, Prieto would be a septagenarian by the time of the 1973 race, but the question of age and health seemingly created no difficulties. Behind Prieto stood Jesús Angel Paz Galarraga, and José González Navarro, president of the Confederación de Trabajadores de Venezuela (CTV) and a mepista vice-president, was also a possible contender. As for Miguel Angel Burelli Rivas, his favorable showing suggested the possibility of another race for Miraflores. The parties that supported him had mixed expectations: for the URD, Jóvito Villalba would be facing his last chance for the long-coveted presidential chair. The electoral defeat of the FND had reduced its importance but, with the virtual withdrawal of Arturo Uslar Pietri from active leadership, the bright and ambitious Pedro Segnini La Cruz was emerging as a figure in his own right. In the FDP, Wolfgang Larrazábal remained characteristically enigmatic but could not be ruled out.

New possibilities existed on both the right and the left. The
unexpected showing of perezjimenismo in the Federal District left
the CCN with an unanticipated congressional representation and
clearly raised the likelihood of an attempted comeback by the
ex-dictator. Toward the opposite pole, a bona fide communist
candidate seemed a distinct possibility for the first time in some
years. It was widely expected, and duly verified, that the
government would fully legalize the PCV under that name, and that
smaller leftist groups would also be permitted electoral
participation. It seemed probable that the communists might
attempt to join a leftist coalition, although it was difficult
to tell; certainly its senior leadership, including Gustavo Machado
in particular, was too old to mount more than an inactive and
purely symbolic candidacy.

Prospects, then, were rich and varied. There was also the
likelihood, based on past experience, that a political unknown
would leap from virtual obscurity to electoral prominence. Thus,
the multiplication of parties, mini-parties, and electoral groups
of various sorts suggested a broad and varied range of options.
More importantly, the larger organizations themselves were in a
state of flux, and the situation of pre-candidacies and nominations
was distinctly fluid. Yet the very process of candidate selection,
as we have already argued, stands not only as the first important
dimension in chronological terms, but as potentially one of the
most **decisive** factors influencing the eventual outcome. Our
hypotheses were derived from two major elements--the degree of
openness in candidate selection, and the status of a nominee
representing an electoral coalition. The first stressed the
preferability for electoral purposes of a competitive nomination
in which the choice was dictated by the party membership and not
by the notables. The second raised the question of an independent
versus a party candidate, as well as the relationship between
components of a coalition candidacy. Several different varieties
were to emerge during the selection of candidates for the 1973
campaign.

THE SOCIAL CHRISTIAN PARTY COPEI

For COPEI, the long-sought victory in 1968 had presented not
only an opportunity but a challenge, requiring major changes of
personnel and leadership within the party. COPEI found itself in
need of a new secretary general for the first time in a generation;
a future task would be to choose a candidate to succeed Caldera.
It was to be a long, expensive, and embattled process, the first
act of which unfolded in 1969 with the necessary restructuring of
party leadership. The central requirement was the naming of a
new **secretary general,** and it was with some trepidation and
uncertainty that the Social Christians turned to the task at the
eleventh National Convention in August of that year. The choice
was anything but automatic. Acting Secretary General José Antonio
Pérez Díaz, occupied in the upper house of Congress, was hesitant
about his candidacy; there was strong support for Luis Herrera
Campins, who firmly denied interest. Godofredo González declared

his availability but did not work actively; Pedro Pablo Aguilar attempted to win support for González, whom he presented as the oficialista preference. All the while Arístides Beaujon was conducting the daily party affairs that built grass-roots support.

Beaujon, a hard-working party loyalist from Falcón, was a veteran of the party's middle generation of leadership. Not nationally prominent, he had been one of several deputy secretary generals. Following elections it was Beaujon who devoted attention to party routine while the government was being organized. He therefore entered the convention with less national prestige than his opponents but possessing the indebtedness of many party members for recent favors. Godofredo González, embodying party traditionalism, increased his electioneering only at convention's eve, whereas Herrera Campins stayed out and Pérez Díaz entered late in the game. Beaujon consequently was elected to the post, winning on the second ballot after gaining the support of Hilarión Cardozo and of such younger leaders as José Curiel and Oswaldo Alvarez Paz. The establishment of weekly meetings between the Comité Nacional and President Caldera undertook to assure effective coordination between government and party. The new secretary general began to emerge as a copeyano of national importance and was quoted to the effect that his "political aspirations had not been quenched by winning the party position."[1] In time, a general belief grew that there was little warmth in the feelings of Rafael Caldera toward Beaujon.[2]

The next act in the drama occurred in August of 1971 at the twelfth National Convention. Attention focused once more on the secretary generalship. Three identifiable forces appeared. The so-called traditionalist sector, increasingly identified with the government and termed oficialista, backed a slate headed by Pedro Pablo Aguilar. The forces for renovation within the party, and especially the youth, preferred Herrera Campins but, given his continued reluctance to seek the post, opted instead for the fiery Abdón Vivas Terán, former JRC leader and an articulate champion of communitarianism for the ideological left within COPEI.[3] Arístides Beaujon, less identified with any single sector but enjoying substantial loyalty from the grass roots, campaigned to retain his position. Beaujon's earlier attempt to reach an accord with Luis Herrera Campins--whereby they would have combined forces to seek the secretary generalship for the latter and the presidential nomination for the former--had not proven successful.[4] Herrera, who would have enjoyed the support that went to Vivas Terán as well as additional convention votes, made no public declarations.[5] It was expected that a second ballot would be necessary, at which point the votes of Vivas Terán might be decisive.

Meeting as was their practice in Caracas's Radio City Theater, copeyanos also faced the prospects of a nominating convention only a few months off. Much of the speculation, as well as bargaining for votes, was tied implicitly to probable pre-candidacies. However, there were enough uncertainties Herrera concerning the secretary generalship On the first ballot, the oficialista slate with Pedro Pablo Aguilar received 465 votes, followed by Arístides Beaujon with 332. Abdón Vivas Terán ran third with 133, thus being eliminated from the second round of balloting. The combined votes of Beaujon and Vivas Terán, of course, would have precisely equalled the Aguilar total; over two dozen delegates had not voted, however. The possibility of firmly controlling the bulk of Vivas's votes was slender at best. Moreover, the choice was an ambiguous one. Beaujon was presumably staying in the running for the presidential nomination, whereas Aguilar would be firmly supporting the candidate of the traditionalist sector. For many of the Vivas voters who preferred Herrera Campins for president, there seemed little clear reason for swinging one way or the other. In the end, with another twenty-seven delegates voting, the totals for Aguilar rose by 71 and for Beaujon by 89. Thus the victory for Aguilar was by a total of 536 votes to 421 for Beaujon. A comfortable margin after a second ballot, to be sure, although by no means an indication of certain oficialista control over the party rank and file. Attention then turned fully toward presidential pre-candidacies.

Four men contested the Social Christian nomination: Arístides Beaujon, Lorenzo Fernández, Luis Herrera Campins, and Edecio La Riva Araujo. The former, notwithstanding his loss of the secretary generalship, began stumping the country shortly after the convention, with his official pre-candidacy announced on 19 November 1971. Herrera Campins entered as the choice of reformist, renovating elements within the party; Edecio La Riva unabashedly carried the standard of COPEI's right wing. Fernández, whose unofficial campaigning began before his resignation as interior minister on 22 January 1972, stood as the preferred choice of oficialistas. Even before the close of 1971, the contest had assumed unprecedented magnitude. Each of the four candidates had his own campaign staff, headquarters, public relations, and finances. Newspapers carried extensive advertising for all four, and the general impression was that of a competition between leaders of four rival parties. Adeco Secretary General Carlos Andrés Pérez, while scarcely a disinterested observer, nonetheless expressed a widely held view in his surprise over the economic resources being employed. He found "the abuse of resources disturbing, the origins of which I do not want to give an opinion upon, but which could mean a very dangerous imbalance in the future electoral process. . . ."[6]

All four aspirants had strong credentials, thus further assuring a bruising contest. Beaujon, although lacking an identifiable sector of support, was a sturdy figure who had accumulated many political IOUs through his dedicated toil for the party. Fernández, in addition to having held the key cabinet position in the administration, was a member of the founding generation of COPEI and was politically and personally close to Rafael Caldera. Herrera Campins had also been a ranking party leader since emerging from the youth movement in the 1940s. Although favored by reformist and youth elements in the party, Herrera was by no means a party rebel, having served loyally and effectively for many years, most recently as head of the copeyano parliamentary fraction. Edecio La Riva, outspoken advocate of the party's right wing, also carried a lengthy

record of party service into the convention and was popular with
many who did not share his views. As a realistic matter, La Riva
had little chance of winning the nomination, and even for Beaujon
the probabilities were not great. There was no reason to
anticipate a first-ballot victory by either Fernández or Herrera
Campins, however, opening the likelihood of substantial bargaining
for votes before a second round of voting.[7] The outcome, then, was very
much in doubt when the second Extraordinary National Convention met
on 17 March 1972.

The neutrality of convention authorities was swiftly called
into question. Problems over the housing of out-of-town delegates
led to public complaints by spokesmen for both Beaujon and Herrera
Campins, and only a special meeting of the Organizing Commission
eventually settled the question. Voting began on 18 March with
Lorenzo Fernández receiving 433 votes, Herrera Campins 297, Beaujon
193, and La Riva 33. Efforts to arrange a pact between Herrera
Campins and Beaujon--which would have provided a winning margin for
the former--proved indecisive, as the earlier unwillingness of
Herrera to support Beaujon for secretary general was not forgotten.
Neither was there a firm accord between Herrera and La Riva,
although several followers of the latter indicated their decision
to support Herrera on the second ballot. Lorencista delegations
also were making the rounds but failing to win firm endorsement
from either of the two candidates already eliminated.

Beaujonista votes were certain to divide, as were those of
La Riva. Herrera Campins's vigorously effective pre-convention
campaigning had created considerable enthusiasm about his
availability and continued to generate excitement at the Radio
City Theater. Fernández, a less stirring figure, was nonetheless
familiar to the delegates and clearly reflected the preference of
Rafael Caldera.[8] There was a feeling by outsiders that the greatest
rank-and-file support favored Herrera Campins, but Fernández could
scarcely be counted out. And when the second ballot was held, he
emerged with the nomination by polling 506 votes to 444 for
Herrera Campins. The latter had drawn two-thirds of the additional
votes but still fell short by a margin of 62. Murmurs of quiet
pressure and intervention began to circulate even as Lorenzo
Fernández accepted the acclamation of the convention, an event
made conspicuous by Herrera Campins's absence.[9] The magnitude of
complaints about internal irregularities soon became far more than
murmurs, however. Focus for the controversy was a letter released
to El Nacional through its political reporter Guillermo Pantín--its
basic thrust was to charge that bribery had produced the votes
necessary for Fernández's victory.

The controversial document was a letter addressed to the Comité
Nacional of COPEI, dated 7 April 1972, and allegedly written by
Dagoberto González and César Perdomo Girón--both leading supporters
of Luis Herrera Campins. There were immediate efforts to minimize
its importance. A communique by COPEI's press secretary on 18 April
stated that no such document had been presented to the Comité
Nacional and that González and Perdomo had told the secretary
general that the published text was apocryphal. The same day,

however, González himself told the press that the public copy
represented a rough draft circulating among various party leaders,
after which he and Perdomo would "edit, definitively, an internal
document in which we will make considerations concerning the
Extraordinary National Convention of COPEI."[10] At this juncture
the Social Christian leadership succeeded in pulling a curtain
across any further internal complaints or grievances. However,
the damage had been done, and there were never bona fide denials
of the letter or its contents.

The signers, acknowledging their preference for Herrera Campins,
were prepared to respect the **convention** decision but wrote that
for the health of the party it was important to present a cold
analysis of the process. Therefore, they had "gathered a multitude
of reserves, denunciations, complaints, frustrations and fears."
Among their concerns were the offering of favors and aid as
arguments to gain votes, promises of promotions in the public
administration, and in general, the "persistent campaign identifying
a determined pre-candidate as the favorite of the Government."
The letter cited specific examples of favoritism, many of them
petty--e.g., **Caracas street cleaners'** removing propaganda of certain
pre-candidates while carefully leaving that of one individual
untouched. Those who presided at the convention itself were charged
with partisanship: Herrera Campins was not permitted to greet
delegates informally within the convention setting, but Fernández--
unlike his three rivals, not a convention delegate--**was allowed to**
enter the hall accompanied by cheering supporters, after which he
was invited to ascend the podium. Most grave of all, however, was
"the appearance for the first time in our party struggles of a
phantom who hovers over the moral reserves of our party and to whom
our political adversaries have been referring repeatedly in public
form, symbolized in the tragi-comic figure of the Hombre de
Maletín."[11] In this case, it was charged, there was no single
person, but rather "**numerous** individuals who were dedicated to
such a deplorable electoral practice."[12]

As the writers themselves noted, the opposition had already
picked up frequent complaints and public references to convention
proceedings. Many copeyanos, in the words of the letter, felt a
"sentiment of concern and even of anguish," with the ardent wish
that future correctives restore the recent injuries to the moral
values of the Social Christian movement. Even had there been
serious question about the authenticity of the document,[13] the
fact that convention proceedings could justify the expression of
such sentiments spoke for itself. Certainly the presence of
favoritism and government influence on behalf of Lorenzo Fernández
did a distinct disservice to Fernández himself. Caldera's choice
of his successor, however, implemented by oficialistas with
heavy-handedness and a surprising absence of political finesse,
cast a pall over the nomination. Even if the more serious charges
of virtual bribery and extortion were erroneous, the fact of their
widespread acceptance remained. It was not only the AD that could
later speak of the Hombre de Maletín in its campaign propaganda,
and there was wide public understanding of what was implied. The

events of the nominating convention, then, were distasteful and
divisive, denigrating the past achievements of Fernández.
Whether or not the copeyano nominee was truly the popular
choice of the party or not cannot be firmly established; similarly,
the common contention that Herrera Campins would have made a
stronger candidate can only be a subjective judgment. At the least,
there was serious question about the depth of party enthusiasm for
Lorenzo Fernández, and oficialista pressures on his behalf were
injurious to COPEI. It raised immediate dangers for the campaign.
Confronting the problem, Fernández initiated his campaign by
making the first of several swings about the country. His initial
audiences were largely partisan, as he undertook the renewing of
party faith and unity. This remained his primary task throughout
much of 1972, when ideally he would have preferred to concentrate
on a more positive effort. Neither Herrera Campins nor his
followers bolted the party, but the degree of their campaign
participation remained uncertain. Given their power in many
sections of the country, this was but another potential blow to
the Fernández candidacy. For the Social Christians, the process
of candidate selection had been divisive and for some, both
undemocratic and immoral. It was scarcely an auspicious beginning.

In the subsequent quest for broader support and electoral
alliance, COPEI eventually narrowed its attention to the FDP.
The latter, founded in 1962 by ex-adeco Jorge Dáger and centered
upon the personality of Wolfgang Larrazábal, was sorely in need
of aid. Having won some 275,000 votes in 1963 behind the admiral's
candidacy, the FDP had seen this drop in five years to 240,000
notwithstanding the increased electorate. Since inauguration of
the Caldera government it had been weakened further, with several
of its more effective leaders having resigned. There was some
slight strength in the labor movement[14] but virtually none in
other important sectors; the party was controlled by Dáger and
his son Douglas, with only a semblance of internal democracy.[15]
Dáger's own candidacy had been floated, but the party needed to
arrange an accord with either COPEI or the AD. Larrazábal himself
was most unenthusiastic about such an accord; Jorge Dáger—once
termed an "exquisite politician"—began to explore the opportunities
by the close of 1972.

After several months' negotiations with both COPEI and the AD,
Dáger in late April announced the suspension of talks, convoked
the FDP National Assembly for late May, and flew to Canada to
confer with Larrazábal. One day prior to the opening of the party
meeting, Dáger sent a telegram to the AD definitively ending
negotiations. At the third National Assembly in the Teatro Río on
26 May he withdrew his own candidacy in favor of Lorenzo Fernández.
Dáger told efedepista delegates that he had sought certain
agreements: creation of an Instituto de los Barrios, with
sufficient budget and personnel to deal with marginality in urban
slums; a full policy of political amnesty for all those arrested
or detained for political rather than common crimes; an
international policy that would include relations with all
interested socialist countries (especially Cuba); creation of a

health service to guarantee medical treatment and medicines for the poor; and legislation guaranteeing sustenance to fathers of Venezuelan families.[16] Dáger further stated that the Social Christians had accepted all five points without qualification, and were willing to include some FDP candidates on their own electoral lists. The AD, in contrast, had been either partially or totally opposed to each of the FDP points.

David Morales Bello for the AD had already told the press that the FDP had produced a long shopping list: three ministries, five state governorships, eight embassies, six autonomous institutes, and so forth.[17] Dáger denied such charges and told the assembly that at no point had the FDP asked for such commitments. In terms of traditional patronage, the major example was the Instituto de los Barrios, the director of which would be Wolfgang Larrazábal. Later formation of legislative planchas by COPEI (see ch. 4) was to include several efedepistas, although the FDP also ran its own planchas as well. In the event of a Fernández victory, the benefits for the FDP could be clearly seen; some party members even envisaged a similar coalition in 1978 backing Dáger for the presidency. For COPEI, the single greatest possible benefit was the support of Wolfgang Larrazábal. The FDP argued that its independent strength was 250,000 votes at a minimum, and that they could be delivered to the Fernández column.

Thus the agreement was negotiated and, when on 11 July 1973 Lorenzo Fernández officially registered his candidacy before the CSE, his entourage included both Wolfgang Larrazábal and Jorge Dáger. Later the same day Larrazábal told the press that he would begin campaigning for Fernández the following day in Maracaibo and that he planned to work extensively in the barrios. Saying that Fernández could win alone, the admiral declared that with FDP backing the program of government could be more fully realized.[18]

ACIÓN DEMOCRÁTICA

The devastation produced by its 1967 division was perhaps as profound psychologically as it was debilitating politically. The loss of an election and consequent fall from national power, notwithstanding the narrowness of defeat, was not easily absorbed or accepted. The initial months following 1968 elections were marked by deep gloom and even bitterness, especially at the middle ranks within the party. As time passed and the organizational rebuilding began in earnest (see ch. 4), the presidential nomination began to receive more importance. It was, however, of less urgency or immediacy to the AD than was the case within COPEI. After the third schism in less than a decade, the AD was homogeneous and free from serious internal conflict. Its more immediate task was restructuring and strengthening the party apparatus, without which victory in 1973 would be impossible. Moreover, there were but three realistic possibilities for the nomination, none of whom seemed likely to divide the AD yet again. Most important to the process, of course, was the decision of ex-president Rómulo Betancourt, for the party founder was assured the nomination if he indicated his willingness.

Betancourt was the first ex-president to become eligible for a second term under provisions of the 1961 Constitution, which specified two full terms out of office prior to another presidency. Betancourt had firmly renounced the possibility of another term when he stepped down in 1964, but this was forgotten as time passed. Having been born in 1908, he was certainly not too old for consideration. Some speculated over the state of his health but in the absence of firm knowledge were content to leave that question—if relevant—to Betancourt himself. Having left Venezuela shortly after concluding his presidency,[19] he had spent most of the intervening years outside the country, and this contributed to uncertainty over his possible receptivity to another nomination. Betancourt himself, characteristically keeping his own counsel, gave no indication of his own thinking. Until his views were clarified, neither Gonzalo Barrios nor Carlos Andrés Pérez either could or would strike out on their own. In awaiting guidance from Betancourt while concentrating on internal party affairs, the AD effort to rebuild its structures was maximized. When COPEI's four pre-candidates were stumping Venezuela in late 1971 and early 1972, the AD maintained a calm exterior and patient interior. As Barrios said, the party could well afford to wait.

Only in late May of 1972 did Rómulo Betancourt return to Venezuela to take up permanent residence once again, and congressional maneuvering over the possible candidacy of Pérez Jiménez led to constitutional proposals that might have affected Betancourt as well. These included suggestions that the constitution be amended to prohibit more than one term. COPEI was intrigued by the thought, and the URD and Jóvito Villalba welcomed the possible elimination of an historic rival. Rumors were rife upon Betancourt's return, running from President Rafael Caldera to the man in the street.[20] With the party convention scheduled for August, time was short for the ex-president to announce his decision, as he knew full well. On 21 July 1972 Betancourt informed the nation of his decision. His message was brief and to the point, which he summarized in two sentences: "My return to the country, to live in Venezuela permanently, has reactivated the suppositions of an alleged aspiration on my part to become Chief of State again. Therefore I come to declare in clear and emphatic terms that I will not be a candidate for the Presidency in the elections to be held in 1973."[21]

There seems little retrospective question that Betancourt's course had long been clear in his own mind.[22] The delay in announcing his decision, however, proved a salubrious and wise precaution on behalf of party unity. Having waited until scant weeks before the AD convention, Betancourt had seen to it that the period of pre-convention competition would be brief, thereby minimizing the possibility of serious rifts over the nomination. It became a contest between Gonzalo Barrios and Carlos Andrés Pérez, with scattered backing for Reinaldo Leandro Mora insufficient to make him a serious contender. Sentiment had already largely solidified by the time of Betancourt's announcement. In Barrios the party had one of Venezuela's most brilliant political

intellectuals, a man whose career of distinguished service had
barely fallen short of the presidency in 1968. Cosmopolitan,
refined, subtle in word and manner, he enjoyed particular strength
with independent and intellectual sectors. Yet he was no longer
young, and his professorial attitude seemed out of tune with the
electorate. Carlos Andrés Pérez,[23] most betancurista of all party
leaders, had gone from minister of interior relations to head of
the parliamentary fraction, had led the fight against Prieto and
Paz Galarraga in 1967, and since that division had largely directed
the reorganization of the party. Tough, forceful, and industrious,
he had spent his entire adult life in politics; born in 1922, he
represented the second generation of adeco leadership. As for
Leandro Mora, he was viewed as a political heir of ex-president
Raúl Leoni and as a potential candidate for 1978.[24]

The AD's labor bureau announced its support for Pérez following
the Betancourt statement, after which there were few other public
signs of activity. Already existing advocates or critics of
Barrios and Pérez repeated familiar arguments in their private
conversations: Gonzalo deserved another chance, he would be a
statesmanlike president, he would attract independents, he would
encourage renovation within party ranks; to skeptics he was too
old and his time had passed, he would not be a strong campaigner,
and the party needed new blood at its head. Carlos Andrés was
seen by supporters as the energetic leader of the new generation,
a skillful political organizer, a pragmatic and realistic figure,
a productive administrator, and an embodiment of adeco virtues.
His opponents saw him as too partisan, lacking in flexibility and
breadth, without ideological orientation, unattractive to
independents and hostile to criticism. Both these portrayals were
flawed reproductions of the two men's characteristics and
temperaments but approximated the views of their respective
supporters.

Pérez, who was convinced that the party could not survive
another division or even a wounding struggle for the nomination,
was discreet in his actions and statements during the final weeks.[25]
Moreover, after five years as secretary general he knew full well
that his support was both deep and broad. Similarly, Gonzalo
Barrios wanted neither a party schism nor a rancorous fight for
the nomination. He, too, soon recognized that his own force was
not sufficient to carry the day. Five days before the convention
he announced the withdrawal of his candidacy. In his best form,
the party president announced that he was applying the theory of
the Brazilian military: gana quien más cañones tenga, el resto
se rinde "(Whoever has the most guns wins, the rest surrender)."
With this action, any remaining chance of political bloodshed over
the AD nomination was effectively eliminated. Leandro Mora,
startled by the Barrios withdrawal, himself remained in the race
but was not a serious contender. The National Convention met in
the Teatro California with the outcome predetermined. Carlos
Andrés Pérez was swiftly nominated, with the proclamation coming
on 18 August 1972. The new Comité Ejecutivo Nacional was largely
to his liking, further uniting the party behind its

standardbearer.[26]   Octavio Lepage, with strong support from Gonzalo Barrios, was named to the crucial position of secretary general in place of the candidate; Barrios remained as party president and Leandro Mora retained a high post in the leadership. There was, thus, neither internal pre-convention bloodletting nor post-convention reprisal.

The AD, after years of tumultuous party meetings and serious internal rifts, emerged with well-knit leadership, unified enthusiasm among the rank and file, and a candidate with firm control of the reins. The contrast to COPEI was striking, where the customarily monolithic Social Christians had torn themselves apart in the grievously wounding fight for the nomination. In due course the AD received the support and endorsement of both the PRN and the Congreso del Trabajo.[27] Led respectively by former _adecos_ José Manzo González and José González Navarro, they helped mark the return to the fold of many former party members. Although bringing their own talents and a small group of supporters with them, neither offered the pretense of independent electoral strength that characterized the FDP. It cost the AD very little to secure the backing of the PRN and the Congreso, unlike COPEI with the FDP. The AD had therefore survived the process of candidate selection in better health than COPEI. With Betancourt's artfully timed statement of noncandidacy, the party soon realized that Pérez was its next choice, a reality to which Barrios acceded. Only time would reveal the extent to which other dimensions of the campaign might either vitiate or enforce the _adeco_ unity that Carlos Andrés Pérez carried from the convention into the campaign proper.

THE POLITICAL LEFT

Nowhere was the situation more cloudy following the 1968 elections than with the Venezuelan left. The MEP was the strongest electoral force, although the extent to which its 1968 vote had been essentially that of _adecos_ loyal to Luis B. Prieto was uncertain; Prieto had run some 5 percent ahead of the party's small _tarjeta_ vote, and the durability of the _mepista_ vote could not be assumed. When the party undertook its progressive shift further to the left under the guidance of Jesús Angel Paz Galarraga (see chs. 4 and 6), the size and strength of its constituency became even more speculative. For the URD, its strength sharply reduced in the decade since 1958, the most logical tactic was a shift to the left. The unquenched thirst of its _caudillo_ Jóvito Villalba for the presidency framed the process of selection, with the URD unlikely to support a **nonmember** as it had in 1958 and 1968. For the communist party, the question seemed less one of its own candidacy than the terms under which it would ally, and with whom.

Both the URD and the MEP gradually began to develop the notion of a leftist coalition, guided by the example of Salvador Allende and his Unidad Popular in Chile. Villalba **was vocal in outlining** his view of a revolutionary Venezuelan Unidad Popular, and his rousing rhetoric sharply attacked both COPEI and the AD as bankrupt representatives of the status quo. Claiming for himself the mantle of "nationalistic revolution," the URD chief was an active advocate of leftist coalition. Within the MEP, meanwhile, Luis B. Prieto had been gradually stepping into the background as Paz Galarraga became the party's active leader. Paz strengthened his own internal position vis-à-vis potential opponents, and his role grew as discussions unfolded among the URD, MEP, and PCV. The situation for the communists had been severely aggravated by their own serious internal division, resulting in the December 1971 departure of their more talented and imaginative leaders.

By 1972 the three parties agreed to merge their efforts for the campaign. Representatives drafted the joint statement of principles, which was to provide an ideological base. It was further agreed that the so-called Nueva Fuerza, or "new force," would call a convention to choose its presidential nominee. It was not expected that an integrated list of legislative candidates would be formulated but that the overarching programmatic framework would be pursued by the Nueva Fuerza presidential contender, supported by all three members. Guidelines for the forthcoming congress of the Nueva Fuerza were drawn up with painstaking care. It was agreed that 1,800 delegates would attend in Caracas on 29 July 1972. Each of the member parties would provide 300 delegates from their respective memberships, as well as selecting 300 independent representatives; thus 50 percent of the delegates were to be nonmembers—independents sympathetic generally to the left. Each of the three parties put forward its respective potential nominee: Paz Galarraga for the MEP, Villalba for the URD, and Gustavo Machado for the PCV.

There were numerous endogenous forces that threatened to influence the selection process. The emerging candidacy of José Vicente Rangel for the MAS was more attractive to mepista youth than Villalba; older prietista members of the MEP had misgivings about the affiliation with the PCV, and a Betancourt candidacy for the AD might attract them back into the fold; elements within the URD strongly preferred an agreement or pact with the AD, although Villalba was strongly opposed. The PCV, still reeling from its own recent division, was believed to prefer Villalba to Paz, although no one was really certain. Gustavo Machado, one of the founders of Venezuelan communism, was nearly seventy-four, and his candidacy was purely symbolic. The realistic choice was therefore between Villalba and Paz. It was widely assumed that the urredista would easily triumph. Hero of the Generation of '28, one of the country's finest orators, and among the best-known politicians never to have reached the presidency, Jóvito seemed certain to defeat the quiet, undemonstrative mepista aspirant.

The URD, in recent years an institutional incarnation of its leader, possessed the same traits: rhetorical eloquence, disdain for hard organizational work, and faulty political judgment. The career of Villalba himself was dotted with a series of major political decisions in which he invariably made the wrong judgment or erred in his timing. His opponent, however, was an acknowledged master of political organization whose supporters were working with acumen and industry. With the selection dependent upon 1,800

delegates, half of them at least nominally independent and open to
persuasion, Paz might have been expected to win. On the night of
29 July 1972, that was precisely what happened. Paz received 756
votes, Villalba 671, and Gustavo Machado 341. The margin of 85
votes came largely from two sources--the independent delegates
chosen by the PCV, and 23 members of the URD. A telling commentary
on URD disorganization and lack of preparation was its holding only
277 of the 300 party delegates in favor of Villalba. Mepista work
in choosing its own group of independents, as well as proselytizing
among those of the PCV and URD, paid large dividends. Thus Jesús
Angel Paz Galarraga entered the presidential race with the impetus
of a superbly orchestrated convention victory; Jóvito Villalba was
the great loser.

Villalba appeared on the podium with Paz and Machado following
the convention proclamation, issuing a gracious concession statement
and pledging unqualified support to the Nueva Fuerza and its
candidate. Such was the vigor and force of Villalba's declaration
that it was first believed he and the URD would indeed honor their
word in working as an integral member of the Nueva Fuerza.[28] In
the shambles of its defeat, however, the URD immediately began to
review the situation. Convention procedures had been rigorously
fair and legal; thus younger urredistas, with Leonardo Montiel
Ortega as their spokesman, sharply criticized the failure of party
structures. Recriminations were angrily exchanged, with Villalba
himself saying little. Having taken a leading role in publicizing
the conception of Unidad Popular, his position was especially
awkward. Putting the best face on events, he said that "the
holding of the Nueva Fuerza Congress constitutes for me a triumph
of the cause of popular unity...even though the results of the
election for the presidential candidacy of Unidad Popular did not
favor numerically the initiative of my companions in favor of my
name."[29]

Francisco Faraco, head of the party's Comité Electoral,
rejected internal criticism and pointed an accusatory finger at
independent delegates, whom he charged with denying promised support
for Villalba. Montiel Ortega continued to demand a restructuring
of the party, after which the comitment to the Nueva Fuerza might
be reassessed. While these internal maneuvers continued, with the
URD leadership increasingly divided into senior jovitero figures
and the ambitious younger members,[30] Villalba himself departed the
scene for a two-month world trip. The URD found itself even more
disorganized and confused; further conflict led to the temporary
creation of a Directorio Ampliado, which merely broadened the
forum for debate. Party leaders searched increasingly for bases
to criticize the nominating congress, all the while spreading the
view that the early months of Paz Galarraga's campaigning had
shown him incapable of arousing popular support.

Accusations of bad faith became increasingly common. One of
the villains was alleged to be the PCV, which had supposedly
promised to vote for Villalba at the congress but then reneged;
this was curiously rationalized on the grounds that the PCV feared
Villalba's popular strength and therefore voted for Paz. Paz

himself and the MEP were charged with having circulated rumors that
he would withdraw his candidacy in favor of a political independent
from the left, thus falsely recruiting delegates to his cause.
Former urredista José Herrera Oropeza, a political enemy of Villalba,
was accused of having maneuvered against the URD; why he should not
have been free to do so—having left the URD in 1964—was never
explained. In short, despite continued internal conflict, rancor
was directed increasingly at the party's Nueva Fuerza comembers.
The Villalba defeat became the result of an unprincipled
conspirational plot to obstruct the popular will, rather than the
logical result of political realities and urredista fumbling.
     The URD constantly shook the fragility of Nueva Fuerza unity
through public and private condemnations of Paz's popular appeal.
Some of its members still favored an alliance with the AD, although
the nomination of Pérez made this impractical; others argued that
the honor of both the party and Jóvito had been committed publicly
to the coalition and that withdrawal would be a denial of principle
and integrity. The final outcome was increasingly clear, however,
leading to withdrawal from the Nueva Fuerza and, on 18 January 1973,
the party announcement that Villalba would be its presidential
candidate. On 1 April he was officially proclaimed at the tenth
Congreso Nacional of the URD and began campaigning shortly
thereafter. For Villalba, it was a final quest for the presidency,
as well as a comitment of his personal prestige and influence on
behalf of the URD itself. A group of urredistas who had remained
obligated by the earlier commitment left the URD and, under Jesús
Soto Amesty, formed the Unión Popular Izquierdista (UPI) in support
of the Nueva Fuerza. Villalba himself declared that the URD mistake
was in believing that the MEP and PCV shared its desire for a
program of national revolution. Ultimately, however, "our impression
after all that happened is that with the other two parties as well
as other forces of the Left, nothing interests them but counting
votes and winning some seats in Congress and other deliberative
bodies."[31]
     The splintering of the purported Unidad Popular left Paz and
Villalba vying for the votes of the Venezuelan left. Even before
the withdrawal, however, the left had been divided. The formation
of the Movimiento al Socialismo (MAS) after the 1971 division of the
communist party had cost the latter the great bulk of its younger
members, its more imaginative ideologues, and one of its most
skilled organizers in Pompeyo Márquez. The philosophical and
programmatic distinction was substantial, as a result of which the
MAS stood to the left of the PCV and generally closer to the vision
of a genuinely Venezuelan socialism. Differences of ideology and
outlook between the MAS and the Nueva Fuerza were also real,
entirely aside from the enduring animosity between the MAS and PCV.
For the MAS, in large part born of the world crisis of Stalinism
and further precipitated by the Soviet invasion of Czechoslovakia,
the thesis of the popular front was not valid for Venezuela. Its
distinctive orientation necessitated presentation of its own
presidential nominee and list of legislative candidates. Moreover,
it was important to select a nominee whose own personal qualities

and appeal might further the effort to establish an organizational base for the MAS.

The figure of José Vicente Rangel[32] began to loom on the horizon as a possible candidate. A political independent who' had stood on the left for a decade, Rangel had campaigned for Luis B. Prieto in 1968 and worked in harmony with precisely those PCV leaders who later organized the MAS. Although initially interested in the emerging Nueva Fuerza as an option, Rangel gradually turned away from it. By January of 1972 he was anticipating the probability of being launched as candidate by the MAS and was clearly receptive.[33] He had already been proposed to the party leadership, reportedly by Germán Lairet,[34] and was subsequently proclaimed officially at a party meeting in Maracay. A mass rally in Caracas's Nuevo Circo on 26 May 1972 effectively launched his campaign, and Rangel was out in the field before either Paz Galarraga or Villalba. Later efforts to produce an accord between the Nueva Fuerza and MAS proved futile. By 1973, with the forthcoming legalization of the formerly insurrectional MIR, both Paz and Rangel proceeded to seek mirista endorsement. Although the tangible electoral benefit would be slight, the symbolic impact on the competitors within the left was scarcely negligible.

With its return to legality in 1973[35] after over a decade away from electoral politics, the MIR was led by Simón Sáez Mérida and Américo Martín, who had remained through the lean years of exile, imprisonment, and inactivity.[36] Although some miristas feared possible absorption by the MAS and therefore favored Paz, both Sáez Mérida and Martín strongly preferred alignment with José Vicente Rangel. Despite masista unwillingness to incorporate MIR candidates onto the legislative planchas, it was argued that Rangel's option for victory was superior. Advocates of affiliation with Rangel were strengthened when the URD presumably weakened the Nueva Fuerza by withdrawal. The apparent involvement of the MEP in irregularities over the purpose of voting machines also lessened sentiment in favor of Paz. The fourth Conferencia Nacional was convened on 23 June 1973, by which time the possibility of supporting the Nueva Fuerza candidacy was minimal.[37] There were advocates of the voto nulo--the tactic of casting a blank ballot in protest against the existing system[38]--but sentiment was far greater in favor of a presidential candidacy. Secretary General Simón Sáez Mérida reported to the 230 delegates, summarizing arguments against Paz and recommending the candidacy of Rangel. In convention balloting, Rangel received 188 votes, there was scattered support for the thesis of voto nulo, and Paz was without a vote. In a brief speech Rangel made warm references to old friendships with the MIR and welcomed its participation in "the historic task of constructing socialism in Venezuela...."[39] With the mirista nomination, the choices of the left had been completed; Paz, Villalba, and Rangel stood as rivals in the attack against the existing system.

THE POLITICAL RIGHT

At the other end of the political spectrum, activity centered on Marcos Pérez Jiménez--his candidacy, his sympathy, his commitment, his endorsement. A host of presidential aspirants, some for whom embarrassment might have been expected at negotiation with the former dictator, cast about in search of means to gain his support. Several devoted the bulk of their campaign activities to negotiations with the Madrid exile. The unseemly scramble for perezjimenista approval was propelled by his exclusion from the race. This in turn had been precipitated through an attack of nerves by the parties of the Venezuelan establishment, later nurtured both by opportunism and intermittent flights of democratic theory. The totally unexpected 400,000-vote total for the CCN in 1968 legislative elections had shaken the nation's political leadership. Despite indications that these results were but the latest manifestation of the protest-vote phenomenon that recurred in Caracas each five years, there were concerns that the electorate truly favored a return of the erstwhile strongman. Polls in early 1972 showing Pérez Jiménez to be the choice of as many as 20 percent of the electorate--running second behind Rómulo Betancourt--gave further pause to politicians.

Discussion about means of preventing his possible return to power became frequent. For a time these included the possibility of a retroactive ban on a second presidential term, thereby eliminating Betancourt as well. An option with some broader appeal proposed the institution of a presidential runoff in the event that no candidate received 50 percent of the popular vote. This might have blocked a Pérez Jiménez return to power, with the AD and COPEI uniting in a runoff and thereby assuring the outcome. However, smaller parties, in particular those on the left, were highly critical, viewing the result as indefinitely assuring continuity of the two status parties. In October 1972 COPEI, the AD, and sympathetic independents introduced a constitutional amendment declaring ineligible those adjudged guilty of crimes committed in the course of managing public functions. Drafted by legal experts headed by Godofredo González of COPEI and David Morales Bello of the AD, its subsequent passage in Caracas and ratification by three-fourths of the state assemblies closed the door to another candidacy by Pérez Jiménez.[40]

The AD, which had suffered most seriously at the hands of the perezjimenista tyranny, had first proposed a limit of twenty years following the actual date of judicial condemnation, but this was eventually altered. The arguments combined elements of politics, law, and morality. On one plane, the concern was obviously direct and electoral; it was argued that whatever the theoretical arguments about democracy, it would be suicidal to open the door to Pérez Jiménez. Legal points were more complex but essentially revolved about Article 112 of the Constitution, which spoke of the "unrestricted" eligibility of Venezuelans for the presidency. Third, there were arguments of a philosophic tone. The "pure democracy" position held that there should be no fetters on the right of the people to choose whomever they wished. It was sometimes argued that the people could be relied upon to use wise judgment (e.g., vote against Pérez Jiménez); more cynical views

expressed the idea differently, declaring that the people would
certainly vote for the kind of government they deserved. There
were others who pointed to the ex-dictator's manifold excesses
and violations of both constitutional and moral rights for a decade.
They equated his candidacy with that of a convicted criminal, who
should not receive another opportunity to defraud and defame
Venezuela.[41]

With approval of the amendment, aspirants to the mantle of
Marcos Pérez Jiménez began to maneuver and negotiate. The array of
self-proclaimed perezjimenista parties was legion, with the CCN
itself already having divided. It was firmly controlled by Pablo
Salas Castillo, the "Fouché of perezjimenismo." A native of Apure
who had served for a time as director of social security under the
dictatorship, he had gained apparent influence with the general
beyond his secondary position of earlier years. Exercising firmly
autocratic control over the CCN, including its senators and some
ten of the twenty-one deputies with which it had begun in 1969,[42]
Salas retained tight control throughout the months of discussion,
debate, and uncertainty. The Movimiento Popular Justicialista
(MPJ), which had broken away under deputy Abdelkader Márquez amid
charges of insubordination from Salas Castillo, reiterated its
support for the general but in February of 1973 cast its lot in
favor of Lorenzo Fernández. Retired General Luis Felipe Llovera
Páez, for years the number-two man in the perezjimenista regime,[43]
organized the Partido Nacional Integracionalista (PNI), whose
membership attracted such men as former ambassadors and governors
during the dictatorship.

The alphabet soup of mini-parties went even further. The
Frente Unido Nacionalista (FUN) was headed by its founder and
secretary general Jesús Alejandro Gómez Silva, who had originally
been a supporter of Uslar Pietri and the FND in 1963 and had later
tried vainly to swing that party toward Pérez Jiménez. Like its
founder, the FUN was comprised largely of young professionals and
technicians in their thirties who therefore had not themselves been
active during the decade of military rule. Yet another organization
was the MDI, headed by deputy Raimundo Verde Rojas.[44] A supporter
of Rafael Caldera in 1968, Verde Rojas had joined the perezjimenista
movement only in 1970 and lacked firm credentials in Madrid. In
addition to these, the list of candidates seeking support included
Martín García Villasmil, Pedro Tinoco, and Miguel Angel Burelli
Rivas. The first was a retired general who had served as Rafael
Caldera's first minister of defense. Eventually relieved of his
ministry and retired to civilian status, he immediately undertook
a relentless criticism of the system, its politicians, and its
political parties, including COPEI. He also sought perezjimenista
votes.

Salas Castillo, Llovera Páez, Gómez Silva, Verde Rojas, and
García Villasmil all aspired to the general's blessings. None was
more ardent in his courtship than Pedro Tinoco; neither did the
others match the relative legitimacy of Tinoco's own candidacy. A
wealthy businessman, lawyer, and entrepreneur who had built a
reputation as something of a managerial and administrative genius,

Pedro Tinoco had served as Caldera's first minister of hacienda before withdrawing to prepare his own candidacy.[45]   Supported by the small but well-financed Movimiento Desarrollista (MD), Tinoco sought to create a movement that would embody conservative political values.   He hoped to merge his personal prestige and the availability of financing from the private sector with the votes presumably controlled by Pérez Jiménez.   While stressing the independence of the MD and of his own candidacy from the exiled general, he was equally firm in his insistence upon points of agreement and similarity.   At least implicit was the thought that following a Tinoco presidency, further constitutional revision would requalify Pérez Jiménez and return him to power in 1978.

    Two other presidential candidates remained on the right--Pedro Segnini La Cruz and Miguel Angel Burelli Rivas--only the second of whom seriously sought the endorsement of Marcos Pérez Jiménez.   This had resulted from the success of Segnini in controlling the FND and in gaining its own support.   The contest between Segnini and Burelli, although but a sidelight to the main electoral struggle in Venezuela, was not without its intriguing aspects.   A young Trujillo-born economist, Segnini had played an active role during Uslar Pietri's 1963 presidential bid and had then become influential in the FND, which Uslar subsequently founded.   He served as minister of agriculture under Raúl Leoni during the AD-FND-URD alliance and assumed a position of increasing importance within the party organization.   Segnini worked energetically throughout the 1968 campaign and upon its conclusion undertook the effort to resuscitate the FND, which Uslar Pietri had left on its own.   In the meantime Burelli Rivas stood as the obvious choice for the FND in 1973, and he was offered a position as party leader.   The decision to decline proved a misstep.

    For Burelli, dissolution of the Frente de la Victoria meant that new sources of support were necessary.   He therefore began cultivating his posture as a political independent.   Ultimately, it was hoped that this would draw support from another electoral coalition, most important, to include perezjimenista groups.   It was Burelli's assumption that in due course the FND would join in supporting him.   However, in October of 1972 Segnini convoked the Consejo Nacional of the FND, which officially recognized the pre-candidates--Burelli and Segnini.   Posters showed adjoining pictures of the two men under the slogan entre Burelli y Segnini está el nuestro ("our candidate is either Burelli or Segnini").   Burelli was both surprised and angered; his version of events and commitments was at sharp variance with Segnini's.   Suffice it to say that Segnini, with control of the party machinery, proceeded to solidify his position.   On 8 March 1973 the party convention proclaimed his candidacy.[46]

    By June of 1973, at which time the CSE applied the new constitutional amendment in rejecting the candidacy of Pérez Jiménez,[47] it was believed that the crush of candidates on the right would soon be thinned.   The situation was altered by the course of events in Argentina where Héctor Cámpora, elected president instead of the constitutionally ineligible Juan Perón, had resigned in

favor of the latter. This produced a spate of would-be Venezuelan
Cámporas, who promised to resign the presidency after election and
thus bring about the return of Pérez Jiménez. Gómez Silva, Verde
Rojas, and Salas Castillo all inscribed their candidacies on this
basis, while silence was maintained in Madrid. For the exiled
dictator, there were at least three major alternatives. The first
called for his immediate endorsement of a candidate; the second
dictated a delayed decision; the third was to avoid any public
commitment whatsoever, simply letting events unfold.

The general's unwillingness to make his choice of candidate--or,
at the least, his reluctance to announce a decision--contributed to
growing disarray on the political right. It also held candidacies
which likely would have withdrawn otherwise, and Venezuela found
itself with no less than fourteen officially inscribed presidential
nominees.[48] The stream of supplicants between Caracas and Madrid
increased with regularity, as did airport press conferences, during
which reporters were assured that the speaker was certain of the
general's eventual support. Of this group, only Pedro Tinoco also
proceeded with his campaign apart from bidding for perezjimenista
support. By August it appeared that he was on the verge of winning
endorsement, and he insistently reiterated the fact all the way to
election day. The basis for his claim was an official proclamation
of approval by General Llovera Páez's PNI. The belief that Llovera
remained close to Pérez Jiménez gave further substance to outward
appearances that the decision would be forthcoming. Announcement
in Madrid of the general's ten-point programmatic statement (see
ch. 6) included indications that "his" candidate would have to
subscribe to the proclamation. Most of the aspirants promptly did
so.

By late August the presumed certainty of public support for
Tinoco had been dissipated, while the maneuvering a la Cámpora had
failed to end the uncertainty.[49] Suddenly yet another unexpected
if derivative tactic was announced with the proposed candidacy of
Doña Flor de Pérez Jiménez, wife of the general. In itself a
suggestion that was nothing if not ludicrous,[50] the notion
nonetheless had its transitory value to Pérez Jiménez and especially
to Salas Castillo. The struggle of the latter with Llovera Páez
required the prevention of an endorsement of Tinoco. On 1 September,
Caracas newspapers carried advertisements by the CCN proclaiming
the presidential candidacy of the general's wife, as well as that
of his daughter Margot for deputy from Caracas.[51] The move had
been initiated by Salas Castillo in the frank expectation of
uniting perezjimenistas, a step that was expected to find favor in
Madrid.[52] The next few weeks were filled with continual maneuvering
by the warring sectors. A hurried trip by Tinoco and extended talks
in Madrid led to his subsequent claim that the endorsement was his.
Publication of the document jointly signed by Tinoco and Pérez
Jiménez was in fact no more than a general statement of various
policy agreements.[53]

By October, Burelli Rivas had clearly abandoned any hope of
perezjimenista support, although General García Villasmil made a
last visit to Madrid in a vain bid for endorsement.[54] Tinoco was

proceeding on his own campaign, supported by Llovera Páez and the
PNI but keeping his lines of communication open to Spain. Gómez
Silva and Verde Rojas were sporadically active, and Salas Castillo
continued to maneuver behind the scenes. Pérez Jiménez expressed
frequent doubts as to the relevance of the 1973 electoral process,
anticipating its outcome to be a fraud perpetrated by COPEI and AD
in collusion with one another. He also foresaw the possibility of
a breakdown in the process, with consequent military seizure of
government.[55] Whether these statements reflected his honest
assessment of the situation cannot be determined. Given his own
political career, exaggerated attention to possibilities of either
electoral fraud or military intervention would not have been
unnatural. Alternatively, the general may have concluded that there
was no possible personal benefit in supporting a candidate and
simply employed these arguments to justify his inaction.

Through a telephone interview in late November he charged that
the electoral process was fraudulent and maintained that an
agreement between COPEI and AD provided for their retention of
power in the next ten years. The situation therefore left him with
no choice but abstention, although his followers were left free to
vote for the CCN for legislative and municipal positions. When
asked about his attitude toward Pedro Tinoco, he said that his
recent message to Venezuela had made it clear, and that further
elaboration was unnecessary.[56] Salas Castillo, consistent with the
Madrid message, withdrew his own candidacy before the CSE on 26
November, thus reducing by one the list of presidential candidates.
Gómez Silva was eventually to withdraw only a few hours before the
polling places opened, declining to give his reasons. The 1973
actions of Marcos Pérez Jiménez had contributed, whether consciously
or otherwise, to a fragmentation of the political right and a
proliferation of candidates willing to demean themselves in the
hopes of winning his approval. It appeared likely that, in the
process, the general had forfeited any present or future electoral
strength of his own. Whether this was a result of his
miscalculation, or rather an indication that it was a matter of
indifference to him, could scarcely be ascertained. The end result
was the probable loss of whatever popular support he might have
maintained or increased. The candidates of the right, with the
partial exception of Segnini, were less the product of a genuine
selection process than a reflection of personal ambition
and political intrigue.

The roll of candidates was completed by Germán Borregales and
Alberto Solano. The former, an erstwhile copeyano who had
withdrawn years earlier in protest of its shift from the right,
again offered himself as candidate of the poor, aged, and infirm.
A figure who attracted affection from the public, his presence in
the campaign seemed assurance of the continuity of the process.
Solano, a student of thirty-six who had failed in his 1968 attempt
to be inscribed, presented himself as the nominee of the Fuerza
Emancipadora (FE). His anonymity to the public, to newsmen, and to
Venezuelan politicians was total. With the participation of
Borregales and Solano, along with the withdrawals of Salas Castillo

and Gómez Silva, the number of candidates on election day totaled
twelve.   (See table 12 for an alphabetical list.)

TABLE 12.   Presidential Candidates, 1973

Name	Party	Birthplace	Birth Date
Borregales, Germán	MAN	Coro, Falcón	26 May 1909
Burelli Rivas, Miguel Angel	OPINA	La Puerta, Trujillo	8 July 1922
Fernández, Lorenzo	COPEI, FDP, IP, MPJ	Caracas	8 January 1918
García Villasmil, Martin	PSD	Caracas	22 October 1920
Paz Galarraga, Jesús Angel	MEP, PCV	Altagracia, Zulia	20 March 1919
Pérez, Carlos Andrés	AD, PRN	Rubio, Táchira	27 October 1922
Rangel, José Vicente	MAS,MIR	Caracas	10 July 1929
Segnini La Cruz, Pedro	FND	La Sabana, Trujillo	21 November 1924
Solano, Alberto	FE	Puerto Cabello, Carabobo	1938
Tinoco, Pedro	MD, PNI	Caracas	4 October 1927
Verde Rojas, Raimundo	MDI	Juangriego, N. Esp.	16 March 1929
Villalba, Jóvito	URD	Pampatar, N. Esp.	23 March 1908

Selection of the four leading candidates--Fernández, Pérez,
Paz, and Rangel--demonstrated experiences consistent with the
hypotheses posited. The respective copeyano and adeco nominations
tended to support the relevance to electoral prospects of open,
competitive procedures. The former saw an intense contest which,
at the convention, was neither free nor unfettered. The favoritism
of convention authorities toward Lorenzo Fernández, further
manifested through oficialista pressures in support of President
Caldera's preferences, clearly damaged party prospects. It is
quite possible that the former minister of interior relations might
have won the nomination without such intervention. The point,
however, is that post-convention bitterness and disunity was
engendered by the process of nomination; certainly it created an

early handicap for Fernández. By contrast, the withdrawal of the
AD's Betancourt and Barrios paved the way for a smooth and
harmonious nomination. The AD emerged with an unchallenged
candidate whose legitimacy as the party nominee was apparent.
Unlike Fernández, Pérez began his campaign with full support and
unity of purpose within the party.

The selection of Jesús Angel Paz Galarraga reflected a blend
of elements. His successful nomination at the Nueva Fuerza congress
stemmed from open competition with Jóvito Villalba and Gustavo
Machado. Even the most partisan members of the URD initially
conceded that the competition had been genuine and honest.
Moreover, Paz's legitimacy as the mepista contender had been clear.
His nomination was also consistent with our hypotheses concerning
coalition candidates, to the extent that the three constituent
members of the original Nueva Fuerza had explored and rejected the
alternative of an independent candidate before evolving the
procedures for the nominating meeting.

The selection of José Vicente Rangel was less readily
applicable to our hypotheses. Although the choice of MAS party
notables, he was essentially without opposition and the rank-and-file
membership was so small as to be negligible. Thus the issue of
imposition from above was never germane. Subsequent endorsement
by the MIR reflected the dominant sentiment of its small membership.
The fact that Rangel was not a member of either the MAS or MIR,
given the circumstances of both parties, is not seen as affecting
our hypothesis regarding the preference for party rather than
nonparty candidates.

Finally, all four nominating processes confirm the contention
that candidates of uneven coalitions enjoy an advantage over those
of an equal coalition. The COPEI-FDP-MPJ support for Fernández
was subsequently to suffer, despite its unequal quality, by the
concessions pried from COPEI by the FDP. The Pérez candidacy was
immune to such problems, given the extreme weakness of the PRN and
Congreso del Trabajo. Rangel was also largely if not totally free
of such problems, given his tacit agreement with the masista strategy
of ignoring the MIR, the Comité de Unidad Revolucionaria (CUR),
et al. With Paz, despite the unquestioned inequality between the
MEP and PCV--following the URD withdrawal--there was to be in
actuality a practical degree of evenness. For Paz assiduously and
tirelessly acted as if he were indeed the candidate of a coalition
with members of equal importance. Even before the URD went its
own way, the Paz candidacy was functioning as would that of a
coalition of equals. This was to be a distinct disadvantage to
Paz, whatever the symbolic value of his determination to balance
the ideas and recommendations of his lesser supporters.

4. CAMPAIGN ORGANIZATION

The importance of party structure and organization can scarcely be **exaggerated in Venezuelan politics. While not itself sufficient** for electoral and political success, the organizational dimension has high salience. It was the solid grass-roots support for the AD, built through years of organizational activity, that carried the party to power in 1958 and kept it there for a decade. The shattering of adeco machinery by the prietista division in 1967, coinciding with the emergence of COPEI as a party with efficient national organization, led to the shift from AD hegemony toward a turnover system. The respective phenomena of Wolfgang Larrazábal and Arturo Uslar Pietri in 1958 and 1963, based upon transitory appeals to the politically disorganized Caracas electorate, soon withered on the vine in the absence of organizational fertilization and nourishment. As the new campaign got underway, there was good reason to believe that once again the organizational factor would be crucial to the outcome. In the introductory chapter we identified five **components** of campaign organization: centralization fusion, regularization, institutionalization, and financing. We hypothesized that to maximize electoral prospects, campaign organizations should be both centralized and fused; that specialization should embrace a close relationship between permanent party organs and special electoral organs; that neither institutionalization nor personalization was necessarily superior, but depended upon the style and preference of the candidate; and that financing required the utilization of both internal and external sources. It will be useful to hold in mind our propositional statements while dissecting the elements of each campaign.

THE SOCIAL CHRISTIAN PARTY COPEI
During the years following Rafael Caldera's successful bid for the presidency, COPEI retained the revised party structure that had been developed by Caldera and José Curiel for that campaign. The degree of specialization and centralization so notable in 1968 was retained virtually intact. Copeyanos, justifiably proud of their

1968 performance, saw little reason to tinker with their apparatus. Indeed, an almost mystical faith in the party machinery pervaded COPEI, most particularly among the bright young técnicos responsible for its daily operation. A mechanistic attitude prevailed, based on the conviction that manipulation of the apparatus guaranteed desired outputs. This tone predominated throughout the Fernández campaign; even in the final weeks, with the party's candidate encountering difficulties, doubts were assuaged by a brash assurance that by pulling the correct levers campaigners could make the machinery deliver a victory.

The extent to which copeyano organization changed after 1968 was best measured in terms of personnel. With the freeing of Caldera from party obligations and his departure from the position of secretary general after more than twenty years, organizational leadership was effectively dispersed. Caldera's absence from active party direction created a leadership vacuum that could only gradually be filled.[1] At its post-election national convention in August of 1969, COPEI experienced for the first time a competition for secretary general, with Arístides Beaujon the eventual winner. As he assumed organizational control, many ranking copeyanos entered the government, including such stalwarts as Fernández, Arístides Calvani, Rodolfo José Cárdenas, and José Curiel. José Antonio Pérez Díaz was occupied as president of the Senate, while Luis Herrera Campins and Pedro Pablo Aguilar directed copeyano parliamentarians. Such youth leaders as Eduardo Fernández and Abdón Vivas Terán were also incorporated into the administration. Given this situation, Beaujon staffed the organization with fellow members of COPEI's middle generation of leadership and with younger technocrats.

Not until the eve of the campaign did the pro-Caldera oficialista wing of the party assert full control—placing loyalist Pedro Pablo Aguilar in the secretary generalship and urging the candidacy of Lorenzo Fernández on the party. The struggle to oust Beaujon as secretary general and to block the presidential candidacy of Luis Herrera Campins was successful but cost the party dearly. Although both Herrera Campins and Beaujon eventually accepted the outcome and later campaigned on behalf of Fernández, the internal wounds were not easily healed. Moreover, oficialista efforts to punish the herreristas, and in some cases beaujonistas as well, sapped the vitals of the party just as the campaign became intense. Given these problems of personnel and of personality, the copeyano campaign organization required the strength of leadership that only its presidential candidate could exert. Whether by deliberate choice or temperamental inclination, Lorenzo Fernández failed to provide such leadership. The result was a dispersion of authority, the absence of unified action at the apex of the structure, and internal contradictions that in time produced a rift between the candidate himself and the party leadership. COPEI's campaign ship became a vessel without a firm hand at the helm; even more accurately, perhaps, it could be described as a highly seaworthy craft on which the captain lackadaisically permitted a host of officers to quarrel over the course, the direction, and even the weather conditions.

Six men were most responsible for the copeyano campaign: Rafael Caldera, Lorenzo Fernández, Pedro Pablo Aguilar, Eduardo Fernández, Oswaldo Alvarez Paz, and Rafael Salvatierra. For President Caldera, continuation of the work undertaken by his administration was at issue, as well as the continued success of the party he had created and forged through years of political toil. His commitment to the candidacy of Lorenzo Fernández increased the stakes. Rightly or not, he viewed the election in considerable part as a plebiscitary evaluation of his administration, thus further increasing its importance. The candidate hoped to prove himself on his own right. After decades of service at Caldera's right hand, victory for Fernández would mean both personal vindication and his own opportunity as chief of state. In the case of Aguilar, a shrewdly calculating leader who had risen to national prominence in recent years, a victory for Fernández would further strengthen the oficialista wing, while association with a successful campaign could move him toward a possible future candidacy of his own.

The other three men came from COPEI's rising younger generation, all under thirty-five years of age. Eduardo Fernández, a brilliant young lawyer and politician whose rise had been meteoric, had served Caldera closely throughout the 1968 campaign, after which he became sub-secretary to the presidency before later returning to full-time party activity as deputy secretary general under Aguilar. Largely successful in emerging unscathed from the struggle over the presidential nomination, he continued to enjoy a warm relationship with Rafael Caldera. When in August 1973 he was postulated as the first candidate for deputy from the Distrito Federal--a position once held by Caldera--Fernández's satisfaction was enhanced by his affection for the president, as well as the obvious political symbolism. Already he was widely presumed to be a likely copeyano candidate for president at some future date. Neither Alvarez Paz nor Salvatierra shared either the prominence or the breadth of spirit of Eduardo Fernández. The former, nephew of Jesús Angel Paz Galarraga and brother of mepista Fernando Alvarez Paz, had experienced difficulties in earlier years while the pro-Caldera leader of the JRC. Bright, articulate, and arrogant, he became the national campaign coordinator. Rafael Salvatierra had inherited from José Curiel the responsibility for the party's electoral machinery and technical services, serving as sub-secretary general for electoral organization.

The Comité Nacional held effective control over the organization, although the convention was recognized as the ultimate authority, as with most other Venezuelan parties.[2] With Rafael Caldera in Miraflores and the party presidency largely a symbolic post,[3] the position of secretary general was especially crucial, even more so than those within the especial Electoral Commission. The overall structure was highly centralized, as had always been the case with the Social Christians. Authority from the Directorio Nacional was perhaps never so strongly exercised as during the 1973 campaign insofar as regional and local authorities were

concerned. This was best illustrated during the process of
constituting the party's legislative and municipal planchas or
lists, a task of enormous complexity and delicacy. For COPEI as
the government party, the excess of aspiring officeholders over
available positions aggravated the problem greatly. It was further
complicated by the necessity of incorporating independents, as well
as leaders of COPEI's electoral ally, the FDP.

The Comité Nacional had announced that the party's regional
bodies were empowered to choose their own candidates, but that the
Comité was reserving one-third of the positions for its own
designations. An informal truce between the party's three rival
internal groups--oficialistas or tradicionalistas, herreristas, and
beaujonistas--was endangered at the outset. Young copeyanos,
imbued with the spirit of renewal and renovation, insisted upon
larger representation of junior party members. Favorable positions
were of course being demanded by the FDP, as well as the MPJ and
lesser groups.[4] A series of meetings were held by COPEI's district
assemblies and regional directorates at the close of July, making
recommendations that were presented in alphabetical order to the
national leadership. A special seven-person Comisión de Planchas[5]
was created to meet with local and regional copeyanos before making
presumably final recommendations to the Comité Nacional. The
formation of the planchas, despite the elaborate ground rules,
proved taxing. Before its conclusion, the national leadership was
forced to intervene directly in three states, each of which was
important to overall electoral strategy.

Lara, Bolívar, and Zulia were especially hard hit, although
COPEI also encountered knotty problems in Táchira, Guárico, and
Apure. The situation in Lara was potentially explosive, for the
state was a stronghold of Luis Herrera Campins. In early July of
1973 the Comité Nacional declared the Lara party in a state of
reorganization and, despite opposition from both Herrera Campins
and Beaujon, intervened directly. Both the party president and
secretary general in Lara were passed by, although eventually
included on COPEI's planchas. The intervention was received
unhappily by Herrera and his followers, including Governor Rafael
Andrés Montes de Oca.

Anti-herrerista motives were also involved in interventions of
state leadership in both Táchira and Guárico. The Guárico
situation was aggravated further by the decision to postulate FDP
leader Jorge Dáger for the first Senate seat. Similarly, the naming
of Wolfgang Larrazábal as first senator from Sucre displaced none
other than Rafael Salvatierra himself. In Trujillo, a leader of
COPEI's Comité Regional attacked the Comisión de Planchas for
"rewarding militants whose public conduct is suspect...with
legislative and administrative posts." He warned that COPEI's vote
in December would be disappointing. His words were to be prophetic.

The situation in Bolívar epitomized both the inherent problems
of the process and the centralized nature of COPEI's organizational
structure. In a state where the party was traditionally weak, local
leaders had labored arduously for several years to strengthen COPEI.
Ildemaro Martínez, a loyal bureaucrat of the Caldera administration

who had been marginal to Bolívar politics for some years, was placed first on the slate of deputies while Angel Zerpa Mirabal of the FDP was second; Luis Pilioneta, inactive for some time, was number three on the planchas. Strong protests were lodged in person by Bolívar leaders in Caracas, but insistence by national leaders on their decisions consequently weakened the regional campaign.[6] In December the copeyano vote in Bolívar was disastrously low. Zulia can be cited as one further example of the centralization of party decision-making. Some two years before elections President Caldera had appointed a ranking party leader, Hilarión Cardozo, as state governor. The intention clearly was to strengthen the party in Venezuela's most populous state and, after initial grumbling by zuliano leaders, the choice appeared wise. When congressional lists were first drawn up, however, internal problems erupted. A dispute involving Governor Cardozo and Public Works Minister José Curiel on one side, and Interior Minister Nectario Andrade Labarca on the other—all three zulianos, and with aspirations for higher office in the future—threatened a public quarrel.[7] Three young Zulia deputies were ultimately replaced, each of whom had opposed the Fernández presidential nomination. Only one was eventually returned to the planchas but was moved to a less favorable position on the lists for Falcón.[8]

In brief, the arduous work of putting together its lists left serious problems for COPEI in several states. Deviation from the traditional practice of automatically postulating local and regional leaders provoked no small amount of internal distress. Toward the close of the period in which planchas were due in the offices of the CSE, the special Comisión de Planchas was meeting around the clock at a secluded locale outside Caracas. If nothing else, the excruciating experience gave further testimony to the centralized nature of the campaign. In contrast, COPEI was less successful in exercising horizontal authority over independent groups and micro-parties that also supported the Fernández candidacy. Although the many local and state "Independents for Lorenzo" had been largely copeyano creations and were easily constrolled, the same was not true of other groups, and most particularly the FDP. While consultation with FDP leader Jorge Dáger was frequent, the canny efedepista always kept the interests of his own party foremost; neither he nor Admiral Larrazábal were necessarily amenable to copeyano views. For COPEI, the nature of the alliance was such that the overall structure became diffused in practice, belying the fused organizational charts.

As in the past, COPEI's organizational campaign structure was highly specialized rather than regularized. No other party evolved as complex electoral machinery. At the broadest level, COPEI was grouped into three divisions assigned respectively to policy, execution, and "service." Policy was the responsibility of the Comité Nacional and subsidiary subcommittees; its execution was the direct responsibility of Secretary General Aguilar, Deputy Secretary Eduardo Fernández, and four additional sub-secretaries. The so-called service division included the finance committee and provided general support for the other two divisions. Effective coordination of the campaign, including liaison with the candidate and his personal staff, was the continuing responsibility of Oswaldo Alvarez Paz. The massive array of electronic equipment and specialized campaign technicians--of which more shortly--was directed by Rafael Salvatierra as party sub-secretary general of electoral organization.[9]

The 1968 electoral structure was again employed, stressing vertical control and permitting designation of electoral officials by the party leadership in addition to officials chosen by regular internal party elections. As Caldera and Curiel had reasoned, Venezuelan political and administrative divisions dated from 1904, and in many cases were no longer consistent with reality. Thus party structures paralleling the national administrative structure were inadequate for electoral purposes. COPEI therefore divided Venezuela into nine zones, each the responsibility of a zonal coordinator, or Coordinador Zonal (COZ).[10] The zonal coordinators were assisted by 23 Coordinadores Zonzales Adjuntos (COZA). They were supported in turn by 348 Coordinadores Regionales Adjuntos (CORA). At the bottom of the structure were local Comités de Base, which grew through the campaign and numbered some 16,000 by election day. National leaders had the authority to replace or reassign the coordinators at will, thereby enhancing structural centralization.[11]

The pride and joy of _copeyano_ campaign specialists was their electronic center housed in the drab, three-story Santa Ana Building in Boleíta, situated in an industrial suburb of eastern Caracas.[12] A permanent staff of more than one hundred communications experts, radio and electronic technicians, computer operators, and public relations advisers were assembled by Rafael Salvatierra far in advance of the elections, and the number more than tripled as the campaign approached peak activity. Although the Boleíta operations were conducted in an atmosphere of happy informality, they were also characterized by secrecy. Reminding visitors of a military encampment, plans and projects were labeled with code names, filed in secret archives under lock and key, and further protected by tight security arrangements.[13] Boleíta workers spoke of Operación Delta, Operación Gama, Operación Arauco, and the like. In all, some two dozen separate "operations" were undertaken, outstripping in complexity, personnel, and expense the activities of opposition organizations. Drawing extensively on party workers for a variety of field operations throughout the campaign, the electoral center had mobilized over 80,000 by election day. Operación Delta over a period of months had trained and prepared that number of _copeyano_ activists for tasks culminating at the voting _mesas_ on 9 December, including official party representatives and witnesses who were to help assure the purity of the vote and defend the interests of COPEI.

Operación Gama[14] typified the thinking of Salvatierra and his coworkers, entailing as it did a three-month national electoral census conducted by some 22,000 _copeyanos_. Initiated in September 1973, party workers visited 600,000 homes in thirty towns and ten states. Upon completion of initial contacts, COPEI told a press conference in early November that the results were favorable to

Lorenzo Fernández. Emphasizing that Gama was a census rather than
a poll or survey, Melchert and Salvatierra nonetheless maintained
that the results had a 91 percent degree of reliability. Of 701,
173 Venezuelans visited and interviewed, 255,168 (36.4 percent)
reportedly supported Fernández for president, with 272,433 (38.9
percent) opposed to him and the remainder undecided.[15] It was
further claimed that projections of the census--the bases for which
were unexplained--assured COPEI's candidate 43 percent of the vote,
presumably more than ample for victory. Importantly, a further
phase of Gama called for return visits that were intended to sway
undecided voters. Even more elaborate and ambitious, however, was
the multiphase Operación Arauca with which the Boleíta Center
expected to cap its 1973 activities in a blaze of electronic
wizardry.

     Arauca promised to announce electoral results long before
either the CSE or any of the other parties.[16] Committed to
providing Venezuela with presidential returns only four hours after
the closing of voting tables, COPEI further promised complete
totals within twelve hours. Thus by 6 A.M. of Monday, 10 December,
the outcome would be fully known. Operación Arauca was audacious
in concept and massive in scope. A sketch of its configurations
provides fuller appreciation of both the technical skill of COPEI's
organization and its propensity toward mechanistic manipulation of
hordes of faceless individuals. At the base of the pyramid serving
Arauca were party committees for each electoral mesa (over 15,000
in 1973) manned by anywhere from three to thirty members.
Throughout the day they would be responsible for working at the
mesa, witnessing its operation, and, at the close of voting, taking
a copy of the mesa vote totals to a nearby local headquarters.
Each such committee received orders as to the time and place where
the information was to be taken. Totals would then be transported
to a party office in the capital of each municipio, and from there
in turn to the appropriate distrito capital. Totals would be
summed at the district level and reported by telephone or telegraph
to respective state capitals. The next step was communication to
one of thirteen electronic centers (Centros de Teleprocesamiento)
dispersed throughout the country.

     Each such terminal was equipped with machines capable of
processing the data, recording them on magnetic tapes, and sending
them by direct telephonic cable to a central electronic brain in
Caracas. There COPEI had already fed extensive data into its
memory bank, including the total number of votes per mesa,
municipio, distrito, state, and urban center; the number of votes
COPEI had received in 1968; projections by party strategists of
necessary margins in critical areas; and so on. Bulletins would
be issued frequently by OPIMIR, the press office for the candidate,
which had also set up a network of sixty radio stations in the
interior. Elaborate facilities for press, radio, and television
were prepared in Santa Ana for receiving and disseminating the
bulletins, and a smaller facility was also set up in
"La Muchachera," Fernández's home. Arauca was subdivided into six
categories, each responsible for a different aspect of reporting

the vote totals; Operación Arauca Uno would report solely on the presidential race, for example, whereas Cinco was assigned the more ambitious and longer task of processing and recording all votes. It was estimated that upwards of 90,000 party members or sympathizers would be mobilized for the task on election day and night, moving across the country by foot, horseback, car, motor launch, and plane in order to get the votes on the way to Caracas. Some 1,200 would be working in Boleíta to process, analyze, and release the data.

Perhaps owing in part to the exceptional degree of specialization in the COPEI organization, the candidate himself relied less heavily upon a personal staff than have some major presidential candidates in recent years. Whereas the 1968 Caldera campaign had been a blend of institutionalization and personalization, for Fernández it was more the former. After his long years in COPEI, it would have been surprising had he not relied heavily upon the special campaign apparatus. Alvarez Paz and Salvatierra both interacted regularly with the candidate, who placed greater faith in them than in many senior copeyano leaders. Luis Mariano Fernández was influential in the campaign and served his father faithfully, as did other family members. To sum up, the predominant characteristics of the COPEI campaign organization were centralization, diffusion, specialization, and institutionalization.

Regarding finances, the extraordinary profligacy of campaign expenditures is spelled out in chapter 8. Our present concern is with the source of funds. Certainly for COPEI they were multiple. According to Adolfo Melchert, the sources were the two customarily cited: dues from party members and contributions from sympathetic independents. In accordance with well-established copeyano practice, party members were obligated to pay a fixed monthly sum, pegged to their salary and to family size. Statutorily this quota ranged from 19.50 to 1,010.00 bolívares per month, with the latter sum contributed by Rafael Caldera. In 1972 COPEI claimed 760,000 inscribed members, although only 570,000 were classified as active. It was estimated that some 150,000 bolívares per month were raised through membership dues. Funds were also raised through dinners, raffles, and social functions, with the remainder coming from private sources.[17] For COPEI as for the AD, only a small portion of expenses could be met by membership dues. In the final analysis, large contributions from private individuals and business firms were necessary to meet campaign needs. The Social Christians' electoral organization was unquestionably the largest and most extensive in Venezuela--technically skilled, systematically structured, and dedicated to the victory of its candidate and legislative nominees--in organizational terms a marvel to behold. Whether the mechanistic precision and impersonality of the copeyano apparatus would engender unfavorable voter response remained moot.

ACCIÓN DEMOCRÁTICA

The organizational task confronting the adecos following the 1968 elections was of a different order and magnitude than that of COPEI, with the very survival of the party in question. Although

there was pride in the unprecedented act of accepting a narrowly
unfavorable vote and delivering government to the opposition, this
was small consolation to a party undergoing such a withering ordeal.
The immediate task was a replenishing of the decimated party
structure and a renewal of adeco spirit and morale.

Concluding that past organizational patterns were fundamentally
sound, the party chose not to alter them drastically, concentrating
rather on rebuilding with existing personnel while seeking renewed
support at the grass roots.[18] With the return to full party
activity by adecos who had served in the Leoni administration, the
AD could devote unstinting efforts to its organizational challenge.
The central figure was Carlos Andrés Pérez, who had become secretary
general in 1968. Although Gonzalo Barrios had returned to the AD
as party president following his 1968 loss to Caldera, his role was
more that of the senior statesman, leaving to Pérez the task of
rebuilding and reorganizaing. Strongly supported by other party
leaders and encouraged from abroad by Rómulo Betancourt, Pérez
undertook his work with the inexhaustible vigor and determination
that have since become his political trademark. Traveling,
speaking, consulting at all levels, he helped to convince the
discouraged that the events of 1967 and 1968 had been transitory
rather than decisive. The leadership that emerged after 1968
worked smoothly and collaboratively. In part because of the
severity of problems facing the AD during this period, a high degree
of teamwork was achieved. This was to continue into the campaign
itself. The actual selection of the candidate had assured a
minimum of post-convention animosity. As a consequence, the AD
emerged from the convention and sallied forth into the campaign
with a confident, well-organized, and strongly united party. Where
Lorenzo Fernández was forced to dedicate his first post-convention
efforts to the binding up of internal wounds, Carlos Andrés Pérez
and his party were fully prepared for the fray. Moreover, the AD
was not suffering from the internal disunity that had been
increasing in COPEI. The close-knit leadership that had evolved
from the dark days of 1967-69 was to carry over into the
organization of the campaign itself.

While party elders Rómulo Betancourt and Gonzalo Barrios
provided important advice and counsel, especially on broad strategy
questions, they were less central to the purely organizational
effort. The single most important figure was the presidential
candidate himself; others were party veterans Octavio Lepage,
David Morales Bello, Luis Piñerúa Ordaz, and Reinaldo Leandro Mora.
By mid-1973 the young leader of Causa Común, Diego Arria, also
assumed an important role. The AD campaign effort was largely free
of the divisions of outlook, objectives, experience, and age that
plagued COPEI. Single-minded concentration upon winning elections,
unencumbered by serious infighting between divergent currents and
generations of leadership, was reflected throughout the adeco
campaign. Secretary General Octavio Lepage, who had succeeded
Pérez in that key position, was a widely respected intellectual of
forty-nine who had risen through years of quiet industry. Often
identified with Gonzalo Barrios, he had nonetheless maintained his

independence through the years, combining with breadth of intellect and vision a forceful and articulate partisanship in defense of the party. Luis Piñerúa Ordaz was a quietly unassuming figure who served with dedication and effectiveness as secretary of the organization. While Lepage was overseeing the entire party effort and assuring effective consultation with the candidate, Piñerúa skillfully handled the nuts-and-bolts activities. Leandro Mora, a former cabinet minister under Raúl Leoni, was employed as coordinador general de independientes. David Morales Bello, a distinguished if acerbic lawyer who had become active with the AD only in recent years, served as campaign coordinator. By the final six months of the campaign, the independent Arria became a key figure, contributing innovative and creative dimensions to the campaign. This group of men, combining their talents with skill and collegiality, provided well-coordinated direction to the campaign organization, all under the direct and constant leadership of the candidate himself.

The adeco organizational structure basically paralleled Venezuelan administrative subdivisions, with organs at the state, district, and municipal level. Although there were ad hoc campaign groups of independents, along with the special metropolitan Caracas group under Luis Manuel Peñalver, the AD did not follow COPEI's practice of creating a separate array of regional and zonal organs. Its rather traditional structure was nonetheless centralized, with vertical control exercised from headquarters in Caracas. As with COPEI, this centralization was vividly illustrated by the process of forming and ordering the planchas. For the AD, the apparent shortage of available positions for aspiring office-seekers had never been more serious. In 1958, after ten years of exile, the problem had been manageable. In both 1963 and 1968, the recent departure of leaders in the respective arsista and prietista disputes had diminished the size of the pool. By 1973, however, the situation was different. Just as COPEI had been pressed to find positions for such allies as the FDP and MPJ, the AD was faced with the inclusion of representatives from both the PRN and the Congreso del Trabajo. There were inevitably independents to be considered as well.

The passage was by no means a tranquil one. In the end, however, the AD negotiated these treacherous waters with less damage than did COPEI. The party's National Executive Committee (the Comité Ejecutivo Nacional or CEN) reserved fully 50 percent of the available positions for its own disposal, an action that was not adopted without resistance from state and sectional organizations. Municipal Committees first made their recommendations for local candidates to District Committees, which after deliberation forwarded names to the party's Sectional Executive Committees (Comités Ejecutivos Seccionales or CES). By late July the respective sectionals were sending their selections to Caracas. Acting with as much flexibility as possible, the CEN then proceeded to wrestle with the final configuration of the planchas, calling members of the sectionals to Caracas for discussion of particularly difficult cases. In addition to local

and regional pressures, the AD was concerned with the demands of
its important labor and peasant wings, while also anxious to
introduce new blood through the inclusion of deserving youth
leaders. In the end the verdict of the CEN was final, and its
exercise of authority consistent with organizational centralization.[19]
    Perhaps the single most awkward situation came from Nueva
Esparta, where the AD had suffered through the prietista division
and concomitant loss of labor leader José González Navarro and
Prieto himself, both natives of the island. Guillermo Salazar
Meneses, whose family had long been prominent in local politics,
remained loyal to the AD at the time of the division and lost his
congressional seat in the process. By 1973, however, González
Navarro had in turn left the MEP, organized his Congreso del
Trabajo, and aligned himself with the AD. He hoped to become a
candidate from Nueva Esparta once again. After heated controversy
at the state level and unhappy debate in Caracas, the party
acceded and placed González Navarro at the head of the Senate
list. Salazar Meneses was assigned the first deputy seat from
Barinas, which assured his return to Congress but did little to
help the party campaign on the island.[20] For the PRN, its leaders
were considered for various state lists before José Manzo González
was named first senatorial candidate from Monagas and Miguel García
Mackle second for the lower house from Falcón. Less serious
complications were encountered in placing prominent independents
on the planchas, such as Diego Arria heading the list of deputies
from Miranda, Marcos Falcón Briceño the Federal District deputies,
and Ramón J. Velásquez as senator from Táchira. With vertical
control exercised through centralization, the AD organization
achieved substantial fusion in its horizontal relationships.
Agreements with the PRN and the Congreso del Trabajo were
relatively straightforward. The PRN had declined to a miniscule
force, while González Navarro's recent departure from the MEP had
allowed little time in building the Congreso. Moreover, both PRN
and Congreso leaders had been leaders of the AD in earlier years,
and it was not difficult for the AD to deal with them. As to
independents, the AD was less concerned than COPEI with the
erection of a massive structure of organized groups. As a
consequence, the task of coordinating with independent entities
was relatively susceptible to party guidance. Reinaldo Leandro
Mora, assisted by former URD leader J.M. Domínguez Chacín,
exercised vigorous but flexible guidance to the effort.[21] Beginning
more than a year before elections, the AD brought together an array
of groups under the overarching Unidad de Relaciones con los
Independientes y Organizaciones Periféricas, created as a dependency
of the national electoral commission. Comités Pro-Candidatura
de Carlos Andrés Pérez were created in the majority of municipal
capitals. By October of 1973 some fourteen hundred committees of
independents had been established, over three hundred located in
metropolitan Caracas. Each had a minimum of thirty members.
    Composed of a mixture of adecos and independents, the
committees were free from party discipline and acted with a degree
of autonomy. At the same time, party members could influence their

activity.   In mid-October a so-called National Congress of
Independents Favoring the Candidacy of Carlos Andrés was convened
in the Caracas Hilton, at which 2,900 delegates received Pérez and
other party leaders. The AD approach toward independents varied
somewhat from that of COPEI, with greater emphasis placed upon the
cooperation of independents with party members. Non-adecos were
brought into the campaign actively and in some parts of the country
were of considerable importance. As a consequence, the AD was less
involved than COPEI with groups of independents totally outside the
party structure. The AD approach simplified its task of horizontal
communication and authority, and under the sure hand of Leandro
Mora, the campaign organization was essentially fused, unlike COPEI.
     The contrast between the two major parties in terms of
specialization and regularization was also evident, although more
a matter of degree than kind. The AD's electoral commission under
David Morales Bello was important to the campaign effort and
justifies classification of the overall structure as specialized.
However, it was closely coordinated with the regular party structure,
whereas that of COPEI under Alvarez Paz and Salvatierra stood as a
virtually separate entity. The AD's permanent party organization
was more central to the campaign than the Social Christians'. So
it was that Secretary of Organization Luis Piñerúa Ordaz was of
particular importance to the Pérez candidacy. The usual local
branches, municipal committees, and district and state organs
endured, but their roles in the campaign effort were diminished.
The past practice of weekly meetings and assemblies had become
politically frayed, with party loyalists disenchanted by repetitious
gatherings at which the same faces appeared and reappeared. In the
AD view, therefore, such orthodox organizational ploys were
incapable of effective penetration for electoral purposes. For the
1973 effort, emphasis was placed instead on those termed activistas.[22]
     Not necessarily a party functionary, the "activist" was an
unpaid volunteer,[23] committed to the AD campaign, who provided an
important communications resource for the organization. Representing
the party vanguard at the grass-roots level, the activista was to
help in the dissemination of the party message while feeding back
suggestions, criticisms, and comments to the leadership. With an
estimated 70,000 activistas spearheading the effort,
bureaucratization was minimized. The AD believed that although ortho&
party structure remained important for the wide array of routine
matters that required regular attention, it was no longer adequate
for communication between the leadership and membership. Only
utilization of more direct and personal proselytizing as embodied
by the activistas, in conjunction with independents working under
Leandro Mora and Diego Arria, would suffice.
     The distinction between copeyano and adeco organizational
specialization was also mirrored in the parties' respective efforts
to train and mobilize workers for election day. With COPEI, such
projects as Operación Gama and the several Operaciones Arauca were
centered in the specialized campaign apparatus operated from
Boleíta. AD, however, placed such responsibilities under
Organization Secretary Piñerúa. Also given to the use of code names,

the AD undertook such projects as Operación Mosca and Operación Satélite. The former, "Operation Fly,"[24] was very roughly similar to COPEI's Operación Delta. It too concentrated on preparing thousands for work at the electoral mesas on 9 December. The AD assembled a team of 182 technicians and professionals to provide training throughout Venezuela. An additional 2,600 "instructors" were to extend such training on a local basis. Some 80,000 party members and sympathizers eventually underwent orientation outlining the duties of serving as witnesses and workers at individual mesas. One week before election day, final review sessions were conducted. In addition, Operación Mosca organized a team of 2,000 lawyers and 1,600 coordinators to provide last-minute technical and legal advice.[25]

The basic rationale was set forth in Piñerúa's prologue to the AD pamphlet, which was distributed throughout the party. "Operación Mosca is a conjunction of activities and measures conceived and designed to guarantee that the vote of Venezuelans is expressed and registered with rigorous purity. It is not solely a mechanism to win votes, but also to protect and defend the free and correctly emitted vote...not only that which favors Acción Democrática and Carlos Andrés, but also that which favors other candidates and parties...."[26] Vigilance in defense of the purity of the vote was a basic obligation of all citizens, and party workers were exhorted on the gravity of their responsibility to Venezuela and to the AD. As one AD leader editorialized, "Neither hunger, thirst, nor sleepiness should divert these men and women into abandoning their posts and their mission...."[27]

The task of reporting the vote to party electoral headquarters was organized under the rubric of Operación Satélite. With basic objectives similar to those of Operación Arauca, the more modest adeco effort was designed to concentrate on the competition between Carlos Andrés Pérez and Lorenzo Fernández. The backbone of Operación Satelite was a team of 1,800 coordinators and 500 communicators. The former were assigned the task of supervising party workers at the electoral mesas, as well as gathering electoral data after the close of voting. Each coordinator was responsible for a number of contiguous mesas, running as high as ten in number. With the closing of a mesa and the first tabulation of results, the coordinator would relay the information to a communicator stationed at a party reception center. From there the communications process would move by reserved telephone lines to strategically located cities throughout the nation. The party had divided the country into three zones—West, Central, and East—of which forty-one terminals were located in the interior and another twenty-one in metropolitan Caracas. The latter were equipped with a small computer possessing a three-item memory capacity: number of mesas, the vote for Pérez, and the vote for Fernández. A center for receiving and analyzing data was located in San Bernardino, a residential section of Caracas, where over one hundred volunteers labored under the direction of Leopoldo Sucre Figarella and Héctor Silva Calderón. A dozen technicians were also to be assigned to the center, from which the AD planned to announce up to 90 percent

of the Pérez-Fernández returns within four hours of the closing of
mesas. Results were then to be relayed by closed-circuit
television to Pérez's offices in another section of the city.

Adeco organizational specialization, then, was somewhat
distinct from COPEI's. Coordination between regular party bodies
and the specialized campaign structure was effectively maintained,
and the Secretariat of Organization played a more central role than
was true for the Social Christians. The total organizational effort
was also institutionalized rather than personalized. With Pérez
having spent his entire adult life as a party member, there was
little need for a personalized staff functioning separately. His
aides, though important to the campaign,[28] were fully integrated
into the total machinery. Pérez's vigorous and unremitting
leadership of the campaign helped to assure communication and
exchange of views within the apparatus, for the candidate's
personal imprint was strong.

As with COPEI, the AD's expenses demanded reliance upon all
available sources. A detailed analysis of expenses in chapter 8
suggests that the AD expenditure was of a magnitude comparable
to COPEI's (excluding government activities on behalf of Fernández).
Income from membership dues could no more finance AD's campaign
than it could COPEI's. By party statute all members were obligated
to pay a minimum of one bolívar monthly, with an internal scale
requiring more substantial contributions from officials.[29] With
the AD claiming a membership of some 920,000 internal funding was
grossly inadequate for campaign needs. Contributions from
independents and sympathizers were obviously sought, while the
usual extensive financing from private business and commercial
interests was imperative. The party also relied upon fund-raising
dinners, special drives, raffles, and social gatherings with the
candidate or other ranking party leaders.[30] The adeco campaign
structure, in short, was less massive and complex than that of
COPEI but was effectively and tightly organized. Centralized and
fused, with its electoral specialization well integrated into
the overarching party apparatus, it proved to be flexible, efficient,
and responsive. Directed by an active candidate whose organizational
experience within the party was extensive and supported by a
well-coordinated team of imaginative party leaders, the AD had
successfully rebuilt the machinery that five years earlier lay in
ruins.

THE POLITICAL LEFT
For Jesús Angel Paz Galarraga, José Vicente Rangel, and Jóvito
Villalba, problems in organizing a national campaign were
substantial, and some of the obstacles were insuperable. Each
lacked the resources to combat COPEI and the AD on an equal footing.
The leftist candidates therefore were forced to adopt measures
intended to compensate for existing disadvantages. For Paz, one
of the fine organizational talents of contemporary Venezuelan
politics, problems included the unwieldy coalition that constituted
the Nueva Fuerza. José Vicente Rangel, in contrast, was a political
independent whose experience had been generally remote from

organizational matters. If Paz was the political organization man
par excellence, Rangel epitomized the lone wolf who for years had
been a solitary voice speaking for the left in Congress. As for
Villalba, the deterioration of the URD affected every structural
aspect of his campaign.
     The Paz campaign had been built out of the 1968 race. The
mepista secretary general undertook a characteristically quiet but
carefully conceived plan of action. Assuming active leadership
of the MEP with the concurrence of Prieto, Paz gradually tightened
his control while leading the party toward the left. In the
process, his fellow maracuchos became increasingly influential
while prietistas gradually declined in importance. The eclipse of
Prieto's nephew Antonio Espinoza Prieto[31] and the withdrawal of
Mercedes Fermín[32] were illustrative, as was the restructuring of
the regional leadership in Zulia. The naming of Adelso González
Urdaneta as secretary general in the May 1973 National Assembly
further solidified Paz's position within the MEP. Enjoying the
firm backing of party president Prieto, Paz was enabled to
concentrate more fully upon the organization of the Nueva Fuerza.
Owing to the determined independence of the Partido Comunista de
Venezuela, the task was difficult.
     Perhaps the high point of PCV collaboration and support came
at the Nueva Fuerza nominating convention. Despite frequent
consultation within the campaign command of the Nueva Fuerza,
communist leaders firmly maintained their independence. The PCV
Central Committee proclamation supporting Paz's candidacy was
typical. Written largely by Guillermo García Ponce of its Buró
Político, the document stressed the importance of defeating Carlos
Andrés Pérez. "For us the candidacy of the upper bourgeoisie, and
the most reactionary one, is that of Acción Democrática."[33] This
treatment of Pérez as the most undesirable of the pro-system
candidates was at variance with Paz's contention that there was
no meaningful difference between the AD and COPEI nominees. The
PCV also focused sharp criticism on José Vicente Rangel and the
MAS. Rangel, himself a wealthy man, was accused of hidden ties
with capitalism and the domestic oligarchy. Indeed, a major
objective of the PCV was to outpoll the MAS in the legislative
and municipal vote, and this influenced its decision to postulate
its own slate of candidates. With only a small number of
municipal candidates jointly representing the PCV and MEP, it
remained for the latter to incorporate independents and
sympathizers of the Nueva Fuerza into its own lists.
     For the MEP itself, the campaign organization was strongly
centralized. Paz's control, exercised through Secretary General
González and Secretary of Organization Siuberto Martínez, was firm.
The party's Comité Político Nacional was supplemented during the
final months of the campaign by a smaller, seven-person Comisión
Político-Administrativa[34] which met regularly. The MEP structure
was thus specialized, while Paz's direct involvement lent an
institutionalized dimension. Indeed, the single most striking
characteristic of his campaign was the heavy attention he devoted
to its every aspect. His organizational reputation was based not

only upon shrewd political insight and years of experience but on his concern with detail. Campaigning actively with only a small personal entourage, he expended substantial time and energy on matters that in COPEI and the AD could be delegated to others. Whereas Luis B. Prieto in 1968 had been able to rely on Paz for the handling of myriad organizational details, Paz himself lacked a counterpart in 1973. The broader coalition organization provided less than effective support, thus adding to the candidate's burdens.

Efforts were undertaken to create an overall Nueva Fuerza structure that might function as a team operation.[35]   At the apex was the Directorate, an advisory body with overall campaign responsibility. Each of the coalition members were represented, and important independents also belonged. Directly beneath the Directorate was the Comando Electoral Nacional, with two members of each party. The Comando in turn received reports and recommendations from the Comisión Coordinadora, which was involved with daily and routine tasks. At the base of the entire organization were the Comités Populares, formed along geographic and regional lines. These committees functioned at the grass-roots level--campaigning, canvassing, propagandizing, and proselytizing.[36] They were extremely variable in effectiveness. Efficiency was greater where local mepistas dominated or virtually monopolized the committees. At all levels, in fact, the greatest strength and effort came from the MEP.

The relative degree of communist independence, with the comitment to the Nueva Fuerza more ritualistic than genuine, weakened the alliance organizationally.[37]   The Machado brothers and Jesús Faría voiced their views at the highest level of the coalition, but largely in an advisory fashion. To the extent that the PCV was active in the campaign, it worked for its own interests. The so-called Democracia Popular Venezolana (DPV) of former copeyana Carmen de Valera, with its appeal limited to one state, had little to contribute. Even the UPI, formed on 8 March 1973 by ex-urredistas who refused to accept Jóvito Villalba's self-serving withdrawal from the Nueva Fuerza, was limited to the individual efforts of a few individuals, notably Jesús Soto Amesty and Narciso Romero. Of great value to the campaign was José Herrera Oropeza, a political independent who served as campaign coordinator for the Nueva Fuerza. For all practical purposes, the coalition organization was diffused. Certainly the heart of the Paz campaign remained within his own MEP, and much the same was true of financing.

The Paz candidacy was more seriously handicapped by limited funds than Prieto's five years earlier. The difficulty of negotiating bank loans, serious for the MEP in 1968, became impossible by 1973, while expenses were greater than ever before. The MEP received its proportional contribution from the CSE in accordance with Article 154 of the Suffrage Law; although limited, this source was important. Otherwise, funds came primarily through the contributions of members and supporters, estimated at some 55,000 bolívares per month.[38]   Unlike Rangel, Paz himself was not a wealthy man. The unanswered question concerned charges that the

Soviet Union provided backing to the PCV, and through it to the
Nueva Fuerza. These allegations were predictably denied. Whatever
the possible extent of foreign financing to the PCV, there is
nothing to indicate significant communist contributions to Paz.
If the campaign of Jesús Angel Paz Galarraga demanded and
received unremitting personal effort on the part of the candidate,
it nonetheless possessed some degree of organizational skill and
experience. It also enjoyed the national stature of Luis B.
Prieto. For José Vicente Rangel, in contrast, few of these factors
were present; consequently, his campaign was overwhelmingly
individual in cast. There was but negligible grass-roots
organization to rely upon, and masista advisers were largely
novices to the politics of a nationwide presidential campaign.
Circumstances therefore militated toward individual efforts by the
candidate. Rangel enjoyed freedom from disciplined party influence,
and the impact of his campaign was far more personal than party
based. The MAS and MIR needed his candidacy more than he needed
their support. Thus Rangel's position was enhanced in the
articulation and elaboration of the campaign, if at the price of
markedly uneven organizational support.

For the MAS, whose early operational style was collegial,
there was reluctance to shape a complicated table of organization.
Having reacted strongly against internal party bureaucratization
within the PCV, the MAS was chary of falling into similarly
constricting patterns. Not until June of 1973 did the MAS create
a Comité Ejecutivo Nacional to complement its guiding Comité
Central.[39]   As national electoral secretary of MAS, Juvencio
Pulgar served as Rangel's campaign manager, coordinating activities
and handling necessary arrangements. Party Secretary General
Pompeyo Márquez and Organization Secretary Teodoro Petkoff, probably
the most prominent masistas nationally, exercised strong influence
within the organization. Sharing a determination to achieve
primacy on the Venezuelan left, they insisted upon independence of
action rather than collaboration with the smaller groups backing
Rangel. Thus the MAS sought to centralize its structure while
building strength in local areas; at the same time, its conscious
sectarianism attempted to marginalize others from the Rangel
campaign. Consequently, the MAS was organizationally diffused.

As early as June 1973, members of the so-called CUR went
directly to Rangel,[40] urging that his image be that of candidate
for the entire left rather than predominantly that of the MAS.
Later complaints were lodged with Rangel by other leftist groups
on the periphery of his candidacy,[41] but none as serious as those
of the MIR. Following its June 1973 decision to support Rangel,
the MIR tried unsuccessfully to participate extensively in his
campaign. Shut out of the planning process by the MAS, MIR's only
recourse also took the form of appeals to the candidate. In
September mirista Secretary General Simón Sáez Mérida issued a
public call to the MAS proposing full participation in the final
stage of the campaign. Sáez Mérida contended that all supporting
forces should come together as equals, thereby demonstrating
Rangel's ability to mobilize a unified array of leftist forces.

His plea was of little avail. Although the candidate himself
consulted with a variety of advisers and friends, most regular
exchanges came with the MAS, while Pulgar and his staff continued
to manage operational matters. The resulting lack of horizontal
coordination meant a sharply diffused effort, one that may have
served the needs of MAS rather than José Vicente Rangel's.

Less than three weeks prior to election day, masista-mirista
problems again surfaced in a dispute over respective tarjetas. The
complaint was initiated by the MAS, concerned that the similarity
of tarjetas might cost it votes "mistakenly" cast for the MIR.[42]
A party bulletin, citing the possibility of confusion while
complaining that the MIR enjoyed a better position on the boleta
electoral, urged its members to work hard in clarifying the
question for voters.[43] Sáez Mérida retorted a day later that the
Rangel candidacy represented the left and belonged to all the
people of Venezuela. He also noted that the MAS had chosen its
position on the boleta long before the MIR; if the masista
placement were inferior, it was the fault of the MAS itself. The
masista claim was termed "absurd." In implicit criticism of MAS
sectarianism, the MIR stressed again the need for a unified left
as inordinately more important than "quotas" of votes for its
several components.[44] By the close of the campaign, barriers
between the MAS and MIR were substantial. Except for Rangel's
closing campaign rally in Caracas's El Silencio, he was rarely
joined by leaders of both parties. Regional or local collaboration
was sometimes effective,[45] but this was unusual at the national
level.

In large part, then, the bulk of campaign planning devolved
upon the MAS.[46] Certainly Rangel found the party his major source
of support. Juvencio Pulgar coordinated the specialized
contributions of experts in various aspects of the campaign.
Economists, sociologists, and other sympathetic professionals
donated their services; among the more important were José Augustín
Silva Michelena, Marcos Negrón, Jacobo Borges, and Fernando
Travieso. The noted sociologist Silva organized polling activities
while others concentrated on communications techniques. Instruction
and information were provided to "communicators," whose tasks went
beyond orthodox political proselytizing. They also engaged in
dialogues and discussion groups, which the MAS developed as an
important part of its campaign. These and other techniques were
evolved to compensate for financial constraints on more traditional
methods. Such activities were marked by informality, openness of
exchange, and spirited collegiality. Constructive and imaginative
ideas sometimes resulted, although dispersion of effort and lack
of cohesion were also present.

The magnitude of financial problems was brought home early,
for the impressive rally in Caracas's Nueva Circo that launched
Rangel's candidacy cost some 60,000 bolívares. Fund-raising dinners
and parties were widely used to generate revenue; this source was
tapped on virtually every trip by the candidate to the interior.
Contributions from other sources were limited, and the newness of
the MAS ruled out earlier savings. Among the most controversial

contributions of the entire campaign benefited the MAS to the tune
of 100,000 bolívares, the sum awarded by Venezuela's Instituto de
Cultura y Bellas Artes (INCIBA) as a literary prize to Colombia's
famed Gabriel García Márquez. Copeyanos in particular objected
to García Márquez's gift, coming as it did from government funds.
The Colombian noted his desire not to profit himself and to leave
the money in Venezuela; given his political beliefs, the choice
was clear. There were few similarly large contributions to the
Rangel campaign, and the candidate had to rely substantially on
his own personal funds.

After Jóvito Villalba's decision not to honor the Nueva
Fuerza commitment came statutory reforms of the URD Directorio
Nacional at the party's April 1973 convention. Internal authority
was further centralized, and urredista Political Secretary Leonardo
Montiel Ortega gained greater personal power. Soon named chief of
the Villalba campaign, the party técnico and parliamentarian was
sorely handicapped by the desolation of party structures. There
were defections from the traditional leadership; a major blow was
the resignation of Manuel López Rivas, long a close associate of
Villalba and once a cabinet minister. The URD created a special
campaign unit with de facto powers as campaign coordinating body
empowered to override regular party structures. Villalba often
met with Montiel Ortega and his advisers, but for the most part
he followed his own inclinations throughout the campaign. URD
efforts to mobilize brigades of party faithful for nationwide
proselytizing proved sporadic. Villalba himself campaigned
energetically throughout Venezuela during the final months of the
campaign, often with minimal local support.

THE POLITICAL RIGHT
        The remaining candidacies were largely bereft of campaign
organization. Few could even claim the existence of a structure
outside metropolitan Caracas. Burelli Rivas, García Villasmil, and
Verde Rojas were limited almost entirely to individual efforts.
The case of Segnini La Cruz was but slightly better. Only Pedro
Tinoco deserves a further word here, although his travels were
directed more toward Madrid than the Venezuelan electorate. When
endorsement from Pérez Jiménez became clearly impossible, there was
little remaining opportunity to employ the weakly articulated
structure that had been created earlier. José Ignacio Andrade had
become Tinoco's campaign manager, undertaking establishment of a
Comando Electoral Unificado. Incorporating representatives of both
the Movimiento Desarrollista and the PNI, it attempted to organize
similar entities regionally. Results were highly spotty, and local
sympathizers often failed to receive support or encouragement from
Caracas. With the passing of time, General Felipe Llovera Páez
assumed an increasingly important role in the Tinoco camp. He was
more influential than either Andrade or Guillermo Morón, the
historian who attempted to forge intellectual legitimacy for
desarrollismo.
        In the final analysis, none of these later candidacies
undertook significant organizational work. What did matter,

FIGURE 8. Summary of Organizational Characteristics of the Four
Main Actors--Presidential Campaign of 1973

Actors	COPEI	AD	Nueva Fuerza	MAS-MIR
Candidate Selection	By manipulation and consent	By consensus	Ad hoc, by coalition consensus	By consensus
Campaign Structure	Highly centralized, diffused	Centralized, fused	Centralized, diffused	Centralized, diffused
Electoral Structure	Highly specialized	Specialized	Specialized	Specialized
Candidate Role	Institutionalized	Institutionalized	Institutionalized	Personalized
Financing	External, internal (+ gov't aid)	External, internal	Internal	Internal
Campaign Efficiency	High	High	Low	Low

however, were the structures elaborated by the four major contenders,
infused by party leaders and molded to varying degrees by the
candidates themselves. These appear in figure 8. Certainly the
capacity for a victorious effort was present only for COPEI and
the AD. On the left, both Paz and Rangel faced insuperable
obstacles in financing their respective campaigns. With the former,
centralization, specialization, and institutionalization were all
derived from the MEP, while horizontal relationships with the PCV
produced organizational diffusion. For Rangel, the amorphous and
weakly articulated masista structures assured relatively meaningless
centralization, while the role of the candidate was paramount.
     The contrast between COPEI and AD was more evident than in
1968. There were important qualitative differences in centralization
and specialization. Excessive Social Christian centralization
proved dysfunctional, as illustrated by extreme difficulties with
the planchas. The effective exclusion of elements that had
contested the Fernández nomination underlined organizational
narrowness. Moreover, the exaggerated degree of specialization
led to uneven and halting relations between the candidate's closest
advisers and the regular party leadership. Fernández himself,
whether consciously or otherwise, so heavily relied upon his
campaign advisers that coordination with traditional Social
Christian structures was faulty. Ties with the FDP also proved
less than satisfactory. By the final weeks, Larrazábal and Dáger
were campaigning in ways intended to maximize FDP objectives, and

COPEI was ineffective in attempting to fuse efforts on behalf of Fernández.

The Pérez candidacy enjoyed more moderate centralization and specialization, permitting a healthy and collegial balance between national and regional leaders. Cooperation between the special electoral commission and regular party leadership also proved felicitous. Fusion with such minor collaborations as the PRN, Congreso del Trabajo, and even Causa Común was effective; to be sure, such groups appeared less important to the Pérez campaign than that of the FDP to COPEI. In terms of our hypotheses, AD enjoyed an advantage in its organizational fusion as compared with Social Christian diffusion. Both parties sought financial support from all available sources; they also demonstrated that institutionalization and personalization do not proffer a meaningful basis for discrimination. Our theoretical notions on centralization and specialization, stated previously in propositional form, do not affect the content of our model. We would argue that the exaggerated degree demonstrated by COPEI in 1973 was prejudicial to its electoral fortunes. On strictly organizational grounds, the overkill introduced by the Social Christians, believing themselves at the peak of their powers, raised questions that sought resolution in the popular verdict to be rendered on election day.

5. STRATEGIES AND TACTICS

Formulation of strategies and their implementation preoccupied party leaders no less than organizational dimensions. The competitive 1968 experience had convinced doubters of the importance of searching and intensive preparations.[1] The possibility of a close race in 1973 underlined the necessity for carefully designed strategies and tactics. The outcomes of the nomination process, especially in COPEI and the AD, inevitably influenced strategic and tactical directions, and the posture and policy of the Caldera government added its own impact to the elaboration of campaign messages. Certainly the Social Christian campaign placed heavy reliance upon the record of the administration. The adeco perspective, for the first time in its history, was that of an opposition party seeking a return to power. From the left, the Nueva Fuerza, MAS, and the URD sought both electoral and institutional objectives. The first two were also committed to advancing the cause of socialism while weakening and ultimately destroying the existing capitalist system. For the forces on the right, the plotting of campaign policy wavered wildly in response to the whims of Pérez Jiménez in Madrid.

In some cases the ideal types proposed in our introductory chapter emerged in unadulterated form. More frequently, a given campaign embraced a mixture of approaches in wooing the Venezuelan voter. In addition to respective electoral or institutional objectives, campaigns could adopt an overarching strategy of either consensus or conflict, each of which encompassed two separate subtypes. Similarly, tactical implementation could be classified in terms of inducements or disinducements, each separable into material and symbolic forms. It was hypothesized earlier that the most efficacious strategies are mixed, with the balance weighted on the side of the consensual. Furthermore, a blend of reinforcement and recruitment subtypes is most likely to augment electoral prospects. Similarly, the tactical deployment of a campaign must utilize a combination of material and symbolic subtypes. Application of our schema should help to sort out the complexities of strategies and tactics during the long embattled months of campaigning.

THE SOCIAL CHRISTIAN PARTY COPEI

Intent upon renewing its lease on power, COPEI adopted a two-pronged strategy that blended both consensual and conflictual elements. Party planners, confident of victory from the outset, were influenced less by concern over retaining the presidency than with maximizing the margin of victory. Reasoning that failures in government performance were the result of congressional weakness, copeyanos emphasized the mounting of the largest possible legislative representation for 1974-79. While reinforcement was believed assured through the retention of existing supporters, recruitment was regarded as attracting those independent and nonparty voters required for increased strength in Congress. In following through on consensual approaches, tactics of inducement were used, placing the heaviest possible reliance upon the government record. Both material and symbolic messages were disseminated. At the same time, the Social Christians directed sharp attacks against the AD and especially its candidate. The conflictual strategy was less realigning than it was discrediting, intending destruction of Perez's public credibility. Tactical disinducements were diverse, often following a path of criticism and vituperation. COPEI largely disregarded its other rivals, seeing the AD as its only serious opponent.

The thinking of Social Christian strategists was molded by two basic, deeply held assumptions, the validity of which was rarely questioned. First was the unbending certainty that the administration of Rafael Caldera was the finest in living memory. The supreme leader of COPEI, in the view of the party, had provided such exceptional leadership that the election of his close friend Lorenzo Fernández was unquestionable. Thus the only issue was the final margin of victory. Secondly, many of the copeyano campaign leaders had little respect for the AD and outright scorn toward Pérez. The AD was seen as the deteriorating vestige of a once-great party, its vitality and popularity sapped by three internal divisions.[2] Its leadership had allegedly passed from the hands of giants to pygmies, with the candidate himself a political mediocrity. There was more than a touch of snobbery toward Pérez, an andino of modest origins who lacked a college degree.[3] Such attitudes contributed to the fulsome confidence that so characterized the Social Christian leadership while providing powerful underpinning in justifying strategies. The reinforcement strategy was argued on electoral grounds. Noting the progressive increase in COPEI strength over a decade of elections, matched inversely with an adeco decline, COPEI found good reason for confidence in its party strength. Retention of the faithful seemed to offer few problems. It was the additional recruitment strategy that brought into play the government record. Thus, Pedro Pablo Aguilar told a Cumaná audience at El Chipichipazo in August that Fernández guaranteed a continuation of Caldera's good works, and that a congressional majority was necessary to avoid the obstructionism of the AD. Ten years of arbitrary, even "despotic" government by the AD had left few Venezuelan homes untouched, and its talk of a crusade against poverty was "rank hypocrisy." Only a Fernández government would assure the continuity of development and progress under **true liberty**.[4] Eduardo Fernández wrote of Lorenzo as the single candidate capable of meeting Venezuela's social and economic needs. He was programmatically committed to the "work of government initiated under the mandate of President Caldera. His fundamental purpose is that of propelling those policies forward with audacity and with decision."[5]

The weekly Tuesday meetings between copeyano leaders and President Caldera at La Casona often provided further strategic testimony. Following such a gathering in late **October,** for example, party spokesman Eduardo Fernández alluded to COPEI's concern with governmental responsibility toward the elections, citing its commitment "to maintain a pacific, civilized electoral campaign, abiding by the norms established in this regard by the Consejo Supremo Electoral." He continued by linking praise for the administration with party interests: "When the Social Christian party received the government in 1969 it found a situation of budgetary deficit; today there is a surplus. This is the result of the government's political intelligence, especially in the management of our oil resources.... We have followed a firmly nationalistic line in defense of our principal export product, and that is what has permitted the notable improvement of the country's fiscal and budgetary situation."[6]   Similarly, the president a month earlier had held a special meeting with COPEI's national directorate, expanded by the presence of several cabinet members, to evaluate Caldera's 1968 Program of Government. The president himself spoke for over two hours, and following the meeting Abdón Vivas Terán provided an array of figures and data for the press, concluding with praise for the "highly positive" accomplishments of the administration.[7]

Given the party's clear intention of continuing Caldera policy lines under Lorenzo Fernández, such declarations were to be expected. It remained for the candidate himself to express his personal commitment. Before the Asociación Pro-Venezuela Forum, for instance, **he stated**"categorically" his complete solidarity with the present government, promising to continue its programs of development, economic independence, and progress with the framework of democratic liberties.[8]   Lorenzo was equally firm at the presentation of his Program of Government in November. Reading a condensation at the Hotel Tamanaco, he declared, "I am solidly with the present government. I am conscious and proud of the immense work it has achieved. My government action will be directed to deepen, affirm, and project this work within the ideological and philosophical bases, and the objectives of transformation contained in the Program of Government presented in 1968."[9]   Indirect persuasion was also suggested through the administration's own publicity (also see chs. 7 and 8.) **The** constant appearance of newspaper advertisements hailing the achievements of one or another government entity presumably enhanced public evaluation of the existing record. From a copeyano perspective, this contributed to the consensual strategies on which great confidence rested.

COPEI's tactic of inducement therefore emphasized material considerations tied to the widely advertised accomplishments of the government. Symbolic factors were linked to President Caldera and to nationalistic pride. The former, whose public image was stylistically elegant, represented Venezuela in almost regal fashion at affairs of state. His travels abroad were fully publicized in Venezuela, with his international stature a symbolic inducement. More directly linked to Lorenzo Fernández was Caldera's policy of pacification and reconciliation, which Fernández had administered while minister of interior relations. The candidate was portrayed as the great unifier and pacifier. Future vistas of still greater social harmony and familial concord were projected for a Fernández presidency, with progressive, peaceful nationalism the byword.

Confident of its party constituency, COPEI concentrated on those independents, women, and youth from whom it hoped a congressional majority would emerge. Incentives were tailored for each group. With women, there were assurances of their participatory importance. Meeting a Caracas assembly of Mujeres por la Paz in September, Lorenzo Fernández promised to honor feminine aspirations, pledging defense of their rights while praising their contributions to Venezuela. The following month he told a rally of women in Maracay that he would break social structures that had retarded national progress, specifically those affecting "mothers, wives, daughters, and in general all the women of the country...even the humblest." His government would be free from any form of discrimination, with full equality for all. "There cannot be distinctions drawn within the Venezuelan family, because the family is the true essence and the true justification of our society...hands that rock the cradle of a child are the same that are writing the new history of Venezuela."[10] In the final months of the campaign the candidate also urged larger families upon Venezuelan mothers. Staking out a position directly opposed to that of Pérez on population problems, he stirred up criticism and dismay even within COPEI itself. The climax of his campaign for women's votes came at a large Caracas rally of lorencistas in November, where a torrential downpour scarcely dampened spirits, but created a colossal traffic jam. Doña Olga de Fernández, as ever a major asset to her husband, was featured at most such meetings.[11]

The earliest findings of COPEI's pollsters had suggested widespread public desire for personal security and domestic peace. The party had consequently inferred the wisdom of projecting Fernández as conciliator and unifier—a fatherly, nonpartisan figure with a vocation of service to his people. In Fernández's words, his candidacy was "national, and belongs to the majority of Venezuelans, not merely to the parties officially supporting me.... My government will give top priority to the 'have-nots' of society, with greatest concern directed toward the most humble...."

Moreover, employing a phrase common to his campaign, the Social

Christian cited his past record as councilman, minister, deputy, and senator. "I am well-known for what I have done and achieved for the Venezuelan pueblo in the past, over many years of work·and dedication. I do not talk or offer as much as some, but my record shows that I deliver. I am willing, even anxious to be judged by history on the basis not of what I said or offered, but rather by what I have done."[12] Similar statements were frequently presented to independents. Tactics consisted of mobilizing impressive numbers through the party machinery, inviting participation in the discussion of national problems.[13] The effort culminated in November with a jornada of independents in Caracas. A series of policy proposals were presented to Fernández, inviting the voice of the independent into the policy process. Such activities were massively publicized, with advertisements citing names of dozens of lorencista independent committees as evidence of the candidate's appeal to nonaligned sectors.[14]

Allusion has already been made to the conflictual strategy of discrediting, which was tied to COPEI's original promotion of the polarization argument. Private polls as early as the beginning of 1972 reported that COPEI would be the beneficiary of electoral polarization. Thus the Social Christians promoted the notion for many months, concentrating their fire on the AD as the only serious opponent.[15] Not until mid-1973 did this tactic begin to be questioned, and eventually reversed. In the final months of the campaign COPEI argued instead against polarization. In August 1973, for example, Electoral Sub-Secretary General Salvatierra denied the existence of polarization; he expressed confidence in Fernández's victory margin while seeing several candidates realistically competing for second place.[16] Copeyanos also waxed enthusiastic over reported rises of popular enthusiasm for Paz and Villalba to support the contention that polarization was a desperate adeco myth. The columnist "Sanín," for one, devoted a host of columns to praise of the Paz and Villalba campaigns, concluding with pontifical speculation about the identity of the candidate who would run second to Lorenzo.[17] COPEI knew full well, however, that defeat could only come at the hands of the AD, and its strategy of conflict centered there.

The method was a classic of electoral politics. The presidential candidate firmly maintained the high road, while verbal assaults were lodged by others. Fernández told countless audiences, as with a group of Yaracuy farmers in early August, that "Nobody has heard me utter a single insult, aggression, or lie; and this is precisely because what I earnestly want and seek is to unite my people."[18] The same could not be said of paid party advertisements, nor of many ranking Social Christians. The thrice-weekly full-page "Copei Dice,"[19] prepared by the National Secretariat of Information and Propaganda, provided sharp and sometimes abusive handling of Pérez and other ranking adecos. The most partisan declarations were those of Pedro Pablo Aguilar and Oswaldo Alvarez Paz. Consistently hostile, Aguilar was to be especially cutting during the tumultuous battles over poll results and alleged milk hoarding (see ch. 8). A characteristic utterance was his accusation that the AD was mounting a propaganda circus while "promoting the interference of foreigners in elections,...an absurd and gross maneuver." COPEI, in contrast, possessed sufficient maturity not to rely upon falsification.[20]

Campaign Coordinator Alvarez Paz was vociferously articulate. An October editorial, for example, expressed his hope that the AD would continue to nominate candidates with such limited qualities as Pérez; the intense aggressiveness of the adeco campaign had discredited the party; the more Pérez appeared on television, the greater the Fernández advantage; no strategy could save from defeat such a candidacy as that of Pérez; and the adeco aspirant had no known credentials to support his bid for the presidency.[21] Alvarez Paz also joined the thick of the controversy in November over polling and the milk scandal, accusing the AD of attempting to colonize Venezuela on behalf of foreigners.[22] COPEI's junior partner, the FDP, also added fuel to controversy, most often through its Secretary General Jorge Dáger. One editorial column, for instance, after advancing the startling claim that in any part of Venezuela one could find ten Pérez billboards to every one for Fernández, charged that the AD's previous decade in power had featured bribery, official ventajismo, and the squandering of vast sums of public moneys.[23]

Perhaps inevitably, the lowest blows were largely anonymous and without attribution. By their very nature, these permitted only denial by ranking party officials while damaging rumors continued to circulate. The gravest charges from the COPEI camp were directed at Carlos Andrés Pérez--one questioned his nationality, the other his sense of humanity. On the first count, allegations suggested that the adeco candidate was actually Colombian-born. The potential effect was double, raising the question of his eligibility for the presidency as well as planting the suspicion that he was a foreigner.[24] Although official records decisively disproved the accusation, it resurfaced periodically. Political graffiti and sidewalk comments did not discard the question of nationality. If nothing else, however, the charge was at least susceptible to factual refutation. This was not true of vague characterizations based upon Pérez's activities while minister of interior relations a decade earlier. Thousands of unidentified posters, distributed nationally, depicted him as an assassin of innocent Venezuelans.[25] Portrayed as attempting to flee a sordid past, he was presented as epitomizing the worst features associated with a "cop" image.

Critics of Carlos Andrés could and did point to his earlier career as an unbending prosecutor of leftist activists, citing chapter and verse to document their view. His ready response was to recall the wave of revolutionary violence and terrorism that Venezuela experienced during that era. Moreover, the image of a tough, no-nonsense individual was extensively employed by adeco communications experts (see ch. 7). However, the more insidious claims could scarcely be confronted by rational debate. In addition to such broad generalities about the deterioration of the AD and the mediocrity of its leadership,[26] more specific charges were also lodged. Perhaps the most frequent was that it was hoarding foodstuffs basic to the daily Venezuelan diet. The development of this theme was largely a response to AD criticisms of government economic policies. COPEI argued that the AD was buying up huge quantities of foodstuffs, hereby creating false shortages for the average Venezuelan, all in purely partisan electoral interests. Two courses of action were attributed to the adecos, both based on the premise that massive purchases had been made. The most frequent version charged the AD with unadulterated hoarding; by purchasing commodities and creating market shortages, a false campaign issue was being created. A less implausible variant on the theme contended that the AD was either giving away or reselling products at less than market price. No evidence of such activities was provided, even during the Maracaibo milk controversy in November. However, thousands of posters circulated periodically with prominence given to the word aCAParADores ("hoarders"), with the initials of the party and its candidate in capital letters. Thus, the conflictual dimension continued in conjunction with the Social Christians' consensual strategies throughout the campaign. In the meantime, consonant with government policy, COPEI leaders sought to move the party image toward the political left, hoping to create a favorable contrast with the AD.

As one of Venezuela's two major pro-system parties, COPEI was essentially centrist, and Rafael Caldera also occupied the center of his party. With the launching of the Fernández campaign, strategists chose to seek a public image more readily distinguishable from that of the AD. Perceiving the impossibility of competing with the AD and Carlos Andrés for right-of-center votes, the choice was therefore made toward the left. Strategists believed that, with more than a half-million young Venezuelans casting their first ballots, a leftward shift would greatly increase copeyano support. The carving out of a responsible, mildly leftist posture would presumably attract some votes that might otherwise go to Rangel or Paz. The development of this broad electoral strategy was attractive to the young party técnicos shaping Lorenzo's campaign, and he himself found it acceptable. Most important, it was consonant with the views of President Caldera himself, who saw his government as having made significant openings to the left while pursuing a responsible nationalism.

This decision was not without risks. While attracting enthusiastic approval from the party youth, it ran counter to COPEI's traditional right wing. The Social Christians also invited the possible loss of nonparty constituencies that, especially within the business community, had long been important to the party. Moreover, there were other alternatives for a voter of leftist proclivities. The Social Christians were gambling that the advantages would outweigh the drawbacks, including the doctrinal image of their candidate, for as our data show (see ch. 10), Lorenzo Fernández was perceived as center-right by the public. Consequently, COPEI was inviting possible dissonance on several fronts.

This is not to suggest that such a copeyano decision was mere electoral opportunism. The ideological evolution of the party had been to the left, and Caldera himself had genuinely reshaped and refined his thinking. Certainly the president had attempted with conviction to pursue firmly nationalistic policies. Such actions as the nationalization of natural gas, the oil reversion bill, and similar pieces of moderate legislation were presented as wholly copeyano accomplishments, demonstrating a form of constructive nationalism previously unknown in Venezuela. In addition, there were increasingly xenophobic statements in 1973, especially regarding petroleum. There were repeated rumors that the government was about to nationalize the industry; equivocal statements from the president and the minister of mines carefully left the issue an open one. Eventually the latter spoke out clearly in advocacy of an earlier reversion than the existing date of 1983, and the possibility of outright nationalization could not be totally discarded. Lorenzo Fernández handled the issue in similar fashion. The official pledge contained in his Program of Government, announced during the final six weeks of the campaign, promised to advance the reversion date without offering further illumination of his views.[27]

The quest for leftist approval was also reflected in foreign policy. Rafael Caldera had long advocated the application of Christian Democratic notions of social justice to foreign affairs. He had developed the concept in several works[28] and upon assuming office undertook the implantation of "ideological pluralism" in international relations. In practical terms this meant a reversal of the so-called Betancourt Doctrine[29] and the opening of diplomatic relations with regimes of all ideological stripes. Caldera applied the concept vigorously and by 1973 was moving in the direction of renewing relations with the government of Cuba. The prospects of prompt recognition were strong. While a logical extension of Caldera's "ideological pluralism" and a natural act to crown his foreign policy, the electoral value was not overlooked. Steady movement toward the reestablishment of relations was abruptly halted by the September 1973 events in Chile. These will receive fuller treatment in chapter 8; for the present it need only be noted that both the recognition of Cuba and the copeyano strategy of seeking support from the left were called into question.

In assessing electoral forces on a regional and state basis, Lorenzo Fernández's strategists saw little need to tailor their broad approach to local pressures. Indeed, a feature of Fernández's campaign appearances was his relative absence of precise formulations regarding the problems closest to his particular audience. The projection of past electoral patterns, however, led to the creation of certain priorities, among which Zulia ranked high. With the country's second greatest population, it was seen as crucial to the campaign. Elsewhere the Social Christians believed that prevailing patterns of opinion and support were fairly solid. The oriente was regarded as lost to the AD, with little hope for a strong copeyano showing. The llanos were also viewed with some pessimism, except for the presumed bulwark of

Barinas. COPEI believed itself to be strong in such urban centers as Valencia and Barquisimeto, and metropolitan Caracas was regarded as slightly favorable to the AD. In the Andes Pérez was obviously strong, yet this traditional heartland of the Social Christians must surely be treated favorably. In short, it was believed that broad regional patterns were reasonably firm and subject to changes in degree rather than kind. Zulia and its estimated 500,000 voters, then, was seen as the key—if not to the anticipated triumph of Fernández, at least to the margin of victory.[30]

In 1968 COPEI had capitalized on the division of the AD to win Zulia, polling 24.1 percent of the small tarjetas. The MEP, several of whose leaders were based in the state, ran second with 20.3 percent, leaving the AD third with 19.4 percent. Although competition between the MEP and AD had continued through the intervening years, the relative success of the two rivals was difficult to calculate, especially in the light of the presidential candidacy of the zuliano Jesús Angel Paz Galarraga. For COPEI, the overriding goal was that of amassing the largest possible advantage over the AD. More than a year prior to elections, party stalwart Hilarión Cardozo had been appointed governor, with his clear task that of enhancing copeyano prospects. Relying heavily on a large-scale program of construction and public works, Cardozo was a vigorous and visible governor, one whose work was assidously identified with COPEI. Effectively backed by Public Works Minister José Curiel Rodríguez and Minister of Interior Relations Nectario Andrade Labarca, themselves both zulianos, Cardozo sought to forge a permanent copeyano bulwark out of what had traditionally been a source of adeco power. Projected goals varied, but there were Social Christians who foresaw victory by as much as 200,000 votes, especially if Paz could hold much of the 1968 mepista vote.

To summarize, COPEI was confident of Lorenzo Fernández's victory and thus concentrated upon "winning big" as a means of gaining congressional strength. A blend of strategies was adopted, with consensual efforts stressing the recruitment of nonaligned voters. Conflictual assaults upon the AD and its candidate provided a steady negative accompaniment throughout the campaign. Tactics also reflected the combination of strategies, with enthusiastic if perfervid inducements of copeyano prosperity and happiness counterposed by gloomy forecasts of adeco incompetence and irresponsibility. Overriding all else was reliance upon the presumed popular strength of the government and a fierce conviction among campaign leaders that the eminence of Rafael Caldera made the election of his chosen successor a foregone conclusion. This unshakeable faith in the plebiscitary dimension of national elections assured the centrality of the government to the campaign.

ACCIÓN DEMOCRÁTICA

Facing an imposingly organized foe that counted on the active backing and aid of the government, the AD in 1973 confronted the newest of the historical landmarks that had dotted its volatile

history. The campaign presented a challenge, conceivably of mortal
dimensions. Moreover, its ranking leaders genuinely believed,
whether mistakenly or not, that the copeyano administration had
failed Venezuela and that another five years would entail grave
consequences for the republic. The choice of campaign strategies
was therefore of both immediate and long-range importance. As with
the Social Christians, the AD adopted a mixture of objectives and
methods to be implemented. Similarly, the party concentrated its
concern and attention on but one rival, convinced from the outset
that COPEI was the only serious opponent. The AD was strongly
suspicious of copeyano tactics and fearful of government
manipulation of people and policies on behalf of Lorenzo Fernández.
It was a virtual act of faith with AD campaign leaders that COPEI
would spare no expense or effort to retain power and that political
trickery would be the rule rather than the exception. Adecos were
highly sensitive to the slightest hint of wrongdoing by their
opponents and unfailingly swift to react. In setting forth the
broad priorities and emphases of the campaign, party planners worked
within a highly charged atmosphere, redolent with mistrust of COPEI.
Its attitude toward the rival candidate was less of suspicion than
of lack of respect, for the AD regarded Fernández as a weak
candidate and was unanimous in its view that Herrera Campins would
have been infinitely more difficult to defeat.[31] Several other
COPEI leaders were regarded as unscrupulous political hatchetmen,
however. Opinions of President Caldera varied in some regards, but
were in agreement as to his political astuteness and determination
on behalf of the party he had founded.

    Adeco strategies included both the consensual and conflictual,
as well as several subtypes. Reinforcement was perhaps the most
direct and straightforward, requiring few subtleties. Confident
of their solidarity, the AD maintained the involvement of the party
faithful through direct participation in the lengthy campaign.
Carlos Andrés Pérez, eminently adeco and for some four years the
party secretary general during a period of unremitting
reorganization, saw little need for concern. Reinforcement took
place throughout the campaign, but was less significant than other
electoral activities. Recruitment played a central role, regarding
both noncommitted forces and former adecos. The AD undertook many
efforts similar to those of COPEI. In addition, however, major
attention was devoted to the wooing of former party members who
had been inactive in recent years. Believing that the AD remained
the nation's majority party--in its historic slogan, the true
partido del pueblo--a fundamental strategy was to reattract such
leaders. With his famous expression that "adeco es adeco hasta que
muere," the task was undertaken by the indomitable Rómulo
Betancourt.[32] The ex-president was to prove impressively
successful.[33]

    Those who rejoined the AD on behalf of its candidate--in many
cases swayed by affection for Betancourt and responding to his call
to join together in the struggle against COPEI--constituted an
important congeries of former party notables. The list included
Luis Augusto Dubuc, former interior minister and president of

Congress; José Angel Ciliberto, once prominent in the second generation of party leadership; José González Navarro, labor leader and for years the adeco president of the Confederación de Trabajadores Venezolanos; José Manzo González and Miguel García Mackle, who had left to form the PRN in 1962; Ramón Quijada, former president of the Federación Campesina de Venezuela; former miristas Gumersindo Rodríguez, Rafael José Muñoz, and Alí Bustamante had already rejoined the party. There were indications that Raúl Ramos Giménez, who had led the arsistas out of the AD in 1962, was considering a return had it not been for his fatal illness.[34] For those who formally headed small political organizations, adhesion to the Pérez candidacy and inclusion on adeco legislative lists suggested the possibility of formal reentry to the AD following elections.[35] The success in this rerecruitment of highly skilled political veterans, many with sizable personal constituencies, provided important impetus in the drive to attract former party sympathizers.

A less striking but important form of recruitment concentrated on political independents and unaligned voters, with organizational guidance from Reindaldo Leando Mora and his coworkers. Like COPEI, there were "independents" who, although not formally party members, were well known to be strong sympathizers and supporters. Typical of such individuals were former Foreign Minister Marcos Falcón Briceño and newspaper columnist and essayist Guillermo Feo Calcaño. In a somewhat different category was Ramón J. Velásquez, a distinguished son of Táchira who had served for a time in the Caldera cabinet.[36] His decision to join the adeco campaign was an unhappy blow to COPEI, which had hoped for his support. Where Lorenzo's appeals for independent votes were paternalistically reassuring, those of Carlos Andrés were sharply admonitory. Characteristic was the Pérez speech to nearly three thousand representatives of independent committees convened in the Caracas Hilton:

> I am going to offer a most important reflection: Venezuela lives in a moral crisis. There is discomfort and skepticism in vast sectors which feel that the activities of politicians lack moral bases and concepts....I consider this circumstance extremely grave for democratic life. Democracy is a system of life, not merely a system of government....Democracy based on a subtle concept: national consensus. When a country believes that it is a system of life and of government, democracy cannot be defeated, but when on the contrary this concept is vanishing...democracy is converted into the weakest of systems....Latin America today offers us the most dramatic example of this reality.[37]

The AD was pursuing several forms of consensual strategy while it was employing the conflictual. Of greatest importance was that of discrediting, which the party directed at both the government and at COPEI. It was exceedingly tricky, requiring both unerring political instinct and an unflappable manner. Given the intimate intertwining of the government and COPEI on behalf of Fernández, the AD's attempt to separate the two proved both impossible and unnecessary. Criticisms of the copeyano candidate became in effect attacks on the government; responses to party spokesmen inevitably included the administration as well. The role and position of Rafael Caldera was, for the adecos, the most sensitive and trying ingredient. Criticisms and exchanges with COPEI inevitably involved government members, and the Social Christians were swift to reinterpret adeco statements as direct attacks upon the president. The AD, although indeed critical of the administration, dared not go too far in that direction. Beyond a certain point it would have been possible for the president adroitly to characterize campaign criticisms as disloyal irresponsibility toward the office of the presidency. For the AD, engaged in a serious combat in which little quarter was asked or given, there was an ever-present danger of overstepping the bounds of propriety in statements involving the president.

The AD preferred to leave its sharpest attacks for leaders other than its candidate. Pérez, however, while scrupulously avoiding disrespectful references to either Caldera or to other presidential candidates, was prepared to respond to charges initiated by the opposition. Owing in part to his greater accessibility to the press than Fernández, the AD candidate was less removed from partisan exchange.[38] His strongest direct involvement in controversy came in early September, at a time when the adecos were especially aggrieved by what it viewed as increasingly blatant government intervention. Concern had escalated with a dispute provoked by Miguel Angel Burelli Rivas. Appearing on a morning television program, he strongly implied that he had been approached by COPEI; if he would concentrate his public attacks on the AD, alleged Burelli, he would in turn receive financial assistance from COPEI. The resulting uproar was tremendous, with selective transcripts showing different wording by Burelli. President Caldera chose one version for discussion, opposition parties another. In subsequent interviews Burelli was imprecise about the details, although his general reputation for integrity led some to suspect the worst. It was within this contex that Pérez wrote Caldera on 6 September.

Referring specifically to the Burelli accusation, the candidate rejected a public denial by COPEI and decried its countercharges of "infamy and calumny" against Burelli. Citing the allegation as but the latest evidence of government ventajismo, Pérez voiced fears that "the democratic institutional future of the Republic is being compromised." Recalling an audience with the president held the previous May, at which Barrios and Lepage had joined the candidate, Pérez urged Caldera to produce full elucidation of the Burelli charges.[39] Two days later, citing what he regarded as unsatisfactory comments by the president at his weekly press conference, the AD nominee again insisted upon clarification. In addition, he repeated charges of government interference in the campaign process. Referring among other items to an election poster showing pictures of Caldera and Fernández

side by side,[40] he alleged that government offices were working in
complicity with COPEI. "I issue a call to national public opinion
to be fully aware of the grave political situation that this
illegal and antidemocratic government intromission into elections
is creating; and at the same time I issue the warning that moral
damages of imponderable magnitude are being created, which will
require great effort in order to reestablish decency in the
public administration."[41]

Generally, the two most frequent adeco spokesmen of its
conflictual strategy were Gonzalo Barrios and Octavio Lepage,
respectively the party president and secretary general. The two
men provided a temperamental serenity that helped to moderate even
the more bitter partisan exchanges. Barrios's major sounding
board was his weekly editorial column in El Nacional.[42] Writing
with the semantic subtlety and intellectual sophistication that
had long been his hallmark, Barrios spoke out frequently in
criticism of exorbitant campaign expenditures, arguing that
copeyano overspending might well boomerang against its candidate.
For Barrios, Fernández's campaign messages were characterized more
by quantity of resources than by qualitative creativity. Noting
Fernández's reported comment that he asked his friends not where
they came from but, rather, where they were going, Barrios
suggested that such a maxim, employed by the French in recruiting
its Foreign Legion, was especially disquieting in the case of
COPEI campaign funds.[43] The former adeco presidential candidate
was no less piercing in discussing the role of the government.

During a mid-August interview, he expressed representative
AD views on administration interference. "One has the impression
that the prime duty today concerning those in official positions
is the supplying of financial and human resources for the campaign
of Dr. Lorenzo Fernández. Personally I believe that this will not
prevent his defeat, but experience demonstrates that it will be
necessary to design very rigid legislation to prevent such
occurrences in the future."[44] Similar views emerged regularly,
including a later response to copeyano proposals for a pact
pledging recognition of election results. Following a disquisition
on legitimacy and crime which included references to Napoleon, the
Hapsburgs, Romanoffs, and Juan Vicente Gómez, Barrios argued that
sociological as well as juridical realities should be considered.
Drawing a distinction between electoral abuses and fraud, he
maintained that COPEI had been abundantly guilty of the former,
but that he believed the latter would not occur. "This is an
optimistic chronicle. It does not impute to COPEI the intention
of committing fraud. It simply suggests the freedom of
opportunity to do so. For the rest, the AD—which in fact would
not do so—shares with its contender an interest in the legitimacy
of December results."[45]

It was Secretary General Octavio Lepage, however, who
shouldered the heaviest burden as AD spokesman. While agreeing
that the Venezuelan chief of state deserved respectful treatment,
he contended that there was a norm of behavior for the president
that was being violated. The president was not maintaining a

neutral position as arbiter and moderator of party disputes; the
issue of presidential impartiality had reached a state of crisis.
"We note with distress that President Caldera disdains the warnings
of the oppositions...and, moreover, accentuates the polemical tone
of his public expositions," promoting his party's candidate
without dissimulation. In a further barb, Lepage contended that
Caldera was on the move more than COPEI's candidate himself, "to
the point that we would not be surprised to see him [Caldera] in
the barrios, if Wolfgang Larrazábal does not do enough there to
compensate for this weakness of Lorenzo Fernández."[46] Such attacks
were among the few to draw explicit if measured comment from the
president. Refusing to be "intimidated" by such partisan attacks,
Caldera staunchly insisted upon his right to continue with tours
of the interior and discussions with the citizenry, as he had
been doing throughout his administration.[47] Thus his government
would continue exercising its duty of explaining and presenting
its programs and works to the people of Venezuela.

Lepage soon issued a riposte rejecting the president's
stance. Drawing a contrast between Caldera in 1973 and Leoni
during 1968, the AD leader claimed that the latter had traveled
relatively little during those months and even named new,
independent governors in states where the campaign was particularly
virulent. Quoting a Caldera article published in June of 1968 in
El Universal that considered the damage to any chief of state who
departed from a neutral role, Lepage fully concurred. Further
citing a June 1968 speech by Caldera in Barinas, the adeco
wholeheartedly supported its contention that the government should
remain apart from a partisan campaign. "Up to the present the
opposition parties--and especially Acción Democrática--have shown
extreme tolerance toward the progressive abandonment of his
neutrality on the part of President Caldera. At no time has any
protest reached the aggressive tone that he used against
ex-President Leoni, in spite of its being unjustified. This
attitude of ours responds to a matter of principle. We believe
firmly that verbal excesses, especially against the Chief of State,
damage democratic institutions."[48]

Even in his final pre-election column, the secretary general
returned to the strains he had been orchestrating with precision
for months. Echoing widespread expressions of concern about the
employment of advanced techniques of commercial propaganda, he
decried the creation and manipulation of candidate images as
contrary to the essence of democracy. Claiming that the AD
preferred each voter to consider the issues carefully, he argued
that the copeyano approach was fundamentally undemocratic. The
government party, in a two-year campaign, had "based its electoral
strategy on the indiscriminate and abusive use of propaganda, in
which it has invested an impressive quantity of millions of
bolívares...." Copeyano strategists had relied upon obsessive
propaganda intended to brainwash the people into voting blindly,
without considering the programs being presented. It was consistent
with COPEI's campaign strategy, he concluded, that its candidate had
rejected Pérez's standing invitation to a television debate.[49]

Much of the AD's conflictual strategy, then, dealt with its deep-seated concern over what it viewed as improper intervention in the campaign on the part of the government. This stood in contradiction to the copeyano effort at discrediting the AD and especially Carlos Andrés Pérez. In the thrust and parry that raged back and forth, COPEI's defensive denials of ventajismo were coupled with aspersions on the character of the adeco candidate; the AD attempted to defuse copeyano attacks while continually voicing its disapproval of President Caldera's activities. The inevitable result was an intensity and intolerance exceeding that of previous campaigns.

The AD also employed a strategy of realignment. Directed primarily at the MEP and the URD, it was linked to the rerecruitment efforts of Rómulo Betancourt and relied substantially upon his personal prestige. The party founder had remained in the broadest sense the AD's grand strategist, turning with patriarchal determination to the task of bringing all adecos back to feast again at the family table. His success in attracting once-alienated former leaders of the party has already been noted. Betancourt also sought both a renewal of rank-and-file fervor and the backing of nonparty sympathizers. Largely avoiding party rallies and assemblies he began traveling during the critical closing stages of the campaign, usually accompanied by Gonzalo Barrios. Visiting major cities in the interior, Betancourt and Barrios met quietly with independents and sympathizers, urging their support. Old loyalties, affection for Betancourt, disagreement with the leftward shift of the MEP, and a determination to defeat COPEI were all factors in the success the former president achieved.

Scattered public appearances testified to Betancourt's commitment and participation;[50] he consistently left the spotlight to Carlos Andrés Pérez. Perhaps his single most important public declaration came with the celebration of the AD's thirty-second anniversary. Presenting the only speech of the evening, the ex-president delivered a vibrant summary of party history while incorporating ringing statements in defense of Venezuelan democracy. Bringing an audience of 3,000 in the Caracas Hilton to its feet repeatedly, he recalled his words of 1941 when, at the founding of the party, he had proclaimed that "Acción Democrática was born to make history in Venezuela." Listing the many programs and policies the AD had instituted, he further predicted that with Pérez's anticipated victory in December, greater opportunities and challenges yet lay ahead.

> There must be profound social and economic changes. The situation in Venezuela...cannot be a pyramid with a pinnacle of too many rich and a base of impoverished who scarcely reach subsistence levels. Reform can be made without the necessity of methods imported from abroad.... This means that we Venezuelans of all social classes must achieve reforms, feeling that democracy should have profound social content. The 500,000 abandoned children that exist in Venezuela are a disgrace to the State and a disgrace to Venezuelan society....

Fellow citizens. I have nothing to ask nor to aspire
to. Twice I have received the honor and responsibility of
directing the destinies of Venezuela from Miraflores. I
do not have riches nor perquisites to which I aspire. I
am speaking as a Venezuelan who, above all else, loves the
land and the people where he was born and with whom I have
lived, and therefore I conclude in making a burning and
Venezuelan call that the elections of next December 9th,
which in my opinion will carry Carlos Andrés Pérez to the
Presidency of the Republic, be realized within a civilized
and proper climate.[51]

Throughout the campaign, periodic defections from other parties
suggested the possible momentum of adeco realignment strategy.
Without great publicity, local and regional urredistas and mepistas
sporadically declared their support for Pérez--here a labor leader,
there a peasant organizer. Overt admission of this AD undertaking
surfaced only once during the campaign, with a brief but hectic
flurry provoked by Octavio Lepage. Sharing his party's view that
polarization was a reality, the secretary general remarked to
newsmen that the AD was receptive to an electoral accord with the
MEP and URD. The response was deafening. Copeyanos treated the
statement as symbolizing last-ditch desperation by Lepage.[52] A
prompt telephone call from the candidate in Mérida to the secretary
general precipitated rumors that Pérez was angered by Lepage's
comments. Predictable denials of an electoral accord from both
mepista and urredista leaders were cited at length by COPEI, with
Pedro Pablo Aguilar speaking of the AD's virtual admission of defeat.
The initial impact undoubtedly cost the party a publicity round to
its antagonists. In the broader perspective, however, it was
consistent with a strategy that would bear succulent fruit on
election day.

Carlos Andrés Pérez told the press in Mérida that there had
not been conversations with the MEP or URD. However, "there is
no doubt that at the present, polarization, which has not been
decreed nor organized by any party, is bringing a confrontation
of the candidacies of the government and myself; thus the
democratic sense of the country is going to bring to my candidacy
many votes that in other circumstances would go toward other
opposition parties...."[53] Lepage indicated that there were no
insuperable obstacles to the hypothetical possibility of an
accord. But notwithstanding the existing refusal of party commands
to negotiate an agreement, polarization between Pérez and Fernández
was a political reality that would be "increasingly accentuated as
the campaign goes forward, to the point where the clear majority
of the electors, at the moment of voting on December 9th, will
choose between one party or the other, between one candidate or
the other." He provided perhaps the clearest single public
statement of adeco strategy on this point:

> To speak of electoral polarization is not an insult
> to the leader of one or another party, nor for presidential
> candidates. It is the inevitable result which stems from
> the political dynamics of the present.
> It could be thought that, for the sake of political
> urbanity, it is preferable to maintain a discreet silence
> on this reality, but time is moving on, with scarcely four
> months of the campaign remaining. As the moment of
> elections is nearing, it is becoming necessary to clarify
> the electoral panorama, so that Venezuelans can duly
> orient themselves, and so that unfelicitous confusion
> can be cleared up....[54]

Party inducements and disinducements have already been
suggested. Both reinforcement and recruitment efforts employed
such tactics as appeals to former party members, assurances of
renewed adeco glories, and pledges to implement new programs.
Furthermore, the influence of Betancourt in attempting to regroup
the country's formerly majority party was powerfully employed.
Disincentives focused upon COPEI, the Caldera government, and the
national problems that would presumably worsen in the event of
a Fernández victory. As with COPEI, tactics were largely national
in scope and application. The major distinction lay with
respective candidate styles, for Pérez stressed narrow local
issues and problems appropriate to his audience, while Fernández
was less inclined to alter his customary generalizations. The
AD's regional and state planning was broadly consistent with
COPEI's, and the importance of Zulia also loomed large. Where
copeyano strategists sought a massive victory based upon a
triumphant landslide in Zulia, the adecos believed that by holding
the Social Christian margin to a minimum--somewhere under
75,000-80,000--its strength elsewhere would assure the party a
new lease on power.
     Traditional adeco loyalties were expected to carry the
oriente, and the hope for regaining mepista votes promised a
comfortable margin. The llanos were expected to favor the AD,
notwithstanding COPEI's force in Barinas. The Caracas vote was
also expected to favor the party; the AD saw the only question
being that of Rangel's appeal, which it believed competed with
COPEI far more than itself. There was considerable concern about
Lara and Barquisimeto, and Leandro Mora labored long and hard
in trying to fortify local efforts. Pride and anticipation
characterized assessments of the Andes, for the AD foresaw the
possibility of winning the traditional copeyano regional bulwark.
The returning Luis Augusto Dubuc was effective in Trujillo,
while esteem for Ramón J. Velásquez enhanced prospects in Táchira.
Most important of all, obviously, was the fact of Carlos Andrés
Pérez's Andean origins. Overall, the AD felt that even pessimistic
assessments suggested a substantial lead outside of Zulia.

Reduction of COPEI's strength was therefore accorded high priority. Homero Parra was a key figure in the party campaign throughout the state, as well as in Maracaibo itself. Organizational progress in 1973 was marked, and party strategists fel increasingly hopeful about party strength outside Maracaibo. It was scarcely coincidental that Pérez paid particular attention to Zulia in the climactic weeks of the campaign.

A review of adeco strategy reveals a conjucture of varied campaign appeals. Convinced of polarization, the party shaped many of its plans with this in mind. AD campaigning also reflected two additional elements. First was the necessity of reconstituting the once-massive party and of reestablishing its majoritarian, multiclass political character. Second was pronounced sensitivity toward government ventajismo and electoral extravagance. Whatever the empirical realities, AD leaders deeply mistrusted COPEI on electoral tactics and intentions; some were openly fearful of electoral fraud in the event of a close vote tally.[55] It was believed necessary to respond swiftly and sharply to each and every Social Christian attack. Moreover, convinced of partisanship on the part of Rafael Caldera, the AD was determined to hold and maintain the initiative. If administration acts could not be stopped, at least they would be held up for public scrutiny and criticism. Here again the major spokesman was the secretary general. A newspaper column succinctly presented Lepage's views, and those of the AD: "...COPEI and its government have a true electoralist obsession. They are only concerned with those things that, independent of their real importance, can add votes, without taking into account a rigorous order of priorities established to meet the necessities and problems of the country.... In their strategic laboratories the copeyanos are preparing worse things. But their game has already been fully discovered. They have been unmasked. They cannot deceive anyone, and public opinion is going to impose the sanction that they deserve on the 9th of December."[56]

CANDIDACIES OF THE LEFT
For Jesús Angel Paz Galarraga, the fundamental objective was both electoral and institutional. Although a candidate backed by the MEP could scarcely accept the impossibility of victory, Paz Galarraga was nonetheless presenting a substantially different candidacy from that of Prieto in 1968. His coalition, advocating national liberation and patterned after the Allende experience in Chile, faced tasks that had not existed in 1968. Paz was not only presenting himself as the successor to Luis B. Prieto but as leader of a force promising emancipation from the systemic domination of COPEI and the AD. Competition with José Vicente Rangel also complicated the task. While the candidate of the Nueva Fuerza maintained outward optimism throughout the campaign, it is highly improbable that he anticipated victory on 9 December. However, the goal of besting Rangel was important.

Pacista strategy stressed both consensual and conflictual strategies. With the former, the candidate was attempting to draw together supporters of his own MEP with communists and leftist

independents. Furthermore, he was driven to conflictual measures
in his opposition to COPEI-AD domination. Calling for the
implantation of a new and different system, Paz was forced to lean
heavily on conflictual strategies. Ideally, realignment would
draw away supporters of the two large systemic parties; copeyanos
would leave their party in dismay over government shortcomings,
while adecos would realize that total bankruptcy had befallen
that once-great party. The discrediting strategy was to be
employed as well and was intended to convince the electorate that
the capitalist system was inherently incapable of resolving
national problems. The latter goal required an extensive
cataloguing of Venezuelan shortcomings, a strongly negative
element.

Paz constantly emphasized the basic incompatibility of the
Nueva Fuerza with either the Social Christians or the adecos:
"Above all else, the fundamental basis of our electoral policy is
the defeat of the status parties, that is, Acción Democrática and
COPEI...."[57] He methodically hammered out the theme that there
was no significant difference between COPEI and the AD, that they
were, in his well-worn phrase, "two sides of the same coin."
Critiques of existing conditions in Venezuela were invariably
directed at the "status" parties' coordinated efforts in defense
of international capitalism and the domestic oligarchy. Paz's
audiences were frequently told that COPEI and the AD resembled an
amorous couple--after squabbling angrily during a campaign, they
then went to bed for the next several years before returning to
marital arguments once again.[58] In short, the fifteen years prior
to 1973 provided evidence of the incapacity of "capitalismo
adecopeyano." The system that had emerged bore the name democracy,
but it was a formalistic democracy. Paz spoke of the hollowness
of the system, in which the role of oligarchical interests
permitted domination by the two largest parties while true
democracy and individual socioeconomic freedom were wanting. In
the words of a prominent mepista, the Nueva Fuerza was pursuing
a strategy demanding an anti-imperialist struggle, "a struggle
against the powerful interests of the criolla oligarchy which
can only be achieved by the unity of the people."[59] In other
words, an offensive against the system implied equal treatment of
COPEI and the AD.

Belief in the similarity of COPEI and the AD was a basic act
of faith for the Nueva Fuerza. Paz did occasionally narrow his
campaign comments when circumstances dictated, however. The
events in Chile prompted attention to hemispheric Christian
Democracy, thus inviting comments concerning COPEI.[60] An editorial
by the Nueva Fuerza candidate[61] placed major culpability on the
Partido Demócrata Cristiana for events in Santiago, drawing
parallels for Venezuela. Here, while the left was fighting by
pacific, electoral means, a government determined to perpetuate
itself was pursuing all possible officialist ventajismo to suppress
revolutionary forces--money, influence, and bribery. Even
intervention by the chief of state was employed, and the few
responsible voices in COPEI were ones lacking any power of decision.

Latin American Christian Democracy, in brief, was employing its bases in Santiago and Caracas to continue exploitation and injustice.[62] Paz's remarks about the AD were more general, but occasional references were made to his former membership. Prieto had been severely taxed in dealing with the issue in 1968; by 1973 the question was somewhat muted. The Nueva Fuerza candidate often spoke of having struggled unsuccessfully within the AD to achieve a solution to social and economic problems. Among his more impressive campaign appearances was a visit to the University of Zulia in mid-September. The first presidential nominee to visit the students, he followed an uninspired speech with a vigorously persuasive performance in a question-and-answer session. A frank admission of failures while an adeco leader, combined with an impassioned statement of principles and commitment, elicited a strongly positive reception.

In his final pre-election article, Paz depicted the choice as between the parties of status and his "Unidad Popular" alternative. "Our formula will resolve, consequently, the dramatic social problems that could not be solved by the traditional alternatives represented by AD and COPEI in the last fifteen years."[63] A comparable stance toward the "status" parties was adopted by Luis B. Prieto, who worked actively for Paz. Both in the press and on the campaign trail, he was outspoken.[64] COPEI and the AD were employing mass communications as if selling a commercial product and had gone far beyond the saturation point. Lorenzo Fernández spoke of youth and the family, while the people asked about unfulfilled promises by the Social Christian government; Carlos Andrés demanded development and an end to poverty but ignored questions about adeco failures from 1959 to 1969. Only Paz carried a genuine message--unity of the pueblo--and a true promise--national liberation. Despite the opposition of imperialism and oligarchy, the Nueva Fuerza candidate was offering a program of emancipation. "His purpose is to redeem for the nation the right to decide its own destiny, [which is] now in the hands of entrepreneurs who exploit its riches."[65]

Paz therefore placed strong emphasis on conflictual strategy in denouncing the two dominant parties and Venezuela's existing socioeconomic structure. At the same time, the effort to establish his primacy on the political left required a separate strategy. In the early months of campaigning Paz followed a conflictual approach toward Rangel and the MAS; there were periodic exchanges between the Nueva Fuerza and MAS candidates. This reached its most public stage in June 1973, exacerbated by the mirista decision to support the Rangel candidacy. For Paz, the Rangel candidacy was dividing the progressive, revolutionary sector. Moreover, the MAS was interested in winning congressional seats and only then proceeding with plans, while the Nueva Fuerza already constituted an option for power. It was Rangel's reluctance to negotiate, not that of Paz, that had proved the obstacle to unity.[66] Paz's own willingness to step aside in the interests of a unified left had elicited little response.

The Nueva Fuerza candidate expressed doubts about the sincerity of Rangel's alleged interest in a unified left. Paz noted that an invitation from Rangel to discuss possible negotiations had been addressed only to the MEP, excluding the PCV, UPI, and DPV. He proceeded to reiterate the mepista thesis that socialism in Venezuela was not immediately around the corner and that a gradual program of educating the masses was among the necessary intermediate steps. Masista criticism of this position was unrealistic. If the revolutionary process was to reach fulfillment sooner rather than later, the program of nationalization that the Nueva Fuerza was proposing would be necessary; so too would acceptance of the fact that socialism in its most pristine form could not be swiftly established.[67]

Paz's statement drew a swift rebuttal from José Vicente Rangel, who told the same correspondent for El Nacional that it ill behooved Paz Galarraga to comment on his, Rangel's, sincerity. It was Paz and the MEP who sought self-aggrandizement, and the Congress of the Nueva Fuerza existed for the sake of the party, not the Venezuelan left. Moreover, Paz was peeved over the decision of MIR to support Rangel. Rangel insisted upon his willingness to speak with anyone in exploring a unitary electoral formula for the left and maintained that "we insist unyieldingly on a policy of dialogue and an outstretched hand."[68] Paz's strategy concerning the left was soon modified into consensual form. The nominee made but the most fleeting of references to his rival, preferring to stress Nueva Fuerza support. While lamenting the lack of unity, he reassured audiences that following the elections it would be effectively realized. In the meantime, he repeated the declaration of the popular novelist Miguel Otero Silva, an independent supporter of the Nueva Fuerza and senatorial candidate, that four-fifths of the Venezuelan left was gathered together behind Jesús Angel Paz Galarraga.

Tactical implementation of his strategies was predictable and straightforward. Inducements were provided by explanation of the Nueva Fuerza program, ranging from nationalization of petroleum and iron through free milk for infants and young children. Such material promises were supplemented by symbolic appeals to freedom of choice from foreign intervention and to liberation of Venezuelan society. Disinducements concerning Rangel merely suggested that his was not a realistic electoral alternative; of course, COPEI and the AD symbolized all that was fundamentally wrong about Venezuelan life and politics. Attacks on domestic oligarchics and foreign imperialists were sharp but generally reasoned and civil in tone. The entire tenor of Paz's campaign was one of deep concern and commitment, flavored with moderation and rationality. The contrast in personality and style with Prieto was striking. Especially in the concluding weeks, it was the inimitable Prieto who directed the most colorful and uncompromising blows at the opposition.

The travel itinerary of the final days of the campaign, as Nueva Fuerza leaders toured together, was highly suggestive of the

Nueva Fuerza's tactical assessment of regional strengths and weaknesses.[69]   Ever since 1968 elections, Zulia had stood as the bulwark of the MEP; a strong showing there was a key to the Paz candidacy, and he had shaken up the regional leadership drastically, with his nephew Fernando Alvarez Paz playing a central role.[70]   In the oriente, where a number of influential adecos had also joined with Prieto in 1968, it was hoped that strength might be drawn from former urredistas.   Support was regarded as promising in Lara, Portuguesa, and Falcón. Elsewhere the picture was spotty, while Caracas represented the most serious problem. Basically, electoral strength--all of it essentially mepista--was believed to be concentrated first in Zulia and second in the oriente. Although the leadership privately recognized the high improbability of victory, a comfortable margin over Rangel was anticipated. Paz's support, it was believed, included segments of organized labor and the peasantry, as well as representatives of other groups, whereas Rangel's appeal was seen as limited to university youth, predominantly in greater Caracas.[71]

In strategy the MEP was dominant but found itself plagued by the inconstancy of the communists. Clearly most concerned with asserting its supremacy over the MAS, PCV statements tended to concentrate on bitter anti-masista and anti-rangelista polemics.[72] Although willing to benefit from any electoral successes of Paz, the communists were less than generous in their support.[73] Recurrent rumors of a secret understanding with COPEI flourished. Less than two weeks before elections, an interview with Eduardo Machado raised the specter of a secret communist strategy. While repeating the PCV commitment to the Nueva Fuerza, Machado observed that the defeat of Pérez was of great importance. Using agile phraseology, he suggested that "given the grave danger represented by a victory for Carlos Andrés Pérez, one cannot discard the possibility that important popular sectors would assume an attitude [favoring Fernández]." In contradiction to the pacista view that the AD and COPEI were virtually identical, Machado declared that COPEI had raised "a series of very real questions, such as pacification policy, ideological pluralism, nationalism, and other actions that the Communists, although natural adversaries of the present government party, have to recognize."[74]

The night of the interview, a local communist candidate at a Paz meeting in San Félix read a speech dispatched from Caracas headquarters that heavily stressed the importance of defeating Pérez.[75] Despite slightly equivocal clarifications by other communist leaders, there remained uncertainty over a possible PCV strategy of clandestine accord with the Fernández forces. The implications for post-election events were grave. By the conclusion of the campaign, the emergence of José Vicente Rangel as a figure of national prominence, accompanied by the firmly independent stance of the MAS, assured future strife on the Venezuelan left. Rangel and the MAS, unlike the Nueva Fuerza, had based their strategy largely on institutional objectives. There was little expectation of winning power, but rather of spreading party doctrine, winning respectability in public eyes, and creating

an electoral base on which to build. In February 1973, for example,
Rangel said that a win was unlikely and that his purpose was to
promote and strengthen socialism in Venezuela.[76] Rangel later
would hint at the possibility of victory: "The success of
socialist policy...is beyond discussion. Polls and meetings
make it manifestly clear that socialism is now, once and for all,
an authentic option to power."[77] Yet he **never deluded himself** with
an expectation of victory.[78] In a phrase employed widely during
the latter weeks of the campaign, he told his followers that
chances of victory were bright; he then added with special
emphasis that should he not win, he would be prepared the day
following elections to carry on the fight for socialism.

Rangel's strategies, though broadly similar to those of Paz,
nonetheless differed in some respects. Given his heavy reliance
on the MAS to the virtual exclusion of other groups, he was
largely spared Paz's problems of coordinating plans with a
recalcitrant or dissenting ally. Application of conflictual
messages toward the existing system were naturally basic, and
there was little discrimination between COPEI and the AD. Writing
to contradict the notion of polarization, he insisted that "AD and
COPEI represent the same. The reply to the crisis of copeyano
government cannot be the experience that the country lived during
the ten years of adeco government." Later in the same article
Rangel continued: "Do they not represent the same interests of
the great bourgeoisie and of foreign investment?... It is [very]
clear that AD and COPEI constitute the two faces of the same coin:
the coin of hunger, unemployment, repression and the dependency
of the country."[79] Criticism of the two parties' fifteen-year
stewardship was brusque and relentless. When COPEI's Aguilar
called upon all the presidential candidates to denounce the
October death of three National Guardsmen, for instance, Rangel's
ire was unbridled:

> The Secretary General of COPEI has no authority to
> issue summons to presidential candidates of the Venezuelan
> Left concerning the death of three national guardsmen,...
> and these declarations are no more than an impertinence
> on his part.
>
> Not only does Pedro Pablo Aguilar lack moral authority,
> but no Social Christian can properly issue a summons of
> this nature, as I have already shown that the Christian
> Democrats have a double standard of morality....
>
> It is even more grotesque that a party whose
> counterparts in Chile participate in massacres against
> the Chilean pueblo, now demands hypocritically this type
> of definition with regard to Venezuela.[80]

José Vicente was no less cutting in exchanges with the AD,
but perhaps the most wounding words were directed toward the sins
of capitalism, especially those of domestic oligarchs. The MAS
pledge to expropriate the property of leading economic groups in
Venezuela--such as the Vollmers, Mendozas, Boultons, Salvatierras,

et al.--provided grist for the campaign mill. In the words of
masista ideologue Teodoro Petkoff, the expropriation of "powerful
plutocratic groups" would help to break the dependency that
prevented the building of a socialist society. Though apologists
might call them "progressives" or "philanthropists," for Petkoff
their role was quite different.

> They are responsible for a permanent climate of social
> tension and violence. Their opulence insults the poverty
> of the majority. Any plan for changing the fortune of
> the poor classes, unless it expropriates that immense mass
> of wealth, will be vain chatter. Concepts like income
> redistribution, the elevation of the standard of living,
> full employment, and the like, are used today as electoral
> rhetoric, for they are meaningless if the pushbuttons of
> the economy and of power continue to be pushed by the
> Mendozas, the Vollmers, the Zuloagas and the Machados, the
> Boultons and the Tamayos, the Zarikians and the
> Benacerrafs....[81]

The heaviest criticisms came in September, when the MAS denounced
an alleged plot by Fedecámaras to promote an anonymous antisocialist
campaign.[82] The alleged commitment of 2.5 million bolívares
committed to this publicity effort was characterized by the MAS
as proof of Rangel's ascending campaign drive, as well as the
insidious nature of oligarchical techniques.[83]

Conflictual treatment of the Nueva Fuerza declined as the
campaign progressed. The Nueva Fuerza was viewed as representing
neo-reformism of a social democratic type. The background of Paz
and the MEP nourished apprehension about any commitment to genuine
socialism. The Nueva Fuerza seemed a straightforward mechanical
transplant of the Chilean experience, with little refinement for
Venezuelan traits and idiosyncracies. The Nueva Fuerza was also
regarded as an opportunistic and unnatural coalition susceptible to
bureaucratization and immobilism. To Rangel, the coalition showed
little likelihood of introducing the total transformation of
Venezuela's capitalist and dependent society, which he saw as
indispensable.

Focusing disinducement tactics on the reputed evils of the
existing system, José Vicente Rangel gave particular attention to
symbolic incentives on behalf of recruitment strategy. He regarded
it as important to demonstrate his acceptance of existing rules
of the game. This became more salient with the acceptance of
support by the MIR in June 1973. Rangel himself had established
his personal credentials during a fifteen-year career as
parliamentarian, but the MAS was a new organization and, to many
Venezuelans, unknown. The MIR was associated by those who
remembered it with the violence of the early 1960s. Rangel
consequently devoted frequent attention to the issue. In early
1973 he spoke out forcefully in behalf of the place of free speech
under a socialist system, although conceding that such privations
as food shortages might be incurred during the initial stages of

such a regime.[84]   He stressed similar views in a dramatic if
controversial appearance before the Pro-Venezuelan Forum in
October.   "We are not worshipers of violence for violence's sake.
For us the essential thing is social transformation at the lowest
possible human and economic price.   But [it is] a transformation
for the people, who do not want to continue living in a society
of rich, but in a society for all."[85]

Members of the MIR also stressed their disavowal of violence.
Américo Martín, its leading theoretician, commented that the MIR
was fully committed to electoral participation.   "We in MIR see
a bottling up of Venezuelan capitalism.   Dialectical analysis of
the social classes reveals two paths of departure...one
fascist-bourgeois and the other socialist-proletariat....   They
are logical and natural alternatives in the present crisis....   The
MIR is trying, with other revolutionary sectors, to fill a
vacuum...."[86]   Throughout the campaign, Rangel repeated his
assurances.   "I believe in liberty and in the necessary ideological
pluralism of free men.   The Venezuelan road to socialism takes
into account the tradition of a pueblo which, despite being a
poor colony, mirrors American freedom.   We need criticism and
disagreement.   It is worth running the risks of freedom rather
than falling into the rigid bureaucratization that a minority
might impose.   I do not fear criticism....   All sectors supporting
my candidacy agree in this."[87]   There was equal readiness in
responding to a COPEI call for a multiparty agreement to accept the
election results.   MAS Secretary General Márquez promptly declared,
"We have no ambiguity over it, and it is therefore opportune to
note, in response to Aguilar's declarations, and without implying
a polemical rebound, that it is just as important that both
President Caldera and the government party express, without
equivocation, their willingness to respect an electoral victory
of José Vicente Rangel, of socialism."[88]

Five stages of the campaign were projected, commencing with
the initial rally in Caracas's Nuevo Circo on 26 May 1972.   That
opening mass meeting in the capital, planned and coordinated by
José Agustín Silva Michelena, effectively kicked off the first stage.
Pinpointing the "eight poles of the capitalist system"--Caracas,
Maracaibo, Valencia, Barquisimeto, San Cristóbal, Maracay,
Ciudad Guayana, and Puerto La Cruz--it produced large meetings in
each of these so-called nuclei of dependent economic power in
Venezuela.   The second and third steps consisted of the creation
of bases in the eight polar cities, promoted by the candidate's
visits.   The fourth, which concluded in mid-October 1973, took
the form of an intensified version of the preceding.   Still
relying heavily on Rangel's personal effort, it saw the candidate
visiting hospitals, markets, jails, and generally poor barrios.
The concluding phase, broadly resembling the first, presented
another series of large assemblies but expanded beyond the eight
polar centers to include most remaining state capitals as well.[89]
The final act was held in Caracas's El Silencio.[90]

Initially there was a general impression that the candidate's
appeal was limited to university students in metropolitan Caracas.
Increasingly large crowds in different parts of the country

gradually began to bring this assumption into question. Skeptics
were challenged by an early September meeting in the
capital--"Caracas Socialista"--which demonstrated both masista
organizational capabilities and the breadth of RAngel's appeal.
With the crowd predominantly young, and the program featuring
protest songs, the music of Theodorakis, and innumerable
anti-imperialist and anti-yankee effigies, it also drew thousands
who did not fit stereotyped images of the MAS. At the least, it
helped to suggest taht the Rangel campaign offered more than its
belittlers were suggesting. As the campaign progressed, it became
evident that the Rangel personality was an appealing one. There
was belief that particular support might be forthcoming from
Bolívar, where Germán Lairet headed the MAS and Rigoberto Lanz
directed the MIR. Otherwise, prospects seemed founded largely on
the personal style of José Vicente Rangel. It remained true that
the MAS, seeking to seed the turf for future political competition,
relied heavily upon dialogue and exchange. Beyond and above that,
the undeniable charisma of Rangel provided the most striking
appeal for the radical left.

Jóvito Villalba and his URD advisers contended that fully 60
percent of the electorate was free of party affiliation and
independent in spirit. It was hoped that the electorate might be
swayed by the rhetorical brilliance of "Maestro" Villalba. The
basic strategic configuration was conflictual--in enumerating the
failures of COPEI and the AD--and consensual--in characterizing
Villalba as a figure faithful to the Bolivarian image. Charges
against the two strongest parties were similar to those of Paz
and Rangel, but without the socialist rhetoric and programs. "My
candidacy does not form part of the electoral game of the status,
but is an instrument to open the way to the historically planned
revolutionary change desired by all Venezuelans.... The present
status constitutes a permanent conspiracy against the Venezuelan
people and national independence.... We believe and affirm that
the present economic, political and social status, if maintained
unaltered, constitutes a permanent conspiracy against the work of
Simón Bolívar."[91]

By July the URD was claiming publicly that fully seven of
every ten Venezuelans were undecided, and the candidate continually
scoffed at the "myth of polarization." If in 1968 two such eminent
figures as Caldera and Barrios each polled less than 30 percent of
the vote, the 1973 candidates could scarcely be doing as well.
Villalba's candidacy made polarization completely absurd. "The
Venezuelan people are capable of granting victory to a candidate
who tryly represents the guarantee of an independent economic
development and an efficient and rapid solution for the anguished
situation of hunger, unemployment and insecurity that the majority
of the Venezuelan people presently suffers."[92] At his official
inscription as candidate before the CSE, Villalba outlined five
fundamental objectives: the rescue of presently exploited national
resources from the colonial or semicolonial system; termination
of the existing subjection of society to great monopolies and
foreign oligopolies; creation of jobs and education at all levels;
improved income distribution for all citizens; and a guarantee of

government under law and within the constitution.[93]
        Urredista strategy also grasped at the thin hope that
perezjimenista support might eventually be forthcoming. Despite
Pérez Jiménez's annulling of the 1952 electoral victory of Villalba,
the URD indirectly wooed the ex-dictator. Its opposition to the
constitutional amendment that disqualified Pérez Jiménez was a
singular example. The struggle against polarization was constant.
When Lepage's statement concerning possible URD and MEP support
for Pérez appeared in August, Villalba vehemently denounced the
"insidious campaign" of both AD and COPEI, even while conceding
that "half a dozen to a dozen" former URD ministers and governors
had gone to the enemy. With his fire for polemics undiminished,
he told the press that "I am a pacific and mild man, but when they
attack me, I know how to respond, thanks to possessing a magnificent
tongue...I believe it my duty to reestablish the truth clearly,
categorically, and unwaveringly in the face of propaganda unleashed
primarily by the AD but on a lesser scale by that of COPEI, with
the purpose of confusing the Venezuelan people about my
candidacy...."[94] The only direct response was the wry comment of
Gonzalo Barrios a few days later that Jóvito was being "somewhat
theatrical."

THE POLITICAL RIGHT
        The thinking of the remaining candidates was generally
simplistic and, in most cases, could scarcely have been otherwise.
Burelli Rivas adopted a strategy not wholly unlike Villalba's.
Thus his criticism of COPEI and AD was consistent and vehement,
as were his attacks on government ventajismo. At one juncture
he charged President Caldera with having lost his composure
during the 1973 contest.[95] The AD was equally responsible for
the crisis in which Venezuela lived, however, and repudiation of
both parties was inevitable and necessary. Employing what critics
charged as scare tactics, Burelli also spoke ominously about the
existing system. Hinting broadly that elections might even be
disrupted or disputed, he voiced fears over "what could happen
before or immediately after December 9th," when a "popular explosion
could burst forth...."[96] With his conflictual contentions couched
in more dire language than Villalba's, Burelli based his more
consensual declarations upon his independent status. Believing
that all the parties were in the process of repudiation by the
voter, he presented himself as the only true independent alternative.
        While Burelli and Villalba were both hopeful of perezjimenista
support, it was Pedro Tinoco and the host of self-proclaimed
surrogates for the former dictator who relied most heavily upon a
possible endorsement. For such men as Raimundo Verde Rojas and
Alejandro Gómez Silva, personal advancement was uppermost. The
series of transatlantic treks to seek the ear and voice of Pérez
Jiménez--customarily concluded by falsely positive claims of
approval upon returning to Caracas--reflected a tasteless and
ludicrous opportunism. While this characterization was also
applicable to Tinoco, he was the only one enjoying standing
independent of the general. Hopeful of drawing significant support

from rightist elements, Tinoco and his strategists also sought the
approval of entrepreneurial sectors as well as of the middle class.
The Tinoco strategy assumed the existence of substantial
conservative elements in Venezuela. Although the candidate
rejected such terminology, the entire thrust of his campaign was
founded on the premise that a strong, untapped vein of electoral
conservatism was accessible.

    Overall, then, a wide array of strategies and tactics were
adopted (see matrix in figure 9). On the right they were
simplistic, whereas those of the left were circumscribed by an
anti-system orientation. Both COPEI and the AD presented
intricately designed blends. With the confidence of certain victory,

FIGURE 9. Negative Inducement Matrix

Actors	Targets	Messages
COPEI	AD	Mediocre leadership Arbitrary in power Hoarding Soft with foreigners
AD	COPEI	Extravagant in administration Gov't/presidential interference Campaign overspending Corrupt campaign practices
MEP MEP MEP MEP	AD COPEI AD/COPEI MAS	Betrayal of party doctrine Dismal record in power Supporters of oligarchy, dependent on international capitalism Unrealistic option
MAS MAS MAS	AD/COPEI MEP Nueva Fuerza	Representatives of bourgeoisie Reformist, not revolutionary Opportunism, ill-suited to Venezuela

the Social Christians were consensual in presenting a candidate
pledged to extending and magnifying the purported triumphs of the
administration. Neglecting everyone but the AD, they denigrated
its importance and maligned its candidate in bluntly insulting
fashion. This conflictual strategy was designed to underline the
qualitative differences between the candidates while redirecting
the eyes of the voters toward the positive accomplishments of the
Caldera government. The copeyano emphasis on the plebiscitory
character of the contest produced an element new to post-1958

elections. The AD necessarily developed a more vigorous recruitment tactic than COPEI, reaching out for former party members and supporters. The conflictual strategy toward COPEI drew the record of the government heavily into the electoral debate. Although official ventajismo was an old and familiar trait, the nature and extent of partisan debate over the government itself was much more germane than ever before.

As hypothesized in the introduction, COPEI and AD assiduously constructed strategies combining the consensual and conflictual. There was heavy emphasis on the latter, especially as the battle came to focus on the government record. In tactical implementation as well, a variety of subtypes were employed. The 1973 competition, unlike that of 1968, presented a direct confrontation between two candidates who largely ignored all others. The elaboration of strategies and tactics, while articulated within the context of a struggle for immediate political success, emanated from ideological and doctrinal concepts deeply rooted in party history. We must therefore proceed to an examination of these conceptual and philosophical characteristics.

6. IDEOLOGIES AND PROGRAMS

Venezuela is no exception to Germán Arciniegas's observation that the intervention of intellectuals in Latin American political life is less singular than the high degree of such participation.[1] Certainly the history of Bolívar's native land is replete with examples of intellectual leaders' sharing in political responsibility. It was not until the impact of Marxism in Venezuela, however, that political organizations began seriously contemplating philosophical and ideological verities, attempting to unify their policy preferences and their world view. From the Generation of '28 through the most recent presidential campaign, a wide array of Marxist interpretations and adaptations have been expressed. Christian democracy, social democracy, and developmentalism are more recent schools of thought to have emerged on the national scene. For the contemporary parties, theoretical and doctrinal positions have sometimes shifted during recent years, contributing to party divisions and reorganizations. Some parties have been strikingly flexible, adjusting pragmatically to the exigencies of given political situations; their critics have accused them of opportunism and even of retreating from ideology. Others have insisted on rigid and unbending adherence to basic postulates, whatever the transient pressures.

During the fifteen years since restoration of constitutional rule, Venezuelan party doctrines can, for the sake of classification and coherence, be grouped under the rubrics of the "three R's": revolutionary, reformist, and rightist. As COPEI and the AD have increasingly dominated political affairs after 1958, there has seemed a growing convergence between the two, as COPEI from the right and the AD from the left have moved toward one another in the political center. With the internal bureaucratization of both parties and increasing entrenchment in power, the two have come to represent to opponents a new status quo. Well before the 1973 elections, the term "El Status" was being applied in pejorative fashion to both copeyanos and adecos. Perhaps a more apt term would have been "the new establishment," for despite the apparent profundity and force of COPEI and AD penetration into national

political life, their permanence could not be taken for granted.
Neither were public affairs stagnant or immobile, as the term
"status" implied. Systemic contours were basically the same, but
many dynamic shifts were taking place within existing parameters.
By 1973 Venezuela had seen a renewal of political thought and
expression on both the left and right. The electoral spectrum had
never been broader than in the period immediately preceding 1973
elections. Our attention will be directed largely at party
platforms and programmatic proposals, with broader ideological
elements reduced to a minimum.[2]

THE SOCIAL CHRISTIAN PARTY COPEI

COPEI has followed an exceptional ideological trajectory from
its 1936 origins as a Catholic student movement to the
administration of Rafael Caldera. Initially a quasi-falangist,
ultranationalistic group that violently opposed the equally
immoderate leftist leadership of the Federación Estudiantil
Venezolana (FEV),[3] its emergence in 1946 as a political party
tempered only slightly its fundamental conservatism. During the
trienio, parliamentary disputes between COPEI and the AD were
vehement; the annals of the Constituent Assembly were enhanced by
brilliant debates between Caldera and the famed adeco poet Andrés
Eloy Blanco. Through the decade of the 1950s, however, COPEI's
ideological stance gradually shifted away from its original
conservatism. Experiences during the perezjimenista decade
contributed to some extent, and the growing influence of a younger
generation of copeyanos also provided a more progressive ingredient.
Furthermore, new orientations within the Roman Catholic Church were
also being felt. Until the post-World War II era, reformist
elements of Catholicism were largely muted. Pope Leo XIII's
encyclical Rerum Novarum, an historic statement of the Church's
social concerns, was still discussed with prudence and discretion.
Following the war, however, the fortunes of social catholicism
began to flourish.

    In Europe, thriving Christian Democratic parties emerged,
precisely in the countries most affected previously by fascism.
Chile's Partido Demócrata Cristiano began to reach beyond its
falangist origins, and the "Social Christian" COPEI reflected
broader trends in Venezuela.[4] Subsequent papal declarations of
John XXIII and Paul VI provided further impetus to currents that
were scarcely unnoticed by the Venezuelans.[5] After 1958, COPEI
came to occupy a stance quite dissimilar to that of earlier years.
To be sure, in both 1958 and 1963 candidate Caldera was widely
regarded as a pro-business leader, and his public image stood to
the right of the AD. The victorious campaign of 1968, however,
offered the country an exceedingly detailed program[6] confirming the
social consciousness being articulated by Caldera and most other
party leaders.[7] Moreover, COPEI was by no means monolithic in its
ideological view of the world. Although there had been a few
defections from the party by conservatives unwilling to accept
redefined positions,[8] there remained a vocal and articulate right
wing, best personified by Edecio La Riva Araujo.[9] Moreover, the

JRC had been the seat of strongly leftist views for years. The intellectual appeal of communitarian thought also attracted serious attention, although never widely reflected by the party.[10] The intellectual history and dissection of these ideological themes is beyond our present purpose.[11] In examining the copeyano program for the campaign, however, we must keep in mind the heterogeneity of Social Christian thought. The angrily disputed convention victory of Lorenzo Fernández, signifying as it did the victory of oficialista forces within COPEI, assured the programmatic continuity desired by President Caldera. For some, the continuism implied by the Fernández nomination signified a defeat for the party's left. Not merely the radical proposals of the JRC were to be ignored, but the moderate leftism of Herrera Campins and his followers as well. On the other hand, oficialistas began stressing what it insinuated as a leftist course by the Caldera administration. Citing measures adopted on petroleum and natural gas, praising "ideological pluralism" in foreign policy, and dropping repeated hints about the possible recognition of the Castro government, they argued that Lorenzo Fernández represented indeed a progressive orientation with mild leftist overtones. It remained for campaign statements and the party program to clarify such issues.

Four major sources provide a picture of the Fernández program on behalf of the Social Christians in 1973: his address before Fedecámaras in May; a similar appearance in October before the Asociación Pro-Venezuela; the candidate's official Program of Government announced on 9 November; and his responses to a lengthy interview by El Nacional also appearing that month.[12] In his appearance before Fedecámaras, as on the later occasions, Lorenzo Fernández stressed the virtue of the individual and the importance of a government commitment to human resources. Near the outset he asked rhetorically, what should be the fundamental objective of government? The answer he gave was, "for me, of transcendental importance: man. An inversion of values cannot be accepted. The State, the economy, science, technology, have to be at the service of man." Priorities should remain clear, that man not be enslaved by the science and technology of the state: "development has content. It should have content. It is not as simplistic as some think, having only economic growth. In the first place, development has a doctrinal content. Development has to consider all man's aspects. The economic, of course, but also the philosophical, the scientific, the cultural, the artistic, the sporting.... That is, man must be understood within his whole being. Development cannot be the patrimony or beneficial factor for exclusive social sectors. This would be the negation of development. I repeat, development, conceived within a doctrinal criteria, has to be for all men."[13]

The humanistic concern received continuous attention. In his official government program, the introductory passage, "Objectives of Action," pledged that the "human being will continue being the center of action for my government. In this sense his mental and physical development, by means of nutrition, health, sports and education, will receive priority attention. This is an indispensable requisite to having certain and well paid work, which in its turn is a necessary condition for owning an adequate home in which an authentic family life can be realized."[14]   Similarly, the platform reiterated the commitment to the individual by means of promoting a multifaceted development.

> The fundamental objective of government action is man. The advancement of man is achieved by means of development, and development is achieved with work. I pledge my effort to end unemployment, so that all will have certain and well paid work. As President of the Republic I am going to orient, stimulate and promote a profound, ample and just development, and an audacious and nationalist economic development, guaranteeing liberty, order and peace. The goal of social development is the integration of the community and the participation of all its members in the benefits of development. The first objective of social development is integration of the marginal people, those who have the least, the poor. Therefore within my government there will be special treatment and priority attention for those who today have the fewest opportunities. I want the marginal people to be converted into active factors in a process of development, and not as passive elements in a paternalistic government action.[15]

Fernández also stressed the individual in his public appearances, invariably citing "development" as the magical formula, which would then be broken down into social and economic elements. He told his audience at Pro-Venezuela, as he had previously to Fedecámaras, that economic development was inadequate without social content. To ignore this fact would be a grave mistake, and he explicitly intended to bring about an economic growth that would take into account the necessity for social progress. "I am going to help as I did when I was Minister of Development, but with the condition that people benefitted by this economic development are aware that they are the bases of sustenance for social progress: work, integration of the marginal people, the guarantee that a Venezuelan father can live knowing that he has a job, that he has better income, that he has the right to health for himself, for his sons, for the Venezuelan mother who is giving so many children to the motherland, to that mother that her maternity be guaranteed dispensaries for her children, schools, education...."[16]

Lorenzo Fernández included under social development such topics as education, health, housing, employment, youth, sports, and the family. The careful reader could see that there were far more generalities than concrete proposals, but the familial style of the Fernández candidacy shone through. His platform on education, for example, affirmed the necessity of accelerating existing policy, "introducing innovations" that, however, were not itemized. Listing a series of commonplace objectives fully consonant with existing patterns, these were to be implemented

through such actions as administrative reform of the Education
Ministry, more rational application of budgetary allocations,
coordination of planning, and periodic revision of plans and
programs.[17] Housing problems were to be met by largely
unelaborated measures including a program of popular credit for
improvement of low-income homes, the stimulation of housing
cooperatives, and increased incentives for construction by the
private sector.[18] Virtually all of the proposals had appeared in
similar form in the 1968 COPEI program.

A new entity put forward in the 1973 platform was the
Instituto de los Barrios. Incorporated into the candidate's
program in response to the FDP, it was intended largely to
centralize and coordinate the labors of existing government
agencies working in urban slums. Thus it would "facilitate the
integration into society of the hundreds of thousands of
Venezuelans who inhabit in subhuman conditions the barrios that
form a ring of misery in the principal population centers of the
country. The creation of this Institute will permit the orderly
channeling of diverse efforts...for the benefit of marginal
sectors, and consequently will be a factor of prime importance in
the execution of programs of social development."[19] The party
program also promised the creation of a national health service.
Although presented only in outline form, it was intended as an
autonomous institute which would integrate and restructure "the
budgets and medical assistance services of the Ministry of Health
and Social Assistance, the Venezuelan Institute of Social Security,
state governments, including that of the Federal District, and
other dependencies of the public administration."[20] This national
health service, perhaps more than the Instituto de los Barrios,
seemed essentially an administrative regrouping of existing
entities, and did not receive heavy emphasis during the campaign.

Sections of the program dealing with social development
included brief references to sports and to "the triumph of youth."
Much more thorough attention was given to issues of population
and family planning. COPEI's basic position was consistent with
existing Church doctrine, much of it drawn directly from the
Second Vatican Council's "Declaration on Responsible Parenthood."
The family was depicted as far more than a simple conglomeration
of individuals united by ties of blood. Rather it was "a communion
of beings united by ties of love to realize the human vocation
of solidarity and guarantee the survival of the species and of
fundamental values. Therefore the perfection of society depends
to greater or lesser degree on the perfection of the family. For
a society to live in peace it is necessary that peace find its
initial place in the spirit of families. For that it is necessary
that the government create the conditions necessary to guarantee
a climate of protection to the family institution."[21] Consequently,
COPEI pledged itself to treat the family as primary cell of
Venezuelan society: it would especially provide "protection for
the large family...the family with 3, 4, or 5 children lacking
economic means...protection to the abandoned mother, especially
to the abandoned mother, a tragic problem for Venezuela."[22]

Indeed, there was substantial public concern over problems
of child neglect and abandonment, and Fernández's response included
a statement on family planning. "I will stimulate family education
to permit each couple to assume responsibly the task of bringing
children into the world and educating them with love and care. No
coercive action will be permitted to improve a limitation of births
contrary to the will of the couple. The State will not decide the
number of children that each couple can have but it will see to it
that fathers assume full and integral responsibility for the
children brought into the world. I will be implacable with those
men who sprinkle children onto the world, only then to forget
them."[23] Such legitimate expressions of Catholic doctrine were
unlikely to produce public controversy, but extemporaneous remarks
by Lorenzo Fernández lent themselves to debate. Replying to a
question before the Pro-Venezuela Forum in classic pro-natalist
terms, he declared: "I continue to insist that Venezuela is a
territory of 906 thousand square kilometers, full of riches, but
hardly twelve million inhabitants. The solution of our problems
is not in stopping population growth but in the capacity of being
efficient in the administration of the country."[24] The same
message was often repeated: "Venezuela's principal capital is its
human capital," and therefore Venezuelan mothers were petitioned
to give "more children to the motherland."[25] Problems of poverty,
inadequate education, and similar maladies would be resolved by
his government through administrative efficiency and careful
planning.[26]

This first half of the program, in short, failed to indicate
significant change from that of Rafael Caldera five years earlier.
Admirable if unexceptional generalities reflected a broad sense of
humanity, but there was little of an innovative nature. The
proposals most widely disseminated in the copeyano campaign--creation
of an institute for the barrios, a national health service, and
establishment of a ministry for social development--appeared to be
administrative rearrangements to assure a more efficient usage of
government resources. The first of the three, of course, was also
part of COPEI's commitment to Wolfgang Larrazábal in return for
FDP support. But what of the latter portions, treating of economic
and political development? Here the language was more precise and
the thinking more clearly expressed. While the official program
was still in the process of preparation,[27] the outlines of
Fernández's thinking emerged with considerable clarity before
Fedecámaras.

Industrialization was a driving motor of Venezuelan economic
development. From the level of the family and artesan through small
and medium industry, the state would continue the protectionist
policy of past years. Heavy industry would be scrupulously
defended by a Fernández government. The candidate termed his ideas
"interventionist."

Within a socialist conception, interventionism has as
its objective the displacement of private activity, so
that it is absorbed by the State as its own. Within

> the conception that I have, interventionism is the
> direct action of the State, by means of democratic
> planning, in benefit and for the stimulus, protection
> and development of private activity itself. When I
> was Minister of Development I was a very interventionist
> Minister....
>   I will be interventionist, then....I believe that
> basic enterprises should be in State hands to guarantee
> to private activity that is developed about them, the
> best conditions and guarantees for their functioning,
> their growth and their success.[28]

In the subsequent presentation of Directrices, the message was
similar. The state would provide all possible support to
industrialization. The slogan of "democratizing production" was
coined and was defined as access of the majority to ownership of
the means of production. "I want a country of owners and not of
proletarians. So just as in the countryside a law has been
established which says that whoever works the land to own it has
the obligation of the State to help him become an owner, similarly
in industry more and more opportunities and incentives must be
given for the ever increasing small and medium owners who form a
solid basis for true economic democracy." Heavy industry, "the
true base for our autonomous development," would also receive
further momentum from the state. Petroleum, iron, aluminum, and
steel would continue to surge forward, while government investment
in these and similar industries would grow. A fifteen-year
national steel plan would be initiated, to make Venezuela a
producer of 10 million tons of steel annually.[29]
    The apparent extension of state participation in the economy
was consistent with the leftward trend being advertised by COPEI,
and campaign proposals regarding industry provided solid support,
as did the section on petroleum. The tacit agreement of
presidential candidates not to drag oil into the campaign arena
(no petrolizar las elecciones) was largely honored. In May
Fernández told Fedecámaras that the decisions of the next president
concerning petroleum would commit future generations as well as
the present one. "Therefore, I consider that no man, and no
party, can or is authorized to assume the tremendous responsibility
that it means to formulate a petroleum policy by their own
conception, without making a great national consultation. I have
said that I am prepared to advance reversion before 1983.... But
the decision would be the consequence of consultation."[30] It was
some months later when Fernández made explicit his intention of
advancing the reversion date. He also declared that the Orinoco
Tar Belt would be developed by Venezuelans.

> I am aware that the period corresponding to my
> government is that in which fundamental decisions
> will have to be taken in petroleum matters. I am
> going to advance [the date before] 1983 and

consequently the country should prepare itself to
assume great responsibilities.
The decision on this matter, nevertheless, cannot be
the fruit of emotional impulses but the product of
careful studies that will permit us to act in the
most adequate form and at the most opportune moment.
Therefore, I propose to accelerate the termination
of studies already initiated by the present government
and to effect a great national consultation with the
participation of all interested sectors.
We are master of the largest known deposit of
petroleum in the western world. It is estimated that
the Orinoco Tar Belt, more than 600 kilometers long,
contains more than 700 billion barrels of oil. This
belt will be explored and exploited by Venezuelans for
the benefit of the Venezuelan people.[31]

The other economic pole--agriculture--was subjected to less
searching analysis, despite public insistence that it would receive
high priority from a Fernández government. Fedecámaras was assured,
"I recognize the necessity for agricultural sectors to obtain
adequate remuneration, and the search for instruments that will
assure adequate remuneration.... For the private agricultural
sector I have conceived of open and clear support, and I am going
to ask the support of Congress for a more audacious development,
for I believe...in audacity."[32] Admittedly, the national
agricultural crisis was a political complication, for the Fernández
campaign could scarcely disclaim the policies of the Caldera
administration. The party platform merely promised "to deepen the
change initiated in 1969, in the light of experiences which
agriculture has had, on the national as well as the international
level, with the goal of guaranteeing good nourishment for all the
Venezuelan population...."[33] The rubrics would be "accelerated
agricultural growth," "efficient, modern and integral agrarian
reform," "rural development," and "conservation and promotion of
renewable natural resources."
    Turning finally to "political" development, the program dealt
successively with international and domestic policy, following
closely the molds of the Caldera administration. "International
relations will be conducted within the norm of international social
justice," with more developed countries obligated to carry a
greater burden than the less developed. Venezuela under Fernández
would maintain relations with all the countries of the world. The
candidate promised a foreign policy guided "by democratic
nationalism and by the conviction that it is possible for peoples
with different forms of government, but united by the common desire
to achieve integral development in true democracy, to maintain
correct diplomatic relations." As for the hemisphere, the new
COPEI government would "maintain the closest relations with brother
countries of the continent and will contribute to forging a Latin
American bloc that can defend not only the interests of our
countries but also those of the developing world." In short,

"democratic nationalism that orients Venezuelan policy will be
able to achieve its objectives if a true Latin American nationalism,
ample and generous, is stimulated...the cooperation with Latin
American peoples will be the cornerstone of our foreign policy."[34]
The hallmark of internal policy was viewed as an extension of
Caldera's pacification policy. Fernández, minister of interior
relations during the initiation and implementation of the policy,
was openly proud of his role. When questioned before the
Asociación Pro-Venezuela, for example, he spoke of continuing
pacification but under somewhat different conditions. He viewed
pacification as more than extending permission to Venezuelans
outside the law to rejoin the democratic process. It was necessary
"to create a climate in which all we Venezuelans can live in
Venezuela as such, enjoying that exceptional condition...and I
can therefore guarantee you that I am going to propose from the
Presidency of the Republic an Amnesty Law so that there is not a
single Venezuelan who [must] stay outside national territory."[35]
The Social Christian platform pledged a law of amnesty and was
suffused with assurances of liberty, freedom, harmony, and respect
for a pluralism of views. The armed forces would enjoy Fernández's
confidence, the public administration would be operated honestly
and openly, while he would "advance the transformation of State
structures in a decisive and audacious manner." The platform
concluded: "The Venezuelan pueblo knows my life and knows that I
am a man in whom it can trust. These DIRECTRICES PARA UNA ACCION
DE GOBIERNO represent the synthesis of what I propose to impel
from the Presidency of the Republic with the help of all men and
women of good will. These are my pledges. They are our pledge,
that of all who wish to unite for the immediate conquest of the
future."[36]
The sum total of Lorenzo Fernández's campaign program did not
yield to facile characterization. Humanitarian expressions of
social consciousness, stated in Social Christian terminology, were
both lengthy and imprecise. Pursuant to COPEI's defense and
advocacy of government policy under the Caldera presidency, the
1973 platform elaborated existing programs. Indeed, an array of
new, different, and precise proposals would have represented a
tacit departure from the lines of party evolution, hinting as well,
criticism of the copeyano administration. Thus, COPEI discussions
of social policy marked out few new departures. In the economic
realm, more concrete statements gave assurance that a strongly
activist, interventionist bent might be anticipated, guided by a
pronounced nationalism. Industrialization would be accorded high
priority, and the policy of regionalization promoted by the Caldera
government would be continued. As to agriculture, the crisis of
the countryside was ignored. Foreign policy was viewed as following
the Caldera concepts of international social justice. It was this
area, far more than any others, that gave some substance to the
"leftism" being heralded by COPEI's campaign managers.
There was less than perfect consistency between the orientation
of the official program and that being promoted by the candidate and
his public relations experts. The former, though genuinely

progressive, revealed too few elements to justify a label of "leftist." At the most, Social Christian strategists could merely hope that the platform might realistically appear to the left of the adeco program. In public pronouncements, however, Lorenzo Fernández insisted on the leftist label. Although an understandable strategy that was by no means unreasonable, this did incur certain risks. The course of the campaign, and particularly its rhetoric, could scarcely be attractive to rightist elements. At the same time, the leftist current within the party caused pressures from the opposite doctrinal wing. In 1966 and 1967 Rafael Caldera, preliminary to launching his campaign, labored mightily to contain divergent elements within the party. Only his personal prestige and political acumen made it possible for COPEI to overcome ideological divergencies at that time. By 1973, with a different man carrying the party banner, the problem was again evident. The tradition of party discipline and internal loyalty prevented the kind of fragmentation so common to the Venezuelan party system, but it could not remove tensions and stress.

In any event, the avowed programmatic direction of the 1973 copeyano campaign insisted upon its position to the left of center. Lorenzo Fernández, calling for ideological pluralism at the international level and promising that the domestic policy of pacification in all its implications would be writ large, followed a path that Rafael Caldera and Social Christian oficialistas approved. The voter was assured that this would be achieved under the paternal wisdom and filial warmth of Lorenzo Fernández. The candidate's words during a November interview might well sum up the "nationalist, democratic" program he espoused:

> I am going to realize a policy of social progress that has as its bases of sustenance economic development. I have announced that I am going to create a Ministry of Social Development and a Ministry of Economic Development; that I am going to pursue a nationalist policy whereby I will not negotiate with the Orinoco Tar Belt because, as I have said, it will be explored and exploited by Venezuelans for the benefit of the Venezuelan pueblo;...creation of an economic development to generate new and abundant sources of work that mean better living conditions for Venezuelans. And an audacious policy to train our youth in such a form as to assume the challenge that faces them, that of directing the destinies of a great country that is being forged and will be a reality in the year 2000. In other words, to realize the immediate conquest of the future.[37]

ACCIÓN DEMOCRÁTICA

Ideologically, the formative years for the founders of the AD extended from the youthful protests of university students in 1928 until the coming of the trienio government. These years saw a swift recession of early Marxist influence. As Betancourt later wrote, there was a seeking of "a truly American doctrine or ideology or set of answers."[38] Conflict with the communists by the PDN prior to the 1941 founding of the AD completed the political and ideological break.[39] By 1945 the party had come to a Social Democratic position, advocating centralized government control within a democratic context. The economic system was to be democratized and guided by the state; electoral provisions embodied principles of participatory government. With its seizure of power in 1945 the AD adopted a posture that was clearly radical. An apt self-appraisal was that of Leonardo Ruiz Pineda, a young leader from Táchira later assassinated under the Pérez Jiménez dictatorship: "We are a multiclass party of the revolutionary left...called to fulfill the democratic and anti-imperialist revolution with the participation of all political, economic and social forces interested in the transformation of the country. Within this undertaking we have at their posts of action all Venezuelans desirous of administrative honesty, economic and social peace, economic nationalism, agrarian democracy, industrial progress, the exercise of public liberties and popular sovereignty."[40]

The 1958 return following a decade of exile saw the party chastened by its earlier experience. President Betancourt and senior adecos believed that the stability and preservation of party government demanded high priority, and reforms were approached in a gradualistic fashion. To young party leftists, such contentions were but an ingenuous rationalization of what was seen as betrayal of the party's ideological raison d'être. The resulting cleavage led to the separation of the AD left in 1961. Specific party declarations on program and policy appeared with the publication of basic party "theses" in 1962,[41] and basic objectives were subject to only modest revision in the years that followed.[42] Although the arsista party division in 1962 lacked ideological importance, the same could not be said of the 1967 battle. The ultimate separation of those who founded the MEP largely removed the moderate left. Thus the years between the 1968 and 1973 elections saw a broad homogeneity of thought within the AD, in contrast to COPEI.

To its opponents, the AD no longer possessed ideological commitment. The party responded that its Social Democratic definition was clear and that indeed there had been a remarkable consistency through its performance both in government and in opposition. To a sympathetic observer, "Acción Democrática is a party that responds to the theoretical postulates of social democracy....Within the concept of social democracy the party is committed to and fights for the effectiveness of liberties, the profound modification and democratization of the national economic structure, the establishment of a government rule which permits the free play of social forces, breaks the feudal relations of property in the countryside, intervenes adequately in industrial production, develops commerce and protects sectors with the least resources."[43] The reorganizational effort after 1968 neither required nor undertook major reconsiderations of party doctrine. The adeco platform that was developed revealed the proposals with

which the party would face the future. With the announcement on
28 April 1973 that Rómulo Betancourt would chair the party commission
assigned the drafting of the program--and Betancourt's brisk
assurance that he intended to exercise a strong hand in the
process--interest in its content rose.

In addition to the official platform, major programmatic
statements included the candidate's acceptance speech, his message
on the occasion of the AD's thirty-second anniversary, Pérez's
appearance before Fedecámaras, and the interview in the series
appearing in El Nacional.[44] Pérez's acceptance speech, presented
long before initiation of the Betancourt commission, helped to
presage the full statement that was announced some fourteen months
later. He introduced his remarks by saying that his ideas, "which
will constitute the orientation of my Program of Government, are
an ideological expression of the party that nominates me, shared
throughout my public life."[45] Among the policy areas that resounded
most heavily during his campaign were the war on poverty,
agricultural and agrarian reform, education and culture, and
industry. With the first, he pledged a "pact with the poor," a
theme that was elaborated in the months ahead. For Pérez, this
was not "a demagogic claim to awaken solidarity and support from
the national majorities lacking goods or resources sufficient for
subisitence." What it did mean was an equitable distribution of
well-being throughout all strata of society.   "The reality of our
country is that half the population lives in unacceptable conditions
that cannot be justified in any fashion....We have to create more
wealth, but we are obligated to better distribution."[46]

Development was offered as a solution, relying heavily upon
industrial decentralization and regional development and taking
place within a framework elaborated from the bottom up, "to raise
the economy from the bottom of the social pyramid. In this fashion
industrial, commercial and agricultural enterprises will grow,
because the general enrichment of the country will grow."[47]
Agriculture would receive vigorous government support. In decrying
the crisis in the countryside, he denied that the AD program of
1959-69 had been unsuccessful, singling out the present government
for failing to update, amend, and reorient the initial agrarian
reform to meet changing needs. "The failure of all Latin American
development plans is owing to their failure to achieve a process
of agricultural and livestock development growing at the same
rhythm as industrial expansion. The challenge that I accept is
that of demonstrating that agriculture is not the Cinderella of
national development, but the true engine of industrial
development."[48]

Although agriculture therefore was of highest priority,
industry would not be neglected. Praising the policies of the AD
in the 1960s, he argued that the moment had come for urgent new
decisions reorienting the course of industrialization. Pérez
promised attention to industries linked with the external market
and contributing to Andean economic integration. The petrochemical
industry would also receive particular attention. Two basic
commitments were stressed. First Pérez proclaimed his belief that

basic industries should be in the hands of the state; however, he
was open to the possibility of creating mixed public-private
enterprises where it would meet the national interest. Secondly,
acceptance of the participation of foreign capital in industrial
development required strict supervision and government limitations.
"We will act with a healthy nationalist criteria, understanding
this to be the defense of national interests but without any
isolationist or xenophobic sentiment in denial of indispensable
and growing international interdependence. Our nationalism is
Latin American and follows unhesitatingly the clear paths of the
thought of Simón Bolívar."[49]
     The acceptance message provided few specifics but mirrored
the general areas of greatest concern to the candidate. Moreover,
it was but the first of reiterated calls for meaningful national
political understanding. In concluding his September 1972 speech,
Pérez termed his words "not a challenge to the political adversary
but a dialogue by means of differing ideological foci. There
are no abysses among democratic political groups in Venezuela....
We do not suggest that any one abandon ideological trenches.
Controversy and polemics are the essence of politics. But another
thing is cooperating for the creation of a climate that favors
debate, conciliates gratuitous hostilities and overthrows violence
in national political life...."[50] Pérez later would promise to
call upon other parties in organizing his administration. In this
he went further than Lorenzo Fernández, whose own proposals for
national unity invariably avoided references to the composition
of his administration. The adeco candidate said that his "will
not be a hegemonic government; it will not mean party hegemony,
it will in no way exclude other national sectors that...wish to
deliver their efforts in the construction of that Patria that
we must forge in the next five years of government to consolidate
in effective fashion representative democracy in our country...."[51]
By the close of the campaign Pérez was specifying that he was
prepared to negotiate with all political parties--including the
left--and at his Caracas mass rally in late November specified
that his cabinet would include independents and members of other
parties.
     The introductory passages of the official Acción de Gobierno
were to link economic development with the struggle against
poverty. Given the centrality of the antipoverty theses in Pérez's
campaign, it is useful to quote at some length:

          The advance of the country implies that the gross
          national product is increasing in sustained and
          accelerated form. Nevertheless, in the search
          for that growth one cannot obliquely disregard
          the aberrant and intolerable contradiction between
          the apparent high per capita income of Venezuelans
          and the inescapable reality that a large part of
          our compatriots live oppressed by extreme poverty.
          The quality of life of all Venezuelans has to be
          what orients our concerns. By means of such

instruments as tax action, full employment, aggressive
and renewing impetus to agriculture, national
revitalization of light and medium industry, and
programs of social improvement which should be changed,
and under my government will be changed, that pyramidal
structure of Venezuelan society, in which a few rich,
overly rich occupy the pinnacle while at its broad
base are hundreds of thousands of very poor families
collecting barely enough income for precarious
subsistence.[52]

Running nearly eighty pages, the adeco platform was divided into
eighteen separate chapters. As already noted, there was deep
concern over the stagnation of agriculture; renewed industrial
development was promised; and extensive administrative revisions were
recommended as necessary to assure structural modernization.

Venezuelan agriculture, as Fedecámaras had heard, required
investment from both the public and private sector. The
infrastructure indispensable for modernization of the agricultural
process had to be generated largely through the actions of the
state, with technical assistance programs greatly enlarged.
Expansion of credits was also necessary. "There has to be important
support from the private sector most especially for managerial
credit, and it must be achieved on the basis of a variety of
stimuli that the State must create, so that private capital will
indeed go there."[53] The section of the platform entitled
"reconstruction of agriculture" proposed numerous policies under
subsections dealing with crops, cattle and livestock, forests, and
fishing. All were directed toward a series of fundamental
objectives, with the overriding concern "to guarantee Venezuelans
the satisfactory supply of agricultural products which constitute
their basic diet, at remunerative prices for producers and
accessible to popular sectors. Abundance of production will be the
best protection against speculation derived from scarcity and
inefficient controls."[54] The adecos made it quite clear, then, that
an agricultural renaissance ranked very high among their priorities.

The theme of "new industrial development" presented four broad
goals: better income distribution, closer ties between industry and
Venezuelan natural resources, integration of different branches of
industry, and increased exportation of manufactured products. Basic
industries, under state aegis, would receive high priority from the
Plan of the Nation, and the role of government loomed large. "The
New Industrial Development will be realized principally by means
of State action as a promoter of activities. The elaboration of
plans will have the highest priority. Small and medium industry
will receive the preferential treatment which it deserves as a
large employer of hand work and of prime national materials; at the
same time, large industry will count on specific incentives to
facilitate their action; and its financing will be guaranteed
principally by means of the participation of the State as shareholder
and by means of the granting of guaranteed credits."[55]

Administrative adjustments, finally, would include major
reorganizations of the Corporación Venezolana de Fomento, the
Industrial Bank, and regional corporations, all to be reshaped
within the plans for decentralization outlined elsewhere in the
program.

Like his Social Christian rival, Pérez was convinced of the
intimate interrelationship of social and economic factors. His
speeches and statements were constantly tracing relationships back
and forth between policy areas. For the sake of analytic
presentation, however, it is possible to segregate proposals
falling into the area of social policy. Health and education stood
out; the former provided one of the sharper differences between
Pérez and Fernández. Where Lorenzo urged Venezuelan mothers to
give more children to the country, promising that his government
would deal effectively with infant abandonment and related maladies,
Carlos Andrés quoted appalling statistics and spoke of family
planning. "It is enough to point out that 52% of Venezuelan
children are illegitimate and that existing legal dispositions to
protect those children and the mother are not well developed. The
80% of infant deaths between the ages of 2 and 4 years have
malnutrition as the direct or indirect cause." The figures
continued. "There exist around 283,000 abandoned children in the
metropolitan Caracas zone. Some 65% of adolescents are not enrolled
in any school and among electors aged 18 to 23 there are many
thousands of illiterates (13% in the last elections). Only half of
the youths who want to enter the labor market can obtain employment
and, finally, there has sprung forth with gravity and on a large
scale all kinds of maladjustments in our youth, including the
remorseful problem of drugs, which require rapid and effective
solutions."[56]

The candidate returned to the problem in his final interview
with El Nacional. Irresponsible paternity lay at its roots. "In
Venezuela 52 percent of all children are born of accidental unions.
Each hour 60 children are born, that is, one child a minute, while
thirty are born abandoned—half. Annual infant mortality up to
the age of a year is 20,000. Of those 500,000 who are born in the
year, 23 percent are of illiterate mothers and 46 percent of mothers
between the ages of 15 and 24 years." Among various remedies, "we
have to create throughout the country a Center of Family Orientation,
and within it the Family Planning also indispensable to our
expressed objectives."[57] New educational programs would help
contribute to family orientation and protection, and a ministry of
youth was proposed. Taking the idea from a 1968 campaign promise
of Gonzalo Barrios, the 1973 party standardbearer termed such a
ministry "an organism for study and integral attention to juvenile
problems, which will orient and coordinate official and private
action in this field of such high interest, while its functioning
will be manned with the fullest participation of youth sectors
themselves."[58]

Problems of education also preoccupied Pérez, as stated
during questioning by Fedecámaras. His denunciation of existing
policy began with allegations of great squandering of funds—a common

adeco tack in its criticism of the Social Christian government.   In
Venezuela for the years 1968 and 1969, he stated, "36,000 children
were enrolled in first grade.   For the years 1970 and 1971, of
those 36,000 who should be in third grade, we find instead only
14,000.   And in 1974, undoubtedly, we are going to find 4,000 or
5,000 students in third grade....Absenteeism, the misery of the
poor classes, the lack of a social policy in support of education,
etc., provoke this disgrace."[59]   Venezuela required nothing less
than a veritable educational revolution.   In chapter 10 of the adeco
program, four prime objectives were outlined: quantitative
expansion to meet ever-growing demands of demographic increase;
across-the-board modernization of both educational content and
technology; a democratization of the entire process through state
support, with food, health, clothing, books, and transport included
in order to equalize educational opportunities; and administrative
reforms, including promulgation of a new education law to replace
the one still in effect.   Specific programs included preschool
and primary education in particular, with related attention
directed to rural, special, and adult education.   In all, fully
ten pages of the program were devoted to education--the longest
section in the document.[60]

Institutional reforms were proposed, as Pérez first announced
in his acceptance speech.[61]   "A democratic regime, by its very
dynamism, demands transformations to correct mistaken experiences....
Its effectiveness depends in great part on the efficiency of basic
institutions, on intelligent utilization of available resources,
and organic legislation...utilized to bring about structural
modernization."   The strengthening of municipal government would
be based on greater local participation in community affairs.
Judicial reform would be aimed at a greater flexibility and
efficiency, as well as the elimination of privilege.   A Pérez
government would seek the study and implementation of such measures
through creation of a national commission of legislative reform,
which would work with Congress in proposing amendments to the
constitution.   A variety of task forces within the bureaucracy
would also contribute to the reshaping of institutional structures.[62]

The AD and its candidate were careful to exclude questions of
petroleum policy from electoral debate.   In his appearance before
Fedecámaras, Carlos Andrés Pérez spoke in broadly nationalistic
but generally vague terms.   "We have to prepare ourselves for
the best manner in which petroleum passes into being a resource
managed in well-defined national interests.   We have to establish
technical, human, and economic resources, with which we can count
on handling this resource in Venezuelan hands."[63]   What of reversion
or nationalization?   That would depend on the result of necessary
studies and a clear presentation of all viable alternatives.   "I do
not believe that petroleum should become a matter for controversies
and for breaches among Venezuelans.   I believe that oil can be, in
the long run, one of the great factors for union among Venezuelans.
I assume that all Venezuelans have an authentic nationalist
sentiment to conserve this resources for ourselves and to project
it toward future generations."[64]   The decision about taking

possession of the industry before 1983 "must be submitted to prior
and profound studies. Venezuela must not wait for 1983 to take
decisions related to reversion. It is foreseeable that the nearing
of reversion will move the multinational firms to take maximum
advantage of time and of the wells, with a minimum maintenance of
the installations and undesirable exploitation of petroleum
holdings. If this circumstance prevails, reversion would have to
be advanced."[65]

In his official program, much of the section on energy and
petroleum was a recounting of the past AD role in the evolution
and formulation of petroleum policy. Policy statements differed
only slightly from those issued months before, for reversion at
some juncture prior to 1983 was clearly if indirectly stated.
Concern over activities of foreign corporations was more explicit.
"Lacking but a few years before reversion of the greater part of
present concessions to the Nation, the private companies are
maintaining their exploration activities at minimum levels, and
we run the risk that our industry, by not incorporating new
techniques and because of an absence of investments and proper
maintenance, may be deteriorating at an accelerated pace when we
find ourselves at the point of delivery of the concessions, with
equipment spent and an obsolete technology. For these reasons,
it does not appear possible to wait until 1983 for the State to
assume full management of the petroleum business."[66]   A Pérez
government would also undertake geological studies of the Orinoco
Tar Belt, which would begin to be developed "when that meets our
own interests." The Corporación Venezolana del Petróleo would
bear major responsibility for petroleum and energy policy.

International politics would be conducted with respect for
existing commitments and allegiance to fellow Latin American states.
Basic reorganization of the Organization of American States would
be sought, and Venezuela would work on behalf of the Comisión
Especial de Coordinación Latinoamericana (CECLA) as an exclusively
Latin American organ. The new government would also "intensify
the country's participation in efforts of Latin American integration,
preserving in clear and cordial tone the interests of Venezuela
toward those similarly legitimate ones of brother countries....
Our action in the movement of Latin American integration presumes
a maximum effort to articulate an active international policy
that assures just participation of our country in world trade...."[67]
Significantly, the AD would no longer employ the Betancourt
Doctrine in questions of recognition; indeed, its policy resembled
that of COPEI, without the phrase "ideological pluralism." As
Pérez explained frequently, the doctrine had been used to meet
circumstances of the times. The AD had returned to power during
a period when dictatorships were falling and believed that excessive
diplomatic tolerance by democratic forces had previously
strengthened such despots as Trujillo, Batista, and Pérez Jiménez.
Consequently, the doctrine was a logical norm; but the decade of
the 1950s was long past.[68] As the program declared, "the
international scene at the moment, particularly the Latin American,
is different from that of years ago....Changes operating in Latin

America, most of them as the result of deeds of force, have
determined that the majority of governments in this part of the
western hemisphere are not the product of freely emitted suffrage.
Not to maintain diplomatic relations with these regimes would
result, in the present historical moment, in an unrealistic
attitude....In the universal orbit, our government will maintain
the principle of diplomatic and commercial relations with all
countries of the world."[69]   As for Cuba, nothing was said in the
Acción de Gobierno.   However, Pérez recognized desirable aspects
of renewed relations with Cuba.   In his view the Castro government
seemed no longer to be backing insurrection in Latin America.
However, he believed firmly that the initiative should come from
Havana, not Caracas.   It was a Venezuelan request that had led to
OAS action against Cuban interventionism in the first place; thus
Pérez thought it inappropriate for the Venezuelan government now
to take the lead in moving toward a restoration of ties.   "Given
the original circumstances, I think it reasonable that the
Venezuelan government should not be the one to take the first step
on the road to the reestablishment of relations with Cuba."[70]

On the whole, the Pérez program fit the Social Democratic
rubric.[71]   In its nationalism it was similar to the Social Christian,
and indeed many of the commitments were quite similar.   The two
programs shared an interventionist bent, as well as an emphasis on
industrialization with extensive government participation.   Regional
growth would be encouraged, while social development was regarded as
as ineluctable element of economic progress.   Both candidates
promised improved health and housing facilities, and educational
reforms were viewed as important.   Domestic tranquility and harmony
would be sought, although Pérez went further than Fernández in
assuring that his would be a nonsectarian, nonhegemonic
administration.   Foreign policy would also follow similar lines,
although attitudes toward recognition of Cuba differed in degree.
Despite such parallel stances, however, there were also evident
differences.   Within the context of the campaign competition, as
seen in various contexts, the Social Christian intention of
essentially maintaining existing policies was challenged by adeco
promises of change.   For COPEI, the molds of the Caldera
administration were to be preserved, whereas Social Democratic
forces regarded the government as having failed in many areas.

One fundamental difference lay in the strong AD commitment to
the countryside, to provincial and rural Venezuelans.   Mindful of
the party's historic origins in the campo, the AD in this sense
proposed a major shift of priorities.[72]   Its determination to
revive local governments and agencies was but a further manifestation.
In certain policy areas the adecos voiced somewhat more explicit
language than did the copeyanos--most notably in education and
health matters.   As the leading opposition party the AD could more
readily articulate explicit new proposals than could COPEI.   Yet
for each of these contenders, occupying essentially the political
center, specifics were not always necessary; indeed, as apparent
front-runners in the campaign, a substantial degree of programmatic
vagueness had its value for both.   It was also to be expected that

the views of Fernández and Pérez would respectively represent the
political "ins" and "outs." Lorenzo, addressing several hundred
thousand at his climactic Caracas rally on 5 December--"El
Caracazo"--declared: "I have prepared myself to be the President
of my Motherland, to realize the social, economic and political
transformation that the country demands. I have a clear
consciousness of the responsibility that I am to assume....I go to
Miraflores with a clear and exact consciousness, to continue the
work of Government of which I feel myself proudly supportive,
namely, the work realized by President Caldera, and I am going to
continue and to deepen that reality....I am prepared to continue
the social, economic, and political transformation of the
Venezuelan pueblo."[73] In contrast, the adeco candidate criticized
the administration, believing that the next five years would be
crucial to Venezuelan democracy. He saw certain parallels between
contemporary Venezuela and Cuba of the late 1940s and early 1950s,
when the failures of party government paved the way for first
Batista, and then Fidel Castro.[74] As Carlos Andrés told Fedecámaras:
"I believe that we are at a transcendental historical crossroads;
if we are not capable of giving meaning to Venezuelan Democracy,
in the next constitutional period Democracy can be shipwrecked.
Consequently, it has become indispensable that all sectors of
national life, businessmen, political parties, all Venezuelan
institutions, must together forge a consciousness of this reality
in which our country lives."[75]
    It was inaccurate to deny differences in program or candidate,
therefore. At the same time, however, both parties occupied the
broad middle ground of the national political spectrum. Moreover,
whether spurious or not, there was a doctrinal distinction that
was widely perceived, as many viewed COPEI and Fernández to the
left of the AD and Pérez. Major business interests identified
with Fedecámaras clearly preferred the adeco to the copeyano
candidate. It was largely the Marxists who denied significant
ideological differences; from their perspective, both parties fell
within the capitalist rather than socialist camp, and any
distinctions between them were meaningless. However, there were
indeed programmatic contrasts, and the voter had ample reason to
anticipate that a Social Christian or Social Democratic
administration from 1974-79 would be anything but identical. It
was, of course, both the philosophical and ideological task of the
Venezuelan left to deny this fact, urging the necessity of moving
away from the establishment parties and politics. Such was the
burden of the candidacies of Jesús Angel Paz Galarraga, José
Vicente Rangel, and Jóvito Villalba.

THE POLITICAL LEFT
    The Nueva Fuerza program strongly resembled the political
doctrine of the MEP.[76] The mepista statement, adopted by an
Asamblea Nacional in August 1970, was prepared and edited after
lengthy consultation among numerous party bodies and organs.
Strongly influenced by Demetrio Boersner, the party secretary of
doctrine and training, this "Political Thesis" described the MEP

as a "democratic socialist party of Venezuelan manual and
intellectual workers." Two fundamental objectives were affirmed:
Venezuelan national liberation and construction of a socialist
democracy. It was to these goals that all party doctrine and
political activity was directed. National liberation was understood
as "reducing foreign influence of an imperialist character on the
life of the country, and directing and planning economic and
cultural development in independent form."[77]

Socialist democracy or democratic socialism--terms that were
used interchangeably--were understood as meaning "a system of
organization characterized by the effective domination of
intellectual and manual workers' majorities over the principal
means of production and distribution of riches, for a just
distribution of national income, and for the planning of development
for the benefit of the popular masses...with neither exploited nor
exploiters,...the division of society into antagonistic classes
would be overcome, with the springing forth of a new type of free
man, harmonious and capable of unlimited spiritual and intellectual
evolution."[78] For mepista theoreticians, the goal of liberation
was the most immediate, for without it democratic socialism
remained unattainable. However, the two goals might be sought in
tandem, depending upon the idiosyncrasies of a particular country
and era. Venezuela, it was argued, had shown that the bourgeois or
capitalist classes, even when possessing nationalist elements,
were not disposed to join with the popular classes in progressing
through stages of national liberation. Moreover, when the masses
began to acquire a greater share and participation in the national
patrimony, capitalists would assume increasingly conservative
positions. Therefore, "the popular character of the process must
be manifested from the very beginning by means of fully
democratic-socialist actions and transformations. If theoretically
national liberation and democratic socialization are two successive
stages, in practice they would be virtually simultaneous."[79]

For the MEP, the rise to power of popular forces could be
effected by electoral, nonviolent means under a libertarian,
constitutional regime. A mepista government would place under
state control the basic sectors of the economy and all natural
resources. Moreover, growing participation in developmental
decisions would be extended to the popular masses, until ultimately
the political, economic, and cultural apparatus would be fully at
the service of the workers. Basic industries would then be
nationalized, as would all essential services and public facilities,
and independent national planning would be undertaken. Further
policy steps would include income redistribution; a recasting of
education, health, and housing policies; the introduction of
cooperatives; the replacement of capitalist by socialist agrarian
reform; and effective municipal control over lands. The ultimate
objective was creation of a social order without antagonistic
classes, in which all workers were transformed into a single class
of citizen producers, remunerated in terms of their ability and
their contribution to the collectivity. Principal means of
production would be nationalized and directed by the state, while

medium and small enterprises would remain in private hands, but in democratized form including the participation of workers and employers in management and planning. In the end, "for those who conceive of the liberation of Venezuela as a state in the liberation of the world, revolutionary policy is nothing but a means to accelerate the flowering of a new type of man, superior to the present in wisdom and in kindness."[80]

In discussing its ideological bases, the MEP viewed Marxism as indispensable to universal revolutionary thought, and also as vital to meaningful social analysis. However, its tenets were not to be accepted uncritically or without application to specific conditions. Marxist theory itself demanded a critical confrontation with changing reality, and those tenets that do not withstand the test of time should be discarded. Those Marxist bases most utilized by the MEP were its method of scientific analysis and the notion of class struggle. Even then, however, doctrine must be carefully reasoned and understood, for unlike Marxism-Leninism, "democratic socialism does not accept absolute dogmas and believes that all truth proclaimed at one moment could require later revision."[81] The key mechanism is free discussion between workers and intellectuals, with a plurality of opinion crucial to democratic socialist unity. Although classical socialist doctrines are important, inspiration must also come from post-Marxist empirical social science, including modern developmental theories.

Democratic socialist ideology, then, encompassed multiple sources: "the democratic tradition, pre-Marxist socialism, Marxism and its revisions, modern theories of development, and respective national revolutionary doctrines of each country."[82] Six fundamental ideas are presented as summarizing mepista thinking, beginning with mankind's history of struggle between oppressed majorities and oppressed minorities. This experience underlines the necessity of creating a society free from class antagonisms and contradictory interests. Second, progress toward democratic socialism requires the struggle and ultimate triumph of the exploited and the oppressed. Third, the historical process suggests the existence of stages that cannot be skipped. Thus national liberation precedes democratic socialism, and the struggle against colonialism in all forms is of prime importance. The fourth point insists that social ownership must gain primacy over individual ownership; its many forms include nationalization, self-management, and cooperatives. As to the contemporary international world, democratic socialism cannot be identified with either of the great power blocs but constitutes a third force independent of geostrategic power alignments. Finally, democratic socialism is internationalist rather than insular.[83]

The MEP's position might be described as a moderate and flexible form of socialism. Eclectic in intellectual derivation, independent in policy formulations, adaptable and responsive to specific national characteristics and problems, it could be regarded as a pragmatic application of socialist thought to rectify existing inequities and injustices. The 1973 campaign platform itself took two related forms--one, a lengthy itemization of

programmatic bases, the other an accompanying fifteen-point
summary.[84]   The latter presented nationalization as an important
tool for the Government of National Liberation; within the first
twelve months petroleum, iron, banking, insurance, and credit
industries and institutions would be taken over by the administration
with large latifundios expropriated. The land would be delivered
immediately to peasants working them, who would additionally
receive a variety of credits, both on individual and cooperative
bases. Socialist agrarian reform would "direct its action toward
the liquidation of the latifundio and the large land holding, in
order to create the bases for true emancipation of the peasant,
making him master of his land and his own existence...."[85]

A wide variety of social measures were to be implemented
immediately upon assuming power. For former pediatrician Paz,
among the most important was the daily providing of one-half liter
of milk "to the millions of poor children who belong to families
with monthly income of less than 500 bolivares."[86]   The price of
medicine would be reduced 20 percent from existing levels, and food
prices from 15 to 20 percent. Wages and salaries for the workers
would be raised, while the government would also introduce a
"moving salary," that is, an "increase of salaries in relation to
the cost of living and the productivity of businesses."[87]   Food,
medicine, and rent prices would be frozen at a lower level, and a
policy of full employment would be introduced through social
protection of existing unemployed and the application of strike
insurance plans. The Social Security system would be drastically
overhauled, and special committees of workers and professionals
would be consulted in the process of restructuring and then
operating it. "This 'single Health Service' will give protection
in its preventive as well as curative aspect to all Venezuelans
without exception, including not only medical aid but...the supply
of medicines at reasonable prices or gratuitously, in accord with
the Social Security System that will definitively be established."[88]

In the international field, economic relations would be
strongly affected by the nationalization program. Foreign
investment, as Paz explained, "will be limited to determined areas
in which national capital has no competence, and regulated...in the
percentage of reinvestment that can be made in the country."[89]
Within the western hemisphere, Venezuela would meet its existing
diplomatic and treaty commitments, including those embodied in
the Andean Pact. Overall, policy "will be dictated solely by the
interest of our pueblo and of all pueblos submitted to identical or
similar neocolonialist domination and penetration."[90]   Venezuelan
sovereignty would be exercised through relations with all countries,
and the Nueva Fuerza program specifically listed Cuba, Vietnam,
Korea, East Germany, China, Bangladesh, Guinea, and Tanzania. The
existing contract with the North American military mission would
be canceled, for Venezuelan armed forces "possess a high technical
level and do not require the presence of foreign military missions."[9]

The Nueva Fuerza's initial policies would be highlighted by
nationalization and by a variety of measures relating to wages,
prices, food, medicine, and rent. The breaking of the ties of

dependency with foreign imperialist powers, especially the
United States, would receive powerful impetus. In building a
structure capable of eliminating poverty and internal exploitation,
government control of the basic industries would be central. Small
and medium industries and enterprises would not be affected. Paz
believed that Venezuela had to progress gradually and patiently
toward socialism--the socialism that he said was not yet "just
around the corner." Imperialist structures, domestic national
oligarchs, and generations of embedded tradition made an immediate
transformation to full-blown socialism both unrealistic and
impossible. However, it was urgent that the task be started. With
the defeat of imperialism and oligarchy well under way, the road
to national liberation would beckon more clearly, opening the way
to the development of true socialist democracy. This was an
ideological recipe for moderation and gradualism which, on both
philosophical and pragmatic grounds, was sharply opposed by José
Vicente Rangel and the MAS.[92]
        The origins of the MAS have direct bearing on the ideological
orientation of the Rangel campaign. It was in December of 1970
that the PCV divided, with those who left the PCV organizing the
MAS the following month. Those who departed sought the formation
"of an anti-dogmatic revolutionary instrument, open to new
contemporary realities, removed from any sectarian spirit and...
with sufficient capacity to put in motion appropriate initiatives
and to advance without vacillations toward the configuration of a
union of the people around socialism."[93] The PCV internal
conflagration had been fueled by Petkoff's criticism of the Soviet
invasion of Czechoslovakia,[94] and the aging leadership of the PCV
had opposed any departure from its rigid orthodoxy and pro-Moscow
tradition. The subsequent publication of Petkoff's ¿Socialismo
para Venezuela?,[95] an essay in doctrinal self-criticism   the
communist leadership rejected,[96] came but a few months before the
withdrawal of those who then created the MAS.
        The ideological fertility of Petkoff's writings cannot be
detailed here, but the broad orientation provides background to
the campaign program. He demanded a critical analysis of doctrine
and policy as a basis for the formulation of new positions. Party
bureaucratization and the survival of Stalinist attitudes were
criticized, and the importance of applying Marxist theory to
Venezuelan reality was stressed repeatedly. Extended analysis of
recent national history was developed in the process of calling
for a new, truly popularly based revolutionary struggle, "a
confrontation between the poor and the rich, among those who have
and those who do not have--to translate the expressive English
phrase of haves and have nots. All the abstractions that we
revolutionaries employ--imperialism, neo-colonialism, etc.--can be
reduced to a simple and comprehensive formula: for Venezuela to
rise from below, so that it can realize its historic destiny of a
small world power, the poor, those who have nothing, must throw
out of power the rich and expel the Americans from the country."[97]
Orthodoxies about the stages of revolution were challenged, and
it was argued that the workers constituted but one of several

socioeconomic sectors necessary for achieving socialism in Venezuela. Overriding all else was the insistence upon internal dialogue, self-criticism, and doctrinal flexibility in the quest for true revolution. "Understanding the reality of this decade of the 70s...is an unpostponable task if we try to shape a contemporary revolutionary reply to contemporary problems and find a Venezuelan socialist solution to the many specific ills of Venezuela."[98]

Linked to masista ideological commitments was the outlook of its candidate, a political independent. His views rested less on philosophical grounds than on a profound social conscience.[99] This contributed to a blend of theoretical and pragmatic perspectives in the campaign platform. The tone was aptly suggested by Secretary General Pompeyo Márquez at the official inscription of the Rangel candidacy on 19 June 1973. "The struggle that we have undertaken against the imperialist system in our country has brought us to present to the Nation a program of transformations that serve to liquidate injustice, inefficiency, and a harmful type of contemporary life for the immense majority of Venezuelans. We believe that in denouncing the present state of things...we must utilize all possible means to confront that system concretely, in spite of the institutional opportunism that is put into play, along with repression unleashed against those who question it."[100] The Programa del MAS, in conjunction with Rangel's appearance before Pro-Venezuela and with Tiempo de Verdades, provides a clear picture of the campaign ideology and doctrine.[101]

The Programa itself was presented by Rangel on 22 June 1973 in Caracas's Hotel El Conde.[102] Divided into eight chapters, the document began with an introductory accounting of the ills of Venezuelan society. Setting forth a diagnostic-analytic approach, it moved swiftly into a structural analysis of contemporary Venezuela, which stood out as the highlight of the Programa. A searing critique of capitalist dependency in Venezuela combined deductive reasoning with a heavy reliance upon socioeconomic data. For example: "Characterization of dependent capitalism is founded on evidence that foreign capital today occupies a position of frank domination in the fundamental branches of our economy. Its power controls absolutely the primary exporting sector (petroleum, iron) and carries decisive importance in the manufacturing industry and in commerce and services. Put another way, it dominates more than two thirds of the production of goods and nearly 40 percent of the Gross National Product, generating more than 70 percent of the fiscal income...and 96 percent of export business."[103]

Rangel had written along similar lines, denouncing Latin America's servitude to North American economic interests. "Evidently we must continue subsidizing with our resources the powerful nation of the North: misery subsidizing opulence. You have here an absurd relationship that positively cannot continue."[104] The portrayal of Venezuela continued through sections on the formation of dependent capitalism, the exploitation of the workers, the privilege of capitalists, and the structural crisis of dependent capitalist growth.

Moving from sharp criticism of reality to a somewhat utopian

image of an idealized "new society," the Programa envisaged a
humane system that relied upon participation and self-management
of economic activities. Bureaucratization and rigidification of
the state were recognized as potential evils to be avoided. Dangers
of statism could not be disregarded, for "in an organization like
the State, as historical experience shows, tendencies are manifested
to generate private interests and conservative attitudes and to
convert into privilege the fulfillment of its social role. In all
this the fundamental thing would be criticism, divergence or protest
of popular origin, so that the socialist society will be absolutely
legitimate and recognized as such...."[105]
    A subchapter on the ultimate withering of the state was
inserted as further evidence of alertness to inherent perils.
Workers' organizations at various levels would participate in
economic enterprises, contributing to decisions about production,
the distribution of income, investment policy, the setting of
pay, and all other matters of importance. "Besides, part of the
property socialized will be entrusted to workers' cooperatives.
Thus certain functions and channels of distributions can be
submitted to the control of producers or consumers."[106]
    Specific policy recommendations gave flesh to the programmatic
skeleton. There would be extensive nationalization, although
concentrated almost entirely on heavy industry. Petroleum was
included, although the MAS emphasized that it was not justifying
its nationalization on a priori ideological grounds.
Nationalization within the capitalist model would merely fortify
the power of Venezuelan capitalism. Therefore it was important
that oil be truly "socialized," a process to be placed at the
service of all Venezuelans. Nationalization would not be applied
universally throughout the economy, for the program anticipated
different degrees and forms of individual property alongside
society-wide ownership of the largest enterprises. Attention and
assistance to small and medium industries would permit a mutually
beneficial collaboration of owners and the state. "Medium and
small businesses, for their part, will be able to have in the new
planned economy the security of full utilization of its productive
potential, as well as markets and a level of benefit compatible
with social ends." Such measures would lead to the establishment
of a new system of ownership and property. "In it the decisive
place will be occupied by a public or social area, in which will
be concentrated the fundamental means for the realization of new
economic activity. It will have, besides, a mixed area, that is
the fruit of agreements between businesses and institutions of the
social area and those private ones in which interests and
motivations...are compatible with those appropriate and essential
for all society. And there can exist, finally, an area of private
property constituted by small and medium businesses within the
limits and under the social control already shown."[107]
    Nationalization of Venezuelan capitalists' enterprises--a step
not contemplated in the Nueva Fuerza platform--drew the greatest
public attention when the program was first unveiled. Chapter 2,
entitled "Basamento y Función del Poder Político," first specified

twenty "supermillionaires" whose property was to be immediately expropriated; then followed a second hierarchy of national capitalists, and last a third category consisting of managerial figures representing powerful ecnonomic enterprises that included important foreign interests.[108] Foreign-owned or dominated enterprises would be taken over by the socialist state. Dependency, which inside Venezuela included the exploitation of the provinces by the monopolistic capitalism of the central core, would also be attacked through the high priority to be assigned budgetary allocations for the countryside. Industry would be reoriented so that its development would be based on domestic needs rather than the vagaries of the international market. And similarly, foreign trade policy should derive from Venezuelan industrialization, instead of the reverse, thereby "also serving to break colonial dependency."[109]

Among proposals in the social realm were an increase of workers' wages, a rise in employment, more public housing, reduction in the cost of public services, provision of free medical services and effective public education, and liberation of Venezuelan women from oppression. Not as fully articulated as earlier sections dealing with ownership, property, and the means of production, such recommendations nonetheless received serious attention from the candidate himself. His appearance before Pro-Venezuela dwelt at length upon social and human problems. It was the very inhumanity of capitalism that was the great evil, for it had accentuated marginality, poverty, and underdevelopment. Thus, he argued, 50 percent of the population in metropolitan Caracas lived in ranchos; 70 percent of all Venezuelan children were undernourished; foreign monopolies and their agents were systematically despoiling the economy of its natural riches at the same time that the human environment was deteriorating. Only socialism could bring a halt to the domination of national life by money and material values that mitigated against the interests of over ten million Venezuelans.[110]

The diagnostic tone of the MAS program contributed to its strength of presentation. Perhaps the opening words best summarized the foundation upon which it rested: "The simple observation of Venezuelan reality teaches us that our society functions in a manner opposed to the interests of the immense majority of Venezuelans."[111] For José Vicente Rangel, this underlying conviction in the manifest incapacity of the existing system to improve conditions determined his campaign. The concluding words of Tiempo de Verdades give added flavor to his disillusionment with the present but abiding faith in the future:

> There is a place for hope for Venezuelans. The extraordinary richness of the country, the human quality of our people, prepare the way for faith and for the struggle. Economic groups, foreign capital, parties that serve those interests, in short, all the present establishment work for the cultivation of pessimism....

The country is in frank retrocession. It
is impoverished day by day, industrial and
agricultural indices decrease, an immense mass
of money has to be dedicated to subsidize food
stuffs and purchases from abroad, unemployment
grows, education is dislocated and the system
of assistance is in crisis. For more than ten
million Venezuelans there is no alternative
within this system. Only a minority is
benefitting from national wealth. And what must
be realized by the majority of exploited, of
marginal people, is that the rich and the
privileged can live in that manner, in opulence
and extravagance, by the exploitation of others.
The day that the majority of Venezuelans decide
to put an end to that exploitation, social and
economic imbalances will end. Factories can
continue functioning without the control of the
rich; the real order, based on justice and the
distribution of wealth, can replace the disorder
and chaos of capitalism. Men and women can open
the way to the conquest of the new society. The
only thing that is needed is organization, to
participate, to struggle until the defeat of
pessimism, to take consciousness of power, of
that immense popular power that only socialism
can achieve in Venezuela.[112]

Although treated as a leftist candidate, Jóvito Villalba
largely defied ideological or programmatic categorization. His
criticism of the "status" parties was no less damning than that of
the Nueva Fuerza or MAS, but his program lacked doctrinal definition.
A thirteen-point grab bag of promises couched in campaign rhetoric,
the platform included the following: "war to the death" against
the high cost of living and hoarding black marketeers; creation of
a ministry of employment, with jobs for all citizens; compensation
of half-salary and 10 percent per child to each unemployed family;
a strong government against crime; autonomous universities and
schools, with aid to popular and democratic education; an end to
political repressions, and total amnesty for perezjimenistas and
for the revolutionary left. Among other planks of his "Bolivarian
revolution" were agrarian reform with abundant land, credit, and
technology; a health service with socialized medicine; prompt
nationalization of petroleum and iron; immediate reform of the
income tax law "so that the rich minority pays the 500 million
bolívares necessary to help the abandoned"; extension of the labor
law to the peasantry; and opposition to the culture of oil and
imperialist dependency, to be replaced by a "cultural revolution
for youth and creation of a ministry for Scientific Investigation
and Advanced Studies."[113]
    The Villalba interview with El Nacional provided his fullest
statement.[114] On the subject of oil his position was less

unqualified than the platform had suggested. Stating that Venezuela could not wait until 1983, he also maintained that reversion procedures were incapable of protecting national interests. Nationalization was desirable for three reasons: the increased demand on the international market, and Venezuela's need to be free from United States influence; his belief that 95 percent of the technical employees were now Venezuelan; and the preparation of CVP to increase its responsibility while Venezuelan firms operate formerly foreign enterprises. However, Villalba believed that nationalization should be undertaken only by a strong government which, in addition to enjoying a popular consensus, had also called military men from active duty into important government posts. Tied to this was Villalba's further contention that foreign investment should be subjected to greater limitations. It should never be permitted through credit, which meant national savings; neither should it be oriented toward commerce or the service sectors; and it should be applicable to industrial areas only if technology had to be imported, and then only temporarily. These and lesser measures, then, made up the platform of the movement its candidate variously termed bolivarian, nationalist, revolutionary, and leftist.

THE POLITICAL RIGHT

The Villalba program lacked clear bases or orientation, but the same was not necessarily true of the Venezuelan right. Pedro Tinoco best expressed the views of that persuasion. Publication of his book El Estado Eficaz in August 1973, which Tinoco described as containing the basic message of the Movimiento Desarrollista, provided the foundation for his program.[115] The electorate was offered two basic norms—government with authority and administration with efficiency. "This means a government capable of satisfactorily providing essential public services, to give protection and security to the people and to utilize our great public resources to promote national development and the well being of all Venezuelans."[116] The crisis for Venezuela was not that of the political system but rather one of growth and development predicated upon structural and functional deficiencies. Desarrollismo or "developmentalism" meant not an abstract dogma or ideology but an administrative approach to the development of man and of Venezuela. The former treasury minister told one interviewer that desarrollismo "is the intense promotion of development, giving force to decisions required to expand all productive efforts and to achieve the greatest number of qualitative advances in different techniques and in the very quality of life."[117] The maladministration that the nation had experienced for decades was the root cause of national ills.

Tinoco advocated reforms at various levels within the public administration. First were structural reforms permitting the substitution of new and streamlined mechanisms. As outlined in El Estado Eficaz, the practical effect would have been to consolidate and centralize national administrative bodies under a small number of virtual "super ministries," with geographic dispersion from Caracas tightly controlled by the authority of a small number of

individuals.[118] He would introduce a form of managerial control
whereby the state would carry forward direct action in the field of
production and services, converting existing inefficiency into
desired effectiveness.[119] For Tinoco, "the errors of Public
Administration were owing less to parties and to men than to the
existence of antiquated structures, of inoperative systems and of
inadequate procedures." The sole solution was that of "modernizing
its structures, its systems and its procedures."[120] The consequence
of such reforms would be a mobilization of Venezuela's human
resources within an open, pluralistic society. Democratic planning
and free enterprise would carry the day.

Desarrollismo, Tinoco argued, would lead to an expansion of
society's productive forces, with administrative reforms permitting
a truly scientific and systematic strategy of development.
Embodying a technologically inspired faith in progress and the
dominion of objectivity over emotion, Tinoco implicitly shared a
belief in "the end of ideology." As one observer noted,
"Desarrollismo is a movement of ideas and principles of a
programmatic character, which has as it objective the effort to
resolve complex national problems. When it is presented as
anti-ideological it is because it establishes the primacy of the
objectivity of analysis in place of the emotionalism and very
unilateral nature of political partisanship, just as technical and
scientific treatment is the first step toward a solution,
substituting for demagogic manipulation with electoral or
proselytizing ends, as the majority of existing parties are
accustomed to do."[121] Tinoco spoke to Fedecámaras of "the fruit of
democratic planning,...in whose formulation all those who were
going to be agents or executors of essential tasks would be
involved." With the creation of the "estado eficaz," essential
principles of modern administrative science "which have permitted
the achievement of the diverse economic miracles of this century,
are applied to public management, and we will be able to have an
efficient state, efficient management of development, and efficient
promoter of development."[122]

Without delving into the details of Tinoco's official Programa
de Gobierno, we can select a few proposals to provide a sense of
the full orientation. Views on petroleum policy were strikingly
different from those of most other candidates. Tinoco's basic
thesis held that Venezuela should sell as much oil as it could at
the highest possible price. The Orinoco Tar Belt was a resource
that should be exploited commercially at the earliest possible
time. The country would thereby be in a position to increase
production and sales in the near future. "When demand for a
product is rising, when the price is rising, and when one has vast
and immense quantities of the same, that is the moment to increase
activity in order to augment substantially the country's income."
To those who argued that oil in the ground is of more value with
prices rising, he retorted that the rise in prices of products
bought with petroleum income vitiated the argument. Better, in his
view, was maximal production in order to undertake "an ambitious
program of expansion of all our basic industrial activities, in

priority areas, where clear natural advantages favor us, such as those of steel, petrochemicals, gas, and aluminum."[123] Another source of disagreement with other candidates was his unenthusiastic view of Venezuelan membership in the Andean Pact. He regarded entry as having been unwise and ill-timed, seeing the Caribbean rather than Andean region as geographically the most logical for Venezuela.

As the campaign progressed and Tinoco's efforts to secure the endorsement of Pérez Jiménez became more urgent, he frequently referred to the former dictator as Venezuela's "first desarrollista," suggesting that Venezuelans did not appreciate the qualities of the Pérez Jiménez government until after its departure.[124] Tinoco was to terminate one of his several transatlantic flights of supplication to Madrid with an explicit avowal of Marcos Pérez Jiménez's own message to the electorate. Presented in mid-1973, the former dictator's so-called Decalogue of Shame was indicative of perezjimenista thinking.[125] "The great evils that presently exist in Venezuela," it began, "have the common characteristic of being avoidable evils, and if they have succeeded in putting down roots, it has been by the ineptitude or bad faith of many governments and the ingenuousness, passivity and irresponsibility of the minorities which govern. Therefore, such evils merit the classification of shameful, and therefore the Decalogue that contains them must be titled THE DECALOGUE OF SHAME."[126]

Ten were cited, each followed by brief elaboration: delinquency, rancho, underemployment and unemployment, bureaucracy, public debt, clandestine immigration, partisan penetration of institutions, deterioration of services, economic colonialism, and incapacity for recovering and defending territory. Guilt was placed squarely upon the AD and COPEI, with highly selective and frequently noncomparable data employed to enhance the perezjimenista image. This was followed in turn by ten remedies for the sins of the decálogo, sometimes referred to irreverently as the dictator's "Ten Commandments." Sections calling for the reform of state structures, the national economy, the constitution, and public education were singularly devoid of specific content. Proposals for a "new internal policy" and "new foreign policy" were similarly imprecise. Venezuelans were assured of a worsening array of national evils should they vote for either COPEI or AD. The Madrid exile characterized his own ideals as those of authentic nationalism.

Of the other programs, little need be added. With one exception--Miguel Angel Burelli Rivas--none contributed to the programmatic debate.[127] Although Burelli was not a serious contender, his views on a variety of institutional and electoral problems would merit attention in studying possible systemic reforms for the years ahead.[128]

For an overview of the programs of the major candidates, see table 13.

Table 13. Programmatic Emphases, 1973

	Development and Society	Human Resources	Agriculture	Industry	Foreign Policy	Special Emphases
Fernández	Fundamental concern for individual; social along with economic growth; state responsibility for all citizens	Education for all; attention to family; end of unemployment; population growth without controls; Instituto de Barrios	Acceleration of growth; general modernization; progress; favors agroindustry	Strong support of industrialization; increasing role of state; protectionism; rationalization	Ideological pluralism; recognition of Cuba; support for regional and Latin American collaboration	Continuation, extension of programs of Caldera administration
Pérez	Reorganization, modernization of state; juridical reforms; revitalize initiative; attention to problems of marginal citizens	Education for all; war on poverty; improve distribution of wealth; full employment; controlled population growth	Highest priority; central to economic development; structural reforms; protection of small farmer	State control of basic industries; strict supervision of foreign capital; regionalization	Reorganize OAS; openness to relations with Cuba; support for regional and Latin American collaboration	Rural development, agricultural progress the key to national development; need to prove viability of democracy in Venezuela
Paz	Full socialization; remove domestic and international imperialism; eliminate internal exploitation; state control of all resources	Income redistribution; reduce food and medical prices; free milk for children; wages pegged to prices; socialize medicine	Nationalize agroindustry; create collective farms; liquidate latifundio and emancipate peasant	Nationalize industry and basic services in twelve months; limit foreign investment; participation of workers	Extend relations to Cuba, China, North Vietnam, etc.; cancel contract with U.S. military mission; fulfill existing commitments	National liberation through socialist democracy; gradual evolution toward socialism; neutralize COPEI and AD; follow Chilean example (until September)
Rangel	Rescue have-nots of society; emancipation from capitalism; worker participation; nationalize domestic capitalists; emphasis on human problems	Free medical service; strict price controls; liberate women; increase wages, employment; confront inhumanity, marginality	High budgetary priority; emphasize domestic, not international markets; eliminate exploitation	Nationalize basic industry; state collaboration with small and medium industry	Extend relations to include all socialist regimes; support Latin American organs; isolate U.S. from hemispheric organizations	Eradicate domestic and foreign imperialism; devise distinctively Venezuelan model; importance of dialogue
Tinoco	Streamline administrative structures; centralize national organs, agencies; expand productive forces; such development meets all problems	Improve education; more mobs; improve capacity of population; better health services	Increase productivity by improved managerial methods; previous reforms failed from incompetence	Improve small and medium industry; full reliance on managers, technicians of private industry; general expansion	Pro-U.S. policies; improve Caribbean ties; deemphasize Andean regionalism; close ties with Brazil and similar regimes	Administrative efficiency; priority to private interests and foreign investments; increase oil production

PART III
CAMPAIGN IMPLEMENTATION

7. STYLES, IMAGES, AND COMMUNICATIONS

No other political campaign in Latin America has been as richly endowed with political communications, use of media, and intensive public relations activities as the Venezuelan campaign of 1973. For two years the voters were inundated with an outpouring of propaganda; methods ranged from traditional outdoor rallies to the most modern of media techniques. Slogans, singing commercials, television specials, automobile caravans, movie shorts, billboards, public opinion polls, press conferences, partisan newspaper editorials—every imaginable method was tried at one time or another. The extravagance of expenditures was such that only COPEI and AD could mount full-blown efforts. For the others, a variety of measures were employed in hopes of compensating for limited funds. Criticisms of the campaign centered not only on its length and cost, but upon the content of political communications. A distinction was frequently drawn between propaganda and publicity, with the former regarded as legitimate and necessary transmission of political information, and the latter concerned with the selling of a candidate as if a commercial product.

With few exceptions, the individual campaigns incorporated both presentational and participatory elements, although emphases varied greatly. Furthermore, the personality and style of a candidate bore directly on the image that could or should be projected. Certainly the quality of personal style as well as the image of political leadership was central to the task of political communications. Efforts were made to maximize the relative strengths and reduce the weaknesses of presentational and participatory techniques. Given the importance of personalism in Venezuelan politics, all of these were of crucial importance in projecting a candidate before the electorate. Our VENEVOTE data suggest that the participatory dimension was by no means diminished by the spread of mass media techniques.[1] When asked if they attended campaign meetings, 33.9 percent of our respondents replied in the affirmative, and 15.5 percent had gone to several. Moreover—testifying to the personal aspects of Venezuelan campaigning—58.7 percent had been close to or personally met one of the candidates. By the time of our survey 17.7 and 17.4 percent reported contact with Fernández and Pérez respectively, followed by 7.2 percent for Rangel and 4.7 percent for Paz Galarraga.

Presentational exposure reflected the particular importance of television and radio. A total of 63.8 percent had listened to a speech, and 17.8 percent claimed to have heard "many" such programs. Asked more specifically if they had seen any of the candidates' television programs, 55.6 percent replied in the affirmative. As to reading, 56.8 percent reported having read about the campaign in newspapers or magazines. This broke down into 38.8 percent who had read "a little," 12.7 percent "some," and 5.3 percent "much." Asked more generally about the campaign, 48.2 percent of the respondents said that someone had tried to influence them in favor of a specific presidential candidate. Slightly over half reported interest in the campaign; it was of "great" interest for 18.5 percent and of "some" interest for 34.7 percent, leaving 46.8 percent professing none whatever. At the same time, 93.8 percent believed that the results of the presidential election were important, and 68.2 percent stated that it mattered very much to them which party won. The level of citizen attention and involvement, in short, generally confirmed the intuitive judgments of candidates and party leaders. And by 1973, the expansion of the Venezuelan media guaranteed ample facilities for the implementation and dissemination of political messages.[2]

THE SOCIAL CHRISTIAN PARTY COPEI

Lorenzo Fernández was scarcely a figure unfamiliar to national politics. Born in Caracas on 8 January 1918, he was educated at the Colegio La Salle and at the Universidad Central de Venezuela, where he graduated summa cum laude in law in 1942. Fernández and Caldera had first come together in the tumultuous university climate immediately following the death of Juan Vicente Gómez and the transfer of authority to Eleazar López Contreras. When Caldera founded the UNE on 8 May 1936, he was accompanied by some hundred students, among them Lorenzo Fernández. In a short time Caldera and Fernández were fast friends and trusted political colleagues, an association that carried the two young students to the leadership of the Republic. Fernández and Caldera were among the small group that began publishing the weekly UNE in August 1936; the first Congress of the UNE was convened in 1939; formation of Acción Electoral carried Fernández to his first elected post as a municipal councilman in Caracas, while Caldera and Pedro José Lara Peña[3] went to Congress. The organization soon assumed the name Acción Nacional, and COPEI itself came into existence on 13 January 1946. The JRC was founded in 1947, with its leaders numbering such important future Social Christians as Luis Herrera Campins, Rodolfo José Cárdenas, and Valmore Acevedo. Caldera and Fernández remained in effective control of the young party, with the former the theoretician and the latter more concerned with practical matters. Both served in the Constituent Assembly.

Though not endorsing the military golpe de estado in 1948, COPEI attempted to remain active politically until the perezjimenista electoral fraud of 1952. Thereafter Caldera and Fernández were at their lawyers' desks and remained largely outside public affairs until the final days of the dictatorship. Upon the restoration of elected government and the coalition government under Rómulo Betancourt, copeyano participation included that of Lorenzo Fernández as minister of development.[4] Later, when COPEI opposed the Leoni government under the slogan Autonomy of Action, Fernández was of indispensable assistance in beating back an internal challenge to Caldera's domination. Once Caldera assumed the presidency in 1969, Fernández was appointed to the crucial Ministry of Interior Relations and twice served as acting president during Caldera absences from Venezuela. Resigning from the cabinet on 22 January 1972 to seek the presidential nomination, he was chosen the Social Christian candidate on March 18.

The events surrounding the nominating convention contributed to a public image that was somewhat misleading. Fernández was more than simply a friend of the chief of state, for by the time of his nomination, he had spent more than a quarter-century in political life, including service as councilman, deputy, senator, and cabinet minister, while laboring at the right hand of one of Venezuela's most brilliant party organizers and leaders. An administrator and executive by nature, Fernández was a somewhat pedestrian public personality whose forte lay in individual exchange and small group discussion. An avuncular figure whose speeches were less than incisive, the nominee appeared older than his years. Rarely appearing without his tabaco cumanense--the fine cigars produced in the Cumaná area--the portly candidate projected a personal style and appearance that contrasted with that of Pérez.

Fernández's first task had been binding up the wounds left by the intensive pre-convention campaign and the bruising events at the Teatro Radio City. For several months he worked toward a renewal of party unity. This process was still continuing when the adeco nominee began his own campaigning. COPEI, having thus lost important initiative in the communications arena, was soon forced to react to the Pérez image of firm leadership and a strong hand. Fernández could not compete directly with Pérez on such grounds; style, temperament, inclination, and even health mitigated against it. Consequently, the campaign image the Social Christian experts began to project was that of Fernández as pacifier, as paternal unifier of the Venezuelan family.

Thus the tranquil, comforting father figure of Lorenzo was opposed to Carlos Andrés's drive and dynamism. COPEI had little choice in its presentation of the candidate, and its campaign managers insisted that, as Alvarez Paz remarked, "We have projected the image of Lorenzo Fernández as he is, neither adding nor subtracting anything." When the candidate returned to the campaign in early 1973 after several weeks in Europe,[5] the party began to intensify its efforts. If, as some believed, the contest with the AD were to be characterized by the opposition of COPEI's implacable party machinery to the vitality of Pérez, then the communications effort would have to be maximal. Fernández placards inundated the nation, and especially Caracas, which one foreign journalist

described as covered not by meters, but by acres of pictures,
posters, and slogans.[6] The dimension of such Fernández propaganda
was unprecedented, outstripping even the very substantial adeco
effort. Major arteries were awash with thousands of triangular
green pennants, and a smiling Lorenzo beamed down on passersby from
walls, lamp posts, and billboards.[7]

The slogans were numerous, none of which really caught hold.
Among those used more widely were: Siga sonriendo, Lorenzo
Presidente ("keep smiling, Lorenzo President"); Y este año, Lorenzo
("and this year, Lorenzo"); and Lorenzo es liberación ("Lorenzo
means liberation"). All were relatively bland and lackluster. In
the latter stages of the campaign, emphasis on Fernández's
unification of the Venezuelan pueblo was stressed in such phrases
as el hombre que está uniendo al país ("the man who is unifying the
country"). A sixteen-page Sunday supplement in July, hailing the
eleventh of the month as the "national day of popular unity,"
presented the candidate at the apogee of paternal affection for his
people. Amply illustrated by pictures of the candidate exchanging
greetings and abrazos with Venezuelans of different ages, sexes,
and occupations, the tabloid pressed the theme of unification to
the heights of repetition and exaggeration. His ceremonial trip
to Europe was described as a mission by which he carried to the
world the message of a united people, an event "without precedent
in Venezuelan political history as prologue to a new united
Venezuela." Among others were, to cite but a few: "Venezuela is
united with Lorenzo because the hour has arrived for those who
have least"; "We Venezuelan women who believe in peace as a base
of progress are united with Lorenzo"; and "from house to house,
street to street, village to village, Lorenzo is unifying the
country."[8]

The candidate's personal appearances consistently emphasized
massive meetings at the expense of individual contacts. Typically
he would fly from Caracas toward the end of the week, spend two or
three days in a large urban center, then return home once again.
During a campaign visit the copeyano machinery was heavily employed
in assuring the largest possible mass rally, replete with music
and entertainment, local leaders, and electronic gimmickry. The
candidate would eventually appear, deliver a brief speech, and
depart the podium. Far less time was spent in direct personal
contact by Fernández than by Pérez, Paz, and Rangel. Thus COPEI's
campaign managers in large part converted the mass
rally—traditionally viewed as a participatory technique—into a
presentational form. The apparatus produced the crowds, the
entertainment and festivity were provided, the candidate spoke from
the platform, and then he was gone. Smaller meetings with local
notables were sometime held, but these too were less frequent than
with other candidates. Thus the Fernández campaign trips, which
concentrated on cities rather than smaller towns and villages,
permitted the candidate to be seen by throngs of thousands, but
with less personal exchange and dialogue than his opponents.

For the other candidates, a return to the capital from the
field was an opportunity for meeting with party strategists, a

press conference, a day or two stumping the barrios, and television
appearances--in short, continuing campaign activity. For Fernández,
however, the time in Caracas was, at least to the public eye, one
of inactivity.[9] To cite a typical instance, the Social Christian
candidate spent over two weeks in mid-August virtually without
public campaigning. Although his taped television programs
appeared, there were only two live appearances--one an indoor
speech to the Venezuelan Association of Executives, and another to
a similar group. Otherwise he was presumably secluded in his home.[10]
In the meantime, Wolfgang Larrazábal was in the barrios of Caracas
on Fernández's behalf; FDP Secretary General Dáger was stumping
the interior in the company of Pedro Pablo Aguilar; and Eduardo
Fernández and others on the Comisión Electoral Metropolitana were
also campaigning daily. Although by the conclusion of the
campaign party advertisements spoke of Lorenzo's making his fifth
swing of Venezuela, the fact remained that monster meetings based
on official party organization were the order of the day and that
the candidate's personal effort was far less arduous than that of
his rivals.

COPEI's public relations experts did their utmost to disguise
the candidate's relative inactivity. A typical copeyano newspaper
advertisement would fill the top third of the space with a large
picture of Fernández and the hours of his weekly television
programs, while large print urged the reader to see on television
a friendly president in dialogue with his people (vea por televisión
a un Presidente amigo que dialoga con su pueblo). Beneath this
was the second portion of the advertisement with a box listing
locations and times for local party rallies in metropolitan Caracas;
although the candidate would not be present, another headline
proclaimed Lorenzo Un Presidente Amigo. The bottom third announced
that "Zulia was united with Lorenzo," and there was a picture of
the candidate greeting a small child. The picture might have been
taken anywhere and any time; Fernández's most recent trip to Zulia
had been more than a week earlier. At the very bottom was
additional prose informing the reader of the outpouring of warmth
for the candidate at the recent meeting in Cumaná; without saying
so, there was a clear implication that Fernández had appeared.
Actually, however, the Cumaná rally had been the so-called
Chipichipazo at which Dáger and Aguilar were featured speakers.[11]

Fernández had three weekly programs that were broadcast on
television and radio: "Lorenzo Invita," "Uniendo al País," and
"El Mensaje de Lorenzo."[12] Formats emphasized discussion between
the candidate and a small number of guests; in other cases there
were film clips showing Fernández on the campaign trail. Copeyano
media and public opinion experts who played an important role
included Paco Correa and Carlos de Gregorio. North American
campaign specialist Matt Reese, a Washington-based consultant who
had once worked for John and Robert Kennedy, provided additional
counseling. Press relations were the responsibility of the
Secretaría Nacional de Información y Propaganda, under the direction
of Carlos Rodríguez Ganteaume. Among its other responsibilities
was the thrice-weekly full-page advertisement "COPEI DICE," over

250 of which had been written by the close of the campaign.[13]   A
separate agency served as the official press office for the candidate
himself. Coordination between Fernández's press service and the
party information office was imperfect, although sufficient to avoid
obvious public error or contradictions. The nominee also received
publicity from the FDP, as well as the various groups of independents.
     An important media issue for the Social Christian campaign was
the question of a television debate with Pérez. The first such
exchange by presidential contenders had been a highlight of the
1963 campaign, when Rafael Caldera and Arturo Uslar Pietri appeared
together.[14]   It had not been possible to arrange similar meetings
in 1968, although the televised exchange between Arístides Calvani
and Ramón Díaz over alleged fascist elements in the copeyano
campaign platform had provided an exciting program.[15]   For 1973,
while various candidates sought public exposure in debating Pérez
and Fernández, the adeco candidate ignored them and pressed his
own challenge to his copeyano rival. The AD was confident that
its candidate would more than hold his own and announced its
willingness to work out necessary details. The Social Christian
campaign managers wanted no part of such an exchange, although the
candidate himself was unafraid. Once Fernández had been convinced
to abstain, it remained for COPEI to put the best face on its
rejection of the challenge.[16]   Oswaldo Alvarez Paz told one
interviewer somewhat laconically that it was unwise, for the AD
"would use the debate as a boxing ring."[17]   The AD, seeking the
maximum advantage, then began publicizing its challenge widely.
     In a public relations ploy which its experts regarded as
daringly brilliant,[18] large adeco advertisements appeared with
flanking pictures of Pérez and Fernández, announcing the time and
station for their respective television programs. The major
caption asked its readers "which of these two men is best prepared
to govern Venezuela?" In the best commercial vein, Venezuelans
were being asked to try and compare.[19]   Alvarez Paz denied any
fear of confrontation, arguing that there was no reason for
Fernández to play the AD game, or to provide Pérez additional
exposure. As Fernández had completed over six hundred days'
campaigning before the people, there was no purpose in a special
program to explain the distinguished career with which all
Venezuelans were familiar.[20]   The candidate himself later responded
to a question before Pro-Venezuela, saying:

> I am not going to fall into foolishness over the
> debate because a person who is going to govern the country
> cannot go on television to conduct guerrilla actions before
> his people. That candidate expresses his program of government
> on television and I express mine; then there is no sense in
> our going on television to express our programs of government.
> I do not have to go on television to say that I graduated as
> a lawyer Summa Cum Laude, that I have been professor and
> teacher for over 20 years, that I practiced my profession
> successfully, that I participated successfully in private
> business, that I have been Councilman, Deputy, Senator,

Minister of Fomento and of Interior Relations, Ambassador, and on two occasions Acting President of the Republic. But if one speaks of expressing his antecedents and his merits for struggle, while some went into exile to struggle there against the dictatorship, I myself stayed here....To go on television to express personal foolishness makes no sense for one who aspires to govern a country.[21]

The AD understandably returned to the question of a debate frequently, and eventually COPEI and its candidate fell silent on the challenge, which was never accepted.

Party propagandists staunchly maintained the themes of pacification and unification of the national family. Lorenzo was increasingly described by the slogan Lorenzo, un Presidente Amigo,[22] and pictures of the candidate with his wife, ten children, and assorted grandchildren were widely displayed. The pace of campaigning was not altered until the very end of the campaign, when he met seven mass rallies throughout the country in eight days, concluding one in Caracas on December 5.[23] Even then, the pattern was that of large popular mobilizations, and Fernández's appearance was treated more like a triumphal reception than a candidate explaining his program and asking for votes. In public speeches he was expansive with generalities and parsimonious with specifics; his platform style was lugubrious and funereal, occasionally broken with somewhat abrupt and agitated interludes. This inevitably placed a burden on copeyano media experts, and the perhaps unavoidable response was to increase the propaganda in volume and magnitude.

As already suggested, however, quality and creativity were not hallmarks of the Social Christian campaign. The Fernández image, if an unexciting one, was perfectly valid and yet was never fully effective. Party experts produced massive amounts of propaganda, apparently hoping to overwhelm the voter; in short, the more the better. Figures and numbers were to help convince the electorate. Examples are legion: the party announced that during his Pro-Venezuela appearance, the candidate answered 101 questions during 152 minutes, touching on a total of 141 different themes or topics; more than 600 days' campaigning were hailed as demonstrating an unprecedented commitment to the Venezuelan people; the national "Unity March" organized throughout the country for 24 November claimed the mobilization of "over one million Venezuelans in 200 different locations'; advertisements in the final weeks cited the thousands of people to have been visited by Fernández during the thousands of kilometers he had traveled in a given state, with appropriately impressive if meaningless figures filling in the blanks. Time and again COPEI's propaganda spoke of the biggest, the best, and the most. Even granted the natural exuberance and partisan hyperbole of an intense campaign, the claims were sometimes extraordinary and generally had little meaning unless the reader concluded that Fernández was so certain a winner that he too should vote for him.

The candidate himself was far from alone in the campaign. A

major asset was his wife Doña Olga, an attractive and exuberant
woman who thrived on public appearances. Both Wolfgang Larrazábal
and Jorge Dáger campaigned on behalf of Fernández; the two
efedepista leaders campaigned both singly and with copeyanos, as
Larrazábal sometimes accompanied Fernández and Dáger went with
Aguilar. The final weeks of the campaign, however, saw them
spending more time in areas where the FDP was hopeful of a good
showing and less in urban barrios--especially Caracas--where
Larrazábal might fill the vacuum. From COPEI itself, Fernández's
three rivals for the nomination were nearly invisible. Herrera
Campins did campaign some, largely in rural areas where, as he
noted after the elections, Fernández had not often gone. Edecio
La Riva was removed through appointment to an ambassadorial post,
while Arístides Beaujon was rarely in view at all. José Antonio
Pérez Díaz stayed near his post as president of Congress, and
COPEI's acting president Godofredo González was only occasionally
in the public eye. Eduardo Fernández labored arduously with the
electoral commission for metropolitan Caracas, which he chaired.
Other than the candidate himself, the party figures most in the
public eye were Pedro Pablo Aguilar and Oswaldo Alvarez Paz.

Of course, the Social Christian of greatest eminence, Rafael
Caldera, was scarcely irrelevant to the campaign. We have already
noted some of the exchanges between COPEI and the AD concerning
charges of government favoritism and ventajismo. Aside from either
direct or indirect support and influence from the government,
however, the copeyano campaign on behalf of Fernández was distinctive.
To begin with, it shared the supreme self-confidence of the
government and of Fernández--what critics viewed as arrogance--that
electoral victory was assured, indeed inevitable. But the
experienced politicians did not allow this to prevent hard work and
industry on behalf of the candidate. The consequence it may well
have encouraged, however, was the certainty that the cause was
just and that little real convincing or persuasion was necessary.
Imagination and intelligence were largely lacking in COPEI's media
presentations. The quality of campaign appeals was given fleeting
attention in the effort to outproduce, outsell, and outshout all
opposition, and most particularly the AD. Copeyano communications
excelled in volume, but not in quality.

The personality and style of Lorenzo Fernández was regarded
by some as a disadvantage. Certainly he stood in contrast to the
other leading aspirants, and the presentational nature of his
campaigning was strongly dependent upon both the party machinery
and its public relations experts. At the same time, however,
Fernández's political career had not been without substantial
accomplishment, and his own temperamental proclivities were by no
means inconsistent with the posture of the government and of COPEI.
It could be argued that the candidacy of a warm and fatherly man,
dedicated to an undramatic but progressive extension of government
policies, could prove appealing to the electorate. Yet there
seemed good reason to suspect that the party might have done better
in presenting its nominee in the best possible light.

Copeyano electronic festivals projected a hollow atmosphere, one that was scarcely improved by the frequently lackluster performance of the candidate. His speeches were disjointed in presentation, lacking in sustained momentum, and studded with jarring non sequiturs. Fernández's funereal tone, especially evident in radio commercials, induced somnolence rather than enthusiasm in the voter. Most importantly, COPEI failed to devise a media strategy that might utilize the candidate's individual qualities in a manner calculated to arouse public interest. Rather than undertake an effort to adapt to Lorenzo's own style and personality, the party campaign managers attempted instead to bury the public in public relations techniques and gimmickry. This helped to insure that the loss of initiative to AD image-builders in 1972 was never to be regained, and that the adeco surge in the final weeks of the campaign would not be matched.

ACCIÓN DEMOCRÁTICA

With the selection of Carlos Andrés Pérez, the AD leadership passed from the hands of its founding generation. Often a controversial figure, Pérez had risen to prominence through a traditional political route--ability, industry, and good fortune. Born in the Andean town of Rubio, Táchira, on 27 October 1922, at an early age he was drawn to politics, which suffused the air in which he developed. Under the tutelage of fellow andino Leonardo Ruiz Pineda,[24] he joined the PDN in the post-Gómez period at a time when it was cooperating with the communists in clandestine activity. Years later Pérez would say that it was he who put up the first communist propaganda in Rubio.[25] Later sent by his father to study in Caracas, he promptly became active in the newly organized AD. At age nineteen he was a delegate to the first party national convention. Four years later he interrupted his studies in law to become the private secretary to provisional president Rómulo Betancourt.

With an office in Miraflores, he learned of political power and its uses at the highest level from a master of the art. Upon the election of Rómulo Gallegos, Pérez became a deputy and short months later joined congressional president Valmore Rodríguez in the vain effort to set up a separate government in Maracay as the military overthrew Gallegos. Arrested, he began a decade that carried him in and out of prison and to eventual exile. He first returned to the study of law in Bogotá, but Colombian Conservatives engaged in the persecution of Liberals there soon proved hostile to adecos, whom they regarded as communists. After narrowly escaping death at the hands of Colombian security forces, he was delivered to their Venezuelan couterparts. From Andean jails he was sent to Puerto Ayacucho in Amazonas and finally expelled from the country once again. He followed Rómulo Betancourt to Cuba, but that visit also proved shortlived when Fulgencio Batista's March 1953 seizure of power made the country inhospitable to the Venezuelans. The next stop was Costa Rica, whose President José Figueres was sympathetic to the adecos. Nearly five years were to pass, with Pérez working on the pro-Figueres daily La República. With Pérez Jiménez's nocturnal flight from Venezuela on 23 January 1958, Pérez and the adecos joined the flood of returning political figures to the country. The 1958 elections returned Pérez to Congress as a deputy from Táchira, but he was called to government as director general of interior relations. In 1962 he succeeded resigning Minister Luis Augusto Dubuc and was projected more dramatically into political prominence. By the time of his accession to the office, the FALN had switched their strategy from rural insurrection to urban violence. Pérez was Betancourt's most effective lieutenant in those tumultuous days. To the left he became the bête noir of imperialist repression, and his unquestioned toughness created a "cop" image. Supporters saw him as a highly dedicated leader whose contribution had been central to the preservation of an elected, constitutional government being attacked by forces enjoying support from abroad. At the time, COPEI and Rafael Caldera were high in their praise of Pérez's performance and dedication.[26] Pérez's own view of his role has often been expressed: "It was a war, a war against subversion that we had to win."[27] During the years of the Leoni government Pérez served as AD parliamentary chief. A leader of betancurista forces, he was intimately involved in the long internal struggle that finally erupted in 1967. Becoming secretary general, Pérez worked with that stubborn tenacity sometimes ascribed to andinos. Although not without his critics within the party, Pérez entered the campaign with substantial support, and for the AD the legitimacy of his candidacy was unquestioned.

Customarily beginning the day with an hour of exercise, weight-lifting, and judo, Pérez was a brisk, no-nonsense administrator, a compulsively hard worker, and a vigorously physical person. Combined with his political reputation as being tough and disciplined, Pérez presented a clear personal style; the candidate himself made the fundamental decision to carry his message and present himself to every corner of the nation. He also determined that the emphasis would be placed on participatory techniques, although the presentational would not be ignored; that is, he would seek maximum direct personal contact, giving this priority over more traditional mass rallies. The AD candidate therefore initiated the peripatetic style that continued throughout his campaign, walking from airports to the center of towns, striding through slum areas, ever seeking direct contact with individual voters. This was soon to result in what party managers later characterized as a campaign with a common denominator--a unity of image and word.

A market study conducted by CORPA, the publicity firm responsible for the Pérez campaign, had confirmed the party belief that the Venezuelan electorate most desired strong, forceful leadership in its next chief executive. Régis Etiévan,[28] the head of CORPA, recommended a vigorous image. The slogan of Democracia con energía was adopted; although some feared that is was too strong, the candidate himself was pleased. So it was that the major AD slogan emerged. The picture of a smiling, happy candidate walking through throngs of joyous supporters was developed. The

party saw advantages in the "cop" image of its candidate, but it
also wanted to dispel the aversion of voters who might regard him
as rigid and inflexible. As Pérez toured the country, therefore,
his advisers worked to present him as openly engaged in frank
dialogue with his fellows, all the while maintaining a vigorous,
active dynamism. Although to some it appeared a contradiction in
terms, the undertaking proved highly successful. The candidate,
resolved to take his campaign to the people, conducted himself with
the tirelessness of an athlete. Dressed in colorful sports clothes
or sometimes in white, he would start a caminata or walk at the
head of a throng of followers, moving at a near-run through the
streets. Stopping frequently to greet local elders, pat babies,
and embrace mothers, he would exchange views on local problems and
then strike off again, followed by shoving, bustling crowds.

Pérez's impact was a powerful one, whether hiking five miles
from the airport to town, or sweeping through the streets of a small
village. His speed helped generate even greater enthusiasm and was
to produce a slogan that must rank as a classic in the annals of
Venezuelan campaigning. Early in his campaign during a brisk hike
through a small mountain village, an Andean woman was heard by
reporters to cry out ese hombre sí camina ("that man really does
walk").[29] The phrase was soon taken by Chelique Sarabia and
incorporated into a song of the same title, which became a public
favorite.[30] Combined with a widely used campaign poster--in which
a smiling candidate was walking with one arm upraised in greeting--
it further contributed to the single most sharply etched political
image of the year. Other campaign songs, all composed by Sarabia,
complemented the Pérez campaign. Va de frente y de cara capitalized
upon Lorenzo Fernández's refusal to debate on television, while
another popular song was Gracias a tí, Venezuela ya camina ("Thanks
to you, Venezuela is on the move"). Jingles, commercials,
advertisements, and all other forms of propaganda and of public
relations presented the same image of the candidate.[31] On campaign
swings, Pérez would intersperse press conferences, visits to radio
stations, and dinners attended by local supporters with an
unremitting schedule of caminatas. These would customarily be
concluded by a brief speech of some fifteen minutes; the candidate
would then speed away by auto caravan to another barrio, where he
would descend and hike another mile or so through the streets. The
emphasis was heavily on the informality and vitality of the
caminatas.

Pérez's public appearances invariably left a strong impression.
His Andean-accented Spanish, which critics mimicked, actually served
to underline his modest background and facilitated his appeal to
the popular classes. Apparent immunity to mud, rain, and steaming
heat further strengthened the image of a man of the people, one of
great telluric force. Leaping mud puddles or ascending steep
mountainsides to visit a home--events carefully recorded by
photographers--all contributed in positive fashion. Even the worst
of conditions were not permitted to deter him, as when a torrential
downpour on the mountain hillsides of Caracas slums in Santa
Rosalía sent cascading mud and sewage two feet deep upon the

candidate and his party.[32] A by-product of the Pérez campaign style
was the sustenance and insight gained by the experience. Even at
the conclusion of a long and tiring day, he visibly drew vitality
from contact with the people, and discussions lent further
understanding of local problems as faced by the lower classes. The
experience in Santa Rosalía, for example, was cited by the candidate
privately as well as publicly as having made him understand more
fully the problems of those living in such circumstances.

Like his copeyano counterpart, the adeco candidate had three
half-hour programs on television weekly: "Carlos Andrés Responde,"
"Carlos Andrés ante el País," and "Hablemos con Carlos Andrés."[33]
In the first, he occupied an arena surrounded by risers from which
members of the studio audience asked questions. Some were
occasionally planted, but this was generally unnecessary in that
news developments largely assured that important topics would be
raised. As the campaign progressed, television commercials and
spot announcements were often imaginative and invariably
professional, as was the case with the lengthy special shown shortly
before elections. Among the candidate's advisers, Diego Arria was
especially influential. Having joined the Pérez campaign team some
six months before elections, Arria's arrival by chance coincided
with the death of CORPA President Régis Etiévan. Along with the
expert contributions of CORPA's Sarabia, Viera, and Alfonso
Fernández, Arria provided insightful counsel and guidance.

The AD, like COPEI, also employed foreign advisers. The AD
contracted with F. Clifton White, Joe Napolitan, and Bob and Jane
Squier.[34] Squier, who had a $50,000 contract with Arria's Causa
Común, spent one week monthly in Caracas working with Venezuelan
media specialists; Napolitan spent three to five days monthly in
the country. Both COPEI and the AD were touchy about charges of
foreign interference in the campaign, which is why the use of such
advisers did not become public knowledge until a story appeared in
the Washington Post.[35] Napolitan explained that the activity was
not clandestine but that publicity was undesirable in view of
sensitivity over the importation of gringos. Reese, who provided
assistance to COPEI, initially refused to comment about his
involvement on behalf of Fernández. After a brief flurry between
Pedro Pablo Aguilar and Octavio Lepage the issue was dropped, since
both candidates were using such advisers. The general view was
expressed by Lepage, who told a press conference that the advice
concerned strictly technical matters, centering on the designing of
the newest techniques to reach the masses. The "technical" nature
of the assistance was offered as justification of the contention
that foreigners were not influencing national politics.[36]

The AD press campaign included the predictable "Página de
Acción Democrática," nearly two hundred of which had been published
by election day. This thrice-weekly full-page advertisement was
prepared by the party's Departamento Nacional de Información y
Propaganda,[37] with Antonio Stempel París playing an active part.
The appearance of a similar "page" by the PRN, presumably financed
by the AD, provided additional propaganda. An extremely useful
vehicle was also adopted in early October through weekly breakfasts

with the press. The candidate, meeting each Tuesday morning in the
restaurant El Portón, would make announcements and then open the
gathering to questioning. The timing was shrewd, for it was on
Tuesdays that President Caldera normally met in La Casona with the
leadership of COPEI, an occasion that generally produced favorable
news. Pérez's breakfasts thus helped to counteract possible
copeyano campaign propaganda while assuring the adeco candidate
wide attention in the media. The absence of a similar session with
Fernández may also have been advantageous to Pérez.[38]
     The pace of the candidate's campaign endured to the end,
although the pattern of travels was altered in late October.
Instead of the intensive swings through a particular state or
area--five days in Bolívar, four in Barinas, and the like--Pérez
emphasized so-called relámpago or lightning trips. Thus he would
fly from Caracas to a relatively populous area, hike through
selected portions of town, conclude with an evening meeting and
appearance, then return to the capital. He also gave extra
attention to certain critical locations, including Caracas,
Maracaibo, Valencia, and Barquisimeto. The latter was chosen for
the official presentation of the party platform on 17 November.[39]
There was the inevitable mass rally in Caracas on 29 November this
and Fernández's rally the following week were the two largest
meetings in Venezuelan history.[40] The climactic event for the AD
campaign was held on 6 December, the last day of the campaign.[41]
Implementing an idea suggested by Diego Arria in July, Pérez
conducted a marathon caminata in Caracas, marching from Catia in
the west to the Plaza Altamira in the east. Accompanied by a
festive, cheering throng which filled the streets along the route
for a good dozen blocks in front and behind, he covered the
distance of some twenty kilometers in under four hours, concluding
with a speech at the party's outdoor campaign site in Plaza
Altamira. It provided a dramatic, impressive, and characteristic
ending to the AD campaign.[42]
     Despite Pérez's constant motion, others were also busy. His
wife Doña Blanca was a warm and attractive person whose visits to
hospitals, orphanages, and teas contributed in positive fashion.
The party leadership was also active. Secretary General Lepage was
quite visible, and party president Gonzalo Barrios devoted time to
his weekly columns in El Nacional, while holding press conferences
and representing the party at public affairs. Rómulo Betancourt,
although far from uninvolved in the campaign, remained out of the
public eye. Only such events as the party anniversary celebration
in September, the presentation of the platform in Barquisimeto, or
the closing rally in Caracas drew him to a podium. As Betancourt
told the press in typically picturesque and picaresque language,
he was active in the campaign but was not "mitineando."[43] However,
on 9 November he launched a twelve-day trip to the interior.
     Accompanied by Barrios, Betancourt paid daily visits to a
number of state capitals, as well as Cabimas in Zulia. Meeting in
small groups at lunches, conferences, and interviews, he discussed
the party program, on which he had lavished time and attention,
especially such subjects as decentralization, the interior, and

rescue of the agricultural sector. Along with Barrios, he also
stressed the importance of tolerance and moderation in the
preservation and strengthening of Venezuelan democracy. Speaking
in Maracay during the uproar over the Maracaibo milk controversy,
for instance, Betancourt declared: "I have faith in Venezuelans,
in political parties, and in the certainty that they will not
continue using calumnious instruments that not only go against a
party, but against the democratic structure of Venezuela. I have
faith and confidence that utilization of the lie, like the
Australian weapon the boomerang, returns against those who use it.
I have faith that the President of the Republic...will assure the
realization of elections within a civilized debate."[44] During his
tour as well as in a later visit to the oriente in early December,
he repeated these themes at length.

The campaign of Carlos Andrés Pérez, in brief, had several
notable qualities. Foremost was the distinctive personal style of
the candidate. Linked to this was a communications effort that
blended harmoniously with the Pérez style. The evident unity was
beneficial to the image being projected, one that was lucid and
unambiguous. Technically the adeco campaign was less overpowering
than that of COPEI, yet it showed greater imagination, flexibility,
and creativity. There was a spark and a flair which, for whatever
reason, the copeyanos failed to capture. The direct personal role
of Pérez himself, carried out for more than a year, was important.
Certainly it provided a strong participatory ingredient that was
largely absent in Lorenzo Fernández's campaign. Thus the AD
candidate, supported by an effective blend of public image and
communications techniques, generated a momentum matching his
energetic style; its populistic quality was consistent with adeco
traditions and built steadily as election day neared.

THE POLITICAL LEFT
The nomination of Jesús Angel Paz Galarraga launched the
zuliano on what could prove the culmination of a long political
career. Yet his candidacy for a leftist alliance including
communist support was quite different from that of the AD, which he
had been steadily approaching until 1967. Born in Los Puertos de
Altagracia, Zulia, on 20 March 1919, Paz studied medicine at the
Universidad Central de Venezuela during the early 1940s, became
active in the AD, and continued working for the party upon returning
to Maracaibo to initiate his professional career. Establishing a
successful practice which eventually brought him the presidency of
Zulia's pediatric association, he also became well known for his
work with the poor. By the fall of the Gallegos government he was
a local leader of some importance. A lengthy period in jail was
followed by clandestine activity in Zulia. With the flight of
Pérez Jiménez, Paz became secretary general for Zulia.

After the election of Betancourt in 1958 and the departure of
numerous party leaders to government positions, Paz became national
secretary general.[45] For seven years he was to retain the key
position, continually solidifying his power and strength within the
party. Betancourt and then Leoni led the nation; the AD presidency

shifted from Leoni to Prieto; such leaders as Barrios, Dubuc, and Pérez served in key ministries; González Navarro and Malavé Villalba concentrated on labor affairs; others were occupied by parliamentary duties; potential rivals from Paz's generation left the AD in the 1962 arsista split;[46] all the while Paz ran the party organization with the canny incisiveness of a chess master. Having enjoyed an independent power base before assuming the position, Paz also began to develop his own policy preferences. These produced occasional conflicts during the Betancourt years, and party differences grew while Raúl Leoni was national president. The dispute between so-called pacistas and betancuristas deepened, with the forces of the latter led increasingly by Carlos Andrés Pérez, and divergences over proposed tax reform increased the rift.

The Christmas season of 1966 saw the decision by Paz to postpone his own candidacy and throw his support to Luis B. Prieto. It appeared at the time a brilliant stroke. Despite Prieto's victory over Gonzalo Barrios in the unprecedented party primary, attitudes and rancors had grown too deep on both sides, however, and the denouement saw the departure of the prietistas and the founding of the MEP.[47] Prieto immediately initiated his candidacy, and Paz served as guiding organizational genius. Following the 1968 elections the zuliano progressively moved the MEP to the left, and on the night of 29 July 1972 was nominated by the Nueva Fuerza. A skilled political organizer whose eventual candidacy for the AD had been prevented only by a herculean conflict that had engaged master politician Betancourt from afar, Paz moved more fully into the public eye than ever before.[48]

A brown-skinned, hawk-nosed man with a dark moustache, he had been referred to as "el Indio Paz" for much of his life. Quiet, contemplative, and somewhat introspective, the candidate had found it temperamentally comfortable to operate behind the scenes. Although sometimes regarded as coldly calculating, Paz to his friends and confidants was a man of considerable personal warmth. Whether or not these qualities could be effectively projected to the public by so complex and private a man was uncertain. Given the limited resources of the Nueva Fuerza, moreover, the effort depended primarily on the candidate himself. Press and information officials in the party worked hard, but their activities were largely such traditional tasks as writing press releases, taking photographs, and printing campaign posters.

Among the more common slogans and banners were those extracted from the coalition: National Liberation, The Popular Nationalist Front, and National Independence. There were calls for an End to Oligarchical Oppression, Economic Freedom, and for Social Justice for All. These and similar mottoes failed to permit a clear distinction from the MAS and lacked widespread popular appeal. For the candidate himself, the nickname of "el Indio" was employed less than might have been expected. Similarly, Paz's medical background was not given particular attention. Only toward the end of the campaign did posters begin to appear with a large photograph of the nominee clad in a medical coat and listening to a stethoscope while examining a small child. Paz himself made frequent reference to his medical experience during his speeches; he would sometimes speak of seeking the presidency in order to minister to the illnesses of his people. Posters, slogans, and similar publicity failed to emphasize this image, however.

Despite the evident talents of the Nueva Fuerza candidate, his political experience had been unarguably traditional. This was reflected in his campaign, for although he believed in relying upon personal contact, he made extensive use of the traditional forms of campaigning, large rallies and meetings. Paz worked hard and energetically in his campaign and believed that a greater expenditure of time would pay electoral dividends. Yet, on a customary day of campaigning, he came into close contact with fewer voters than either Pérez or Rangel, and the numbers who attended his major meetings were inevitably smaller than those for Fernández. In touring a small village, Paz would generally walk in his distinctive, loping stride through the middle of the street, waving to the people on both sides as he passed. However, he was less effective than Pérez or Rangel--the former charging through at breakneck speed, interrupting his walk with handshakes and abrazos, and the latter pausing for conversations of five or ten minutes apiece at several doors in a single block.

A shortage of experienced advance men and similar assistants also created an inefficiency that must often have caused the candidate private misgivings.[49] Too much of Paz's own time was occupied with arrangements others should have spared him. He was a man characteristically painstaking in his attention to detail, and Paz frequently had to attend to arrangements that had been neglected by local leaders. The geniality of the candidate was reflected in his maracucho entourage; although fiercely loyal and totally committed to Paz, it brought to its work an irrepressible spirit and gaiety that was not always conducive to the greatest efficiency. The unevenness of Nueva Fuerza organization was also reflected during tours. Organizational support was substantial in Zulia, for example, though slim in Trujillo.[50] In some instances, it was Paz and his wife who took care of personal as well as professional details while stumping his countryside. None of this could fail to affect his campaign.

Critics to the contrary notwithstanding, the candidate was not a weak public speaker. Neither, however, was he notably eloquent. Troubled with hoarseness in the first months of the campaign, he often spoke at too great length. This difficulty was frequently exacerbated by the inclusion of too many speakers at the same rally, thus tiring the audience before the nominee himself had begun. Paz emphasized the same themes in most of his addresses: the failures of formalistic democracy since 1958; the sameness of COPEI and AD; the contradictions of capitalism and evils of imperialism; and certain elements of his own program, especially such pledges as free milk for children. As the campaign moved toward conclusion, he increasingly challenged the alleged polarization of the vote. Paz also sharply criticized polls, which he charged were paid for by the status parties and therefore were partisan fabrications. He frequently conducted his own encuestas vivas, or live polls, asking

his listeners to hold up their hands if they intended to vote for
him.[51] Another familiar passage stressed the fact that the
electoral tarjeta with the symbol of a plumed Indian was for
another party, not that of the Indio Paz.[52]
    The traditionalism of the campaign was demonstrated by concern
over crowd size, notwithstanding the lessons of 1968 when large
crowds attending Prieto rallies were also striking in their
exuberance. There was substantial attention, directed by Paz
himself, to the positioning of his official photographer and the
use of wide-angle photographic techniques, thus maximizing the
appearance of large crowds. To be sure, the MEP did possess the
capacity to attract a large crowd. The final Maracaibo rally, held
on 4 December, drew a crowd of well over 100,000. Its cost was
some 300,000 bolívares. The Paz campaign applied proper names to
many of their meetings--El Mandarriazo, El Tarrayazo, and El
Toletazo--with the "azo" suffix suggesting the mounting of a blow
against the existing system.
    The two persons most active in aiding the Paz campaign through
personal appearances were Sra. Victoria de Paz and the redoubtable
Luis Beltrán Prieto. Accompanying her husband regularly, the former
overcame initial nervousness to become effective and self-assured.[53]
Having long looked after her husband's papers and gathered
information for his newspaper articles and columns, she was fully
attuned to his program and policies. Prieto's involvement became
public as time wore on, and the "maestro" worked hard for his
associate. With an energy belying his seventy-one years,[54] he
campaigned individually as well as joining Paz for joint
appearances. Prieto still generated great warmth and affection
from his audiences, and his speechmaking was no different than it
had been during his own campaign five years earlier--vigorous and
pungently forthright. For Paz himself, what was necessarily a
predominantly participatory campaign seemed rarely to catch fire.
The dedication of the candidate was best perceived in small forums
rather than in large outdoor meetings. Had the Nueva Fuerza been
equipped with a team of skilled media experts with large resources
at their disposal, Paz might have been projected with much wider
appeal. Instead, the Indio was forced into orthodox and somewhat
old-fashioned campaigning.
    To the left of Paz stood José Vicente Rangel. Although well
known in political circles from years of activity, Rangel was
youngest of the major candidates and the newest to emerge at the
level of national leadership. Born on 10 July 1929, he spent his
formative years in Cúcuta, Colombia, before becoming a student in
Barquisimeto. Upon entering the Universidad Central de Venezuela
to study law, Rangel affiliated with the URD. Active in the
student-based Vanguardia Juvenil Urredista (VJU) from its founding,
he was jailed briefly in 1953 following the electoral fraud against
the URD, then traveled to Chile and some four years of exile.
Continuing his law studies and marrying his Chilean wife Ana
Avalos, Rangel returned home late in 1956 and was active for a time
in the Junta Patriótica, which overthrew Pérez Jiménez. Although
elected deputy from the Distrito Federal in 1958, he was not

immediately prominent among younger political figures. Those
attracting wider attention included Domingo Alberto Rangel and
Simón Sáez Mérida of the AD's left wing; Rodolfo José Cárdenas and
Luis Herrera Campins within COPEI; and for the URD, Amilcar Gómez
and especially Fabricio Ojeda. The next few years were dedicated
primarily to journalism rather than to parliamentary politics,
where he remained in the background.

In addition to working with La Razón and the weekly Pueblo,
from 1961 he became a key figure with the leftist tabloid Clarín.
Rangel's position on the left soon became clear; he denounced
government acts while treating the PCV and MIR with sympathy.
He was also critical of violent tactics, however, as suggested by a
polemical change with then-communist Pompeyo Márquez over dimensions
of the armed struggle. With the heightening of the battle between
the government and the revolutionary left, the official communist
journal Tribuna Popular was banned, leaving Clarín the major outlet
for the left. Although Rangel maintained cordial relations with
Villalba, his position and that of the so-called ala negra (black
wing) of the URD caused complications for the party caudillo.
Following the 1963 elections in which Villalba finished third
without the support of the left, internal party friction was swiftly
exacerbated. Moderate urredistas urged Villalba to try to form
alliances, a course the leftists firmly opposed. Before the
inauguration of Raúl Leoni in March 1964, José Vicente Rangel left
the URD, as did Luis Miquilena, José Herrera Oropeza, Adolfo
Herrera, and others.[55]

Rangel joined others from the urredista left to organize the
Vanguardia Popular Nacionalista (VPN). Founded on 28 February 1964,
it was a movement "guided by revolutionary nationalism" that sought
the liberation of the Venezuelan people.[56]   Rangel tended to play a
solitary role; he devoted his time more to congress than to active
journalism. During a period when most leftists were incarcerated,
exiled, or abstaining from politics, he denounced political crimes
and defended human rights with anger and eloquence, gaining the
trust of the left and grudging respect from his adversaries.[57]   The
merger of the VPN with the arsista-based PRN in August 1966 as the
PRIN was intended to pave the way to a united party of the left, and
Rangel became a sub-secretary general. Marked heterogeneity of
views and interests eventually led to defections and reorganization,
but not until after the PRIN had supported the candidacy of Prieto
in 1968. José Vicente Rangel, returned to the Chamber of Deputies
for the PRIN from Zulia, campaigned for the mepista leader and
argued strongly for the unity of the left. With the
near-dissolution of the PRIN soon after elections,[58] Rangel became
a political independent.

The crisis of the PCV and creation of the MAS in January 1971
became the vehicle for Rangel's presidential candidacy. From the
initial Nuevo Circo rally in May 1972, the candidate began touring
the country, seeking votes and recognition for himself while also
establishing more fully the identity and legitimacy of the MAS.
Rangel began to project nationally the personality and style that
colleagues and associates well knew. It was a powerful if uncommon

one. Rangel was the antithesis of the organization man, preferring
an independent and often solitary role. This candidate was not a
lifetime toiler in the vineyards of a political party, like Pérez
and Fernández; neither was he the organizational strategist and
tactician like Paz Galarraga. Rangel was instead a figure who
charted his own course, reached his decisions in private, and then
proceeded with an unwavering steadfastness. A somberly handsome
man whose youth was offset by a greying moustache and temples,
Rangel was an austere, sober, and rather unsmiling figure. Both in
campaign style and in image, his was truly charismatic.

Although the MAS treasury was even slimmer than that of the
Nueva Fuerza, the voluntary contributions of its communications
experts produced a highly creative and attractive campaign. The
striking if superficial resemblance between José Vicente Rangel and
semilegendary "doctor of the poor" José Gregorio Hernández[59] was
not lost upon his image-builders. Among its principal
presentations was a series of full-length profiles of the candidate
in a dark suit, hands behind his back.[60] Lacking funds for
expensive advertising, the MAS made imaginative use of original
caricatures and cartoons painted on walls. Depicting COPEI, the
AD, and United States imperialism in varying forms, the slogans of
socialism and of national liberation were widely used. There was
almost universal agreement that the MAS wall paintings were the
most outstanding of the campaign.[61] It was noteworthy that only
rarely were MAS murals defaced, unlike propaganda of the other
parties.

Traveling by himself most of the time, totally without aides
or entourage, Rangel conducted an exceptionally individual and
personal campaign. Deeply convinced of the importance of direct
personal contact, his emphasis on walking the poor neighborhoods
of Venezuela rather than holding large outdoor rallies was not
dissimilar to that of Carlos Andrés Pérez. However, the personal
style was almost diametrically opposed to that of the AD candidate.
With Pérez, it was a tumultuous race through the streets,
surrounded by noise and festivity, dominated by the driving
vitality of the nominee. For Rangel, it was a slow, often solitary
walk in which he would converse with a family, often accepting an
invitation to enter a home or shack to talk at greater length.
Rangel obviously saw and was seen by fewer voters than Pérez and
lacked the impact of the AD whirlwind. On the other hand, he
established a degree of conversational rapport that was impossible
for Pérez. Each of the two, in short, had advantages and
disadvantages. Rangel's preference for more than a hasty abrazo
was consistent with masista tastes; the candidate and the party
believed in dialogue, both for immediate electoral purposes and
with a view to long-range political objectives.

The campaign style of José Vicente Rangel, then, was highly
distinctive. A grave, serious countenance and austere, quiet
manner combined to produce an unusual but unmistakeable charisma.
Rangel achieved his impact through the very severity of his
personality. With women of all ages, moreover, his sex appeal was
undeniable;[62] the appeal to youth, on programmatic as well as

stylistic grounds, was also strong. And despite the emphasis on individual conversation and contact, the masista and mirista candidate was a superb orator. Addressing a crowd from the platform, the reserved and restrained candidate was transformed into a fiery, impassioned spellbinder. Well-organized and articulate in exposition, attuned to the mood of his audience and magnetic in holding its attention, he may well have been the best public speaker of the campaign. Certainly the Rangel podium manner was yet another asset to his campaign, and clearly benefited the MAS.[63]

For Jóvito Villalba and the URD, the 1973 campaign provided a last hurrah for the fading hero of the Generation of '28. At sixty-five the oldest of all the candidates, the veteran undertook an active campaign. Relying upon his years of political prominence and unleashing once more his silvered tongue, Villalba stumped Venezuela under the slogan of levántate pueblo ("people, arise"). It was the hour to rise up against the exploitation, waste, and squandering of the recent past. One campaign symbol was the outline of an alarm clock with the phrase "it is the hour to win," and close examination showed the hands pointing at 7 and 3 for 1973. Posters with the traditional urredista yellow showed its leader with his arms upraised. Villalba's own campaigning was earnest and active;[64] however, the party organization was gone, the time past. The propaganda effort of the final weeks, seeking to depict Jóvito as a heavy underdog about to spring an historic surprise, was little more than pathetic. The electorate perceived the weakness of the candidacy and knew full well that there was little reason to take it seriously.

THE POLITICAL RIGHT

With the remaining candidates primarily engaged in the quest for an endorsement from Madrid, campaign activities were less extensive. The partial exception was Pedro R. Tinoco, son of a onetime minister of interior relations to Juan Vicente Gómez. Born in Caracas on 4 October 1927, he was educated in France, Switzerland, and the United States, and graduated from the Universidad Central de Venezuela in 1948. Tinoco entered the world of business and finance as a lawyer and economist, also teaching fiscal law at the Central University and political economy there and at the Universidad Católica Andrés Bello. Tinoco meantime improved his standing and influence with Fedecámaras and with foreign banking and investment interests. Active in the Chamber of Commerce, serving three years as president of the Asociación Bancaria Nacional and also the Instituto de Capacidad Bancaria, he contributed to the founding of the short-lived Asociación Venezolana de Independientes (AVI) prior to 1963 elections. The next few years saw the emergence of the Movimiento Desarrollista, and it carefully maneuvered for advantage before supporting COPEI in 1968. The reward for Tinoco was appointment as treasury minister.

Actively favoring private enterprise and defending large economic interests both domestic and foreign, Tinoco strove for managerial efficiency. Demonstrably able, competent and

hardworking, Tinoco and desarrollismo sought the public image of
efficiency, strength, and order. In August 1973 campaign manager
José Ignacio Andrade declared that the initial effort was to present
the candidate as efficient and capable. The succeeding phase would
change emphases and stress his personal warmth. The first appeared
more successful than the second. The campaign slogan of autoridad
y eficiencia was neither imaginative nor catchy, and its
incorporation into singing commercials produced appalling results.
Tinoco, large, balding and somewhat forbidding, did not engage in
extensive personal campaigning. The determined effort to woo
perezjimenismo was time-consuming and unsuccessful, and extensive
media advertising at the close of the campaign was unexceptionable.
The attitude of the political left was predictably vociferous in
its criticisms;[65] most of the electorate was indifferent.

Of the remaining candidates, Pedro Segnini La Cruz was easily
the most active, touring Venezuela for several months by public
transportation. He gained additional attention when he drove a
Caracas taxicab as a means of meeting voters. At the conclusion of
the campaign he was holding forth nightly in a small park at the
eastern entrance to Caracas' Sabana Grande. The site where Burelli
Rivas had drawn sizable crowds five years earlier, this location
attracted but a few hundred dogged members of the FND, despite the
fluid and florid forensics of Segnini La Cruz. Burelli himself was
not very active, although his press conferences and television
interviews were well covered. General Martín García Villasmil
campaigned little. Along with Raimundo Verde Rojas, Pablo Salas
Castillo, and Alejandro Gómez Silva, more time was devoted to Madrid
visits and counterclaims of perezjimenista approval than to
legitimate campaigning. The final two ultimately withdrew their
candidacies. Germán Borregales made occasional public appearances,
but these were less colorful than his pronouncements. As for Juan
Alberto Solano, we are not aware of any public appearances
following his official inscription as candidate in July.
Presumably, neither was the Venezuelan electorate.

Comparison of the four leading contenders illustrates the
dominant communications characteristics. As depicted in figure 10,
only the Pérez effort placed strong reliance on both participatory
and presentational techniques; for Fernández, the latter received
the greater emphasis. Paz's campaign reversed the copeyano pattern,
with stress given to participatory techniques. For Rangel, the
emphasis was predominantly participatory. In summary, only COPEI
and the AD possessed the financial and human resources to undertake
a major use of both presentational and participatory methods. The
strong preference by the Social Christians for the former reflected
both the outlook of its campaign managers and the predilections of
their candidate. There was an assumption that presentational
efforts could offset a relative de-emphasis on the participatory.
Thus the increasing monopolization of the contest by Fernández and
Pérez promised to be revealing in terms of somewhat contrasting
patterns of campaign communications between the two.

FIGURE 10.   Candidate Images

Candidate	Technique	Favorable	Critical
Fernández	Presentational	Unifier (el hombre que está uniendo al país)	Weak
		Pacifier (pacificación para todos)	Inarticulate
		Progressive (con Lorenzo a la conquista del futuro ya)	Ill health
		Nationalist (defiendo lo de aquí)	
		PATERNAL (un presidente amigo)	CALDERA'S PAWN (amigo del presidente)
Pérez	Participatory, Presentational	Energetic (ese hombre si camina)	Ruthless
		Decisive (da la cara)	Mediocre
		Tough (va de frente)	Unprincipled
		Nationalist (hacia la gran Venezuela)	Uneducated
		DEMOCRACIA CON ENERGIA	COP
Paz	Participatory	Man of the people (el Indio Paz)	Manipulator-politician
		Dedicated (médico del pueblo)	Unprincipled opportunist
		Nationalist (Independencia nacional)	Ineffective leadership
		UNIDAD POPULAR	COMMUNIST
Rangel	Participatory	Redeemer of people (José Gregorio)	Saint with feet of clay (santurrón)
		Forceful (con el puño)	Sinister, dangerous
		True socialist (decídate por el socialismo)	
		Magnetic, sexy	
		Austere, charismatic (JOSE VICENTE!)	Manufactured (hombre de pantalla)

8. CAMPAIGN EXECUTION

The campaign course from nomination to election day was fraught with obstacles and perils for the candidates. Some difficulties were predictable and responses almost automatic; others could not be anticipated and demanded skillful improvisation. Examination of several such episodes, which do not fall neatly into our broad analytic scheme, provides a more detailed sense of the warp and woof of the Venezuelan campaign. Moreover, such events tested the mettle of organizational structures, tactical planning, candidate presentation, and electoral communication at that critical time when the outcome was still very much in doubt.

PARTISANSHIP AND VENTAJISMO

Government intervention on behalf of its own partisan interests is an ancient tradition of political campaigning. Similarly, opposition attempts to tar a government with the brush of interference is a tried-and-true tactic. The charges and countercharges that resounded between adecos and copeyanos provided dissonant chords to the 1973 experience. Accusations of government ventajismo had been lodged against Rómulo Betancourt in 1963 and Raúl Leoni in 1968, but without the vehemence and persistence of 1973. The explanation may have been more circumstancial than deliberate. During the 1963 campaign there was little serious doubt as to the outcome; what might have been termed ventajismo had been more extensive prior to the campaign proper, in the wake of the 1962 adeco division and subsequent maneuvering between loyalists and arsistas.[1] Five years later controversy was based on the AD-MEP struggle, and President Leoni, siding with the former, permitted government officials to provide aid of various sorts. He himself followed the familiar pattern of increasing public appearances during the final stages of the campaign.

In 1973, two general forms of interference were planned. The first centered on the participation of government officials, bureaucrats, and public servants in the campaign. A contrasting type consisted of public appearances, pro-government publicity, and other overt activities that might be viewed as partisan involvement.

Early in 1973 the AD had sent Pérez, Barrios, and Lepage to discuss the matter with President Caldera. Although there was general agreement at the time, by mid-year the AD denunciations had led to sharp retorts from the administration. In his press conference on 2 August the President spoke bluntly.

> I don't know that there is any need to repeat myself. In my expositions, in my press conferences, in my activities, I do not name parties, do not mention candidates, do not intervene in the specific question facing the Venezuelan voter....Now I do defend my Government and explain the acts of the Government, and this is a right nobody can take from me....
>   Press conferences provide constant dialogue, not for electoral purposes, but as an expression of a concept of government, a mode of government, a style of government; and to travel to the country, as I have done and I do frequently in the most simple form, without recruiting people to come to applaud, but meeting them spontaneously, ...furthers dialogue.[2]

The president's position was to remain unaltered: he was continuing the activities of the preceding four years, neither increasing nor decreasing them. It was his task to maintain contact with the people on behalf of the government, presenting and explaining its policies and inaugurating its works. There had not been nor would there be partisan activities on his part.

The AD saw the president's travels and inaugurations as having increased. Public appearances by cabinet ministers were also regarded as constituting clear if indirect intervention in favor of COPEI, as were the many large newspaper advertisements hailing the accomplishments of the administration. Exchanges between the government and AD changed in venue for a time as congressional activities occupied attention during much of August and early September. A previous squabble about respective party attitudes toward the role of Congress had been indecisive[3] but contributed to sharp partisan controversy as the session drew toward its conclusion. Approval of the 1974 budget, reforms of the suffrage bill, and other last-minute legislation piled up, requiring an extension of the session. Copeyano-adeco and government-opposition partisanship turned to legislative maneuvers centered on Carmen de Valera, a long-time copeyana who had defected from the party and was demanding the right to present "serious charges" in the Chamber of Deputies against the Ministry of Public Works. COPEI and the government denied her the right to speak; the AD of course defended Sra. de Valera, and for several days a lack of quorum halted legislative work.[4] A second extension was finally negotiated and the ex-copeyana permitted to speak. Following her rambling presentation of undocumented charges on 23 August, Congress soon concluded its business.

Minister of Interior Relations Nectario Andrade Labarca reiterated Caldera's views in stressing government impartiality and its guarantee of electoral purity. He also argued the right and obligation of the administration to inform the public of its work. "Therefore I do not believe there is justice in calling our action an electoral campaign, for it is the government exercise of mechanisms and democratic processes that the people would be the first in demanding from a Government which has arrived to power on the altar of the public will. Therefore I do not believe that this can be called ventajismo."[5] Such denials were soon superceded by ambiguous but potentially damaging charges of presidential candidate Miguel Angel Burelli Rivas. Appearing on 28 August as featured guest on Radio Caracas TV's "Buenos Días," Burelli had made suggestive if imprecise remarks concerning apparent ventajismo. The AD picked up the issue and its candidate wrote Caldera on 6 September with a formal request that the president intervene against any and all campaign irregularities. Pérez saw the Burelli allegations as suggesting improper partisanship and lamented not only the particular episode but also his fear that "the democratic institutional future of the Republic is being compromised."[6]

The same evening the president addressed the issue at his weekly press conference. Citing portions of the Burelli text, Caldera explained that his examination revealed no mention of an offer of government money. Furthermore, since Burelli was seemingly discussing the role of parties, it should be COPEI rather than the national government that ought to respond.[7] The next day Lorenzo Fernández joined the fray from Zulia by telling an audience in La Concepción that he supported Caldera's right to defend and explain the works of his government. The AD, he added, recognized its impending defeat and thus had little remaining option but to charge official ventajismo. Gonzalo Barrios replied that COPEI's attempt to proposition Burelli was simply "the limit." Continuing irregularities were contaminating the entire electoral process as the country witnessed the unfolding aggression of officialdom. "I fear that if information on the practices that COPEI has invented and developed to retain electoral power manages to penetrate sufficiently the large popular sectors of the country, not even the victory of AD will be sufficient to repair the psychological havoc of the scandal, and so will be reflected negatively in future attitudes. If COPEI wins under the same conditions--a hypothesis that is logical to consider despite its improbability--the deterioration would be precipitated irreversibly toward the extremes."[8] To this were added Carlos Andrés Pérez's statements on 8 September, among his strongest of the campaign. Quoting from what he termed the true Burelli text, Pérez said that the one cited by Caldera was not fully accurate. The crucial portion allegedly read as follows:

> ...It has been suggested to me that I could obtain large
> resources on television if I accept or agree to attacks
> against the Government so that I might say what would
> be agreeable to the Government, for that would take away
> votes from another of the candidates. I do not
> participate in such things. I say to the nation that

this is authentic, it is authentic, it is authentic. It has been insistently proposed to me that I might receive TV commercials, receive means to support my candidacy. And that instead of my attacks on the President of the Republic, I might attack those whom it would be agreeable to attack for the benefit of COPEI and the damage of another candidacy....[9]

Recapitulating AD complaints, Pérez denounced the participation of "hundreds" of public employees at all levels being paid from public funds while working full time on COPEI's electoral campaign. Convinced that he would win despite undemocratic interference, Pérez called on public opinion "to have full awareness of the grave political situation that this illegal and antidemocratic Government intromission into elections is creating; and at the same time I issue the warning that moral damages of imponderable magnitude are being created, which will require great effort to reestablish decency in public administration."[10] Among other examples of government partisanship cited were the complicity of government offices in coordinating the dissemination of COPEI's electoral propaganda, consultation between government and party in their respective advertising, and the distribution of a campaign poster with juxtaposed photographs of Caldera and Fernández. And finally, he added, adeco phones were bugged--a constitutional violation.

For the AD, then, collusion between government and COPEI officials could not be ignored. In addition to the possible effects on elections, such actions were prejudicial to democratic institutions and to public confidence in the probity of the existing political order. Only the president could provide effective remedial action. Interior Minister Andrade Labarca returned to defense of the government, which was "capable of guaranteeing, in accord with legal norms, the absolute purity of the electoral process. Never before has this purity been so well guaranteed, because of the results of legal reforms that the opposition has approved in Congress...." As to AD charges of wrongdoing, the minister welcomed proofs of any such actions. "The government is the most interested party in putting an end to any irregularity, because it does not want the results of the electoral process to be subject to the slightest suspicion of partialities."[11]

The AD fought in the CSE as well as before the public. Campaign manager David Morales Bello led that party effort. In mid-August he spent over three hours before the CSE demonstrating alleged government ventajismo; posters, propaganda, and assorted campaign paraphernalia were shown to the membership. The familiar poster showing Caldera and Fernández side by side was included. First seen in Táchira in January, it had been denounced before the CSE and disappeared; now, said Morales Bello, it had been redistributed in Cojedes.[12] All Consejo members with the exception of COPEI's representative voted for investigation by a special committee. The AD attempted to keep the issue before both the CSE and the public. In early October Morales Bello told the press that there were no signs of CSE progress despite his documentation of "ventajismo oficial." The use of state resources to help the Social Christian campaign, he argued, left the other parties at an unfair disadvantage, as well as being illegal. In actuality the Consejo had indeed been investigating, however, and on 19 October approved a report recommending to the government a voluntary adjustment of its propaganda. Although cautiously and mildly worded, it left little doubt as to its opinion of government actions.

The text of the report by CSE President Luis A. Pietri stated that specific analysis of each individual case was neither desirable nor beneficial. Special mention was made of Article 166 of the Suffrage Law, as well as Article 122 of the Constitution and Article 28 of the Administrative Career Law. The first forbade ministers or government officials from making electoral propaganda, either directly or indirectly; the second declared that public employees served the state and not a partisan political force; the last prohibited functionaries from propaganda or from partisan political activity.

The Consejo Supremo Electoral wants to express responsibly its judgment that the National Government would contribute in a positive way to the best interests of the electoral process now underway, and therefore, would invigorate the democratic system, by adjusting voluntarily--during the weeks remaining until December 9th--the propaganda on its achievements and policies that it normally makes. At the same time, it should avoid any coincidence of official propaganda with that of any candidate or party. The Consejo Supremo Electoral makes this exhortation with the assurance that it find, once again, effective receptivity by the National Executive.

The Consejo Electoral exhorts the political parties to maintain, for the rest of the debate now in process, the civic duty that, as entities of leadership for the citizenry,...supports the best interests of our nationality and of our destiny.[13]

The report was signed by all the members save Eduardo Aguilar of COPEI, who characterized the report as including concepts that might confuse the public. Although a mild and diplomatic admonition, the CSE report intimated that it had indeed found substantiation for allegations of ventajismo. Andrade Labarca replied for the government in a similarly subtle and understated tone. Expressing his interest in the CSE announcement, the minister of interior relations also noted its recognition of the governmental right to inform the public on its programs and accomplishments. The government, he promised, would fully collaborate in order "to help guarantee even more fully the purity of the electoral process."[14]

Neither the government nor COPEI had remained totally on the defensive during the sustained attack of its opponents. While Rafael Caldera and his ministers clung to dignified denials of ventajismo while reiterating the right to inform the public, the party itself launched a counteroffensive. In early October the Social Christians issued a call to all political parties formalizing their agreement to recognize electoral results. Pedro Pablo Aguilar warned against underestimating "the susceptibility of political phenomena to contagion, and the tradition of our country is more that of violence and anarchy than of institutional life and liberties. Therefore in these final weeks of the electoral campaign the candidates and parties must make a great effort to keep the debate within a civic and respectful climate in order to prevent anything which might cause irreparable damage to democratic life, and equally we must agree upon the recognition and defense of the electoral results." Thus, all parties could contribute to formation of a great national conscience by agreeing upon the "honest recognition of the electoral results and acceptance of the will expressed by the people."[15]

Acting President Godofredo González joined Aguilar in disseminating the proposal. The parties reacted with cautious suspicion. Octavio Lepage promised to study the proposal and respond; Gonzalo Barrios reacted similarly, although he told a newsman that Aguilar's proposal was reminiscent of the sign hung over bars in the United States' Old West: "Please don't shoot the piano player."[16] The following day Carlos Andrés Pérez asked that COPEI promise "solemnly and publicly that it will respect electoral results."[17] As the government party, he maintained, only COPEI could deny recognition of the results. Lepage shortly delivered the official AD statement in the form of a five-point document. The party was fully prepared to collaborate with the CSE and to reach agreement with other parties. Furthermore, it requested that all parties and candidates receive equal guarantees, therefore presupposing "that the government maintain neutrality and abstain from interposing its influence and the powerful resources at its disposal...." If COPEI were willing to sign such a pact recognizing the results, presumably the government would also renounce any direct intervention in the campaign. "Only the government is in a position to disregard the electoral results, and to do so would have to secure the support of the Fuerzas Armadas Nacionales. The latter have given convincing demonstrations of their institutional loyalty and there is no reason to think that attitude could change. We are also confident that President Caldera will be at the height of his historic responsibility in doing nothing that might break the respectability and solidarity of the democratic regime."[18] For the other parties, Siuberto Martínez of the MEP was unenthusiastic, and Jesús Angel Paz Galarraga termed the COPEI invitation "highly suspicious."[19] Pompeyo Márquez for the MAS similarly expressed interest but charged the government with responsibility for any public uncertainties about electoral honesty.

As things developed, the pact was never implemented and soon slipped into obscurity. Controversy over the role of the government continued throughout the campaign, and rival positions were clear. For the opposition, and particularly the AD,[20] ventajismo was rampant. Government advertisements in the media were excessive;

bureaucrats were working on behalf of Lorenzo Fernández; and Caldera was dedicating every rock and stone in Venezuela on behalf of his would-be Social Christian successor.[21] Even the CSE had issued a gingerly but unmistakeable rebuke. For the government, President Caldera was acting as he had for four years, continuing his dialogue with the citizenry; with the legal participation of the left, the process was the most truly representative in national history; moreover, the jurisdiction of the independent CSE further underlined the good faith and patriotically disinterested role of officialdom. Rafael Caldera coolly continued with his daily routine while stepping up the tempo of his dedications and public inaugurations. A typical presidential statement was the following, delivered at the October initiation of the Santo Domingo hydroelectric complex in Barinas:

> To be sure, at times the very groups that have contributed to creating and maintaining the rule of liberties, lose the vision of their responsibilities in orienting the pueblo and, in reciprocal accusations, not always well grounded or well evaluated, leave the people who do not have time to study all questions carefully the false idea that liberty does not permit one to construct, and that democratic discussion is a factor which enervates and drains the potential of the country....
>
> I feel obliged to remind all my countrymen that efficiency is proven and is not imcompatible with liberty, that liberty has been the stimulus, and that the very discussion that appears in the sands of political struggle, far from weakening the spirit for creative accomplishment, has been for us a constant nourishment that fills us with satisfaction each time that we advance another stage in the progress and transformation of Venezuela.
>
> When I have spoken to the country of the work of the Government, I have always thought of the large number of Venezuelans, many of them young...but fully qualified in their credentials, their knowledge, and their will for service. To all those who form the great team of government and administration that powers the development of Venezuela, I want to reiterate my full confidence, my sense of solidarity, and my conviction that they will continue working and producing, for Venezuela needs them now more than ever.[22]

THE LEFT UNDER ATTACK

While the government, COPEI, and the AD maintained a drumfire of denunciations over ventajismo, a separate set of issues plagued the Venezuelan left. The first was precipitated by an unexpected public statement of all Venezuelan bishops.[23] Speaking officially for the national episcopate, the document criticized socialism as an electoral alternative. Arguing that construction of a new society should follow neither "liberal capitalism" nor "marxist socialism," the bishops criticized the latter for "its atheist materialism, its dialectic of violence, and the manner in which it understands individual freedom within the collectivity, denying at the same time all transcendence to man and to his personal and collective history.... Its atheist materialist vision does not permit--and the experience of marxist regimes demonstrates this abundantly--the exercise of authentic human freedom...." Therefore, "the believer cannot accept marxist ideology without contradicting his own faith; neither can he adhere globally to the postulates of marxist analysis of man and of society, without compromising substantial aspects of that very faith."[24] The document cited papal encyclicals and other authorized declarations in supporting its position.

At the very outset, Iglesia y Política had stressed its political neutrality in hopes of muting possible criticism.

> Respectful of the plurality of possible political options within the same faith, and keeping in mind the concrete conditions of national reality, the Episcopate has avoided all type of manifestations that could be interpreted as undue intervention in this field.

> This non-partisan position of the Episcopate does not imply indifference to the political, taking this term in the sense of the search for and implementation of everything which contributes to achieving the common good of the country. It is precisely in this sense that we call upon all our compatriots to seek the best paths and instruments to realize a more just and more fraternal society, and one with greater equality and participation.[25]

It was, however, a vain hope. The two presidential candidates on the left complained of Church meddling in politics, then prudently left the issue to fade away. From young dissident Christian groups, however, the document elicited sharp opposition. Several met jointly with the press to announce their own document against the official position.[26] Its leading spokesman was Joaquín Marta Sosa, a former young copeyano leader who was supporting José Vicente Rangel, while Father Martín Soto Ojeda, a communist candidate for the Nueva Fuerza to the Caracas municipal council, seconded the response. Essentially denying the incompatibility of socialism and Catholicism, they attacked the local hierarchy as having "opted in favor of privilege" rather than seeking a Church "at the service of justice and of the redemption of man in this world."[27] An ad hoc group of students at the Universidad Central announced their desire "to create a socialism whose maximum concern is the new man and the new society, where we all can live with the most human, most just, and most evangelistic values." Furthermore, "socialism owes much to marxism but we understand and seek a purer, more transcendent socialism, with all the hope and the spiritual values that Christ has offered us...."[28]

The JRC also joined in debating the participation of Christians

in designing a new and better society. Meeting on 2 August to
evaluate the party campaign at the youth level, the JRC devoted
four hours' discussion to a draft statement,[29] and the approved
version appeared a week later as a full-page advertisement.[30]
Describing its posture as both anticapitalist and revolutionary,
the JRC denounced the capitalist society and dependency to which
Venezuela had submitted. The revolutionary commitment of the JRC
was to the marginal masses and required "the transformation of
present structures and the construction of a new society." As to
the role of socialism in the elections, the young _copeyanos_
proclaimed their pluralist determination to debate and exchange
views with Marxist groups.

> We reiterate our conviction that the fight against
> powerful and imperialist sectors has to be definitively
> won in this electoral process. International capitalism
> and criollo capitalism generously finance other
> candidacies, which are the best expression of a system
> that we have attacked for its petroleum negotiations and
> for its ambitions of consolidating itself as a political
> power in Venezuela by means of FEDECAMARAS. They, more
> than anyone, know that we Christian Democrats are their
> enemies and that we are going to continue confronting
> them. For this very reason, COPEI constitutes today the
> best option opposing powerful and antipopular sectors.[31]

Although the document provided renewed evidence of the wide chasm
separating the JRC from the ideological mainstream of the parent
organization, it differed little from previous JRC statements.
The Venezuelan bishops, their ill-timed effort apparently weakened
further by internal differences, chose not to continue the debate;
consequently both leftist parties and Catholic youth groups turned
their attention elsewhere.
    For the candidacies of Rangel and Paz, the episode soon
passed without having incurred notable damage. A month later,
however, a potentially more threatening challenge was posed by the
business community through an antisocialist campaign which
especially reflected entrepreneurial alarm at the increasing
visibility of José Vicente Rangel. Although there was little fear
of a Rangel victory, members of the business elite worried about
the possible strength of the left by 1978 or thereafter. It was
in mid-September that Rangel first announced that a campaign against
socialism was being planned by Fedecámaras. Showing photostatic
copies of documents to reporters, he charged that a public relations
agency had been hired to disseminate unfavorable publicity, at a
total cost of 2,544,364 bolívares.[32] Paz Galarraga had learned of
the purported campaign at the same time, although delaying public
comments until later.[33]
    Fedecámaras immediately responded that it would neither confirm
nor deny the allegations until the proofs could be studied and, in
the absence of public advertising, the issue receded into the
background. By mid-October, however, the dispute was renewed during

Rangel's appearance before the Asociación Pro-Venezuela Forum. Repudiating Fedecámaras for attempted domination of Venezuela through sheer force of economic and financial power, the candidate repeated his contention that a campaign of 2.5 million bolívares was being directed against his candidacy. A fuller version appeared in Momento later in the month, with Rangel again attacking the "campaign of lies and fallacies" that "the most reactionary economic groups and representatives of monopolistic foreign investment" were conducting. In attempting to close the path to socialism, Fedecámaras was intending to confuse the voter through an anonymous campaign, which was contrary to law. Moreover, the business organization was attempting to act as a political party, thus testifying to the growing strength of the MAS in producing an authentic popular movement.[34]

A Fedecámaras spokesman denied the charges, carefully stating that people supporting the campaign, being anticommunist, would necessarily include some business leaders. This was extended by Fedecámaras president Alfredo Paúl Delfino a few days later. A strong declaration rejected institutional responsibility for the campaign while excoriating the totalitarianism of Marxist systems. Stressing the right of businessmen as citizens to respond to attacks, Paúl declared that the press campaign was an effort "to clarify in the popular mind the collective tragedy that the implantation of socialism-communism...in our country would signify...."[35] Fedecámaras itself had a legal right to conduct such a campaign itself, he observed, but thus far had chosen not to do so. It was not responsible for the campaign; however, it was admittedly sympathetic toward it.

Later identification of the so-called Comité Pro-Defensa del Sistema Democrático removed the taint of anonymity; while the left continued to denounce oligarchical business interests in Venezuela, businessmen struck back in the effort to weaken "socialism-communism." Advertisements featured a series of photographs depicting a conversation between ordinary-looking citizens, with cartoon-like captions presenting the message. In one, a woman discoursed with her neighbor about an absence of freedom but a surfeit of backwardness and misery in socialist countries. Lines were necessary in order to buy food, clothing, shoes, and other rationed goods. Furthermore, such governments converted the people into slaves, while "children belong to the state and not to their mothers, and they are taught that spying and informing on one's parents is patriotic." Finally, the reader was urged "to vote against socialism-communism. Defend your liberty and your rights."[36] The impact of such advertisements was hard to judge, as were television commercials that dramatized similar scenes. Certainly popular Venezuelan attitudes toward communism--as our data report elsewhere--suggest the possible value of such propaganda for business interests. Yet in the midst of the advertising tidal wave that flooded the media as the campaign drew to a close, it is questionable whether either Rangel or Paz were significantly damaged.

The same cannot be said about the impact of events in Chile,

however. Indeed, the repercussions may well have injured COPEI as
well. It was Tuesday, 11 September, when news began reaching
Caracas of the uprising against President Salvador Allende and his
subsequent death in La Moneda. The reaction of the MAS and of
Rangel was to disclaim serious concern. Noting that there had been
no effort to pattern themselves after Allende, the candidate Rangel
stressed the need for Venezuela to find its own route to socialism,
"an experience that cannot be compared with any other in the
continent; we will make our fight on electoral terrain...."[37] He
also viewed the Chilean experience as showing the lengths of
violence and violation of human rights to which capitalist
governments were prepared to go. What failed in Chile was not
socialism but rather the so-called democratic institutions,
Parliament, and an ability to prevent the connivance of military
fascists with Christian Democrats.[38] Despite Rangel's genuine
belief that his Venezuelan course was distinctive, unlike the
Chilean,[39] the MAS feared possible electoral deterioration as a
consequence of the Chilean crisis. In a statement by its Comité
Ejecutivo, it anticipated that Venezuela's dominant class, "in the
desire to exploit to the maximum the Chilean situation to demoralize
socialist ranks, has unleashed its batteries against our movement
and against our candidate, José Vicente Rangel."[40]

The potential injury to the Nueva Fuerza was greater, given
the extent to which it had been modeled after the Chilean
experiment. Paz himself had announced the night of his nomination
that what had occurred in Chile could take place in Venezuela as
well. This was utopian, as Paz doubtless realized, but it was an
effective card to be played in the campaign. In an editorial
written twenty-four hours prior to Allende's death, the candidate
had attacked the pro-golpista conduct of Chile's Christian
Democrats as well as the impact of international imperialist
interests. Transferring the dispute to Venezuelan turf, he had
denounced copeyano efforts to perpetuate its power, including
repression, ventajista use of resources of the state, and
intervention by the president. In Venezuela, the choice by the
left of the electoral path meant the most difficult course to
power, one that the Nueva Fuerza would honor despite officialist
provocations.[41] With the toppling of Chile's Unidad Popular
government by violent upheaval, Paz's electoral card had seemingly
been trumped. The candidate doggedly insisted that Chilean events
simply emphasized the determination with which the Nueva Fuerza
must continue its own struggle.[42]

The Nueva Fuerza took the initiative in calling and directing
the memorial meeting for the thirteenth, in which it was joined by
the MIR and, after initial reluctance, by the MAS. The first time
since 1960 that all the groups of the Venezuelan left were
together at such a public act,[43] speeches were delivered by a host
of figures, including Luis Henríquez Acevedo, who had just resigned
as Chilean ambassador to Venezuela. The final address was an
emotional declaration by Luis B. Prieto, an Allende friend of
forty years. Alluding rhetorically to the visions of Bolívar and
condemning copeyanos chilenos for responsibility in the

assassination of the Chilean president, he assured the audience
that "from Chile comes the bloodied word of Allende to tell us
that the Latin American revolution has begun."[44] Paz called for a
minute of silence at his meetings later that week in Zulia and
Trujillo, while his supporters attempted to turn events against
COPEI. Communist leader Hector Mújica accused the Chilean
Christian Democrats of major responsibility. In early October it
was the Nueva Fuerza that sent a delegation to Miraflores to seek
presidential intercession on behalf of political detainees in
Chile. Special mention was made of Luis Corvalán and other leaders
of the Chilean Unidad Popular, and appeals were sent to Cardinal
Quintero and to Pope Paul VI.

Events in Chile posed no special problems for AD. Pérez and
Lepage expressed sorrow over the death of Allende and the
destruction of an elected government, and Rómulo Betancourt sent a
telegram of sympthy to Allende's widow, reiterating the personal
friendship and mutual esteem dating back to 1940. For COPEI the
Chilean developments were a deep embarrassment. Within the
electoral context, the Social Christians had been attempting to
promote an opening to the left, yet there was strong loyalty and
identification with the Chilean Christian Democrats, and in some
cases strong personal ties of friendship. The JRC, deeply moved
by the emotional impact of Allende's death, found its position
stated succinctly by its former leader Abdón Vivas Terán: "The
behavior of Christian Democracy and of Frei in Chile is neither
justifiable nor acceptable," adding that the PDC bore considerable
responsibility for the tragic and bloody course of events.[45] JRC
Secretary General Julio César Moreno said that the Juventud
"condemns the fascist military golpe in Chile, which diminishes the
freedom and the social conquests of the Chileans of the last ten
years...."[46]

The hemispheric Organización Demócrata Cristiana de América
Latina (ODCA), which by coincidence was meeting in Caracas under
the leadership of Luis Herrera Campins, its secretary general,
condemned the extremism and intolerance of both Marxists and
rightists. Deploring the death of Allende and the spread of
fratricidal passions in Chile, the ODCA specifically denied Christian
Democratic involvement in the golpe.[47] The JRC then compared
events in Chile with the actions of Francisco Franco in the Spanish
Civil War. Moreno announced the JRC belief that events threatened
"to enthrone a dictatorship of eminently fascist qualities" and
promised to urge a continental meeting of the hemispheric youth
organization of Christian Democracy, which would similarly condemn
Chilean fascism. The Caldera government was called upon to break
relations unless the military junta provided a set of guarantees.[48]
Other young copeyanos added their voices to others demanding that
the new government in Santiago not be recognized.

For the senior party leadership, the news had provoked a
swift but inconclusive emergency session of the Directorio Nacional.
Pedro Pablo Aguilar denied PDC involvement and blamed extreme
rightist elements; copeyano parliamentary leader José Luis Zapata
voiced personal regret but opined that the golpe reflected the

majority view in Chile. COPEI attempted to blunt charges against
its Chilean counterparts by newspaper advertisements reproducing a
declaration of PDC President Patricio Aylwin objecting to the
imposition of a new constitution and calling for a return to
elected government within two years. The advertisement bore the
headline, in large print, that "before systematically slandering
one should be familiar with the declarations of the President of
Chilean Christian Democracy."[49]
    President Caldera moved slowly and cautiously. Initial
statements of general concern and regret were followed by three
days of national mourning for Salvador Allende. By 20 September
the president told his weekly conference that he remained committed
to ideological pluralism, strongly hinting at recognition of the
new Chilean government. It followed shortly, although a week later
a cable also went to General Pinochet of the military junta to
"express the aspiration of the Venezuelan people that in our noble
sister country the death penalty not be applied to those arrested
as a result of recent events."[50] Most striking of all was the
administration's breaking of measures leading toward establishment
of diplomatic relations with Cuba. Especially as news of atrocities
and inhumanity escaped from Chile, and the role of the PDC became
increasingly suspect, the copeyano strategy of leaning toward the
left became a source of embarrassment and concern.

FINANCING THE CAMPAIGN
    The sheer cost of propaganda and publicity, multiplied by the
exceptional length of the campaign, can only be regarded as
extraordinary. By 1973 it had reached such proportions as to lie
far beyond all but COPEI and the AD. Even granted the confidential
nature of such expenditures, some general notion is necessary if
informed opinion may be brought to bear on the entire subject. The
estimates and figures presented here are neither precise nor
authoritative but are sufficient to sketch a clear portrait of
campaign costs.[51]
    Official government expenditures can be itemized with
reasonable confidence, although representing but a fragment of the
complete picture. As shown in table 14, the national treasury paid
to the CSE 80 million bolívares from 1964 thorugh 1968, all but 10
million assigned for the 1968 campaign year. The next five years
totaled 108,800,000 bolívares, following the reversion of another
100 million which would have been spent for purchase of the
electronic voting machines. Dividing the 1969-73 figure by the
number of registered voters suggests an average CSE expenditure
of nearly 24 bolívares each (slightly over $5). Of the 1969-73
expenses, some 13 million bolívares went to the parties with CSE
representation, along with costs of CSE publicity, advertising, and
announcements for the press, radio, and television. This was but a
fraction of the total campaign cost, and merely provides a
reasonably accurate starting point.
    The expenditures for COPEI and the AD clearly constituted the
great bulk in 1973. On radio, each short spot announcement cost
15 bolívares. For each of the two establishment parties--which we

TABLE 14.   Funds Allocated to the Consejo Supremo Electoral

Year	Allocation in bolívares
1964	3,100,000
1965	1,100,000
1966	2,400,000
1967	3,400,000
1968	70,000,000
1969	4,000,000
1970	2,900,000
1971	10,300,000
1972	36,900,000
1973	54,700,000

Total 188,800,000

are assuming to have spent roughly comparable sums[52]--one can estimate four such cuñas per hour during a ten-hour period daily. Based on one hundred radio stations, this totals some 21,600,000 for a year. For television, a one-minute commercial ran some 3,000 bolívares; a modest estimate of twelve per day would total 36,000 bolívares; three channels total 108,000 bolívares; multiplied by 30 days equals 3,240,000 bolívares; for twelve months, it totals 38,880,000 bolívares. In the Caracas press, a one-page advertisement cost 3,000 bolívares; at an average of five pages in Caracas and ten in the regional and local press, this comes to 45,000 bolívares daily, or for a year, some 16,200,000 bolívares. For movie houses, underestimating the number at only one hundred which showed political advertising, the weekly total would run 3,000 bolívares, or 12,000 bolívares per month and 144,000 bolívares for the year. Magazine advertisements, somewhat variable, is estimated conservatively at 2,500 bolívares weekly; this amounts to 130,000 bolívares per year; another modest estimate of only ten magazines produces expenditures of another 25,000 bolívares monthly, or 300,000 bolívares for one such valla for a year; at a total of one hundred, this would produce a cost of 30 million bolívares. For afiches or campaign posters, generally costing one bolívar, a calculation of one hundred separate afiches, each of which had 500,000 copies, adds another 50 million bolívares to expenses.

Other items must be included: radio and television specials run at least 1 million bolívares; buttons, flags, pins, and similar campaign gimmickry are one-half million bolívares; another half-million bolívares at least is spent on organizing and conducting large meetings and rallies. Perhaps another two million bolívares goes to polling. We have not included expenses for party activists--which Resumen calculated at 90 million bolívares for a year--nor fees to outside consultants and advisers serving under contract. Neither does this include the fees of the advertising agencies employed. Eliminating all of these additional categories, the generally conservative calculations above still have COPEI and the AD spending approximately 160 million bolívares each.[53]

Estimating that the other campaigns together amounted to another
10 percent, we have 16 million bolívares more. Adding together
all the party campaign totals, along with the CSE expenditures,
produces approximately 450 million bolívares. Divided by 4.5
million eligible voters, the result is 100 bolívares per voter--
slightly over $23 each. Another way of putting it is to say that
the 450 million bolívares were spent to elect some 250 national
congressmen, or an average of 1.8 million bolívares each.

Whatever example one contrives, the conclusion is
inescapable--the Venezuelan campaign was extraordinarily costly.
Moreover, the amount of government advertising, substantially
increased during the campaign period, was of course financed from
the national budget. The total outlay for the Fernández campaign
was therefore effectively larger than that of any other candidate,
including Pérez.[54] The end result was a rising tide of criticism
that followed lines familiar to many countries in recent years:
only wealthy persons could be free of political commitments; the
necessity for large contributions opened the door to bribery,
extortion, and pressure; major economic interests would be able to
control leading parties and candidates; poorly financed candidates
had no practical chance of winning office; in short, politics was
generally being corrupted morally and materially by money. The
crowning event of this "dance of the millions" was a widely
publicized wager of one million bolívares between supporters of
Fernández and Pérez. Oswaldo Llobet, a Valencia merchant, offered
his bet with the pronouncement that Lorenzo's sure victory provided
him confidence that there would be no takers. Three days later
Portuguesa cattleman José Coury Torbay accepted. On 15 November a
full-page adeco advertisement showed Sr. Coury with a check in his
hand saying, "Here is my million for Carlos Andrés."[55]
Arrangements proceeded while some protested what was seen as a
carnivalesque degradation of the electoral process. The two
bettors made publicized visits to their respective candidates,
while the press and magazines covered the story.

POLLING IN THE 1973 CAMPAIGN
    If the use of money produced concern about the manipulative
dimensions of the campaign, the utilization and validity of
political polls was even more controversial. A brief background
of Venezuelan polling is therefore useful. The sampling of public
opinion for political rather than commercial purposes was
relatively new. Political polling was first employed in the 1963
campaign, but not extensively; by 1968 there was heavier usage by
the parties, including efforts to adapt poll results for partisan
purposes.   One summary of published results of 1968 polls
showed the following array of voter preferences:[56]

			10/31-			
Dates:	11/29	11/15	11/12	10/7-11/7		12/1
Caldera	42%	29.02%	25%	24.1%	21.4%	29.1%
Barrios	18	45.05	20	20.9	21.3	28.2
Prieto	24	17.20	27	28.7	20.8	19.3
Burelli	11	8.73	18	23.3	28.6	22.3
Sources:	OPISA	Publicidad Formas	Nueva Voz Popular	Economis- tas Asociadas	Liga de Inde- pendientes	Official Results

Culminating the partisan manipulation of polls was the citation in
a pro-Caldera paper of the findings of "Lou Harris" two days before
elections. The banner headline—unaccompanied by prose or citation
of source—revealed to no one's surprise a comfortable margin of
victory for its candidate: Caldera, 40 percent; Barrios, 29
percent; Prieto, 23 percent; and Burelli, 8 percent. Such
unscrupulous use of both legitimate and phantom polls by the
candidates and parties contributed to inevitable public mistrust of
such "findings." At the same time, however, scientifically sound
and nonpartisan work was being done, especially by DATOS. It was
this organization that had become recognized for the quality of
its political polling—which itself constituted a very small
proportion of its overall survey activities.[57] By 1973, other firms
were also producing increasingly serious and professional findings
to their clients.

DATOS's reputation for accuracy and integrity has been
recognized, based in part upon the general belief—never verified
or denied publicly by the firm—that it had been **remarkably**
accurate during the close 1968 elections. Of others in Venezuela,
the local outlet for the German firm GETAS is well known, as its
relationship with COPEI. During the 1973 campaign, furthermore,
both COPEI and the AD contracted for polling services with various
sources, as well as employing party technicians and experts to run
spot-checks. Rafael Salvatierra for COPEI and Héctor Silva of the
AD played a supervisory role in such undertakings. By 1973 the
sophistication of political leaders had grown with regard to the
polls, if they had not yet become fully appreciative of possible
interpretive **refinements.** They were no longer interested solely
in candidate preferences and popularity soundings but sought
guidance on issue salience and public concerns. The AD, it should
be recalled, had been influenced by survey results in its choice of
image and issue emphasis for Carlos Andrés Pérez. COPEI also
devised various campaign strategies in the light of opinion
findings. This did not, however, deter either COPEI or the AD from
announcements of favorable poll results without giving full figures,
sources, or analysis. Public mistrust and cynicism therefore
continued to challenge the validity and honesty of political polls.

In addition to the existence of unreliable or scientifically
unsound polling practices by some firms, partisan misrepresentation
had added to public skepticism. Inaccurate or ambiguous reporting

also contributed to widespread distrust of the polls. In March of 1973 the generally responsible Bohemia, for instance, issued a widely read story that reported an upward trend on behalf of Lorenzo Fernández. It first declared that DATOS's monthly polls the preceding November and December had given Pérez the lead with 24 percent, followed with Pérez Jiménez and Fernández each at 18 percent; 20 percent were reported as undecided.[58] Nearly six months later another Bohemia story, claiming to have the results of DATOS's three-month polls, proved a melange of confusion and contradiction.[59] Under an eye-catching banner that claimed the projection of a flatfooted tie between Pérez and Fernández on election day, it gave several sets of contradictory figures. Totals between voter preferences for president and for political parties were confused; the bases for alleged projections were not presented, nor could they be deduced from the text, while one table of figures was printed without explanation or accompanying prose.

Charges and countercharges continued to swirl about the polls. In September a front-page headline in the daily 2001, reporting results unfavorable to the AD, produced an angry protest from David Morales Bello. The paper duly printed his objections without providing further information on the previous story, which was both incomplete and improperly identified. Not long afterward Momento, claiming the need to protect itself from litigation, reported on three public opinion surveys identified as "A," "B," and "C."[60] According to the pro-Fernández magazine, the polls favored COPEI. Empresa "A," described as a seven-city survey resembling the DATOS poll for "Pulso," reported for August an intention of 26 percent to vote for COPEI and 20 percent for the AD. This was explicitly compared with July findings of 27 percent for Fernández and 21 percent for Pérez; the switch in terminology from party to candidate, possibly innocent, was not mentioned. Respondents reportedly said that Fernández was "best for Venezuela" in the opinion of 32 percent; Pérez followed with 27 percent. The number of readers noting the different wording and meaning of the questions was doubtless small. Momento then reported that Empresa "B," reporting Caracas only for July, found 26.8 percent planning to vote for Fernández and 24.1 percent for Pérez. On the similar but decidedly nonidentical question of who had the best chance of winning, 42.8 percent indicated Fernández and 28.8 percent Pérez (the totals for this question went over 100 percent). This apparent carelessness in reporting, incomprehensible analysis, or partisanship in presentation unfortunately typified much of the press handling of poll results. It was small wonder that they were shrouded in mists of controversy and disbelief.

A chain of events that brought the copeyano-adeco rivalry to heated intensity began on Saturday, 27 October, in the headquarters of the AD. Octavio Lepage told newsmen that the AD viewed opinion polls as useful for the orientation of electoral campaigns, and that propaganda was not the purpose. In view of widespread public references to alleged polls of unknown paternity, the AD had earlier issued a public invitation to serious firms to reveal their results. Since this had gone unheeded and fraudulent propaganda usage continued, the AD felt it incumbent to release the findings of its own most recently commissioned poll. The secretary general then introduced the North American president of "Gaither International, S.A." who had twenty years' experience with survey work in Latin America; he had reportedly predicted the narrow Caldera victory in 1968.[61] George Gaither proceeded to explain his findings. In a nationwide survey conducted from 5 September to 5 October, using over one hundred survey points and drawing from all social classes, Gaither found the following percentages on voter preferences: Pérez 31, Ferández 27, Rangel 9, and Paz Galarraga 4; the other candidates were under 5 percent, and there were 18 percent undecided. In response to preferences limited to six candidates (Pérez, Fernández, Rangel, Paz, Tinoco, and Villalba), Pérez enjoyed a lead of 32 percent compared to Fernández's 27 percent; Rangel had 10 percent, Paz 5 percent, and 19 percent were undecided.[62]

By the time the story appeared Sunday morning in the press, Gaither had taped television commercials and was leaving the country; COPEI was indignant, and the guerra de las encuestas ("the war of the polls") had broken out anew. AD made wide use of the results, including television announcements in which Gaither, speaking badly accented Spanish, explained the findings. While COPEI initially regarded the poll as totally spurious, it also believed the AD had blundered in using a Yankee to advertise the results.[63] Paz Galarraga, citing mepista membership of 400,000, scoffed at the results and cited his own, on-the-spot, encuestas vivas. Rangel described the surveys as undertaken by desperate groups of the bourgeoisie lacking the backing of the pueblo. Orestes Di Giácomo of the MEP thought it likely that if Borregales could afford to commission a poll, undoubtedly Don Germán would be in the lead! Despite flashes of humor, however, serious controversy loomed immediately ahead.

COPEI initially attempted to ridicule the poll and impugn its author. The party denounced the AD's reliance on a foreigner, who was also charged with violating laws against participation in the electoral process. It also claimed that Gaither International had not existed in Venezuela in 1968, hence could not have predicted the Caldera victory. The Social Christian secretary general charged the AD with a propaganda stunt promoting the interference of foreigners, calling it "an absurd and gross maneuver that helps to cast doubt on the authenticity of other polls." Unlike the AD, he continued, COPEI had the maturity not to release poll results. Aguilar went on to add that GETAS poll results showed Lorenzo Fernández in the lead, as did all of the DATOS polls.[64] In a matter of hours his contentions boomeranged when Carlos Andrés Pérez blithely announced at his weekly breakfast with the press that the latest DATOS poll gave him a lead of 9 percent, some 400,000 votes ahead of his Social Christian rival. He further provided newsmen with a copy of a DATOS report to its subscribers which confirmed his lead of 30 to 21 percent. Whether this version of DATOS findings was valid, the public impact was unambiguous. The adeco candidate, having refuted to his satisfaction the Social

Christian claims regarding DATOS findings, repeated the invitation to COPEI to make public its own polls.[65] Even the apparent DATOS confirmation of a Pérez lead over Fernández faded alongside the most startlingly impolitic public declaration of the entire campaign. During extemporaneous remarks following the weekly conference of party leaders, the copeyano secretary general told the press: "I want to confess that in elections such as those of 1958 and 1963, when in COPEI we appreciated the electoral perspective was not very favorable to us, we had recourse to that trick of inventing a poll and making it public with the idea that some unwary people could be seduced."

The enormity of this gaffe by the combative Social Christian spokesman overshadowed the earlier Gaither dispute, and AD lept to the fray with obvious relish. In less than forty-eight hours radio commercials went over the airwaves, beginning with a recording of Aguilar's voice uttering the damning words; these faded away as the announcer proceeded to denounce such copeyano deceit as further proof that Venezuela needed truthful leaders like Carlos Andrés Pérez. By Saturday the press also began publishing adeco advertisements. A typical one presented the previously cited words of Aguilar as printed in the 31 October issue of 2001, surrounded by a black border. The headline read: "This is the confession by those who use traps and deceit before imminent defeat." Below the boxed quotation was the further statement, "one cannot believe in those who confess to having utilized falsehood and traps to confuse when they have seen themselves defeated."[66] While the local COPEI-controlled Junta Electoral tried to stop further broadcasts of the commercial,[67] the Comité Ejecutivo Nacional of the AD added further pressure by terming as "scandalous" the "grave and compromising declarations of Pedro Pablo Aguilar." Lest the point somehow be missed, it was added that "Acción Democrática believes that Venezuelan democracy needs ethical and responsible participation of its political parties, especially of the largest, on whose action, in large part, its future depends."[68]

The Aguilar statement and its **aftermath**, coming in the **wake** of the Gaither results and apparent confirmation by the respected DATOS survey,[69] left the AD as winner of the guerra de encuestas. Social Christian blunders in response to the adeco initiative gave a great boost to the Pérez candidacy. COPEI's continuing effort to impugn George Gaither, moreover, was at best inconclusive. Oswaldo Alvarez Paz, speaking for COPEI during a tactical withdrawal of Aguilar from the public eye, returned to the theme of Gaither's nationality. "It is inconceivable that a party announces the results one day in a press conference and the same day the newspapers receive page advertisements...and television announcements are produced with a foreigner, a North American associated with multinational companies, stating that a certain candidate is going to win the elections in the country."[70] How long, he added, rhetorically, must Venezuelans stand for such foreign meddling in domestic affairs? Moreover, records showed that Gaither International had not been in existence in Venezuela in 1968. As it developed, there was truth in both the COPEI and AD claims concerning Dr. Gaither; it was true that Gaither International had not been operating in Venezuela in 1968. However, he had been in charge of field work for International Research Associates (INRA), which did indeed exist.

While its communications experts were making the most of Pedro Pablo Aguilar's statement, the AD called another press conference, at which they returned the "foreigner intervention" charge deep into the copeyano court. Octavio Lepage contended that it was the Social Christian party that permitted interference into internal Venezuelan affairs. "COPEI not only maintains German experts in the management of polls"--which he termed "technical" and therefore not interference in domestic politics--but had also contracted services of "planners in the organization of electoral campaigns and in the distribution and handling of propaganda, the manufacture and preparation of slogans, and publicity campaigns." Lepage provided photostats showing Edmund Moser as president of GETAS Venezolana, C.A., COPEI's polling agency. Other documents included the name of Moser as a leading stockholder. "One needs a very straight face," he continued, "to say that 100 percent of that enterprise is managed by Venezuelans."[71]

Moser was also identified as representing Germany's Adenauer Foundation, and reporters were reminded of a story in Der Spiegel the previous year revealing a close friendship between Moser and the Social Christian foreign minister Arístides Calvani. The AD secretary general waxed sarcastic in asking if COPEI did not classify Germans as foreigners; he then observed that COPEI presumably lacked full confidence in its German advisers and thus had contracted Matt Reese from the United States, as well as United States film producer David Sawyer.[72] He further charged COPEI with having sent a representative to the 1972 Democratic convention in Miami to recruit advisers. After telling newsmen that Gaither had been paid some 150,000-160,000 bolívares--which went to Venezuelan representatives and would therefore remain in the country and be taxable--he announced that the AD would do no further polling. Gaither had called the winner for 1973, as he did in 1968. In a final footnote, the secretary general suggested that COPEI might hold a press conference with Moser to make public the data of the GETAS poll.

As the session thus drew to a close, there was little question that the AD had assumed the offensive. Aided by the attack of foot-in-mouth disease that visited itself on COPEI, the AD had gained significantly. Yet there was the possibility of a COPEI counterattack on a totally different front. Whether coincidental or not, this erupted less than a week after the Gaither press conference in the intricate mosaic of ILAPECA and the hoarding of milk.

FROM POLLS TO MILK: ILAPECA

The morning papers on Friday, 2 November, reported that a raid in Maracaibo the preceding afternoon had uncovered 100,000 kilos of powdered milk in an AD printing and publicity shop. Moreover, adeco deputy Eleazar Pinto had been taken into custody. The public functionaries, who had been accompanied on their raid by a battery of photographers, announced to the press that their action had been based on a presumption of hoarding. COPEI began broadcasting allegations that the AD had been hoarding in order to promote a shortage that could be used for electoral purposes. The AD immediately responded that the powdered milk was the legal property of the firm ILAPECA, and that the AD had not used the propaganda shop for several months. The president of ILAPECA also issued a statement affirming that the milk belonged to the firm. Noting that all imports of powdered milk were carried out under authorized quotas from the Ministry of Development, Dr. Alberto Finol declared that ILAPECA currently had an inventory of over three million kilograms stored—the equivalent of over two months' sales. The 100,000 kilos in question, due to a space shortage in ILAPECA warehouses, had therefore been placed temporarily in the building that was raided.[73]

By Saturday the controversy became both confusing as to facts and nasty in tone. Julio César Moreno of the JRC announced that the AD leadership was pursing a conscious policy of hoarding such basic products as sugar, flour, and black beans—all for partisan advantage at the expense of the poor. Deputy Pinto should be stripped of his parliamentary immunity and subject to prosecution.[74] Pro-Fernández forces continued the attack with public statements by Jorge Dáger, who asked that the government "immediately and effectively apply the law, with proper penalties for hoarding."[75] Social Christian media experts, still smarting under the impact of the Gaither-inspired exchanges, wasted little time. Typical of their effort was a colorful advertisement on an outer page of 2001 Saturday, which featured in large letters the word "aCAParADores"; thus the initials of Pérez and his party stood out in the Spanish word for "hoarders."[76]

In Caracas Friday Lepage denounced what he termed the newest copeyano effort to discredit the opposition; Zulia Governor Hilarión Cardozo was singled out as responsible for the ILAPECA affair. The secretary general insisted that the Maracaibo locale had not been rented by the party for several months and that Pinto's presence had resulted from a garbled radio broadcast concerning reports of the forthcoming raid. Secretary of Organization Piñerúa Ordaz added that hoarding seemed impossible when the commodity in question was not in short supply.[77] The major response came the following day in Maracaibo, however, at a press conference conducted by Carlos Andrés Pérez. Speaking extemporaneously and with evident care in choosing his words and restraining his anger, the candidate categorically denied party complicity and called upon both the government and ILAPECA to clarify the situation. Throughout the campaign, he continued, the government party "has produced all kinds of defamatory and damaging propaganda, against me personally and against my party." With this latest recurrence, it would seem that the absence of judicial action was inexcusable. "If the company is hoarding milk in complicity with a political party, the government should take legal

measures...in accord with the law.   And if ILAPECA has nothing to
hide, then it should take legal steps to recover its property....[78]
By Sunday the dispute had assumed yet harsher terms through an
exchange between party presidents Gonzalo Barrios and Godofredo
González.   The adeco used uncharacteristically blunt language.
Responsible Venezuelans, he contended, were increasingly concerned
over a possible crisis of the system, and the AD had responded
through honorable and patriotic opposition.

> In all honesty we affirm that COPEI has not proceeded
> in the same manner.   We have previously denounced its
> numerous abuses, its aggressions and its low blows.   And
> now, in the name of Acción Democrática and as president
> of the party, I come to formulate a denunciation...because
> we are convinced that the proximity of elections and the
> certain perspectives of our victory are spurring
> conspiracies against the reputation of the AD and the
> image of its presidential candidate, sharpening the
> implicit dangers of deceits and attacks contrary to the
> spirit of the regime within which we legitimately make
> opposition and aspire to power.

Publication of favorable poll results on behalf of Pérez had
"unleashed against him and his party a wave of violent and fearful
reactions explainable only by bad advice grown out of desperation."
COPEI's propaganda continued to employ "the fascist concept that a
lie, even if absurd, comes to be believed and supplies a sense of
proven truth if sufficiently repeated."   The AD's moderation was
not limitless "in the face of all the unjust aggressions that are
carried out with the tolerance, not to say support of the public
powers of the Nation."[79]
Acting President González of COPEI, not known as an immoderate
or unduly partisan politician, employed similarly strong language
at a press conference.   He maintained Zulia authorities had
responded to a complaint by citizens living in the neighborhood and
had found the powdered milk amidst AD afiches and campaign
propaganda.   He also assumed that Eleazar Pinto's efforts to prevent
the raid demonstrated probable guilt.   COPEI knew that "AD was
preparing, as a part of its campaign of provocation of artificial
scarcity, the disappearance from the market of various products of
prime popular necessity.   It already happened with sugar, with black
beans, and they were trying to do the same with powdered milk, to
cause a negative popular action against the government and COPEI."
In the past, COPEI had lacked sufficient proof of adeco wrongdoing
but now would request a government investigation of the apparent
violation of the nation's laws against hoarding and usury.   "There
is no doubt that at the end of any electoral process...tense
situations are sharpened by the confrontation of different political
forces.   We have said that we are prepared to contribute with all
our efforts to...lower those tensions as we near the day of the
vote.   But we cannot fail to denounce facts that are prejudicial to
the public such as the promotion of scarcity of products for popular
consumption."[80]

Respective communications experts entered into the fray. On Sunday, 4 November, "COPEI DICE" carried a long editorial entitled "A Delinquent Party." The AD "has been converted into a party hoarding the food of the people, because it wants those products to rise in price while the vultures who want to nourish themselves on the hunger of the pueblo will be enriched."[81] The Social Christians also presented a two-page advertisement with its own poll findings, conducted by an unidentified if "responsible" firm employing "a team of independent, Venezuelan professionals, composed of statisticians, sociologists, psychologists, engineers, and social communicators." They reported a sizable lead for Fernández over Pérez and a strong sentiment that COPEI's government had done a better job than any others the country had experienced.[82] In contrast, "La Página de Acción Democrática" the same day included headlines that Zulia Governor Cardozo "also knows how to falsify scandals" and requoted the "confessions of a sinner named Pedro Pablo Aguilar," reiterating that the AD had long known of copeyano poll manipulation, to which "Dr. Aguilar has now confessed."[83]

Gonzalo Barrios, arriving later the same day at AD headquarters, classified COPEI's charges as a "brazen exploitation of the lie." Furthermore, he was startled that Godofredo González, "a man whom I consider serious and decent, seems to be subscribing to affirmations about hoarding of food products on the part of the AD in spite of knowing that such is not only a falsehood, but a veritable absurdity."[84] COPEI, undaunted by countercharges, began running full-page advertisements featuring photographs of the police and of Pinto taken during the moments of actual occupation. Headlines read that "AD is guilty of the high cost of living, of speculating and hoarding the food of the pueblo." The text spoke of the AD's act as "irresponsibility and cynicism without precedent in Venezuelan political history," and "the most damaging and criminal political maneuver known in the history of the country."[85] With such vehement charges and allegations poisoning the atmosphere, the effort of the press to unravel the case proved difficult and inconclusive. ILAPECA attempted to clarify its own position, only to be drawn more deeply into the political morass.

While the firm's legal department drew up papers requesting return of the confiscated 100,000 kilos of powdered milk, its vice-president José Sabal Machado repeated the argument that in the absence of a milk shortage, hoarding seemed both irrelevant and impossible. The ILAPECA purchase of 500,000 kilos from Holland had been stored in the regular company warehouse, with the exception of the challenged 100,000 kilos, which because of inadequate storage space were temporarily placed in the Maracaibo shop. Guido Gómez, manager of the firm and a member of the AD, charged that his affiliation had led the state government to intervene and noted that there were copeyanos among the directors of the firm. Full-page advertisements were also placed by ILAPECA, citing data since 1967 to show the increase of Venezuelan employees as well as its rise in sales of dairy and milk products to Venezuelans.[86] A letter to the minister of development from Barrios and Lepage on behalf of the AD formally asked that any infraction by the party be indicated publicly. The directors of Fedecámaras issued similar petitions after hearing a presentation by ILAPECA officials but also received no response. Unable to elicit enlightenment from government officials, the AD continued its vigorous protestations. Pérez told his weekly press conference on 6 November that the Maracaibo incident was an immoral and illegal maneuver involving the government and its party; Barrios's column on the tenth, "El Watergate de Maracaibo," lamented the wounding of moral judgment by both the government and COPEI. Insisting upon the certainty of an adeco victory in December, he pledged that the "immediate future will demand of us the choosing from diverse options, by means of a will that combines firmness with honesty and foresight. This undertaking can only be carried through to a successful conclusion by men who, besides inspiring confidence as politicians, also inspire it as administrators. By definition, integrity is one and indivisible."[87] The AD also prepared a advertisements with the word "infamy" superimposed over copeyano pictures of the confiscation; beneath was a reminder of the damaging quotation from Aguilar.[88] COPEI, while continuing to hit the hoarding issue, made occasional sallies against the Gaither poll as well; there was yet a stubborn insistence that all polls showed Fernández winning, producing on the part of the AD a "desperate attitude which obliges us to be more vigilant than ever, because the enemies of the country have found allies in our land. Today more than ever, Lorenzo's firm position in defense of our interests is justified."[89]

Coming immediately on top of the encuesta war, the hoarding squabble brought campaign tempers to a fever pitch. Both Rafael Caldera and Rómulo Betancourt undertook to moderate the climate. The president spoke to reporters in measured and noninflammatory language, promising that a legal investigation was underway. He also noted the inevitable intensification of opinion with the proximity of elections but asked all political parties "not to exceed the limits of moderation."[90] Betancourt, traveling to the interior, repeatedly stressed the importance of the democratic process and the necessity of civilized exchange and tolerance. Despite a wide variation of partisan interpretations, the press voiced a common concern over the deterioration of the electoral climate. Perhaps unconsciously, both parties themselves drew back at least a little from their more immoderate exchanges.

The milk controversy itself was left unresolved. There was never any indication that the AD leadership had indeed undertaken a policy of hoarding--an act which, as a practical matter, could scarcely have been undertaken at such a level as to affect the entire domestic market. Whether there was independent trickery by local party leaders, logically less improbable, was not supported by hard evidence. On the other side, neither was there proof that national copeyano leaders had plotted the affair, nor that Governor Cardozo was implicated. Government handling of the case did appear curious. An order by a Maracaibo judge to return the milk to ILAPECA on 23 November was denied by officials of the Ministry of Development. In late January 1974 the ministry

further announced that the powdered milk would not be returned to
ILAPECA.
     With the full truth of the matter unlikely ever to be
unraveled, it is important to recall the timing of the episode.
Adeco suspicions that it was a carefully planned conspiracy were
not illogical within the heated campaign context, although
corroboration was missing. If nothing else, the entire episode had
distracted attention from the Gaither poll and its aftermath, thus
providing COPEI with an opportunity to recoup its propaganda
setback. Whether or not COPEI or the AD would be believed in the
milk case remained problematic. In the meantime, the campaign
cooled somewhat in temper but remained vigorously competitive.[91]
     COPEI's use of the ILAPECA affair, in summary, was symptomatic
of a more profound weakness in its campaign. Convinced that the
application of a well-financed and powerfully organized apparatus
would produce victory, the party lacked adequate contingency
planning. Thus the only means of response to the negative feedback
of adverse polls was denunciation of the results and degradation of
the methods employed. Unprepared to recognize or cope with a loss
of momentum, the copeyanos lacked an alternative strategy to regain
the initiative. The consequence was a hasty resort to ad hoc
tactical reactions which, added to the evident idiosyncracies of
the Fernández style, threw the campaign effort into disarray.
Unlike the AD, which utilized the results of private polling to
make incremental adjustments in its campaign, COPEI restricted
access to its own polls, creating uncertainty and doubt among
important supporters within the campaign machinery itself. In
short, the ILAPECA episode, though shrouded in mystery, reveals a
major flaw in the conduct of COPEI's campaign.

MANAGING ELECTORAL CONFLICT
     As the campaign process gradually unfolded the CSE remained
near the center of activity. The obvious task of preparing for
and managing the vote on election day was far from its only
concern. The CSE response to adeco charges of government
intervention has already been recounted, and as election day neared,
extracurricular duties accumulated. As the principal legal
institution empowered to oversee electoral activity, the capacity
for problem-solving and conflict management by the CSE became a
crucial element in the process. One of the important areas was
that of propaganda and advertising. It was largely the verbal
violence provoked by the Gaither and ILAPECA disputes that led the
national Chambers of Radio and Television to impose their own
restrictions on political advertising. It was announced on 4
November that all political propaganda would be reviewed by the
Cámara Venezolana de la Televisión. None would be broadcast
without full identification; all would be excluded that might be
"wounding or offensive to the dignity of party institutions or of
political personalities...;" and there would be care to avoid
messages "which can incite public lack of tranquility and contribute
to wounding of the normal unfolding of the electoral process."[92]
     While there was sympathy with the good intentions of the

broadcasting industry, many questioned its authority for such a decision. As the AD noted, although the action was laudable the legal authority was solely that of the CSE.[93]   CSE President Luis A. Pietri announced on 6 November that only the CSE had the power to control or limit political propaganda. On the eighth the CSE approved a set of standards for electoral propaganda: there was a prohibition on all anonymous propaganda, a ban on defamation of organs of the state and its institutions, and prohibition of the use of proper names without permission of the individual. A few days later Pietri initiated a series of meetings with publishers and editors to discuss and clarify relevant guidelines. He especially reminded them of the legal requirement that all electoral propaganda cease forty-eight hours before the start of the vote, which meant midnight of Thursday, 6 December.[94]

The AD requested that the Consejo prohibit all official propaganda from radio and television for the final fifteen days of the campaign. Referring to the 19 October statement concerning government publicity, the party claimed that there had been no appreciable decline and therefore urged that only purely administrative information be permitted. On the fifteenth the CSE released new restrictions, holding political parties to a daily limit of ten television commercials between 5:30 P.M. and 11:30 P.M., and ten for the remainder of the broadcast day; none were to exceed one minute in duration. Each party could also have a weekly half-hour program and a daily five-minute program on each television network. Special events, such as presentation of a program or official closing acts, were exempted. Radio was restricted to a total of one-sixth its time, to be divided equally among the parties requesting it. Each party was limited to a maximum of 1,200 centimeters per newspaper column daily in each paper (approximately three pages); interviews and news stories were excluded. As to official organs and state entities, the CSE decreed that its publicity would be restricted to administrative items, without use of slogans or **phrases** considered as either direct or indirect electoral propaganda.[95]

Later CSE decisions included a banning of all vehicles with loudspeakers from circulating with electoral propaganda except between 10 A.M. and 8 P.M.--a measure observed more in the breach than the promise. Restrictions were also placed on partisan activities in the various Caracas plazas and circles "owned" by one or another of the parties.[96]   Concern was being voiced by mid-November over the existence of COPEI's plans to announce electoral results. CSE President Pietri announced repeatedly that there was no law against any such practice, but that only the CSE returns would be official. With elections nearing, he also made frequent public appearances and statements assuring the electorate of the integrity of the process. A series of meetings were held with the party secretaries general during the final three weeks, as well as with other ranking political leaders. When Pérez Jiménez released his charge from Madrid that the elections would be fraudulent, Pietri responded with a public denial, for

the Electoral Power which we represent will not permit
it; because the personal and political honesty of the
current President of the Republic would never favor it;
because the Fuerzas Armadas Nacionales guarantee...in the
stability of its democratic institutions, respect for the
Fundamental Charter and the impartiality of the vote;
because the democratic political parties, indispensable
factors in all governments of a representative nature,
similarly would not permit an attempt on republican
institutions; and, finally, because the Venezuelan pueblo
is not ready to agree that its sovereign will, expressed
by means of the vote, can be mocked and disowned.[97]

As something less than an afterthought, he also remarked that the
last case of electoral fraud had been in 1952 under the regime of
Marcos Pérez Jiménez.

During the final days of the campaign, repeated messages from
the CSE, from the president of the Republic, and from the Venezuelan
military reassured the electorate of the safeguards and guarantees
attached to the electoral process. At midnight on Thursday, 6
December, official campaigning came to a close. The carnival that
had seized Caracas in the final weeks reluctantly drew to its end,
although the city remained noisy throughout the night. Lorenzo
Fernández had appeared briefly at the Plaza Venezuela for a final
message to his followers; Carlos Andrés Pérez had marched
confidently across metropolitan Caracas, the jubilation of his
companions undampened by afternoon showers, concluding before
supporters in Plaza Altamira; José Vicente Rangel paid final visits
to several neighborhoods, ending with an impromptu speech along
Sabana Grande, without microphone, scrupulously departing as
midnight neared; Jesús Angel Paz Galarraga had already completed
his campaign in El Silencio two nights earlier; Jóvito Villalba led
a final automobile caravan as dusk fell; other candidates had
largely terminated their activities earlier. On Sunday, 4.6
million Venezuelans would be eligible to cast their vote for
parties and candidates of their choice.

Following last-minute adjustments, the voters had the choice
of twenty national political parties; ten regional parties; four
groups of voters designated in certain municipalities; and twelve
presidential candidates.[98] They were to fill the presidency of the
Republic and to elect 225 national congressmen to the Senate and
Chamber of Deputies, 274 members of the twenty state legislative
assemblies, and local representatives of 181 municipal councils.
The voting system, after the three modifications since September
1970 approval of the Suffrage Law, stood ready for application.
The boleta única had three columns bearing the colorful symbols of
some four dozen alternatives. With over 75,000 Venezuelans
scheduled to serve at the 15,011 voting mesas distributed
throughout the country--not including party witnesses and a CSE
secretary per table--all that remained, it seemed, was the voting
and its tabulation. Despite the changes of system and method of
voting, CSE officials had given extensive assurances of total and

unqualified preparations as December approached. The public respected not only the CSE's determined nonpartisanship but also the apparent professionalism of the staff. Further public confidence was built through military participation in Operación República III, with the armed forces providing extensive technical and logistical support.

The computer center installed for the December elections, acquired under contract from Management Assistance Incorporated of Venezuela (MAI), consisted of two electronic computers and accompanying transmission machinery. A copy of the acta from each of the 15,011 mesas would arrive at the CSE and be checked for valid seals and signatures before going to the computer center for verification and transcription. Teams of eighty persons would put the tabulations onto magnetic tapes, with verification following immediately. MAI officials anticipated a 3 percent margin of error in the initial transcription, with verification reducing this to zero. The magnetic tapes would then go to the first computer in groups of twenty, with each group taking but a few seconds. With 60 million characters and 64,000 memory positions programmed, the computer would already have lists of mesa voters and similar data for further verification or rejection of returns. The second computer would project results onto television screens installed in the office of the CSE presidency, for use by the press and for national television.

With the system having a capacity to receive a maximum of 100,000 voters per hour, it was believed that forty-eight hours would be sufficient to complete the process, although 80 percent should be compiled and released publicly by afternoon Tuesday. A trial run on the machinery by MAI officials was conducted a week before elections, indicating all was in good order. The MAI machinery consisted of "third generation" equipment centered upon the IBM 360/30. Its rental was 700,000 bolívares for three months, including operating expenses and cost of personnel. Located in a sealed room under the Centro Simón Bolívar towers in downtown Caracas, it would be retained by the CSE in 1974 for all electoral processing and the subsequent repurification of the Registro Electoral Permanente.[99]

With election day impending, problems with the Registro Electoral suddenly appeared. Tens of thousands of Venezuelans had not been informed of the mesa to which they were assigned, and mesa officials themselves were lacking in information. Seemingly out of nowhere, a major crisis loomed. At first it was believed that relatively few voters had not been properly assigned and informed of their voting mesa. CSE President Pietri announced on Tuesday, 4 December, that in such cases the individual should go to the nearest municipal board, where officials would check and then authorize his voting in the last mesa in his local area. As numbers of puzzled voters began to grow, the CSE on Thursday announced the locations in Caracas of six so-called Pilot Centers of Information and Orientation; these, it was said, could provide or obtain all necessary information on any voter. However, at least two of the sixteen were found by newsmen to be nonexistent, and voters in some

cases had received as many as three separate and conflicting
notices as to their assigned mesa.[100]   Newspaper headlines in
Caracas dailies announced "disorientation," "confusion," and a
"disconcerting" aura. It soon became apparent that the highly
touted Registro Electoral, for a variety of reasons, was seriously
wanting.

A major complaint was the delay in CSE delivery to the voter
of proof of inscription (comprobante) in the Registro Electoral.
The use of the mails in the days immediately preceding elections
was unwise, given the service's slowness and unreliability. The
hiring of private messengers represented a desperate stopgap
measure. Voters still lacking official notification were driven to
a difficult and problematic search for information that was casting
increasing gloom over the proceedings. As the CSE repeated public
assurances of confidence, it was visited on Thursday and Friday, 6
and 7 December, by party leaders seeking clarification. Additional
remedial measures were adopted by the Consejo, which had gone into
permanent session on Thursday. Pietri characterized all problems
as "derived from the change of voting system and from the adoption
of a new institution in the Registro Electoral Permanente."[101]   He
detailed four separate sets of circumstances that might be
thwarting potential voters, issuing remedial instructions for each
of the categories. To be completed by midnight Saturday, these
were designed to assure that all citizens who had registered would
be certain of voting somewhere.[102]   In the meantime, rumors of an
electoral postponement added to the prevailing atmosphere of
concern and uncertainty.

Cables from the Associated Press were reporting that up to 50
percent of the electorate might be unable to vote. Radio Rumbos
quoted Marieli Marrero of the CSE as confirming the figure,
although she soon issued a denial. In the urban centers, lines of
citizens grew as time passed. Three new information centers were
opened Friday for the Caracas metropolitan area, staffed by the
most competent people available. Luis Pietri, unfailingly serene,
issued reassurances that all obstacles had been overcome. Appearing
on nationwide radio and television on Friday night, he again
ascribed CSE problems to "the adoption of new procedures and the
recent reforms of the Suffrage Law put into effect only three months
ago...."[103]   Saturday morning newspapers carried full-page notices
advising the voters of the most recent adjustments. Normality of
proceedings was assiduously and insistently repeated. However, the
AD expressed concern, various party leaders trooped into the CSE
for further discussions, and Miguel Angel Burelli Rivas released
a proposal calling for a pact by the candidates accepting a delay
of elections. Stories of voter confusion were legion: a man who
had solved his own problems lamented that his wife was assigned to
a mesa in San Cristóbal, Táchira; others had been placed on Los
Roques, a sparsely inhabited offshore island. The spirit with which
most Venezuelans accepted the situation was epitomized by the woman
who told a newsman of her gratitude to the CSE for giving her a
chance to see so much of Caracas while seeking the necessary
information!

A new array of adjustments was announced on Saturday night by the Consejo, including the extension of voting hours until 8 P.M. Where problems of registration and voting mesa still remained, electors would be able to vote after four in the afternoon at a local mesa, assuming possession of the proper documents. As advertisements in Sunday's press proclaimed to "the voter who does not know where to vote," those without their registration document, those omitted from the Registro Permanente Electoral, or those placed at a mesa not located near their residence could vote at any polling place in the **parish or municipality where they had** registered--from 4 P.M. on. Additional technical details--cutting the corner of the identity cédula, the inking of voters' little fingers, and the like--were also publicized.

As Sunday dawned on Caracas, the mesas were set up at 5:30 A.M. and opened to voters thirty minutes later. Despite intermittent showers, the voting proceeded without incident. The average wait in in line ran from two to four hours. Moreover, there were those who finally reached mesa officials only to learn that they would have to return again at 4 P.M. In the interior, the bulk of the voting was completed by early afternoon, although polling places remained open until 8 P.M. even if all its registered voters had already appeared. **By nightfall** the electorate had demonstrated, for the fourth time in fifteen years, its commitment to the act of voting. Whatever the preferences of the electorate, the turnout was heavy. Undaunted by the gravity and annoyance of CSE **errors** of omission and commission,[104] Venezuelans had provided an impressive demonstration of civic virtue.[105]

During the day, the press dutifully observed the act of voting by presidential candidates and accompanied President Caldera and ex-president Betancourt to the urns. The outpouring of voters amid an atmosphere of calm anticipation was reflected by the candidates themselves. Lorenzo Fernández breakfasted early, attended mass, cast his vote, and returned to "La Muchachera" to await the outcome. Promising to invite the opposition to join in a government of national breadth and commitment, he also joked with newsmen that he would be intrigued to know how President Caldera had voted. The Social Christian candidate was ebullient in his confidence, happily posing for photographers with both arms and fingers extended in victory signs. Carlos Andrés Pérez arose before **seven** and walked to the voting mesa, remarking that it was his last caminata as a presidential candidate. He predicted victory by over 200,000 votes but was equally unequivocal in promising to respect the verdict, whatever the outcome. Jesús Angel Paz Galarraga voted at mid-morning, expressed satisfaction in having carried his **message** of liberation to the nation's exploited, and said that no impugning of electoral results was expected. He went to Nueva Fuerza headquarters to await the returns. José Vicente Rangel also voted in the morning, arriving on foot and receiving applause from the voters. He praised the final CSE arrangements as positive, pledged respect for the results, then spent the day at his mother's home.

The other candidates passed the day in various ways after

casting their ballots.   Jóvito Villalba received friends, watched
television, and played dominoes.   Pedro Tinoco also entertained
friends at home; Segnini spent the day in FND headquarters; Burelli
praised the voters but repeated his charges of CSE "incompetence";
and Germán Borregales visited several polling places during the
day.   Rafael Caldera voted at Caño Amarillo at 8 A.M., briefly
expressing his satisfaction over the civic process and proclaiming
his pride in governmental guarantees of freedom and equality for
all citizens.   Rómulo Betancourt voted later in the morning at
Altamira's Colegio Don Bosco, praised the electorate, and
characterized Venezuela as having demonstrated itself "a country
apt for democracy."   As Sunday passed--warm and sunny in much of
the republic--respective party electoral teams readied themselves
for the evening's initiation of the vote count, while the CSE was
also believed in prepared.   After nearly two years of political
campaigning, the decisive moment was at hand.

9. THE VOTERS DECIDE:
Winners, Losers, Also-Rans

All was in readiness. The Boleíta machinery was euphoric in anticipation of the copeyano victory which Operación Arauca was expected to verify. At midnight Sunday its first bulletin reported Fernández leading with 7,499 votes to Pérez's 6,722, with all other candidates under 1,000 votes. It was to be the last Social Christian bulletin until midday Monday. Meanwhile adeco technicians in San Bernardino were relaying information to the candidate's headquarters in the Torre de las Delicias, where Diego Arria acted as spokesman. His first announcement gave the AD candidate a total of 94,575 votes to 66,644 for Fernández. Well before dawn Arria told the press that the outcome was increasingly clear. He claimed both Mérida and Táchira for Pérez, as well as Lara. Although conceding that COPEI had improved its position in the oriente, it still trailed there. The pro-Fernández margin in Zulia was unexpectedly small, while the Caracas race was neck-and-neck. By 9 A.M. Monday, with champagne already flowing in the penthouse, the AD was certain of its victory. Its computations of 80 percent of the vote showed a total of 1,268,202 for Carlos Andrés versus 990,940 for Lorenzo. With the margin pushing toward 300,000 the winner seemed obvious.

The adeco announcement elicited angry response from COPEI in the person of the candidate's son Luis Mariano Fernández, appearing in place of Rafael Salvatierra. Denouncing the statement, he explained that COPEI was responsibly seeking to avoid problems by delaying public claims while the vote tally was small. Later in the day Godofredo González also urged patience, praising the quality of COPEI's computing mechanisms but emphasizing the necessity of awaiting CSE returns. However, the impression of Pérez's victory was spreading in Caracas.[1] The afternoon edition of El Mundo headlined his victory; media reporters were referring to him as president-elect; and television personality Renny Ottolina concluded an interview with Octavio Lepage by sending his congratulations. José Vicente Rangel promptly recognized the outcome, while Jesús Angel Paz Galarraga told newsmen that Pérez was obviously the victor. Pedro Tinoco and Pedro Segnini La Cruz also agreed on the

outcome. By late afternoon the AD tally showed Pérez leading
Fernández by a margin both unexpected and irreversible--1,723,268
to 1,325,643. The Comité Ejecutivo Nacional met with the candidate,
then issued a call for serenity to all members and sympathizers.
Gonzalo Barrios further noted, "the data that the AD supplies are
obtained by means of a serious and sincere procedure. We would not
have any interest in revealing a victory that would be denied by
official returns."[2]
    For COPEI, both Boleíta and "La Muchachera" were largely
silent. Alvarez Paz appeared once to issue a brief call for
prudence until official returns were known. By 5 P.M. the
blackboard mounted by the computation center recorded 1,462,123
votes for Fernández and 1,388,776 for Pérez. Eduardo Fernández
referred to CSE errors and further recommended calm to party
supporters. Otherwise, party leaders were nowhere to be found, and
stiff security measures inside Boleíta were rigidly maintained.
Only much later was it learned that ranking copeyanos had repaired
to the candidate's home to recommend his concession. By that time
the outcome had also become clear in Miraflores, and President
Caldera saw the desirability of an official statement from
Fernández. The candidate, however, was totally unbelieving at the
returns and adamantly refused to concede. Throughout Tuesday both
Fernández and party officials were unavailable for comment. The
customary weekly meeting with Caldera was canceled with the
explanation that the Sunday and Monday vigil had left party leaders
too tired. At "La Muchachera" friends and visitors were denied
entrance.
    Announcements from the CSE were coming more frequently by this
time, although totals mounted with plodding slowness (see table 15
for a selection of CSE returns). The final Monday bulletin had
tabulated 270,997 votes--an estimated 5.81 percent of the registered
voters. Pérez had received 121,375 votes for 46 percent, compared
with Fernández's 102,771 and 39 percent. Rangel stood third with
6 percent of the vote, followed by Paz with 3 percent and Villalba
with 2 percent.[3] By the end of Tuesday the CSE had counted 722,783
votes, with Pérez leading Fernández by 48.6 to 37.8 percent. Rangel
led Paz by less than one thousand votes, with each a shade over 4
percent of the total.[4] Jóvito Villalba conceded with a
characteristic telegram to the winner. Insofar as the new government
freed itself from the deviations and mistakes of the present system,
"you will receive my most sincere and disinterested support, while
in the contrary case you will receive our frank opposition."[5] The
continued seclusion of Lorenzo Fernández and of most copeyano
leaders was meanwhile producing growing concern. Private
individuals and business spokesmen, including Fedecámaras and
Pro-Venezuela, urged the necessity of conceding. Finally, COPEI
convoked a press conference for midday on Wednesday, 12 December.
    Secretary General Aguilar announced that the purpose would be
to read a telegram from Fernández to Pérez. It was brief, blunt,
graceless. "Mindful of my democratic convictions and my
responsibility before the country, although the official scrutiny
of the elections held last Sunday has not yet been concluded, I

TABLE 15.   CSE Bulletins--Selected Returns

	Bulletin No. 6 12/10, 11:30 P.M.		Bulletin No. 8 12/11, 1:30 P.M.		Bulletin No. 10 12/11, 8 P. M.	
Total Votes	270,997		615,994		722,783	
Valid Votes	261,395	(96.46%)	591,373	(95.97%)	693,521	(95.95%)
Null Votes	9,602	(3.54)	24,821	(4.02)	29,262	(4.05)
Pérez	121,375	(46.43)	286,094	(48.39)	337,147	(48.61)
Fernández	102,771	(39.31)	225,831	(39.20)	262,477	(37.84)
Paz	8,897	(3.40)	23,585	(3.98)	28,556	(4.11)
Rangel	13,836	(6.29)	25,697	(4.31)	29,490	(4.25)
Villalba	7,392	(2.82)	16,625	(2.81)	20,213	(2.91)
Burelli	2,906	(1.11)	5,147	(0.87)	5,929	(0.85)
Tinoco	2,256	(0.86)	4,086	(0.69)	4,695	(0.67)
García V.	559	(0.21)	1,571	(0.26)	1,911	(0.27)
Borregales	712	(0.27)	1,250	(0.25)	1,431	(0.20)
Segnini	433	(0.16)	942	(0.21)	1,040	(0.14)
Verde Rojas	155	(0.05)	346	(0.05)	401	(0.05)
Solano	103	(0.03)	199	(0.03)	231	(0.03)

	Bulletin No. 12 12/12, 10 A.M.		Bulletin No. 15 12/12, 9:30 P.M.		Bulletin No. 17* 12/13, 8 A.M.	
Total Votes	2,667,558		3,631,411		4,308,703	
Valid Votes	2,555,007	(95.78%)	3,478,293	(95.78%)	4,127,526	(95.79%)
Null Votes	112,531	(4.21)	153,118	(4.21)	181,177	(4.20)
Pérez	1,232,218	(48.22)	1,683,420	(48.41)	2,006,214	(48.60)
Fernández	951,446	(37.23)	1,285,703	(36.97)	1,518,385	(36.78)
Paz	117,122	(4.58)	170,299	(4.89)	210,513	(5.10)
Rangel	118,809	(4.65)	154,458	(4.44)	174,954	(4.23)
Villalba	75,879	(2.96)	105,368	(3.03)	126,401	(3.06)
Burelli	21,769	(0.85)	27,898	(0.80)	31,753	(0.76)
Tinoco	18,531	(0.72)	25,276	(0.72)	28,451	(0.68)
García V.	6,814	(0.26)	9,319	(0.26)	11,198	(0.27)
Borregales	5,700	(0.22)	7,393	(0.21)	8,665	(0.20)
Segnini	3,791	(0.14)	4,971	(0.14)	5,845	(0.14)
Verde Rojas	1,897	(0.07)	2,795	(0.08)	3,521	(0.08)
Solano	1,031	(0.04)	1,393	(0.04)	1,626	(0.03)

*Although this was the final CSE bulletin, minor revisions were incorporated for the offical returns on which the proclamation of the president-elect was based. Those appear in the next section of this chapter.

declare my recognition of your electoral triumph (stop) I hope that
your conduct of government will be for the benefit of Venezuela
(stop) Lorenzo Fernández."[6] Aguilar announced that the candidate's
message had unanimous party support. In the face of what was
emerging as a crushing party defeat, he continued in aggressive
fashion.

> COPEI is affirmed and defined as the political force
> that quantitatively and qualitatively represents a great
> sector of the country. COPEI guarantees by its
> credentials as a party of government and of opposition,
> that in the next constitutional period it will assure that
> juridical principles have effect and that the
> constitutional rights of Venezuelans are respected.
> We have made an extraordinary performance in
> government, a progressive and nationalistic policy that is
> irreversible, and now we are going to complete that work with
> normality. The party has not authorized nor prompted any
> act that could perturb civic normality. We are obliged
> to contribute to the success of the process, to maintain
> tranquility, that the country may enjoy the Christmas
> spirit that has already begun to be felt.

Fernández's concession message was praised by the secretary general
as a "noble and gallant gesture" that would further enshrine his
figure for the Venezuelan community.[7]
    The situation moved promptly toward relaxation and normality.
Within a few hours Luis Alberto Machado had visited Pérez to extend
the congratulations of Rafael Caldera, and the two exchanged abrazos
during a cordial interview. The following day the president spoke
warmly of his forthcoming successor as "a worthy fighter of
undeniable conviction and constancy," while promising to meet
shortly with Pérez, "more frequently than my predecessor did with
me."[8] Pérez reiterated his appreciation to the pueblo, both those
who voted for him and those who chose otherwise. He also responded
to Fernández with a telegram of his own.

> Your telegram that I read today in the press is the
> expression of national sentiment. Your recognition
> honors me. We both lent our presence together with the
> other candidates for the Presidency of the Republic so
> that the people would choose the new President of the
> Republic from among us. We both are contributing in the
> measure of our responsibilities and mutual democratic
> convictions to Venezuela, the victor in the civic content
> of the elections. I congratulate you and express my
> sentiments of consideration and esteem. Your countryman
> and friend, Carlos Andrés Pérez.[9]

On Friday, 15 December, Rómulo Betancourt cited the
revolutionary hero of independence, José Antonio Sucre, to the
effect that "among brothers victory gives no [special] rights."

Gonzalo Barrios reiterated Pérez's statements that independents and non-adecos would share in the duties of the next government, while Rangel and Paz both pledged firm, conscientious, and responsible opposition. On Friday, 21 December 1973, in a solemn ceremony at the CSE before a distinguished audience including President Caldera, ex-presidents Betancourt, Larrazábal, and Sanabria, officers of the judicial and legislative branches, the cabinet, high military command, and invited guests,[10] Carlos Andrés Pérez was officially proclaimed president-elect for the constitutional term beginning 12 March 1974.

ELECTORAL PATTERNS

The 1973 elections again demonstrated the seriousness and constancy with which Venezuelans regard the act of voting. The CSE announced that 4,518,388 voters had gone to the polls--96.9 percent of the registered voters, or an abstention rate of only 3.1 percent. Of those who participated, 3.69 percent cast null votes--166,944 in all.[11] (See table 16 for a detailed breakdown of the final returns.) The rates of abstention and of null votes were therefore

TABLE 16. Final Presidential Returns, 1973

Total Votes	4,518,388	
Valid Votes	4,351,444	(96.30%)
Null Votes	166,944	(3.70)
Carlos Andrés Pérez	2,122,427	(48.77)
Lorenzo Fernández	1,598,929	(36.74)
Jesús Angel Paz Galarraga	221,864	(5.09)
José Vicente Rangel	183,513	(4.21)
Jóvito Villalba	132,829	(3.05)
Miguel Angel Burelli Rivas	33,181	(0.76)
Pedro Tinoco	25,736	(0.59)
Martín García Villasmil	11,567	(0.26)
Germán Borregales	9,393	(0.21)
Pedro Segnini La Cruz	6,185	(0.14)
Raimundo Verde Rojas	4,169	(0.09)
Alberto Solano	1,651	(0.03)

both lower than in 1968, when 5.49 percent of the registered voters stayed home on election day, and 6.38 percent cast null votes. In the latter case, it was probable that use of the boleta única had contributed to the reduction by one-half. The increase of voters over 1968 was slightly over one-half million. Even before the final figures were known--indeed, almost before CSE bulletins themselves began to be issued--it was apparent that the electorate had registered a decision of dramatic proportions. Two phenomena stood out over all others--polarization of the vote and the profundity of the AD victory.

The former was without precedent, and went beyond the expectations of those who had either predicted or sought electoral polarization. The AD and COPEI polled 74.60 percent of the small

card vote; MAS, in third place, had 5.23 percent. Presidential
contenders Pérez and Fernández, incorporating scattered votes on
such tarjetas as the PRN, FDP, and IP, accumulated 85.51 percent of
the valid votes, with Paz Galarraga third at 5.09 percent (including
both MEP and PCV votes). The domination of the two status parties
was overwhelming. In 1958 with the candidacies of Betancourt and
Caldera they had polled 64.44 percent; in 1963 with Leoni and
Caldera, 53.0 percent and in 1968, with Caldera and Barrios, 57.4
percent. Polarization was also broadly national. Looking at the
presidential returns by state, we find for the first time that the
same two candidates ran first and second in each entity. The high
was a combined Pérez-Fernández total of 93.8 percent in both Apure
and Barinas; in no cases was the percentage lower than the
seventieth percentile, with the single exception of Nueva Esparta.
There, with native son Villalba still enjoying popularity, the AD
and COPEI candidates totaled 57.4 percent of the state vote. Such
was the sweep on small cards that only one senator won direct
election from outside COPEI and AD--again the case of Nueva Esparta,
with the second of its representatives to the upper house.
    Polarization and its concomitant economy-of-the-vote argument
had been overwhelmingly persuasive to the electorate. The sheer
number of candidates had, somewhat paradoxically, helped to convince
the voter on an AD-COPEI choice. This was consistent with the
widespread dismay a few months earlier when it became apparent that
some dozen candidates were in the race. VENEVOTE data, moreover,
is supportive. An overwhelming 95.7 percent of our respondents,
when asked, averred that there were too many parties in Venezuela.
Only 2.8 percent said the present number was satisfactory, while
0.6 percent thought there should be more. In short, preferences
seemed to harken back to Venezuela of 1959. The electorate had
seen its only meaningful presidential options as the AD and COPEI
standardbearers. With seven presidential candidates each receiving
less than 1 percent of the vote, and three more polling a combined
total of only 12 percent, the popular decision was emphatic. In
the absence of legislation or constitutional revision placing
meaningful qualifying requirements before would-be presidential
candidates, the electorate simply dealt with the situation itself.
    The sweep for the AD and Carlos Andrés Pérez was unique in
Venezuelan electoral history. Although the candidate drew a
fraction of 1 percent less than had his tutor Rómulo Betancourt in
1958, the national scope and consistency of his triumph was greater.
Betancourt had lost five states plus the Federal District in 1958;
five years later Raúl Leoni lost six states and the Federal
District; in Barrios's 1968 defeat, he won nine and lost eleven
states, along with the Federal District. The Pérez performance was
therefore little short of historic, as he won all but one state--
Zulia by 3 percent--along with the Federal District and both
federal territories. Even the unequal races during the trienio,
including Rómulo Gallegos's 1947 triumph, had been less than fully
national.[12] As shown in table 17, in two states Pérez exceeded 60
percent (Apure and Cojedes); in another ten he was over 50 percent
(Anzoátegui, Barinas, Bolívar, Guárico, Monagas, Portuguesa, Sucre,

TABLE 17.   Polarization by State and Region--Presidential Vote, 1973

Entity	Pérez	Fernández	Total
Nueva Esparta	31.3%	26.1%	57.4%
Sucre	50.6	23.0	73.6
Anzoátegui	54.5	26.9	81.4
Monagas	58.7	27.9	86.6
Bolívar	59.4	29.7	89.1
T. Delta Amacuro	51.4	28.1	79.5
T. Amazonas	55.9	31.3	87.2
Oriente	53.3	26.7	80.0
Apure	65.6	28.2	93.8
Barinas	58.6	35.2	93.8
Portuguesa	51.3	32.5	83.8
Cojedes	60.6	27.2	87.8
Guárico	58.3	29.4	87.8
Llanos	57.6	31.1	88.7
Táchira	53.8	41.2	95.0
Mérida	49.2	43.6	92.8
Trujillo	54.4	38.2	92.6
Andes	52.6	40.9	93.5
Zulia	40.4	43.4	83.8
Lara	46.4	39.5	85.9
Yaracuy	54.3	38.1	92.4
Falcón	49.9	33.3	83.2
West	44.7	40.1	84.8
Federal District	43.1	39.9	83.0
Miranda	48.9	39.1	88.0
Aragua	45.4	38.8	84.2
Carabobo	44.9	40.2	85.1
Center	45.1	39.6	84.7
National	48.8%	36.7%	85.5%

Note: Computed from official CSE returns.

Táchira, Trujillo, and Yaracuy), along with the two territories.
His lowest state total was 31.3 percent in Nueva Esparta, which
still won it, while in Zulia he received 40.4 percent. At the
regional level, the victory was equally massive. In the oriente--
where both mepista and urredista votes were drained away by the
AD--he polled 53.3 percent of the total vote. The llanos gave him
57.6 percent while doubling the Fernández vote in three of the five
states. The West was much closer, but the adeco still won the
populous region with 44.7 percent to Fernández's 40.1 percent.
Lara, a state which had been of deep concern to the AD, supported
Pérez by 46.4 percent to 39.5 percent.

In the crucially important **Center**, containing 36.0 percent of
the registered voters in 1973, the adeco also defeated Fernández by
a clear margin, 45.1 to 39.6 percent. The Federal District, which
the AD had not won since the Gallegos era, went to Pérez with 43.1
percent of the vote, while Fernández received 39.9 percent. Perhaps
the greatest satisfaction of all for Pérez was his sweep of the
Andes, the very heart of COPEI's traditional strength. Pérez won
his native Táchira, captured Mérida for the AD for the first time,
and completed the sweep in Trujillo; his regional total was 52.6
percent, nearly a dozen points ahead of Fernández. Nationally, the
adeco candidate also won by 12 percent of the vote, with the actual
margin slightly over 500,000 votes--that figure also the greatest
of the elections from 1958. The extent and magnitude of the victory
was dramatized by the impact of the small card tally on the
composition of the 1974-79 national congress (see table 18 for a
summary of congressional returns). For the first time since 1958
the party captured an absolute majority in both houses--something

TABLE 18. Congressional Returns, 1973

	Total Votes	4,308,703		
	Valid Votes	4,135,880	(96.01%)	
	Null Votes	171,816	(3.99)	

AD	1,833,730	(44.32%)	PRN	3,490	(0.08%)
COPEI	1,252,761	(30.28)	URI	3,247	(0.08)
MAS	216,473	(5.23)	FE	2,324	(0.06)
MEP	207,785	(5.02)	Alcina	1,571	(0.04)
CCN	178,089	(4.30)	DPV	623	(0.02)
URD	132,780	(3.20)	ARPA	1,536	(0.04)
FDP	51,347	(1.24)	Reina	547	(0.01)
PCV	49,455	(1.19)	Mov. Fam.	520	(0.01)
MIR	42,106	(1.01)	MIA	478	(0.01)
OPINA	30,531	(0.73)	AEI	449	(0.01)
PNI	29,226	(0.70)	ARVI	405	(0.01)
IP	25,928	(0.62)	BIN	298	
FUN	14,604	(0.35)	COPEI/IP	261	
MAN	11,746	(0.28)	FEVO	186	
PSD	11,462	(0.27)	FIPO	124	
FND	10,713	(0.25)	UPV	112	
MPJ	8,079	(0.19)	COP/FDP/IP	26	
DesCom	6,759	(0.16)	MEP/PCV	9	
MDI	6,100	(0.14)	COPEI/FDP		

Note: Announced as definitive results on 15 December, these
were subject to slight alteration following minor CSE revisions.

regarded as virtually impossible given the fragmentation of the
system. Winning both senators in seven states, the party captured
28 of the 42 seats directly contested. The addition of five
senators under the quotient (MAS 2, MEP 2, and CCN 1), along with
ex-presidents Betancourt and Caldera, left the AD with 20 of 49

seats. In the Chamber, its majority was 102 of 200 seats. Application of the electoral quotient produced a total of 17 additional deputies (MEP 4, CCN 3, MAS 3, URD 2, PCV 2, and 1 each for MIR, PNI, and OPINA) (see table 19 for comparison of congressional representation in 1969 and 1974). The adeco sweep was further reflected by gaining control in 157 of Venezuela's 181 municipal councils.

TABLE 19. Congressional Representation, 1969 and 1974

Party	Senate 1969	Senate 1974	Chamber of Deputies 1969	Chamber of Deputies 1974
AD	19	28	63	102
COPEI	16	13	59	64
MEP	5	2	25	8
CCN	4	1	21	7
URD	3	1	20	5
FDP	2		10	
FDN	1		4	
PCV (UPA)	1		5	2
PRIN (PRN)	1		4	
MAN			1	
PSD			1	
MAS		2		9
MIR				1
PNI				1
OPINA				1
Totals	52	49*	213	200

*The total Senate seats for 1974 include two lifetime seats of ex-presidents Betancourt and Caldera.

The COPEI defeat was devastating, despite the overall increase in the total party vote. At the presidential level, the twelve percentage points by which Fernández trailed Pérez was nearly identical to the unfavorable gap between Caldera and Raúl Leoni ten years earlier. The Social Christian candidate led in but a single state, Zulia. The loss in the populous Center was both unexpected and decisive, and the defeat in the Andes was perhaps even more traumatic psychologically than politically. The congressional outcome was also greatly disappointing. Not only had COPEI representation dropped in both chambers, but the total of 64 deputies was essentially inflated, for 18 of the 64 were either independents, members of the FDP, or other non-copeyanos who had been placed on Social Christian lists. Thus its party delegation was smaller than that of the preceding five years. The loss of both Cojedes Senate seats cost the party Hugo Briceño Salas, previously president of the Finance Commission. Others who had remained in the Caldera government instead of running were also lost; Hilarión Cardozo, José Curiel, Nectario Andrade Labarca, Luis A. Machado, Rodolfo José Cárdenas, and Arístides Calvani were among those who would necessarily be outside formal positions from 1974-79. The one bright spot for the Social Christians--to which their leaders naturally gave great public emphasis in post-election analyses--was the substantial increase in the copeyano vote over 1968. The slow rise of the party's national share of the vote, which reached just under 30 percent in the 1968 Caldera victory, had mounted another 7 percent. Never before had a Venezuelan party in government gained rather than lost votes after a term in office.[13] Traditionally weak in the oriente, the party rose from Caldera's 14.6 percent to Lorenzo's 26.7 percent; a larger vote in Zulia helped lift the western share from 32.5 to 43.4 percent; while the electorate in the Center increased from 27.1 percent for Caldera to 39.6 percent for Fernández. Only the Andes showed a regional decrease, from 49.5 to 40.9 percent. COPEI quite accurately stated that in many instances the vote total had equaled or exceeded their more optimistic projections. Lorenzo Fernández's total of virtually 1.6 million votes was, by itself, an impressive one. Such electoral figures were correct, but of course told but one side of the story. While COPEI remained a strong, viable, mass-based party, it had suffered a major setback.

On the left, disappointments were severe. For the Nueva Fuerza and especially the MEP, the outcome was grave. Although Paz Galarraga did finish third, thus leading both Rangel and Villalba, his 5.09 percent was less than expected. The base of support in Zulia nearly vanished, with Paz attracting but 11.5 percent of the state total. In the oriente, where the MEP had drawn 19.7 percent for Prieto in 1968, Paz received but 6.3 percent (along with 0.7 percent on the PCV card). Even in Prieto's native Nueva Esparta, the Paz total (both MEP and PCV) was only 12.8 percent. In Congress, both MEP Senators and four of their eight deputies were chosen by the quotient. Prieto and independent novelist Miguel Otero Silva reached the upper house, and such party stalwarts as Salom Mesa and Oscar Carvallo survived in the lower chamber. Those not returning included Adelso González, Julio Urbina, Angel Fariñas Salgado, and Paz himself. Mercedes Fermín, who had resigned from the party in August, was another experienced legislator who would not return to the new legislature.

There were various explanations for the MEP defeat, but none were more obvious than the evident return of MEP voters to the AD. There were ample indications that Betancourt's phrase had been borne out--adeco es adeco hasta que se muera--and that another slogan had been operable--mepista es mepista hasta que se mete detrás de la cortina negra. A comparison of the 1973 vote for Pérez with the combined totals for Barrios and Prieto in 1968[14] produced suggestive results. These most logically appeared in the oriente, the traditional adeco stronghold that had provided much support for Prieto in 1968. The 1968 total had been 54.0 percent in Anzoátegui, where Pérez polled 54.5 percent; Bolívar had produced 55.8 percent for the AD and MEP candidates in 1968, and Pérez received 59.4. In Zulia, importantly, the 1968 combined percentage was 44.7 percent,

compared with Pérez's 40.4 percent five years later. The Federal
District went from 41.8 to 43.1 percent, and nationally, the figure
had been 44.8 percent in 1968 and 48.8 percent in 1973. Such
returns supported the belief that most votes for Prieto in 1968
had not been converted to the MEP but were won back by AD during
the 1973 campaign. For the PCV, returns were also discouraging,
for the communists had been noticeably outpolled by the MAS; indeed,
the MIR vote for congress was only slightly below that of the PCV.

     For the MAS, results were mixed. Contrary to party
expectations, José Vicente Rangel had trailed Paz. His 4 percent
vote total also fell short of anticipated strength, and Rangel's
total on the large tarjeta, despite mirista support, left him
33,000 votes behind the MAS on the small card. As foreseen, both
Rangel and the MAS showed the greatest relative strength in Caracas.
The contrast with Paz Galarraga was especially noticeable. Rangel
won 9.0 percent of the Distrito Federal vote, but this constituted
36.8 percent of his national total. Only 2.1 percent of the
Distrito Federal favored Paz, representing but 7.2 percent of his
overall vote. Party leaders took greatest satisfaction in the fact
that their legislative total slightly exceeded that of the MEP,
permitting their claim to have become Venezuela's third political
force. Following the application of the electoral quotient, the
MAS enjoyed a total of 2 senators and 9 deputies. Its congressional
delegation included Rangel in the lower house, along with Teodoro
Petkoff, Freddy Muñoz, Juvencio Pulgar, and D. F. Maza Zavala, while
Pompeyo Márquez and Eleazar Díaz Rangel joined the Senate.

     The URD stood on the brink of extinction. Jóvito Villalba's
132,829 votes--3.05 percent--were a bare whisper of the 550,000
(18.9 percent) he had won ten years earlier. Even behind the
independent candidate of the 1968 alliance, Burelli Rivas, the party
had won 440,000 (11.9 percent). Only in Jóvito's native Nueva
Esparta did he receive more than a miniscule fraction of the vote
(25.4 percent). Congressional representation was also decimated,
dropping from 3 senators and 20 deputies to 1 senator and 5
deputies, with 2 of the latter received through the quotient. Party
stalwarts not returning to Congress included Leonardo Montiel
Ortega, Hens Silva Torres, Simón Antonio Pava, and Enrique
Betancourt y Galíndez. Of the two former electoral allies of the
URD, the FDP survived through dint of its 1973 alliance with COPEI,
as 7 efedepistas reached congress on Social Christian planchas.
Even so, it lost Larrazábal and Dáger, who had been senatorial
candidates in states swept by AD. Angel Zambrano also failed to
win another term. For the Frente Nacional Democrático, 1973
sounded the death knell, with congressional representation totally
eradicated.

     The outcome for the right was disastrous. None of the
presidential candidates polled 1 percent of the vote, and only
Tinoco succeeded in obtaining a congressional seat. With the
assistance of the quotient (1 senator and 3 deputies), the CCN
returned Oscar Hurtado to the upper house and Pablo Salas Castillo
to the lower. The competition among perezjimenista groups proved a
clear victory for the CCN over its various rivals. Its small-card

vote of 178,089 (4.3 percent) far exceeded that of the FUN, MDI,
MPJ, Alcina, and Alianza Revolucionaria Patriótica (ARPA).
Meantime, Luis Felipe Llovera Páez, Borregales, Burelli, García
Villasmil, Verde Rojas, Gómez Silva, and Segnini La Cruz all failed
to reach Congress.

The exceptional strength of polarization altered significantly
both the topography of the party system and the composition of
Congress. In addition to the predominance of the two main parties,
most of the remaining popular support was for the left rather than
right. Of those organizations that survived, only one--the CCN--
could legitimately be regarded as right of center. The unprecedented
elimination of parties, in accordance with Article 26 of the Law of
Parties which required 1 percent of the vote, included OPINA, PNI,
MD, IP, FUN, MAN, PSD, FND, MPJ, MDI, PRN, FE, Alcina, ARPA, and
Frente Independiente Popular (FIPO). As for Congress, the turnover
was pronounced; of 252 members, only 120 returned from the previous
term, including those who moved from one house to another. Although
some came back after an absence of five years, including former
presidential candidates Gonzalo Barrios and Luis B. Prieto, more
than half were entering parliament for the first time. If the
outlines and permutations of electoral patterns were readily
accessible, however, interpretations concerning campaign effect and
impact were diverse. Analysis of such views provides further bases
from which we can, with further guidance from our survey data,
return for a retrospective consideration of our original model.
Thus we first turn to the post-election explanations, justifications,
and rationalizations of the persons most directly involved.[15]

THE SOCIAL CHRISTIAN PARTY COPEI
COPEI had genuinely expected decisive victory. Thus Lorenzo
Fernández was stunned, even disbelieving, as the returns arrived.
Oswaldo Alvarez Paz and Rafael Salvatierra, unwavering believers in
the cause and persuaded by their técnicos, found the results
startling. Rafael Caldera, upon recognizing the implications of
mounting vote totals, reportedly said inverosímil, inverosímil
("unbelievable, unbelievable"). Of the more prominent copeyanos,
only Luis A. Machado had been known to express even the slightest
notion that victory was less than an absolute certainty. With
Fernández unavailable, the major post-election spokesmen were
Alvarez Paz, Salvatierra, and Pedro Pablo Aguilar. Theirs was the
task of painting the party defeat in the most favorable light
possible.

Alvarez Paz stressed the rise in the copeyano vote from 1968
to 1973, and therefore maintained that the results by no means
suggested a denial of the Social Christian movement. Never before
had a Venezuelan government party produced an electoral increase on
its behalf. "I believe that the Chief of State...has been the most
illustrious President in Venezuelan history. He is the pride of
Venezuela, and of Latin America. The faith that Venezuelans
deposited in him was not deceived. I believe that many Venezuelans
are already beginning to feel a nostalgia for the grand President
who is leaving us."[16] Hinging his explanations upon the impact of

polarization, he argued that inevitable antiregime sentiment naturally aided the adeco candidate. The enlarged AD vote was drawn logically from other opposition parties, and in the long run the pro-Pérez constituency would prove itself "soft." Consequently, "it can be affirmed that the vote obtained by Lorenzo Fernández is a much more solid vote and of much more conviction, than the vote obtained by Señor Carlos Andrés Pérez."[17] The party faithful should take heart in the fact that, according to COPEI's campaign coordinator, most of the new young voters chose Fernández rather than Pérez. The increase of 600,000 votes for the Social Christians would prove lastingly faithful, therefore, while the additional votes attracted by the president-elect were transitory.

Alvarez Paz's emphasis on the increase in copeyano votes provided the major basis for post-election efforts to rally disappointed members. Nowhere was there a public indication of the possibility that COPEI's votes were themselves a product of polarization and might be no more durable than those of Pérez. In Zulia, he insisted, the party could only be proud of the results. COPEI had set a minimal goal of 180,000 votes, and a maximum of 200,000; yet Fernández received some 230,000 votes. In Maracaibo the Social Christian had won 50 percent of the votes, and after capturing 7 deputies in 1968, had increased the total to 11. Conceding that the margin had been less than desired, Alvarez Paz also argued that the precipitous drop for the MEP, along with the weakness of the URD and CCN, indicated that nowhere did polarization operate more strongly than in Zulia.

Fernández's manager also attempted to meet specific criticisms of the campaign organization and tactics, firmly denying that youth and relative inexperience might have been a factor. Lorenzo Fernández, it was argued, had been surrounded by both young and "not so young" people. There were many who shared in campaign responsibilities, some more than others. "To establish responsibilities on the basis of youth, or maturity or immaturity, is something absurd, a product of meaningless speculations. In COPEI, during the electoral campaign, each one knew what he had to do and the form in which he had to undertake it, so that all our companions who were in Government and all those of us who were working in the party leadership, worked with a perfect identity of thought and of action."[18] Indeed, it was this sharing of campaign tasks that made possible the "miracle" of increasing the copeyano vote by 600,000 after five years of government. Organizational synchronization was perfect, producing a collaboration to "warm the masses" with the candidate's message. Essentially, Oswaldo Alvarez Paz saw an invigorated Social Christian Party, aided by a superb record in government and effective campaign organization, which only through unusual circumstances had lost the elections.

Much the same argument, offered in somewhat greater detail, was stated by his organizational alter ego, Rafael Salvatierra. The copeyano political sub-secretary and técnico par excellence did concede that "Our objective was to maintain the party in power. Lamentably we did not succeed, but it cannot be denied that 1,600,000 Venezuelans said yes to the alternatives we presented."

The margin of defeat was largely a reflection of the ease with which an opposition campaign can be mounted. Moreover, Salvatierra saw many of the voters as having been misled, owing to a lack of full political understanding and insight. "The majority of the people do not know the causes of problems that confront a government, and the opposition took advantage of this to win votes." The vote was in no way a **repudiation** of the Caldera government, although here too the electorate suffered from political innocence. "The policy of President Caldera, absolutely nationalist, is directed at protecting our interests, so that the Venezuelan becomes even more Venezuelan. The results will be seen in coming years. But it is also certain that President Caldera's nationalism was taken advantage of electorally, as we were accused of affinity with the communists, which yielded extraordinary dividends to the candidate of Acción Democrática."[19]

Salvatierra shared with Alvarez Paz an adamant denial of organizational and tactical flaws, although granting that, inevitably, some mistakes were committed. These did not include the youth of Fernández's advisers. "In the first place, all the militancy of COPEI worked in the electoral campaign of Dr. Lorenzo Fernández. Each one in his region and at his level [worked] within his determined responsibilities. I believe that it is a little venturesome to accuse of inexpertness those of us who worked in the campaign, since it is generally recognized that COPEI's machinery was, is, and will continue to be the best organized."[20] He further underlined the point by stressing the youth of the Venezuelan population, also noting that the average age of the party's National Committee was under thirty-five. He also blamed the organizational disarray of the CSE. Referring to the chaos of the final days before elections, Salvatierra argued that the government was held responsible for shortcomings over which there was no control. This point was converted into an attack on AD, which he viewed as having dominated the CSE.

If COPEI had erred, it was in failing to alert the electorate to <u>adeco</u> manipulation of the Consejo, thanks to its commitment to permanent defense of the democratic system. Few voters were aware of the circumstances under which the CSE was operating. Thus, the Social Christians never said that "Acción Democrática had control of the administrative organization of the Consejo Supremo Electoral, and that its leaders bore heavy responsibility for the chaos.... Such was the control of the AD on the CSE, that two days after having closed the period for propaganda, it permitted the AD to publish an advertisement in the press, with the telephones of its networks, to 'inform' the public on [the location of] voting <u>mesas</u>...."[21] Salvatierra, though less outspoken than Alvarez Paz, was firm in stressing that (1) COPEI's electoral loss to the AD notwithstanding, the party was stronger than ever before; (2) the record of the Caldera administration had made a lasting national impact, one upon which COPEI would build in future years; and (3) the campaign strategy and organization of Lorenzo Fernández had been fundamentally sound.[22] Somewhat less unqualified evaluations were presented by the pre-convention party contenders. Edecio La Riva

Araujo, who had been least likely of winning the nomination, was perhaps more disinterested than Luis Herrera Campins and Arístides Beaujon.
La Riva reflected traditionally conservative, aggressively anti-adeco views. His basic posture was one of elegant simplicity: the electorate was essentially conservative and preeminently anti-leftist, thus the copeyano flirtation with the left had been fatal. Suggesting that his pre-convention banner of the machete was comparable to Pérez's democracia con energía, La Riva faulted his party for failing to have insisted on questions of principle. Calling himself a telluric man who knew and understood Venezuela, he saw the country as demanding order, respect, and discipline. Carlos Andrés Pérez, his fellow andino, had also understood this sentiment. La Riva, ever the loyal party member, refused to place the responsibility for defeat on individual shoulders, contending that everyone in the party shared the blame. At the same time, he was critical of the campaign emphasis on pacification, regarding it as running counter to the overriding civic concern for safety and security. For the future, COPEI held the moral power to assure responsible government by the victors. The greatest of all Social Christian duties was that of regaining power.[23]

Arístides Beaujon was guarded in his comments. Preferring to avoid interviewers, he conceded only that COPEI did not enjoy tactical and strategic unity, the ideological consensus necessary for victory. He also retained admiration for the performance of the outgoing government.

> From the first moment at which I knew the electoral result, I believed that Dr. Rafael Caldera should return to the national direction of COPEI, where today more than ever his presence is necessary. He returns with his prestige strengthened by the experience of having been President of the Republic, and with the optimism that has characterized him....
> We feel pride in the work realized by this Government, presided over by our leader Rafael Caldera, which had a profound democratic content, steely nationalism, and a magnificent vocation for the justice and wellbeing of all Venezuelans.[24]

Sharply contrasting with Beaujon's caution was the outspokenness with which Herrera Campins initially addressed the electoral outcome. Although these remarks reflected Herrera's first inclination to grasp boldly for party supremacy—an impulse he soon curbed—they reached further toward an evaluation of campaign errors and misjudgments. Calling for a cold analysis of the defeat, but without internal bloodletting, Herrera examined criticisms being voiced from the party rank and file.
There was a strong denial that governmental elitism had contributed to public disapproval, although some policies had been incompletely explained to the citizenry. Moreover, he praised the effort and style of Lorenzo Fernández. He denied that he had been

shut out of the campaign; his personal campaigning had focused
largely on rural areas that the candidate had not visited.
Nonetheless, Herrera's carefully worded responses did not entirely
mask his disapproval. The study and investigation of the causes of
defeat, he averred, would not be enhanced by a revival of
controversy, and "having been myself a precandidate, I do not
believe it elegant to speak further." Queried about the hombre del
maletín, he also avoided direct criticism. "It is not the time to
disinter observations and charges that have been made about the
course of the 1972 convention, because that was already considered
by the party. Repercussions that it might have had, will have to
be probed by political analysts upon deep reflection over the
results of the electoral process."[25]
    In later statements the senator from Portuguesa elaborated
further on the campaign. None had seriously entertained the
possibility of defeat, given the brilliance of the government record,
the size and magnitude of Fernández crowds, the support of
influential independents, and the technical brilliance of the
electoral organization. The overthrow of Salvador Allende in Chile
had been costly to COPEI--as it also was to MAS--and campaign
statements concerning the recognition of Cuba had been distorted.
Food scarcities and what the public perceived as inaction against
hoarders and speculators further weakened the party campaign; the
ILAPECA controversy, though understandable amid the intensity of the
competition, had not been helpful. Reiterating the importance of
careful and honest reevaluations on the part of the party, he
stated that COPEI had not yet fully absorbed the impact of the
loss. Perhaps most important of all would be a rededication to
basic doctrine and ideology.

> I have the impression that in the years of Government,
> the party disregarded the formation, preparation, and
> elevation of the ideological level of our members and of
> our leaders, and perhaps that explains how a sector of
> youth, which never in sound logic would have leaned
> toward Acción Democrática and even less for its candidate,
> voted in 1973 for that very party and candidate...I truly
> believe that the most urgent thing is for us to return
> more profoundly to the Social Christian spirit...in order
> to be able to continue as an alternative to the great
> currents of materialist thought that exist in the
> country.[26]

    Similar concern over party doctrine was expressed by a more
disinterested copeyano, outgoing president of Congress J. A. Pérez
Díaz. Long one of the most respected Social Christians, he viewed
the tactical and material execution of the campaign as having been
divorced from COPEI's political thought; it was "lacking in
ideological message, an important point that must be examined by
the party." He clearly was critical of alleged elitism by the
leadership. "I believe that one of the things we should review
with great care is that of making the internal democracy of the

party more genuine, so that internal democracy becomes a reality
and not a formal question....What must now be done is to restructure
the party, proceed again to the task of formation, to make a
recapitulation in order to copeyanizar COPEI, to socialcristianizar
once again in the process of recovering the mystique and capacity
of sacrifice that for a moment had been forgotten."[27] Pérez Díaz
also rejected the view that the increased copeyano vote justified
either pride or satisfaction. "There is no doubt that we lost the
principal objective, which was the retention of power. He who
thinks that the party has been fortified by the elections is
mistaken. The main thing was to retain power, and we did not
retain it."

A more extensive and detailed post-election critique,
promulgated at the February 1974 party Directorio Nacional, came
from a prime architect of the campaign--Secretary General Pedro
Pablo Aguilar. The meeting, expected to be the scene of visceral
internal battle and mutual recrimination, provided instead another
example of the Social Christians' characteristic discipline. It
was agreed to leave all party officials in office for a period of
over eighteen months. Thus tempers would have been cooled,
Rafael Caldera returned to party activity, and--presumably--errors
of the Pérez government would encourage renewed unity of thought
and action. Aguilar, a major architect of the party defeat,
therefore prolonged his secretary-generalship rather than being
thrown to the wolves; he also enhanced his position by a systematic
assessment of the campaign. Sharp criticism was directed at the
electoral machinery, which at one juncture was characterized for
"mercenary spirit and false tecnicismo." Coordination among the
Organization Secretariat, the candidate's own staff, and the
campaign press office was lacking. Internal problems led to the
marginalization of many natural party leaders, and copeyano state
governors were not effectively incorporated into the effort.

In addition to such organizational failings, the secretary
general saw the communications effort as flawed. Radio and
television had been inadequately used, the presentation of the
candidate's image and message was lacking in ideological content,
publicity was not pitched to the major concerns of the voter, and
generally poor public relations hindered rather than enhanced the
candidate's effort. As for strategy and tactics, too little
importance was placed on rural areas, direct contact with the
pueblo had not been maximized, agricultural problems had not been
confronted, and the ideological tone of infantilismo izquierdizante
("leftist infantilism") was damaging. COPEI had been arrogant in
assuming that its campaign claims and contentions would be
accepted at face value, the high cost of living and related
pocketbook problems had been underestimated or ignored, and foreign
policy issues had been given exaggerated importance. In short,
Aguilar cited the great majority of shortcomings presented by
nonparty observers.

A striking passage in Aguilar's report to the Directorio
Nacional[28] strongly praised the adeco campaign. He conceded that
COPEI had misjudged the strength of its major adversary. He lauded

the Pérez campaign for its internal unity, the adoption of opportune
political appeals, the effective use of public opinion findings, the
fruitful recruitment of independents, its avoidance of pre-electoral
internal dissension, and the attraction of its former members.
Adeco communications efforts had far outstripped those of COPEI,
winning widespread support in the media while denigrating or
discrediting government policies. Moreover, skill in
counterpropaganda enabled Carlos Andrés Pérez to appear as the
victim of partisan attacks, heightening public sympathy in his
behalf.

Special party commissions were later to undertake in-depth
studies of the campaign, including detailed electoral analysis
through the data stored in the Boleíta computers. Although some
remained a closely guarded party secret, an important statement was
issued be José Rodríguez Iturbe.[29] Drawing upon electoral data
collected and presented by Secretary of Organization Adolfo Melchert
and by former CSE representative Carmen G. de Cuahonte, Rodríguez
Iturbe and Gustavo Tarre Briceño undertook a synthesis of the
party's findings. It was conceded, albeit in partisan fashion, that
the AD campaign had been carefully molded and successfully executed;
for COPEI, there were both external and internal reasons for its
defeat. Extraparty causes were grouped under five headings:
polarization, the cost of living, the turn to the left, adverse
sentiment on the part of immigrants, and regional Andean sentiment.
Internal factors included the world crisis of Christian Democracy
and the impact of the Chilean case, which was circumstantial and
beyond COPEI's control.

As to purely organizational errors, the young zuliano exhibited
a candor that not all of his colleagues shared in electoral
self-examination, pointing to a number of factors demanding prompt
rectification. Among the more serious were the processes and impact
of internal factionalism, personal ambitions and animosities, the
failure to respond to regional and local needs and interests, and
organizational disarray in several states, notably Táchira, Bolívar,
Lara, Guárico, and Cojedes. Moreover, despite mechanistic
efficiency, the campaign had been undermined by the lack of a single
head, as the candidate's staff and the National Directory quarreled
with one another. Additional deficiencies were the absence of
effective campaign slogans, the inadequate projection of the
government record, and the lack of mystique, which offset much of
the innate organizational capability developed by party experts. If
the party were to aspire to a renewed term in power, Rodríguez saw
it compelled to fight even more firmly for an end to social
injustice, to oppose powerful international interests, and in
organizational matters to avoid both leftist infantilism and rightist
recrudescence. Above all else, the worst enemy of COPEI was
"grupalismo," that internal danger of factionalism and favoritism.
"If COPEI wants to exercise National Opposition with dignity, if it
aspires to be spokesman of the country and not of counterposed
interests of subalterns, it has to confront directly the dangers of
grupalismo. If it does not do so, its historic force as the only
democratic alternative will diminish little by little until it is
converted into a vanishing hope."[30]

As this and other dissections of the campaign were undertaken by the Social Christians, their future actions also became partially dependent upon the course of action to be pursued by the incoming administration. With the return of Rafael Caldera, the revitalization of party morale and discipline seemed probable, as well as a reinvigoration of doctrinal commitment. At COPEI's twenty-eighth birthday celebration in January 1974, Acting President Godofredo González helped set the stage for future political competition.

No excuse will be valid if campaign promises [by Acción Democrática] are not faithfully and precisely executed. Among these promises is that of a true democracy, a democracy which watches over rights and in which the government does not persecute and the governed have the right not to be persecuted. A democracy requires the maintenance of order but also requires respect for the dignity of man and, in short, is identified with peace....

Now, at the close of Caldera's term, we maintain without arrogance but with just and legitimate satisfaction that the best government the republic has had was under President Rafael Caldera....

More than ever we are now the party of hope. After today, destiny leads us to new heights--the conquest of the future. Without hesitation or vacillation, we are going to conquer the future--for God, for country, for COPEI.[31]

ACCION DEMOCRATICA

Carlos Andrés Pérez barely paused before plunging into the task of selecting his cabinet, state governors, and the large number of other public officials to be named. In-depth electoral analysis received little attention, but both Octavio Lepage and David Morales Bello remained outside the government to concentrate on the continuing direction of party affairs.[32] In assessing the campaign, the former stressed several major factors: the candidate himself, the strength of the party campaign, the internal qualities of AD as a microcosm of national life, and the errors in COPEI's own campaign. As a personification of the new, invigorated and youthful nation, Pérez had reached the electorate with clarity and straightforward frankness. In contrast with the mentality that emphasized public works and sumptuous construction, the AD nominee stressed more indispensable needs in terms of a rational order of basic priorities. "The voter saw in Carlos Andrés Pérez the mature man it sought for a difficult and decisive period of our historical evolution...a man of the hour for the problems of the times, casting before the electorate a certain image of the ruler needed."[33] Moreover, the personality and style of the candidate were also ideally suited for implementation of the campaign that was designed. "The type of campaign which developed was dynamic, with direct contact of unprecedented, unparalleled magnitude. Never had so high

a percentage of the population met with a candidate as with CAP.
None of his opponents in the recent campaign reached such a high
level with regard to the voters. Citizens, in an exceptionally high
proportion, knew CAP and spoke with him."[34]
The secretary general characterized his party as homogeneous
with its campaign free from internal rifts and firmly united on
behalf of the Pérez candidacy. Thus it was possible to organize the
effort efficiently at all levels and in all parts of Venezuela.
Moreover, organizational strength provided additional support to
Pérez's exceptional effectiveness in attracting independents. In
fact, "never before have the independents been so motivated--to use
a modish word--as they were in this election." The result was an
electoral victory in which fully half of the votes for Pérez were
cast by independent voters. And there was no denying the fact that
Rómulo Betancourt's characteristically graphic description was
accurately portrayed in his "adeco es adeco hasta que se muera."
The electoral outcome had given ample testimony to the continuing
vitality of AD as the leading party in Venezuela.
For critics who had claimed that the AD had forgotten its
origins as a popular party and evolved into an organization at the
service of great national and international economic interests, the
victory had provided revealing evidence to the contrary. The popular
component of the electorate--workers, peasants, and poor sectors of
the middle class--had provided a good 80 to 90 percent of the adeco
vote. Recalling the electoral independence of the Venezuelan voter,
"the free and deliberate vote for Acción Democrática constitutes, in
my opinion, proof that Acción Democrática continues being a great
popular, multi-class, anti-dogmatic movement...explaining our
repeated triumphs in the electoral field."[35] Therefore, he saw the
results as vindicating the party heritage.

It was said by some, especially in some sectors of
the Left, that the AD was a party no longer carrying a
message; a rheumatic, arthritic party in a state of
decadence. The vote of the people cast out that arbitrary
theoretical view in demonstrating that reality was
otherwise, and that the AD continued being the party best
able to understand and interpret the hopes and expectations
of a country conscious that the AD had never turned its
back, and that its earlier governments had achieved a
brilliant administration in the national interest at the
service of the most needy sectors.[36]

Lepage also viewed the Social Christians as having committed
many errors, which worked to the advantage of the AD. What he
bluntly termed a record of failure during its administrative
stewardship had handicapped the copeyano campaign. The 1968 slogan
of cambio had aroused high national expectations, and the subsequent
failure to deliver on promises of fundamental change had cost the
party dearly. The controversies created by the process of candidate
selection were also harmful to the government party, and COPEI had
"missed the mark in choosing the team into whose hands the

responsibility of designing and directing its electoral campaign
was placed." Copeyano strategy and tactics were also imprudent,
both in tying the candidate's fate to the record of the government
and in launching negative attacks against Carlos Andrés Pérez and
the AD.

> I believe that copeyano analysts, in the study which
> they have announced concerning the causes of their defeat,
> should consider, although not publish, the prejudicial
> strategy of not limiting themselves to presenting their
> candidate or exhibiting their credentials to govern, but
> of insisting more on the attempt to destroy Carlos Andrés
> Pérez. This absolutely negative and injurious campaign,
> that was developed by means of flyers, pamphlets, etc.--
> remember the so-called Christmas Fair in Plaza Venezuela
> last December--proved unfortunate for those who did it
> and for those who tolerated it....Copeyanos insisted on
> this campaign to its culmination in the absurd scandal of
> powdered milk in Maracaibo, the consequence of which was
> its reduced margin of victory in Zulia....[37]

In reiterating the president-elect's frequent pledges to avoid
the establishment of a monolithic and sectarian one-party
government--an obvious possibility given the magnitude of the adeco
triumph at the polls--the secretary general reviewed his critique
of Social Christian miscalculations: "the failure of COPEI in
government constitutes a resounding and definitive condemnation to
sectarism in the exercise of power. COPEI was isolated from the
sentiment of Venezuelans and suffered a rejection owing in large
part to the sectarian and exclusivist form in which it exercised
government at all levels. I think that this experience should not
be disdained by adecos, and we should take it into account, so that
we do not ever forget that Venezuela and Venezuelans cannot be
governed in such a manner."[38] Lepage was speaking from the broad
perspective of his position at the organizational axis of the
victorious party. A more narrowly drawn interpretation was that of
Campaign Coordinator David Morales Bello. Like Lepage, he began
by firmly emphasizing the central role of the candidate. From
his point of view, the candidate's robust personality, strength
of thought and action, and style in communications played a
principal role in the electoral success. "At no time did we try to
hide our candidate. Proof of this were the television programs in
Carlos Andrés responded to all questioners and without prior
preparation....The same was true of the programs where
representatives of the communications media were invited; nobody
was ever prepared in advance." Furthermore, the nominee filled his
role with natural ease.

> Carlos Andrés Pérez was not a candidate manufactured
> artificially, in posters, or snapshots. He was an
> honest-to-God candidate, one whom we did not have to hide,
> nor did we have to invent. The National Electoral

Commission of Acción Democrática simply had the task of
looking for means for the pueblo to know the Candidate as
he is. We based it on the authenticity of his personality,
we did not manufacture it. CAP was the center and axis of
everything we did....
        In our campaign, there was always a spirit of fervor.
Carlos Andrés, with his activity, stimulated the people
on this occasion to be not simply spectators but, on the
contrary, active participants in the effervescence of
caminar.[39]

    Organizationally, the robust and unified party effort had
effectively furthered the electoral cause. Barrios, Lepage, Piñerúa,
Lusinchi, Arria, Manzo González, et al., worked closely on the
Comisión de Estrategia, logistical support was dedicated and
efficient,[40] and Rómulo Betancourt contributed his own unique
talents. The campaign manager also singled out a variety of
tactical successes, some of which originated with the candidate
himself. The caminatas, for example, had been proposed by Pérez, a
notion the leadership did not fully grasp at first. Once understood
and adopted, other adecos soon rediscovered the art of walking, as
Morales Bello wryly observed. Release of the Gaither poll had also
been advocated by the nominee; once Pérez had explained his position
and motives, the Directorio Nacional had approved the idea
unanimously. The repeated visits to poor barrios, and especially
the many returns to Zulia, had provided much of the backbone for the
campaign. Morales Bello also had high praise for the effectiveness
of Homero Parra in contributing to the organizational revival in
Zulia.
    Among the issues that helped the AD campaign, none were as
important as the cost of living. Morales Bello denied that his
party had used it for electoral objectives, seeing it as an
inevitable factor in the competition with COPEI.

        The high cost of living has been and is a reality in
the country, with an alarming increase in the course of
the government term now ending. The humble people,
without resources, without means and with family burdens,
have suffered unspeakably, and I have no doubt that this
was taken into consideration at the ballot box....
        We made reference to the lack of an adequate
agricultural policy...for we could not view with disdain
the hunger of the pueblo...it was not demagogy but an
expression of sentiments deeply linked to the sincerity
of the cause that we defended.[41]

He rejected implications that adeco public relations skills misled
or deceived the voters. The party utilization of electronic and
media techniques was praised for its competence, but only as a lucid
presentation of the platform. Moreover, such efforts had become an
integral part of campaign activity in Venezuela.

> Modern life, fully influenced by electronic advances, cannot exclude electoral debate--something of such general interest in connection with democratic norms-- from audiovisual means of communication. That is, authenticity is required, so that the humanistic part of the electoral process and of the expression of popular sovereignty is not replaced by resources oriented toward the deception of those considered susceptible [to deceit]. And I can say, without fear of denials, that our norm never departed from the sure projection of our reality. We had a Candidate with nothing to hide, and he was always presented whole, like an open book.[42]

Looking at the vote itself, the campaign coordinator contended that although many loyalists had indeed returned, there had also been many new voters in the Pérez column. Of the estimated 600,000 young Venezuelans who had cast a ballot for the first time, the bulk had favored AD. This was a testimony to the vigor of the party, even more than to COPEI's campaign errors. Of the latter, Morales Bello singled out the self-sufficient and mono-party nature of the Caldera administration, its coquetry with "castro-communism," and the ventajismo of the regime. In addition, COPEI had conducted the final weeks of its campaign with exaggerated confidence over the outcome. In contrast the adecos--informed by their polls that undecideds ran as high as 18 percent in important populated sectors--intensified their efforts during the concluding stage.

Viewing the campaign and party within a broad national perspective, he also felt that its ideological position was consonant with the mainstream of contemporary Venezuelan attitudes. AD was prepared to restore the good name of leftism in the country, which had been deformed and discredited in recent years by elements subject to international influence. The AD, neither conservative nor conformist, stood as representative of the Venezuelan democratic left, "inspired philosophically by the principles of democratic socialism and pledged to a program of action dedicated to modifying socio-economic structures." This required a just distribution of national wealth, equality of opportunity, and democratization of production, all to be achieved within "a climate of respect for political rights, with the enjoyment of liberty at the service of pacific coexistence...."[43]

For Morales Bello as for Lepage, then, the broadest elements of the adeco electoral success were clear: a powerful and highly attractive candidate, unity of action within the campaign leadership, the support of a vigorous party closely attuned to the Venezuelan pueblo, and the miscalculations by COPEI upon which additional political capital had been produced. Meanwhile, the president-elect drew many of his key campaign collaborators into the new government: Luis Piñerúa Ordaz as minister of interior relations, Diego Arria as governor of the Federal District, Armando Sánchez Bueno as minister of communications, Ramón Escovar Salom as secretary of the presidency, and Antonio Leidenz to the Labor Ministry, among others. Party President Gonzalo Barrios became president of the new Congress, where Jaime Lusinchi remained as the AD's parliamentary leader. With the inauguration of the new administration in March of 1974, the AD faced an organizational situation reminiscent of COPEI's five years earlier, its leadership ranks being **significantly** depleted by appointment to government office. The immediate organizational picture would be subject to the fortunes of the adeco government, coming to office with an aura of even greater public expectancy than had its predecessor in 1969; both opportunities and problems lay ahead. With such experienced figures as Lepage, Morales Bello, and Reinaldo Leandro Mora remaining primarily dedicated to party duties, however, the AD seemed well-equipped for the restaffing and reshaping of its apparatus.

THE ALSO-RANS

On the political left, analyses and interpretations ranged from abstract ideological discussion to hard pragmatic critiques. For the Nueva Fuerza, Jesús Angel Paz Galarraga remained prominent in the continuing struggle to unite and raise leftist fortunes; he was therefore concerned with projecting optimism over future possibilities while rallying the spirits of the severely disheartened MEP. Consequently, Paz devoted attention to both the coalition and to his own party. The zuliano spoke with pleasure of having finished in third place. Polarization had been the major factor in the electoral outcome, with fully 1.5 million votes for the AD and COPEI being the **result** of "economy of the vote" arguments. The disunity of the left had helped to make this possible. "The Left was not capable of unifying with a single formula which would give the exploited and marginals any sense that there was a true alternative of victory. If to this one adds the economic power of the dominant sectors of the national and international economy, plus utilization on a large scale of the means of social communication, we have found the principal reasons for what has occurred in Venezuela."[44]

To inevitable questions about the apparent return of former mepistas to AD, he contended that his party's lists of inscribed members were clearly faulty, although conceding that many who had voted for the MEP in 1968 had undoubtedly favored the adecos in 1973. Paz argued that his votes were truly committed to the MEP and that its membership now saw it in the proper ideological light--as a socialist party. "It is evident that the MEP at its time of origin was a simple detachment from the AD; that is, a Social Democratic splinter of the Left. Nowadays the MEP has been defined as a party which struggles for Socialist Democracy."[45] He lamented his own inability to cope with this adequately and--in private discussion--was candid in recognizing the organizational defects of his campaign. By 1973 these had been magnified in importance as a result of the intensification of public relations techniques, along with the expenses that few parties or candidates could hope to meet.

Party theoretician Demetrio Boersner was more systematic in his explanation of the elections. In approximate order of

importance, he saw the problems as: the colossally expensive
propaganda campaign by the forces of the status quo, copeyano errors
in government, division of the popular forces, organizational and
propagandistic failures by the popular forces, antisocialist
propaganda, the repercussions of the Chilean counterrevolution, and
imperialist participation in the electoral process.[46] Among the
errors of COPEI were its selection of Lorenzo Fernández, efforts to
attract perezjimenista voters, and a host of governmental decisions
which, for Boersner, drove the United States and its economic
oligarchs to back Pérez against the Social Christians. His broader
doctrinal analysis drew upon such assumptions as an antidemocratic
conservatism of Pérez, leftist reformism in COPEI, and the primacy
of international factors. Criticisms of the MAS and José Vicente
Rangel for refusing to join Paz in a united force were sharp.

Boersner did not conceal his dissatisfaction with the Nueva
Fuerza campaign; he laid much of the blame at the feet of the
communists. Neither was the MEP free from errors and
miscalculations, however.

> In the Nueva Fuerza, the MEP suffered
> organizationally from an excess of decentralization and
> of liberalism. The PCV did not succeed in restructuring
> entirely the national organization damaged by the
> separation of the MAS....
>
> Concerning our message, the errors were yet more
> evident. The MEP adopted, during the past four years, an
> advanced socialist doctrine, but did not diffuse it
> sufficiently within its grass-roots militancy, some of
> which retained reformist ideas. The PCV perhaps had the
> error of being too tied to the traditional style of
> Leninist political preaching. The MAS showed its capacity
> to reach the student youth, but had little success with
> workers' masses...[while] the MIR was distinguished by
> having a clear, dialectic and mature political line, but
> its numerical weakness prevented its effective spreading
> of that line on a large scale.[47]

For the future, he proposed a more extensive and effective
propagation of the socialist message nationally, building broad
popular unity through a mutuality of interests and objectives.
The working class remained the core of revolutionary sentiment and
potential strength, although ultimate success required a close
association with the peasantry and with progressive elements of the
middle sector.

Slightly different emphases emerged from Miguel Acosta Saignes,
an unaffiliated intellectual from the Generation of '28 who had
favored the Nueva Fuerza. He was largely unpersuaded by references
to polarization and believed that COPEI was seriously mistaken in
basing analyses on that factor. The propagandistic barrage from
the media loomed larger in his view. Moreover, he believed that a
realistic study of Venezuelan party evolution testified to the
growing strength of two-party phenomena, as exemplified by COPEI

and AD. A more realistic appreciation of this fact by the left would be important for future political competitions. Besides, the fragmentation and individualism of organizations on the left helped rob its candidates of meaningful electoral appeal. The single bright spot he saw emerge during the campaign proper was the precision and specificity with which both Paz and Rangel had presented their programs.[48]

Mepistas avoided more than the briefest of references to their PCV collaborators. Paz Galarraga, determined to broaden his forces on the left, therefore awaited quietly the outcome of bitter post-electoral debate within the PCV. Those communists who had most favored the electoral alliance--Gustavo Machado, Jesús Faría, and Radamés Larrazábal--angrily denounced Secretary of Propaganda Guillermo García Ponce and his followers for having neglected the coalition in campaign advertising. The concomitant preference of COPEI over the AD as "the lesser of two evils" was attacked as disloyal to Paz. The embarrassment over having polled barely 50,000 votes--four times less than the MAS and but a few thousand more than the MIR--helped detonate the explosion that soon rocked the PCV.[49] Discussions concerning "bureaucratic reformism," the presence or absence of "revolutionary optimism," and the proper road to "renovation and renewal" provided neither enlightenment on the campaign nor meaningful guidance for the future of the PCV.

Somewhat more pointed commentaries emanated from the leaders of the Rangel campaign. The candidate himself professed neither surprise nor dissatisfaction with the result. Rangel thought that the third-place finish by the MAS, a new party, was an important achievement. The results strongly indicated the efficiency of the AD organization in reaching and communicating with the many Venezuelans who voted on the basis of daily problems, the high cost of living, poor services, and immediate problems affecting their daily lives. Polarization was a related factor as well, although Rangel viewed it as having damaged the MEP campaign effort more than that of the MAS. Certainly he believed that the MEP, a typically "traditional" party, was in a state of decline. Moreover, the deterioration of traditional parties was an important by-product of the 1973 vote. "We [of the MAS] have surged forth as the first socialist opposition that Venezuela will have had. That is, the leadership of the Left has already passed from reformism and populism to socialism. This is a very important fact from the standpoint of clarifying the [leftist] perspective."[50]

Masista organizational chief Pompeyo Márquez told interviewers that the party's showing had been impressive. Describing the MAS as Venezuela's third political force, he regarded it as having disproved critics who had viewed it merely as spokesman of university students. "The MAS is throughout Venezuela, and in contact with the popular sectors. Of course, our message has great attractiveness--it could scarcely be otherwise--with sizeable layers of youth. And that fills us with pride. We have no reason to disguise ourselves as youths, however, nor should we...."[51] The secretary general reiterated his belief that a Venezuelan "popular unity" molded on the Chilean experience of Salvador Allende was inappropriate. An historical appreciation of the Venezuelan left, he argued, required a rupture of traditional practices and schema. The role of the MAS symbolized a break with the past; the only significant division in the country was that between the vast dispossessed and the small groups of millionaires who owned everything.

> We are going to develop our ideological planning, to advance our elaboration of propositions on the Venezuelan road to socialism, through a knowledge of the country. We believe that the successes achieved by our policy were intimately associated with the anticapitalist and explicitly socialist condition that was expressed. Similarly, we are of the opinion that the limitations of our message were in its inadequate development, in not having known how to describe adequately the design of socialist society as an alternative to dependent capitalist society, with its urgent and immediate problems for the great masses....[52]

Manuel Caballero, an advocate of Rangel as well as of MAS, saw the AD victory as having been assured by the disruptive imposition of Lorenzo Fernández by COPEI. COPEI was also criticized for its apparent effort to court the perezjimenista voter, as well as the assumption that polarization would work in favor of the Social Christians. Thus, the masista ideologue maintained that much of the impact against candidates termed "pro-establishment" had been minimal. As for the left, returns purportedly indicated the clear ascendency of the MAS over its mepista rivals. He saw former prietista voters returning to the AD from the MEP, while PCV strength had been drained off by the MAS. The weak electoral response to the Paz candidacy assured the effective demise of the MEP, leaving the MAS as legitimate representative of the Venezuelan left. "The evolution of the MEP toward socialist positions--or more precisely, at least at the leadership level, Social Democratic--was made clearer through the removal of its more rightist leaders. But public opinion was not confused by such proposals...," and the duplicity of the communists had assured the ultimate failure of the Nueva Fuerza.

Caballero felt it necessary to explain what he viewed as the frankly puzzling fact of the MAS's outpolling Rangel. Added to this was the task of discussing reasons for the "declining" Paz to have led Rangel at the polls. First noting the similarity of vote totals for Paz and the MEP, he saw this as reflecting a tendency toward straight party voting. Furthermore, Paz's familiarity to many Venezuelans through his years as an AD leader, combined with popularity in his native Zulia--where the MAS organization was especially weak--contributed to his small margin. Paz's access to televiewers, though limited, was also superior to that of Rangel. It was also argued that campaign errors included tactical attitudes toward both marginal slum dwellers and Venezuelan youth. With the former, it had been a mistake to assume an anti-system attitude,

which masistas had concluded from the 1968 perezjimenista vote.
Rather, the attractiveness of a strong and forceful leader should
have been emphasized. Moreover, the insistence of party tacticians
in launching relentlessly uncompromising attacks against opponents,
including the country's wealthiest families, was damaging in its
harshness.[53]

Mirista ideologue Américo Martín urged that the entire
electoral process be viewed within a broad historical context and
further maintained that the evolution of mirista policies had been
consonant with domestic conditions. The armed rebellion of a decade
earlier had been appropriate; the subsequent departure from violence
was equally sound. Economic and structural developments during the
Caldera years had prepared the path for electoral participation in
1973. The pragmatic, technically shaped dialectic between the two
parties of the establishment, despite short-run electoral success,
helped open the door for leftist messages. The electorate was
unlikely to respond in the future to sloganeering such as
"pacification" and "democracy with energy." And in the meantime,
the MIR had grown more dramatically than any other force.

With the era of rebellious adventurism passed, the left was
in a position to make large strides in the near future. Yet its
disunities presented a barrier that demanded greater self-abnegation.
The acrobatic opportunism of pacts and alliances from the MEP, PCV,
and even FDP had to be overcome. Too many leftists, as the returns
became known, reacted with panic in a spirit of "save yourself if
you can," thus rendering meaningful unity of action and commitment
even more difficult. Martín, expressing greater public realism
than masistas or mepistas over the prospects of true unification,
nonetheless insisted upon its necessity. The overall picture was
anything but simple and straightforward; in fact, complexities were
in the ascendency. "There are characteristics and shadings that
require the greatest subtlety; but in no way is the game closed,
with a 'mexicanization' of political struggle or a moderation of
the class struggle. From the firm base of social and labor conflict
there opens a broad fan with new forms in order to regain the
initiative and enhance the appeal of the Left."[54]

All such leftist analyses were couched within a framework of
future planning and action. In the case of other losers, however,
there was less to be said. Jóvito Villalba and fellow urredistas
made little further reference to the 1973 race and scarcely
attempted to conceal the impending interment of what had once been
Venezuela's second political party. Wolfgang Larrazábal confessed
the FDP's surprise at the outcome, while crediting both AD
propaganda and its candidate's personality for the AD victory--"Carlos
Andrés Pérez was the most dynamic. That camina, camina undoubtedly
warmed many people." Nonetheless, Larrazábal remained startled by
the vote, and especially after what he regarded as a gigantic
display of popular support for Fernández in Caracas on 5 December.
As to his own contribution, the retired sailor believed his image
with the masses to have retained its appeal despite the years
outside Venezuela.[55] Jorge Dáger, architect of the FDP alliance
with COPEI, was silent on the elections for several months, at which

time he and Larrazábal, amidst charges and recriminations over that
decision, proceeded to divide what remained of the party.
On the political right, post hoc commentary was sparse. The
perezjimenistas broke the silence only long enough for Salas
Castillo to claim his CCN's victory over would-be rivals. For
desarrollismo, Guillermo Morón spoke rather than Pedro Tinoco, who
was already mounting an ultimately unsuccessful effort to secure
a cabinet post in the Pérez government. Morón claimed satisfaction
in what was termed a clear electoral swing to the right. "The
massive support for Carlos Andrés Pérez demonstrates that the
Venezuelan pueblo is conservative. I have said this in my books,
articles, and speeches, and that is why I have had a conservative
political attitude, for I am also Venezuelan." The perezjimenista
voters, in his view, had the alternative of voting for Tinoco or
Pérez, and obviously opted for the latter. In sum, there were
three principal reasons for the Pérez victory. "First, because the
bourgeoisie lept almost totally to the aid of that candidacy. In
the second place, the professional middle classes gave their support
in almost all the country, and in the third place the marginal
classes have continued to be irritated because their basic problems
have not been solved...."[56]
For Miguel Angel Burelli Rivas, seemingly relegated to political
obscurity five years after his strong 1968 showing, the lessons of
the vote were several. In the first place, the intervention of
money was excessive. He faulted COPEI for both an arrogance in
office and a disingenuous leftism that failed to convince the
electorate. Moreover, its presentation of the nominee was
inconsistent with the tone of the Social Christian campaign.
" There was excessive aggressiveness in presenting a man as
'father of the family.' There was a contradiction. Worst of all,
he was a candidate appearing under the sign of illegitimacy,
because within the party he was imposed by fraud." Concerning the
victor, Burelli praised his campaign for the "enormous personal
effort; the unmistakeable sense of his words and the publicity
campaign, which was far superior to that of the COPEI party. In
COPEI they tried out many slogans, changing the theme constantly;
on the other hand, there was a constancy in the effort for Carlos
Andrés. Of course, both campaigns, almost all the campaigns, fell
into the error of promoting men and ideas as if commercial
products."[57]
Speaking of what he conceded was an unduly generous Law of
Parties, which permitted a proliferation of parties and candidates,
Burelli Rivas praised the electorate for applying its own common
sense to the problem.[58] Clearly, the ranks of the also-rans
included both aspiring candidates and formerly vigorous if
secondary parties. Two-thirds of the presidential candidates
failed even to secure a congressional seat through application of
the electoral quotient, and small parties fell by the wayside. The
death knell was tolling for the URD, while the division of the FDP
signaled its effective demise. For perezjimenismo, the CCN was
grievously wounded, the ex-dictator had dissipated any possible
strength, and the lesser factions disappeared. Only on the left

was there a likelihood of future successes, yet the immediate
prospects were dim. The MAS stubbornly rejected meaningful dialogue,
let alone practical collaboration, while José Vicente Rangel drifted
further away; Paz Galarraga attempted to resuscitate the MEP, while
the PCV staggered the imagination with yet another division of its
miniscule band of narrow bureaucrats.

As the magnitude of the AD victory began to be absorbed, the
work of putting together and sorting out the paramount factors in
the 1973 Venezuelan electoral campaign was only beginning.

REALISM AND SURREALISM IN CAMPAIGN 1973

Interpretations of the campaign and elections were suffused
not only with partisanship but sometimes with a strange blend of
the real and the unreal. Campaign directors and participants alike
occasionally suffered from incomplete or distorted perceptions of
reality, as partisan loyalties and hopes clouded judgments. On the
campaign trail itself there were few who did not occasionally
succumb to overly exuberant assessments of crowds and of supporters'
enthusiasm; all too often a candidate's local leaders knew little
of value concerning opponents in the region. The nominee could--and
often did--pass through a chain of towns and villages without proper
advance preparation or briefing; after completion of the visit,
national headquarters would have limited bases on which to judge,
evaluate, and plan future trips. The logistical demands complicated
such matters for all but COPEI and the AD, but even those two
campaigns were sometimes misinformed. It was especially true,
moreover, that the activities, styles, and popular responses of the
candidates were only partially known or perceived by the opposition.

Examples are legion, and though they vary in importance,
provide random testimony to the lack of campaign realism. Thus,
opponents underestimated the impact of Pérez caminatas, failing to
recognize his evident personal impact, as well as the effectiveness
of direct contact; the Fernández appearances, given the mechanization
of the COPEI campaign, were themselves easily misjudged because of
sheer numbers; the belief that Rangel held few formal evening
meetings because of ineffectiveness with the citizenry flew in the
face of clear indications that his choice reflected the educational
emphasis of his campaign; the early lack of enthusiasm toward the
Paz candidacy led to erroneous suppositions that he was incapable of
drawing sizable crowds; carefully selective publicity from Villalba
meetings--especially out of Nueva Esparta--should not have been
taken as indication that significant support for the URD remained.
Hard, practical political intelligence concerning rivals was too
often in short supply. Although leaders plotted campaign tactics
and responded with acumen to public declarations from the opposition,
they were not fully cognizant of developments in the field--where,
after all, the voters were to be found.

It is also true that presumably accepted political folk wisdom
was sometimes illogical. Misleading assumptions were permitted to
go unchallenged. The Social Christians were never fully successful
in dispelling the notion that Lorenzo Fernández has been imposed by
oficialismo. The decision to tie the fate of the candidate to public

perceptions of the Caldera government, moreover, was both unfortunate and myopic. Even the most partisan administration supporter should have recognized the almost universal political failures engendered by efforts to elect a candidate on the basis of his predecessor's performance. The total identification of the Fernández candidacy with the Caldera government defied customary patterns of electoral behavior, as copeyano tacticians learned when it was too late. This was even more unwise in the light of the problems of daily life the electorate was suffering.

Unquestionably, many of these were exaggerated for electoral purposes by COPEI's opponents. Moreover, some were beyond the power of either Caldera's or any other government to remedy. But such qualifications did not change the vulnerability of the Social Christians to such issues. Rising prices, scarcity of potatoes, momentary absence of pasteurized milk, virtual rationing of sugar, expensive importation of other domestically produced consumer items, all of these were almost constantly before the Venezuelan voter. The government did not fully know or appreciate what was being thought and said in the streets of the nation. Lorenzo Fernández as well, instead of attempting to explain or to confront such issues, ignored them or issued denials that flew in the face of daily reality. In fact, a self-confident failure to examine the campaign searchingly and questioningly contributed further to harmful self-deceptions. The candidate's refusal to debate the adeco nominee could scarcely have been less damaging than to have accepted the challenge, and the decision to minimize the activities of party leaders who had not initially supported Fernández was simply a waste of available talent.

Greater sensitivity to public currents might have alerted COPEI to the negative impact of its propagandistic excesses. The extreme tone of many Social Christian campaign messages lost rather than won votes, and Pérez found it possible increasingly to appear as improperly or unjustly criticized. Such slips as Aguilar's admission that COPEI had manufactured false polls in earlier campaigns merely helped to strengthen existing skepticism over the party's public pronouncements. The increasingly obvious growth of polarization, which the party had first proclaimed and then repudiated, provided another discordant note. COPEI simply increased the potential for harm with its repeated denials.

The alliance with the FDP represented another miscalculation. That the FDP claims of electoral strength were believed can be seen only as testimony to the persuasiveness of Jorge Dáger. More importantly, the Fernández strategists never accurately grasped important aspects of the adeco campaign. They underrated Pérez's campaign impact and were slow to recognize that the presumably negative "cop" image of his years as minister of interior relations was neither strong nor damaging. The patient effort to recapture former members of the adeco family was largely overlooked, and mepista strength was consistently overestimated. In short, the all-embracing aura of certain victory prevented that discerning evaluation which could have produced more effective policies on behalf of Fernández. Similarly, it permitted adoption of the "leftist" media image. All these drawbacks could have been pulled together, with their potentially negative impact minimized. Even assuming that polarization and other campaign-related factors may have rendered a COPEI victory impossible, the failings of the campaign leadership turned a reasonably close race in October into a rout on 9 December.[59]

With the victors, post-election analyses understandably stressed the many positive aspects of the campaign, crowned by resounding electoral vindication. The timing of the campaign was impressive, beginning with the artful handling by Betancourt of his refusal to become a candidate once more. The appearance on the scene of Diego Arria, just as the death of Régis Etievan produced a major gap among communications advisers, proved highly fortuitous. For a time there was reason to question the outspoken anger with which the AD attacked government ventajismo, accompanied by increasingly unguarded denunciations of President Caldera. The party presentation of purported grievances before the CSE, presented with a characteristic blend of brilliance and unbridled asperity by Morales Bello, seemed unduly blunt at the time. The periodic attacks by Lepage were also viewed by some observers as dangerously forceful in singling out the activities of the president. Ultimately, the results on 9 December suggested that either the adecos had been wise in such denunciations or else, at the least, copeyano counterattacks had offset negative responses to AD allegations.

Given the magnitude of the Pérez victory, then, it is difficult to mark off serious campaign errors on the part of AD. The AD's criticisms of President Caldera and of government ventajismo emerged, after the fact, as having been reasonable to the electorate. It should be reiterated that at several important junctures decisions were adopted at the recommendation of Pérez despite serious reservations on the part of the Comisión de Estrategia. As Morales Bello indicated, the very idea of repeated caminatas had first seemed foreign to the adeco planners, and the decision to release the Gaither poll was also a reflection of the candidate's wishes in the face of misgivings by advisers. With the explosion of the ILAPECA controversy in the wake of the Gaither presentation, there were a few ranking adecos who, until the returns became unmistakable, entertained reservations about tactics pursued during those tumultuous days.

The AD concentrated upon COPEI as its only serious rival, just as the Social Christians had emphasized competition with the AD. The adecos, confident of their ability to attract perezjimenista sympathizers, were somewhat misled in their assessment of Rangel and the MAS. This is not to say that AD either feared or anticipated a Rangel victory in 1973. Party strategists assumed that Rangel would draw more heavily from Fernández than from Pérez, and thus posed no immediate threat. At the same time there were unrealistically high adeco expectations concerning José Vicente's vote. Especially prior to the spread of polarization, there was a belief that Rangel would poll some of those votes being sought by COPEI in its exaltation of a "leftist" position and would run a strong third, outdistancing the masista legislative vote. Adeco strategists also feared a strong showing by the masista candidate among Caracas slum dwellers. As the labyrinthine contortions of Pérez Jiménez appeared increasingly fruitless, the AD--anticipating from the ranchos a large anti-system protest--foresaw substantial inroads for Rangel.

For Rangel and his advisers, there were the usual underestimates of the Pérez campaign. It was generally believed that the weight of copeyano public relations and of government involvement would carry Lorenzo Fernández to Miraflores. Private assessments of the Nueva Fuerza candidacy were rather mixed. On the one hand, there was a wide consensus that Paz Galarraga was not a persuasive candidate, that the coalition was dominated by essentially reformist rather than revolutionary elements, and that the PCV contribution was irrelevant. However, there were differences of opinion over the enduring electoral vitality of the MEP. It was believed that mepista labor strength was greater than the elections were to demonstrate. Moreover, the extent to which prietista voters returned to the ranks of the AD was not widely anticipated. There was almost unanimous agreement that José Vicente Rangel would run well ahead of the MAS, and that it was the Rangel campaign personality and dogged determination that would pull along masista legislative candidates on his coattails. Petty rivalries between local masistas and miristas, of course, were infantile and harmful to Rangel's campaign.

In the Nueva Fuerza, attitudes were predominantly those of the MEP, with partisan evaluations more the rule than the exception. From Luis B. Prieto on down, there was an impassioned belief in the cause--and in the inequities of other political contenders--which produced an outlook unrealistic in its expectations and occasionally self-righteous in posture. At the same time, the cool sagacity of Paz was the single most important influence. His unruffled deftness in rolling with unexpected punches[60] was combined with the longer view that the 1973 campaign represented a further step in the restructuring of the MEP and the building of a unified left in opposition to the parties of the Venezuelan status. As for the PCV, its somewhat schizoid attitude toward the Nueva Fuerza rendered electoral judgments of little value and questionable quality.

The lesser candidacies produced perhaps the most unrealistic assessments of the campaign. Jóvito Villalba and the URD certainly did not anticipate victory but nonetheless felt that enduring party loyalties and the unquenchable Villalba rhetoric would save the party. It was all too convenient to ignore the obvious deterioration of local organization and of party vigor, arguing instead that the Villalba charisma would capture the fancy of the electorate. Urredista leaders retained the extraordinarily myopic belief that Villalba still retained a relevance to Venezuela. Neither the anachronistic quality of his style and personality, nor the atavistic tone of campaign appeals, were recognized by the dwindling handful of urredista leaders and advisers.

Nowhere was shortsidedness greater than on the political right; none were more poorly attuned to the realities of Venezuelan political life than Pedro Tinoco and Marcos Pérez Jiménez. For desarrollismo, there was little experience with campaigning and scant awareness of what was needed to reach the electorate. Tinoco and his supporters also failed to recognize that entrepreneurial leaders would concentrate their efforts and assistance behind candidates who could hope to win. Finally, the exaggerated emphasis given to perezjimenista strength contributed to the demeaning quest of personal endorsement by the former dictator. As for the general himself, tactical decisions could scarcely have been more flawed, and the result was to leave but a few flickering embers of perezjimenismo in the ashes of his ambitions for vindication.

In sum, the campaign had been an exceptional exercise in civic education, popular participation, and political mobilization. Whatever the criticisms--undue length, excessive expenditure, distortions of advertising messages, and inequities between the two dominant parties and the multitude of opponents--the progressive democratization of the system was evident. For better or worse, it had reached a new level of solidity, maturity, and self-assurance. The fulfillment of its civic duty by the Venezuelan population was exemplary. In the process, the increasing monopolization of the political center by COPEI and AD was evident, strewing the cadavers of lesser parties across the political landscape. Speculation over a shift of the party system followed in the wake of the elections. Some believed a two-party system was emerging; some felt that a unified left might eventually rise as major challenger to the AD. Others argued that the AD was being transformed into a "dominant party," in Duverger's concept: that is, a party far ahead of its rivals in a pluralistic party system, one that identified successfully with national ideas, styles, and doctrines. Clearly the immediate future placed exceptional opportunities and responsibilities on the AD and on Carlos Andrés Pérez. There could be little question that a skillful campaign had carried the nominee to his decisive triumph.

CONCLUSION
The Significance of Political Campaigns

The Venezuelan campaign of 1973 was replete with a panoply of sophisticated communications techniques, political maneuvering, and old-fashioned personal appearances. Such effort was necessary to obtain an electoral decision by more than four million Venezuelans--a verdict that could prove the most decisive of the post-1958 era. Such was the prevailing view of both participants and observers. Members of the 1973 "campaign elite" offered a wide range of justifications and explanations, but there was little dispute about the intrinsic relevance of the campaign. Our own assumption, posited at the very outset, emphasized the fundamental importance of the campaign. As our investigation was launched, we also assumed that in-depth analysis of the Venezuelan case would refine our understanding of campaign participation and mobilization generally.

It therefore behooves us to return once more tho these assumptions. First, we must search out from VENEVOTE the empirical bases for evaluation of campaign effect. Both as a theoretical and an historical exercise, analysis of the data for the campaign **and its impact will permit a comparison with the conclusions of the** actors themselves. This will aid in **corroborating** or contradicting their intuitive and professional wisdom as campaigners; it will also illuminate the ability of campaign elites to evaluate, assimilate, and effectively utilize campaign information. Having derived such findings from the data, we will then need to reassess our original model, seeking to develop an improved research agenda capable of transporting us further toward scientific and theoretical understanding of democratic political campaigning.

EMPIRICAL INDICES OF CAMPAIGN IMPACT
Inevitably, the 1973 Venezuelan campaign produced contrasting effects on individual voters, with the level of interest and participation fluctuating widely. Our data allow the identification and discrimination of differing degrees of campaign influence. To begin with, nearly half of our respondents indicated that someone had tried to influence their voting decision; 48 percent reported a

direct attempt to obtain their vote for a particular party or
candidate. Thus a substantial portion of the electorate had
experienced direct personal contact with campaigners. Clearly, the
long and massive effort to mobilize and influence opinion was
substantial. Complementary evidence is presented in table 20,
which outlines responses to questions involving traditional avenues

TABLE 20. Overall Interest and Involvement in the Campaign

	None	Little	Some	Much
Listening to speeches	36.2%	–	46.0%	17.8%
Reading about campaign	43.3	38.7%	12.7	5.3
Watching candidates on TV	44.4	–	39.7	15.8
Interest in campaign	46.8	–	34.8	18.4
Attending campaign meetings	66.0	18.4	15.6	–
Persuading friends and relatives	73.7	–	15.3	11.0
Doing voluntary work	78.0	(yes = 22.0)		

of campaign exposure and participation.
Responses are ranked by frequency and form of involvement.
The greatest amoung of public interest was generated by campaign
speeches, with only 36.2 percent reporting that they had not
listened to any speeches. By contrast, 22 percent were themselves
involved in campaigning through volunteer work. More broadly, we
find responses segregated into two different categories. The first
four listed in table 20 indicate essentially passive campaign
participation, wherein the role is largely that of spectator. The
last three fall into the realm of activism. Thus the exposure for
the four passive items fluctuates from 64 percent--listening to
speeches--to 53 percent--an expression of interest in the campaign.
The degree of more direct participation ranges from the 22 percent
low for voluntary work to a high of 34 percent for attendance at
meetings. Deriving a ratio from these two ranges, we find about
two spectators for each single activist. This is a markedly high
rate, which indicates an impressively strong level of campaign
participation.
These broad indicators of activity and passivity are but an
introduction to our topic, with further evidence required on the
salience and importance of a campaign to the public at large.
Three direct questions elicited opinion on the importance of the
election itself, the perceived relevance of the identity of the
winner, and the extent to which the campaign helped the citizen in
making a choice. The responses, presented in table 21, underline
a hierarchy of public interest and concern. An overwhelming
majority--some 93 percent--considered the electoral outcome
important, and a more modest but solid majority--68.1 percent--
cared about the winner of the contest. And although a majority
denied being influenced by the campaign, a substantial 42.6 percent
regarded the campaign as having aided them in arriving at a choice.

TABLE 21. Importance of the Campaign

Outcome of the election is important	No	3.9%
	Depends	2.5
	Yes	93.6
Care about which party will win election	No	31.9
	Yes	68.1
Campaign helps make a choice	No	57.4
	Yes	42.6

Such results strongly suggest that the mobilization of forces and the implementation of the different campaigns exerted a pronounced impact on the electorate.

Moving one step further, we sought to probe public opinions of the more attractive and effective campaigns, something not necessarily reflected in the electoral outcome. Respondents were asked their evaluations of the different candidates' campaigns, results of which appear in table 22. These findings must be approached with caution, for our intention was not that of predicting the outcome of the election itself but rather examining the effect of the campaign on the outcome. This being the case, we sought to maximize the likelihood that our respondents had been exposed to the campaign. Consequently, we consciously and systematically undersampled the most fully rural of Venezuela's rural areas; the residents of these areas were the least likely to

TABLE 22. Candidate Attractiveness and Public Contact

Candidates	Most attractive campaign	Candidates met by respondents
Carlos Andrés Pérez	26.2%	17.4%
Lorenzo Fernández	34.5	17.7
José Vicente Rangel	6.2	7.2
Jesús Angel Paz Galarraga	3.2	4.7
Minor candidates	3.2	6.9
None	26.2	41.4
Several	–	4.6

be involved in the campaign or exposed to political messages through the media.[1] This decision created a problem, however, for it had the effect of systematically underestimating the strength and appeal of the candidate and campaign for AD, the most popular party in the countryside. Having registered this caveat, we observe from table 22 that roughly one-fourth of our respondents did not indicate

any choice regarding the candidate to have mounted the best
campaign. Following the same lines, it is evident that nearly
one-half had never met any of the candidates along the campaign
trail.

Upon closer inspection the Fernández campaign--as of early
November 1973 and subject to the restrictions already cited--emerges
as the most attractive, followed by Carlos Andrés Pérez.
Fernández's apparent edge, which does not cancel out when sampling
error is accounted for, is not truly definitive for two reasons.
First, our data were gathered in late October and do not register
the strong wave of sentiment that swung to Pérez in the last month.
Second, there is no one-to-one correspondence between choice of
the best campaign and voting intention. Most models of voting
behavior that appear in the literature do not identify campaign
impact as such, and indirectly refer to candidate personality and
campaign issues. Our data allowed us to measure the impact of the
campaign on voting intention.[2]

Going one step beyond the previous notion of a hierarchy of
citizen involvement and interest, we can differentiate three
separate aspects of campaign mobilization. The first is <u>exposure</u>
to the campaign, including spectator-type campaign behavior on the
part of the mass public. Next is an area of more active
<u>involvement</u>, including participatory activities of several types.
Last, we isolate a realm of <u>concern</u> <u>about</u> <u>the</u> <u>campaign</u> as well as
its perceived impact on the public. Our discrimination of different
levels of intensity within these dimensions of mobilization emerged
from the development of three Guttman scales, as presented in table
23. The respective coefficients of reproducibility and scalability
clearly indicate that each of the three areas represents a unique,
cumulative dimension. At the same time, the results are admittedly
ambiguous about the probable impact of the campaign on the election.
On the one hand, the data indicate that the intensity of
mobilization activities did not reach the highest fever pitch. On
the other, however, the data point in the direction of massive
mobilization in terms of scope. These results, then, provide
evidence of a combination of moderate intensity and wide scope of
campaign mobilization.

Highly persuasive evidence of campaign impact on electoral
outcome, broadly construed, lies in the shift of opinion during the
final month of the campaign. It was during this period that
controversy over the Gaither poll, the Aguilar statement about
manufactured public opinion results, and the ILAPECA milk scandal
in Maracaibo came together to produce the wide victory margin of
Carlos Andrés Pérez. Before examining the dramatic November 1973
impact on the electorate, a broader indication of trends is useful.
This is set forth in table 24, based on DATOS, C.A., national
opinion studies carried out for Voz y Visión, C.A.[3] The indicated
data were in response to the question, "if the elections for
president were to take place tomorrow, for which candidate would
you vote?" As is evident, the <u>adeco</u> candidate led his <u>copeyano</u>
adversary throughout, with his May 1973 margin of 9 percentage
points reduced to a mere 2 by the beginning of November. The

TABLE 23. Guttman Scales of Campaign Exposure,
Involvement, and Influence

Dimension		Values	f^i	Percentage
Campaign exposure*	low	1	410	27.0
		2	343	22.6
		3	559	36.8
	high	4	209	13.7
	CR = 0.9264			
	CS = 0.7760			
Campaign involvement**	low	1	567	37.3
		2	529	34.8
		3	315	20.7
	high	4	110	7.2
	CR = 0.9154			
	CS = 0.7237			
Campaign influence***	high	1	262	17.2
		2	285	18.7
		3	473	31.1
	low	4	501	32.9
	CR = 0.9101			
	CS = 0.6650			

*Includes reading about the campaign, listening to speeches,
and watching candidates' appearances on TV.

**Includes attending campaign meetings, persuading friends
and relatives, and interest in the campaign.

***Includes opinion about the importance of the electoral
outcome, concern over the identity of the winner, selection of
the most attractive campaign, and perception of campaign effect
on voting decision.

number of respondents who declared themselves undecided or refused
to answer had diminished as well, although 19 percent--nearly one
of every five voters--apparently remained open to campaign
persuasion with only one month remaining. The data also suggested
a trend toward COPEI-AD monopolization of public preference, having
increased from 42 percent in November 1972 to 51 percent six months
later, and then to 62 percent by November 1973. Even more
revealing, however, were the findings of DATOS studies specifically

TABLE 24. Voting Intention, November 1972--November 1973

Candidate	Nov. 72	May 73	Nov. 73
Pérez	24%	30%	32%
Fernández	18	21	30
Paz	9	4	4
Rangel	7	8	7
Others	11	9	8
Won't say	19	18	13
Undecided	12	10	6

Source: DATOS, C.A., and Voz y Visión, C.A.; reprinted
by permission.
Note: N=2,500.

designed to analyze and incorporate "don't know" and "won't say"
responses.

These appear in table 25, essentially confirming the narrowness
of the Pérez lead over Lorenzo Fernández as elections neared. The
national probability sample indicated that the adeco candidate's
margin over his Social Christian rival had shrunk to only 3 points.
Thus, at the start of November the DATOS findings were not basically
dissimilar from other sources in the extent to which the margin
between the two leading contenders was too close for prediction of
the 9 December winner. A series of follow-up interviews were
undertaken November 8-21 in four cities: Caracas, Maracaibo,

TABLE 25. Voting Intention, May 1973--October 1973

Candidate	May 73	Oct. 73
	N = 3,000	N = 4,000
Pérez	42.6%	38%
Fernández	31.5	35
Paz	5.7	*
Rangel	8.0	9
Others/null	12.2	18

Source: DATOS, C.A., and Voz y Visión, C.A.; reprinted
by permission.
*Included in others.

Valencia, and Barquisimeto. The results were compared with those
from the same cities within the October national sample. They
indicated a wave of opinion shifts supporting post-election
intuitive interpretations stressing November campaign events as
crucial to the outcome. In essence, two specific speculative points
were largely confirmed: first, that the Pérez momentum at the close
of the contest was powerful; and second, that polarization became a
reality for the voters of Venezuela.[4]

Comparisons indicated an increase of 27.6 percent in support for Pérez, whereas for Fernández the rise was 15.8 percent. Weighting of the previous findings (Pérez 38, Fernández 35 percent) by these percentage increases led to DATOS's final national assessment, with the AD nominee attracting 48.5 percent of the vote, and COPEI's candidate a total of 40.5 percent. The polarization of the presidential vote was 89 percent. Compared with final official election returns, of course, the DATOS projection was highly accurate for Pérez, although Fernández finished some 3 points lower than anticipated. These findings gave impressive support to the contention that the final weeks' campaigning was crucial. Consequently, there was greater weight to the argument insisting upon the impact of the campaign as an important factor in the eventual outcome. To be sure, in one sense it was still necessary to draw inferences from such findings. Had the earlier prediction of a three-point margin for Pérez been maintained but at a higher level, it could be argued merely that the effects of polarization and "economy of the vote" factors were being demonstrated. However, given the fact that the Pérez increase was substantially greater than that for Fernández, the decisive influence of the campaign and related activities becomes an inescapable conclusion.

REASSESSING THE MODEL

Before a concluding recasting of our research inventory for further study of campaigns, we must reexamine the theoretical statement and propositional declarations originally postulated. Democratic political campaigning was defined as a transitory political system appearing intermittently in competitive party systems, whatever the precise composition of a nation's party organizations. Three major categories of variables were identified: the environmental, mobilizational, and implementational, of which only the latter two were susceptible to significant impact from the campaigning itself. It was maintained that the effect of campaigning on environmental variables was only marginal, given their inherently stable quality. Therefore, campaign efficacy-- the probability that the outcome of an electoral contest would be meaningfully affected--was viewed as most relevant in the realm of mobilizational and implementational variables. This leads us to a restatement and synthesis of the evidence that has emerged sequentially in preceding chapters. In doing so, emphasis rests most heavily on COPEI and the AD. Thus--although the 1968 competition could have provided in some ways a richer set of findings--the reality of Venezuela's 1973 campaign, in terms of the model, must be drawn fundamentally from the Fernández and Pérez efforts.

Our major mobilizational **hypotheses were derived from candidate** selection, organization, strategies-tactics, and ideologies-programs. With the first, it was posited that campaign efficiency might be diminished in several ways, and the 1973 case was directly applicable to Lorenzo Fernández for COPEI. His nomination, substantially aided and abetted by oficialista party notables on

behalf of President Rafael Caldera, created serious dissension and
acrimony. Although the vaunted Social Christian discipline
prevented the emergence of splinter candidacies, it failed to
compensate for the initial disillusionment and damage to party
morale that was to afflict the Fernández candidacy. The relative
inactivity of herrerista and beaujonista supporters was damaging,
and the impression of imposition was to plague Fernández's candidacy
for the twenty months which followed. In contrast, the Betancourt
and Barrios withdrawals paved the road to a smooth and unified
nomination of Carlos Andrés Pérez. Thus AD entered the
post-convention period with a marked advantage over its primary
competition.

    For the Nueva Fuerza, the convention victory of Jesús Angel
Paz Galarraga was achieved through legitimate means at the triparty
congress.   However, it resulted in the later defection of the URD;
Villalba's candidacy detracted from the potential strength of the
Paz nomination. The subsequent MEP-PCV coalition, although
obviously composed of unequal partners, was affected by the
candidate's insistence upon deferring to the lesser member. In the
final analysis, therefore, the Paz candidacy bore many
characteristics of an equal coalition. It encountered problems far
more serious than those of the unequal COPEI-FDP alliance supporting
Fernández, even granting the highly favorable treatment the FDP
obtained from the Social Christians.[5] As for José Vicente Rangel,
the nascent quality of the MAS helped to assure his relative freedom
of action in the campaign. This, in conjunction with Rangel's
independence from both the MAS and MIR, left him without serious
problems emanating from the process of candidate selection. Thus
the hypothesis concerning the first element of mobilization was
supported by the experience of the Venezuelan campaign. Carlos
Andrés Pérez enjoyed an initial advantage over Lorenzo Fernández,
Paz was weakened, and Rangel was unaffected by the process of
nomination.

    Turning to campaign organization, we see that the 1973
experience provided even greater support to our hypotheses, with
only COPEI and AD enjoying all the organizational capabilities
requisite for a meaningful drive toward victory. Despite numerous
similarities between the two campaign machines, there were
important distinctions. In the first place, the Social Christian
effort was diffused, unlike that of the adecos. The FDP was
ineffectually tied to the Fernández campaign, and this became
increasingly evident toward the latter stages of the competition.
Furthermore, COPEI's efforts to attract and to incorporate
independents in the campaign were much less efficacious than those
of the AD, where greater organizational flexibility permitted and
encouraged a more significant input by nonparty sympathizers. In
terms of the first hypothesis on campaign organization, the Pérez
effort reflected a centralization and fusion that was absent for
Fernández.

    The other organizational elements--specialization,
institutionalization, and the bases for financing--did not differ
fundamentally between the two parties. In qualitative terms,

however, the coordination of adeco specialized organs stood in contrast to that of COPEI, where internal contradictions and faulty communications between the regular party leadership and the Fernández campaign team mitigated against effective campaigning. The contrast between the two leading nominees and their other rivals was even more pronounced and was generally supportive of organizational hypotheses. For both Paz Galarraga and Rangel, the machinery was essentially diffused. The Nueva Fuerza effort was seriously marred by poor coordination with the PCV, flawed in particular by the divided loyalties of the faction which in May 1974 would break away as the "Vanguard" communists. Rangel in turn was plagued by the MAS-MIR rivalry, which vitiated meaningful campaign collaboration between the two. In both instances, of course, inadequacy of financing was a major factor in the inability to mount a true challenge to the inflated copeyano-adeco party hegemony. Overall, the financial dimension rendered effective anti-system competition a veritable impossibility.

Strategies and tactics also focused primarily on the two centrist monoliths. Those of the right were innocent in conception and naive in application, at the same time assuming a manipulative, antipopulist configuration insulting to the electorate. On the left, ideological formulations and the fundamentally anti-systemic outlook also ran contrary to political reality.[6] Only COPEI and the AD devised and practiced blends that might produce electoral success. At the same time, the two-party domination did not permit effective testing of our hypotheses concerning consensual and conflictual strategies. In a very real sense, the latter element was more heavily accented: for the Social Christians it meant a denigrating attack on "Señor" Pérez and his party, for the adecos an attack on the Caldera administration. Consensual tones were only infrequently sounded, for the respective copeyano and adeco efforts orchestrated the increasingly partisan exchanges. The Social Christians underlined and exaggerated the magnificence of the Caldera record, implying that even the slightest attack was both myopic and anti-Venezuelan; for its part, the AD insisted that ventajismo was at an unprecedented high, thereby adding to the plebiscitory character that was magnified during the campaign's final months.

The mixture of reinforcement versus recruitment strategies was best utilized by AD. Much of this centered on the Betancourt-inspired drive to reattract former supporters. While prietista loyalists were more easily reached as a consequence of the strong leftist shift of the MEP, the fact remains that it was largely reincorporated into active support for the Pérez candidacy. The direct appeal to uncommitted and independent voters was also evident, in contrast with the copeyano recruitment tactic. Especially as the Fernández campaign increasingly stressed the Caldera record, AD capitalized on those economic problems that naturally produced an anti-administration bias. In the final analysis, COPEI's recruitment of nonparty voters was relatively weak whereas AD reached more effectively into the ranks of independent and uncommitted sectors of the public. Our original hypotheses did not include explicit government-opposition factors, owing largely to the multiparty nature of the system. With the monopolization of public sentiment between COPEI and the AD that came to characterize the 1973 campaign, such considerations assumed a position of obvious relevance. Further refinement of the model clearly demands an inclusion of these elements.

In assessing ideologies and programs, our basic posture has been that such elements are relatively secondary to the mounting of an efficacious political campaign. At the same time--as will be documented in Volume II--ideological and programmatic beliefs are by no means absent in the Venezuelan public. Propositionally, we believe that it is advantageous to present programmatic appeals derived from fundamental ideological premises; purely ideological appeals will not suffice to attract a large number of voters. The validity of the argument is suggested by the campaign appeals of both Paz Galarraga and Rangel. Although their campaigns were by no means lacking in ideological content, the primary emphases were narrower and more precise. With the former, attacks on the status parties were secondary to such specifically programmatic pledges as free milk for children, expanded medical services, a freeze on prices, more equitable distribution of national income, and the like. Slogans of an ideological nature, such as National Liberation and Popular Unity, were used primarily as rallying cries to introduce particular issues and promises. Much the same was true of José Vicente Rangel. Broad attacks on the Venezuelan capitalist establishment were couched less in ideological terms than in the reality of haves and have-nots; the electorate was told that humanistic concerns of the candidate would bring about a general improvement of conditions. This, then, was far more programmatic than ideological in nature.

The appeals of the two major contenders were even more programmatic and pragmatic. COPEI nominally based its promises and commitments on Social Christian ideology, and the AD paid verbal homage to Social Democratic populism. Yet in both cases the programmatic element was foremost. We need scarcely repeat that Lorenzo Fernández based his appeals on a continuation of the Caldera record, further illuminated by the "leftist" tone of campaign promises. References to nationalism and to national sovereignty were largely wanting in concrete pledges. The broad generalizations Fernández used in the elaboration of his program were imprecise, despite exceptions over matters of family planning and a reorganization of certain government services. Carlos Andrés Pérez's emphasis on agricultural problems and a decentralization away from Caracas seemed to provide firmer bases for voter decisions. Ideological foundations were even less visible for the adeco candidate than for his copeyano rival. Generally, the AD nominee devoted much more specific attention to the needs of the electorate in different regions of the country. Certainly both of the major candidates leaned away from ideological formulations and, after the overthrow of the Chilean government with the apparent complicity of Christian Democrats, the electorate found both the Fernández and Pérez appeals largely bereft of ideological overtones.

Rather than draw too fine a distinction, we would merely conclude
that the most effective approach will present policies based on
doctrinal premises.
This brings us to the third and final rubric--campaign
implementation. Many Venezuelan critics of communications media
and public relations presentations would argue that implementational
characteristics of candidate appeals are of greatest importance to
the electoral outcome. Our basic agreement with this contention is
evident from our initial proposition, which suggested that
presentation of a clear and recognizable candidate style, whatever
its content, is more important than ideological or programmatic
appeals. Moreover, we would argue that the 1973 campaign was
consistent with the hypothesis that candidate style is the single
most important factor in mobilizing an effective campaign. Both
the 1968 and 1973 experience confirms the common-sense hypothesis
that no single candidate style necessarily maximizes campaign
efficacy.
Moving to communications techniques, we find three of the four
candidates attempting to employ a mixture of both the presentational
and participatory. Rangel was unable to exercise this option
because of financial and organizational shortcomings. Of the two
leading contenders, qualitative differences reflected primarily the
nominees' own preferences of style and temperament. Essentially,
Carlos Andrés Pérez maximized the use of both sets of techniques,
whereas Lorenzo Fernández heavily emphasized the presentational.
It can further be contended that these points of implementational
differentiation also reflected somewhat distinctive perceptions of
the campaign environment. Both COPEI and the AD saw "the optimal
combination of presentational and participatory techniques...[as]
determined by the environment"; with the former, it was an
environment susceptible to public relations techniques and the
manipulation of mass attitudes; the latter believed that such
communication could be fully realized only through the complementary
utilization of direct personal contact.

TOWARD A NEW RESEARCH AGENDA
    In reassessing the research strategy mapped out to guide our
study, several broad generalizations seem justifiable. We believe
that the fundamental importance of the campaign in decisively
influencing a significant portion of the electorate is indisputable.
This further underlines the intellectual relevance of studying
democratic political campaigning. Moreover, it does not seem
immodest to argue that the basic model is sound, although
unquestionably standing in need of further refinement and
elaboration. Although future investigation of political campaigns
can assuredly follow a variety of paths, the threefold taxonomy of
variables retains its validity. The dimensions of environment,
mobilization, and implementation provide fruitful avenues for
further inquiry. It must be repeated: the environmental possesses
overriding influence on the efficacy of campaigning, and it is not
very sensitive to the sometimes circumstantial qualities of a given
campaign. The environmental will invariably provide fairly

inflexible parameters within which the electoral competition transpires. Attention must therefore be focused more directly on the mobilizational and implementational variables.
Of these, the mobilizational stands as the more complex in its ingredients. Its sequential quality remains evident, as it is initiated by candidate selection and **then** followed by tactical and programmatic factors as structured by the organizational. Hypotheses relating to the choice of a nominee require little reworking--at least until broader experience may suggest unanticipated facets of the process. To move further in the area of candidate selection would require both pre-convention and post-convention data, the accurate gathering of which would be awkward if not **unrealistic**. The interviewing of party elites, accompanied by a nationwide sample, if feasible, could theoretically be useful. Thus, for example, COPEI's candidate selection for the 1973 campaign would have been illuminated had there been comparable investigation both prior to and following the convention. Even the most extensive interviewing within the party, either from the leadership or rank and file, would be highly suspect, however, given the individual interests inevitably expressed and protected by the respondents. Data permitting further refinement would therefore have to rest largely on massive national surveys. When Venezuelan political polling becomes sufficiently lucrative to permit Gallup- or Harris-style regularity of opinion testing, the possibilities for analysis will be greatly enhanced. Until then, however, it is scarcely possible for individual scholars to mount and finance such an enterprise.
As for campaign organization, greater insight will come only from stronger emphasis on qualitative judgments. The Venezuelan experience in 1973, following upon that of 1968, leads us to regard our organizational hypotheses as sound but as increasingly secondary to other factors in mounting an efficacious campaign. That is, one now finds general agreement upon the value of centralized and fused organizations, buttressed by specialized organs, and funded by a healthy if not bottomless treasury. Future analytic importance will rest on more qualitative judgments. For example, both the Fernández and Pérez regimes were explicitly specialized. The important distinction, however, came from the smoothly collaborative functioning of the AD party leadership and the candidate's staff of advisers, as contrasted to the dissonance between copeyano party elites and the Fernández campaign team. Similarly, a qualitative element that our model did not meaningfully include was the exaggerated degree of Social Christian centralization, which proved counterproductive to organizational efficiency. The adeco experience in 1973 was more measured and balanced, thus it was advantageous for the candidate. Without stressing the point unduly, let it merely be reiterated that the present model was not sufficiently sensitive to reflect such distinctions in any rigorous fashion.
The strategic-tactical dimension, despite the importance of perhaps circumstantial electoral elements as perceived by public opinion, appears firmly established. In the event of a major shift

of civic attitudes in response to environmental factors, the validity of specific tactical or programmatic campaign decisions might be altered. Nonetheless, a blending of strategies and tactics--as reflected in our consensual-conflictual and reinforcement-recruitment dichotomies--provide durable bases for any further elaboration of this portion of the model. And while we maintain our belief in the proposition that programmatic appeals are rendered most effective if based on explicit ideological premises, this by no means recommends the adoption by a candidate or party of a rigid ideological posture. Whatever the more broadly philosophical rationales that may provide an underpinning for specific programmatic appeals, the latter are most readily transmitted to the voter.

At the risk of implicitly denigrating the ideological element, it is nonetheless necessary to point out that the public will be more responsive to specific policy promises than to broad ideological commitments. A flexibility in applying theoretical formulations to campaign pledges is therefore important. Venezuela in 1973 is an excellent case in point. For COPEI, the "leftist" image intentionally projected before the electorate appears to have been damaging. Be that as it may, such a posture could be derived from Social Christian thought, even if stopping short of an exposition of communitarian thought. Yet an essentially rightist appeal--as would have been presented by such a candidate as Edecio La Riva Araujo--could also have found justification in certain aspects of Social Christian theory. For AD, the **tenets** of Social Democracy permitted the Pérez emphasis on rural problems, agricultural policy, and the populistic "war on poverty." This was consistent with but by no means guaranteed the essentially leftist initiatives of the adeco government when it took office in March of 1974. Without in any sense implying cynicism toward ideological commitment, we would nonetheless insist upon the electoral importance of a capacity to shape programmatic appeals in a variety of ways without abandoning a fundamental orientation broadly derived from ideological bases.

This is of course at variance with the greater rigor found in Marxist formulations. For the true philosophical left, the flexibility of COPEI and of AD indicates nothing more than political opportunism, resulting in policy choices and commitments totally lacking in fundamental theoretical bases. The fact that both Fernández and Pérez could range rather widely to the right or left, still drawing upon the tenets respectively of Social Christian or Social Democratic thought, provides evidence to Marxist analysts of their ideological illegitimacy. Without entering into the debate, we would simply repeat the observation that, whether or not it is **congenial** to one's philosophical or **theoretical** predispositions, the voter will focus on specific policy areas and issues that directly **affect his daily life**. The candidate who is rigorously consistent with ideological beliefs and unwilling to shift or adjust to the exigencies of circumstantial public concerns cannot realistically be confident of the electoral response.

Paz Galarraga could acquire votes by promising free milk to

young children, but not by rhetorical flourishes that deified
national liberation and popular unity. Rangel might attract support
by attacking existing inequities of social policy but would be less
successful in broad-gauged denunciation of the establishment or the
forces of the status. In short, an unbending emphasis on appeals
derived from philosophical bases can be damaging, and a flexibility
in formulating strategies and tactics will likely aid the candidate.
Thus, theoretical refinement of this dimension is somewhat
problematic and resists quantitative analysis. Still, in a country
where, according to VENEVOTE data, 40 percent of the electorate
expresses a preference for a socialist economic system, it will be
possible to legitimize a larger role for socialist parties in the
future. Even allowing for the fact that many of our respondents
did not know what they were opting for with this preference, we
offer this as evidence that the ideologically inclined left must
present its options in a programmatic fashion. Otherwise, a
divided left cannot efficiently tap this meaningful source of
support.[7]

Our third major set of variables is that of implementation.
Here the parameters of empirical testing seem largely to have been
reached. To be sure, longer, more frequent, and improved sampling
of mass opinion may provide small nuggets of additional information.
Basically, however, precision cannot be fully achieved, nor can the
strongly qualitative, subjective element be transformed into more
rigorously testable theory. Probing of the impact of candidate
style, itself a topic worthy of detailed **study** would clearly
require much greater and deeper inquiry into public opinion.
In-depth research, including extensive open-ended questioning,
would be necessary to identify and isolate more fully the mass
perceptions and reactions to individual personality and leadership
style. Even so, this would be strongly influenced by idiosyncratic
factors and in all likelihood would add only a marginal increment
to our model. The dichotomous nature of presentational and
participatory techniques, in conjunction with the blending of
methods we hypothesized as being more efficacious for a campaign,
is similarly resistant to that level of measurement which would
permit empirically clean and conclusive findings.

The future investigation of political campaigning, whether in
Venezuela or elsewhere, should ideally embrace three elements in
its design. To begin with, there should be a panel study based on a
representational national sample, with pre- and post-electoral
waves of interviews. Second, an extensive battery of questions
involving campaign behavior and electoral choice is essential. And
last, campaign influence on voting behavior should be isolated
through multivariate analysis of the variables. In our own case,
resources did not permit the fulfillment of the first requirement.
The pilot study conducted during the summer of 1973 was designed
primarily for purposes of instrument validation. Although it
generated fairly reliable results, it was not feasible to carry out
follow-up interviews with the 250 respondents, for this procedure
could not be extended to our larger sample. As a consequence, our
research strategy embraced three different efforts in compensating

for the deficiency. First, the interviews were conducted as close to the election as possible, although ideally we would have preferred it even later than was the case.[8] Our sampling was so devised as to increase the probability that respondents in our survey had been exposed to the campaign. Beyond this, we formulated a set of questions for the instrument that sought to probe campaign behavior and impact. And last, we undertook additional procedures in pursuing multivariate analysis of campaign impact on voting behavior. This multivariate analysis of campaign effect will be reported separately.[9]

We cannot **eschew** the opportunity to advance certain preliminary remarks. First of all, the major and most decisive influence on voting behavior in Venezuela is party identification. Party identification stands as the leading causal factor, outdistancing all others, regardless of the type of control procedure or form of statistical manipulation. With little hesitation, then, we affirm that party identification is the inevitable point of departure for a model of voting behavior in Venezuela. To be sure, there are other factors, some of which were anticipated in our theoretical model of campaign systems. These include environmental influences (such as previous voting behavior) and mobilizational factors involving individual participation in the campaign and affective responses to the leading candidates. Our model was found wanting and in need of further theoretical refinement with respect to two previously neglected areas. The first embraces campaign-produced evaluative factors such as expectations about the governmental performance of the different contenders, regime evaluation, and public expectations about the impact of such performance. The second area is a consequence of the nature of the 1973 contest itself, which led to a polarization of the electorate--one incorporating both the COPEI-AD cleavage and that between establishment and anti-system parties.

It would be very difficult to lay out in detail the main dimensions of our quantitative inquiry in the space remaining. A description of the full operationalization and analytical techniques would unduly extend this treatment. Second, we would not want to talk about campaign efficiency or impact in a vacuum, as if the environmental variables that we omitted were irrelevant. We have to specify the main sociocultural and economic cleavages that have been politicized in Venezuela. We will devote a major portion of our next volume to elements that are very largely unchanging for campaign purposes but that influence and interact with the distribution of partisan loyalties and other relevant political attitudes. This capsule view of ongoing work in this segment of our broader investigation is not intended as a definitive statement, for at this writing we are still testing and retesting additional alternatives and options. Rather, this is simply to note the intention of subsequently publishing results of our efforts at formal model building, further suggesting that the second requirement of a campaign study has not been neglected in our investigation. It will carry us further on the road from taxonomic model to middle-range theory.

As a final comment, it would be less than candid were we to deny that there are limits to the study of democratic political campaigning beyond which empirical investigation cannot go. There are elements that are sufficiently subjective and qualitative as to resist precise empirical analysis. An electoral campaign will have certain nonreplicable qualities that present a major obstacle to fully satisfactory investigation. Several of the variables occur with an infrequency that **prohibits the number of cases** necessary for valid quantitative conclusions. Overall, however, we stand firm in the conviction that elements of uniqueness in a given campaign are not sufficient to obscure or overpower the more universal qualities. The analysis of parties, of voting behavior, and more broadly of participatory politics, will remain incomplete in the absence of theoretical insights into electoral mobilization and the campaign system.

NOTES
BIBLIOGRAPHY
INDEX

NOTES

CHAPTER I

1. Lott, *Venezuela* and *Paraguay*, p. 46.

2. This short-lived creation of the Liberator encompassed today's Venezuela, Colombia, Panama, and Ecuador.

3. Robert L. Gilmore, *Caudillism* and *Militarism* in *Venezuela: 1810-1910* (Athens: Ohio University Press, 1964), p. 50.

4. Antonio Arraiz, as cited by Juan Liscano, "Aspectos de la vida social y política de Venezuela," in *150 Años de vida republicana (1811-1961)* (Caracas: Ediciones de la Presidencia de la República, 1963), p. 191.

5. As cited in Silva Michelena, *The Illusion of Democracy* in *Dependent Nations*, pp. 42-43.

6. *Ibid.*, p. 49.

7. A pioneering study, first appearing in 1954, is Edwin Lieuwen, *Petroleum in Venezuela* (New York: Russell & Russell, 1964). Less dated information on the topic is found in Franklin Tugwell, *The Politics of Oil in Venezuela* (Stanford: Stanford University Press, 1975), a definitive study of the subject.

8. A useful if somewhat anecdotal treatment is Thomas Rourke, Gómez: *Tyrant of the Andes*.

9. Perhaps the best treatment of *andino* influence on national life is Domingo Alberto Rangel, *Los* *andinos* en *el* *poder*.

10. The expression of political discontent by students who emerged as national leaders by the mid-1940s was the university protest identified as the "Generation of '28." For a detailed analysis, see María de Lourdes Acedo de Sucre and Carmen Margarita Nones Mendoza, *La generación venezolana de 1928*. A briefer account, drawing upon the recollections of several key participants, is John D. Martz, "Venezuela's 'Generation of '28': The Genesis of

Political Democracy," Journal of Inter-American Studies 6, no. 1 (January 1964): 17-33.

11. The AD celebrates its anniversary on 13 September, commemorating its first public assembly at Caracas's Nuevo Circo in 1941. Official permission to organize as a political party had come from the government of the Federal District on 29 July, however.

12. The best single source on the history of the communist movement is Robert J. Alexander, El partido comunista de Venezuela (México: Editorial Diana, 1971).

13. Although inevitably partisan, an indispensable account of this period is Betancourt, Venezuela, política y petróleo. Extensive reliance on valuable source materials enhances many passages in Magallanes, Los partidos políticos. Similar documents in addition to interviews with prominent figures of the era provided the analytic bases for John D. Martz, Acción Democrática: Evolution of a Modern Political Party in Venezuela (Princeton: Princeton University Press, 1966).

14. Electoral figures for the trienio elections were faultily recorded, and detailed returns were destroyed during the Pérez Jiménez government. For a convenient summary and analysis, see Martz, Acción Democrática, pp. 74-78.

15. Contrary to popular opinion, Villalba was not a founder of the URD. Its originators were Elías Toro, Isaac Pardo, Andrés Germán Otero, Eduardo Arnal, and Fernando Simón Bolívar. Villalba was incorporated into the party on 20 March 1946 and swiftly assumed a position of leadership. Soon after the first URD national convention in February 1947, the original founders withdrew, disenchanted with the personalistic role of Villalba. From that time on, the history of the URD was predominantly that of its líder máximo, "Maestro" Villalba. See Magallanes, Los partidos políticos, pp. 465-70.

16. Only recently have the important early years of Venezuelan Christian Democracy begun to receive serious attention. See Naudy Suárez Figueroa, ed., Por los legítimos ideales del estudiante venezolano (Caracas: Ediciones Nueva Política, 1973), especially the lengthy introduction by the editor. This latter also appears as Suárez Figueroa, "U.N.E.: la gestación de una idea revolucionaria," Nueva Política 7-8 (January-June 1973): 3-94. Two historical surveys by copeyanos which include some treatment of the formative years of the movement are Cárdenas, El combate político, and Rivera Oviedo, Los social cristianos en Venezuela.

17. Rafael Caldera's 1947 presidential candidacy, the first of four, was of a symbolic nature. Voters were urged to make him "the youngest president in the hemisphere." At the time he was thirty-one years of age.

18. An excellent examination of educational policy and its implications for private Catholic education appears in Daniel H. Levine, Conflict and Political Change in Venezuela (Princeton: Princeton University Press, 1973). The major proponent of adeco educational reforms for many years was Luis Beltrán Prieto Figueroa. Among his many writings, especially see De una educación de masas (Havana: Editorial Lex, 1951).

19. For a closer examination of these 1952 events, see Leo B. Lott, "The 1952 Venezuelan Elections: A Lesson for 1957," Western Political Quarterly 10, no. 3 (September 1957): 451-58.

20. Only a handful of copeyanos actively opposed the regime or were forced into exile until the latter stages of the dictatorship. The substantial majority withdrew from public life and concentrated upon professional activities.

21. Medina's position in history has become more favorable in recent years. For a posthumously published defense of his government, see Isaías Medina Angarita, Cuatro años de democracia.

22. A fuller discussion appears in Philip B. Taylor, Jr., The Venezuelan Golpe de Estado of 1958.

23. Blank, Politics in Venezuela, p. 26.

24. For a treatment reflecting North American "Cold War" attitudes, see D. Bruce Jackson, Castro, the Kremlin, and Communism in Latin America.

25. For an excellent treatment of the campesinado, see Powell, Political Mobilization of the Venezuelan Peasant.

26. Among the more serious errors of the urban violence was injuring or killing of innocent victims. This emerges in the picture etched by Talton F. Ray, The Politics of the Barrios of Venezuela. Government documents of the single episode that most outraged public opinion, the 29 September killing of innocent travelers on an excursion train, appears in Ministerio de Defensa, La agresión a Mansalva (Caracas, 1963).

27. First was the Vanguardia Popular Nacionalista (VPN), led by José Herrera Oropeza and others from the urredista left wing. The second, the Movimiento Demócrata Independiente (MDI), was formed by followers of Alirio Ugarte Pelayo after his ouster by Jóvito Villalba. The MDI endured beyond the resultant suicide of Ugarte. For a personalized view of the tragedy and its roots, see Bhilla Torres Molina, Alirio.

28. In his reference work Magallanes identifies a staggering total of 159 legally organized parties or groups between 1958 and 1973. Most were short-lived, to be sure.

29. For a partisan but nonetheless useful account, see Alexander, The Venezuelan Democratic Revolution.

30. The experience as junior partner in government served COPEI well in its long climb toward full national power. Shrewd choices by Caldera in the positions demanded--especially the agriculture ministry--helped contribute to the gradual augmentation of Social Christian strength.

31. A sympathetic analysis of extremist activity is Timothy F. Harding and Saul Landau, "Terrorism, Guerrilla Warfare and the Democratic Left in Venezuela," Studies on the Left 4, no. 4 (Fall 1964): 118-28. Also see Fabricio Ojeda, Hacia el poder revolucionario. An analysis of the deterioration of the Venezuelan revolutionary left is Klaus Lindenbert, "Zur Krise der revolutionären Linken in Lateinamerika: Das Beispiel Venezuela," Viertel Jahres Berichte 33 (September 1968): 281-309.

32. Census data are regularly estimated prior to national electoral registration. 1968 figures appeared in Consejo Supremo Electoral, Resultado final del registro electoral, mimeographed (Caracas, 1968). Results of the 1961 and 1972 census are prepared and published by the Dirección General de Estadística y Censos Nacionales. Electoral data appear in the many post-election publications of the CSE.

33. Detailed discussion of electoral mechanisms, as created in 1958 and subsequently altered for the 1973 contest, appears in ch. 2.

34. Caldera's candidacy in 1947--and to some extent in 1958--was symbolic in nature. By 1963, he and COPEI stood as realistic electoral options.

35. These were the "astronauts," "advanced ones," and the more traditional faction named after the araguato--a small reddish monkey.

36. Extensive documentation of press accounts is found in Rivas Rivas, ed., Las tres divisiones de Acción Democrática.

37. The events of this tortuous and controversial series of events will be examined in a later study. The struggle not only epitomized characteristics of internal party dissension and competition for the Venezuelan system, but bore intrinsic if not decisive influence in the unfolding of the party panorama.

38. A letter allegedly sent to his followers by Betancourt dated 15 July 1967 called upon them to expel the "traitorous" supporters of "Sargento Paz." Betancourt has consistently denied writing the letter, both in interviews with Martz in 1968 and in a letter to the editor of the New York Times. Whatever the true authorship, a letter did circulate among party leaders in Caracas which was believed authentic by prietista leaders and deeply wounded many.

39. A detailed recounting of the conflict within the peasant movement appears in John Powell, Venezuelan Peasant, pp. 198-211.

40. Frei in 1964 was charged with receiving funds "from the Christian Democratic Party of West Germany. Probably there is some truth...but it is impossible to confirm...." Gil and Parrish, The Chilean Presidential Election, p. 43.

41. Myers, Democratic Campaigning in Venezuela, p. 104.

42. Martz, Acción Democrática, pp. 215-16.

43. Among the prominent adecos who joined with Prieto were José González Navarro, Braulio Jatar Dotti, Salom Mesa, Said Moanack, Mercedes Fermín, Adelso González, Luis Lander, and of course Paz.

44. Despite Prieto's record of more than three decades in public life, there were many who accepted opposition insinuations of a secret pact with the communists. As discussed below, Prieto's decision not to renounce the declared support of the UPA proved a serious error. Apart from that, it was generally true that his posture was well to the left of his opponents, thereby provoking disquiet among major economic sectors.

45. Unlike his opponents, Prieto was unable to negotiate sizable loans from Venezuelan bankers.

46. Although data are lacking, informed independent estimates calculated the total cost of the campaign at some $20 million. Whatever the precise figure, campaign expenditures were lavish.

47. Members of the Frente often observed that by combining their 1963 vote totals, victory in the four-man 1968 contest would be assured. Few honestly believed, however, that the past personal appeals of Villalba, Larrazábal, and Uslar could simply be summed and handed neatly to Burelli Rivas.

48. Among those employed by AD were Acción Independiente Revolucionaria (AIR), Alianza Popular Independiente (API), Profesionales Independientes del Volante (PRIVO), and Organización Popular Independiente Revolucionaria (OPIR).

49. Such attacks engendered further bitterness on the part of mepista leaders. They remarked that after forty years' friendship and collaboration, Betancourt knew full well that Prieto was anticommunist and was therefore indulging in irresponsible "McCarthyism." Mepistas, including Prieto, told Martz after the elections that even an explicit Prieto rejection of communist support would not have freed him from the encumbrance of such criticism. Prieto himself believed that Venezuelans, long familiar with his public record, would recognize the charges as specious. In the end, this appeared not to have been a justifiable assumption.

50. Partido Social Cristiano COPEI, Programa de gobierno, 1969-1974.

51. It should be noted that of all four campaigns, COPEI's took most seriously the drafting of its program.

52. At one point in the campaign a local humor magazine remarked that with COPEI's campaign calendars proclaiming "only 16 more days until the Change comes," this also meant "only 16 more haircuts for Caldera until election day." Copeyanos with whom Martz was traveling at the time shared in amusement over the jibe.

53. The party colors of AD are white, and it has long been a custom to wave white handkerchiefs at the meetings and public acts.

54. We shall delay until ch. 7 a detailed discussion of the Venezuelan media.

55. Capriles himself received the first position on the copeyano Senate list from the state of Barinas, where COPEI was strong.

56. A sympathetic and well-informed treatment is Richard Gott, Guerilla Movements in Latin America, pp. 214-29.

57. Myers, Democratic Campaigning in Venezuela, p. 144, discusses the debate as lodged against COPEI ideology by Arturo Uslar Pietri and Ramón Díaz.

58. Ibid., p. 148.

59. Foreign press reports to the contrary, the electorate was remarkably patient and the country calm throughout the seven days during which Caldera and Barrios remained within one percentage point of each other as the totals slowly mounted.

60. Pérez Jiménez was eventually disqualified from occupying his seat on the basis of his absence from Venezuela and failure to vote, as required by law. Even in the absence of such a technicality, it remains highly questionable whether he would have assumed his seat, even for ceremonial occasions.

CHAPTER II

1. Of the twenty-four Venezuelan constitutions, that of 1830 was the most durable, remaining in effect for some twenty-seven years.

2. For the 1945-48 regulations, in addition to the 1947 Constitution, also see República de Venezuela, Compilación Legislativa de Venezuela, 1946, pp. 9-35; and Estatuto para la elección de representantes a la Asamblea Nacional Constituyente y garantías ciudadanas, acordadas por el Gobierno Revolucionario.

3. Although women had not been explicitly denied the vote previously, the 1947 constitution was the first to specify equal voting rights for both sexes in all elections.

4. Suffrage requirements are broadly described in República de Venezuela, Constitución de 1961 (Caracas: Imprenta Nacional, 1961), Article 111. Further elaboration appears in Article 7 of the Ley Orgánica del Sufragio.

5. In practice there is little enforcement of sanctions. Among the provisions are the prohibitions--for a year following the elections--against holding public jobs; receiving contracts of any type from the government, at whatever level; initiating administrative actions; or lending services to and being remunerated for public works.

6. When Rafael Caldera assumed the presidency in 1969 there were four such lifetime senators: Eleazar López Contreras, Rómulo Gallegos, Rómulo Betancourt, and Raúl Leoni. All but Betancourt died during the next five-year period; thus, with the inauguration of a new president in March 1974, Betancourt and Caldera were the only remaining living ex-presidents.

7. See Articles 3 and 4 of República de Venezuela, Congreso de la República, Ley de reforma parcial de la ley orgánica del sufragio, p. 20.

8. A professor of mathematics, d'Hondt published his system in two works appearing from 1878 to 1882. They were later approved by an International Conference at Amberes, Belgium, in 1885, which described the formulas as vastly superior to the absolute majority system. The first use of the system was in Belgium in 1899.

9. Luis B. Prieto F., Sufragio y democracia, pp. 56-57.

10. For an excellent dissection of representational qualities, as well as their potential impact for political systems, see Andrew J. Milnor, Elections and Political Stability, especially ch. 4, pp. 71-99. Implications of electoral regulations are also acutely probed in Douglas W. Rae, The Political Consequences of Electoral Laws.

11. John Stuart Mill, Considerations on Representative Government, p. 145.

12. Milnor, Elections and Political Stability, p. 71.

13. For example, the ineffable Germán Borregales, a rightist who stands as a folkloric figure in Venezuelan politics, has repeatedly led his tiny political party into the presidential fray, where his presence attracts votes to its small tarjeta as well. In 1968 Borregales won 0.3 percent of the presidential ballots, while on the small card his party won 24,000 of the 3.6 million cast. Through application of the quotient, his party received one indirect seat in the Chamber of Deputies. Thus Don Germán returned to Congress for the next five years, where he played an energetic and dedicated, if somewhat quixotic role. His case is admittedly extreme but nonetheless reflects the quotient rule in operation. Also looking at the 1968 vote, consider six of the smaller parties (FDP, FND, UPA, PRIN, PSD, and MAN). By direct election, they won zero Senate seats and twelve in the Chamber. With the quotient, however, they eventually received four senators and twenty-five deputies; without the quotient, three of the six parties would have been totally without congressional representation. Here again the basic arguments are clear.

Supporters of the quotient contend that it provides a more just representation, also permitting independent-minded figures who reject the high centralization of the major parties to play an active congressional role. To critics it simply contributes further to the proliferation of parties and candidates to which Venezuela has been subject in the recent past.

A strong critique of the quotient appears in Juan Francisco Franco Quijano, Sistemática electoral, pp. 248-49. His grounds are largely legalistic, arguing that the bases for the quotient are such as to violate constitutional principles of the direct vote.

14. Levine, Conflict and Political Change in Venezuela, p. 240.

15. These and related details appear in Title II of the Ley orgánica del sufragio.

16. For concrete illustration of the multiplicity of CSE responsibilities in the 1973 campaign, refer to ch. 8.

17. For a convenient source of the text, accompanied by the statement of COPEI in justification of the amendment, see Nueva Política 6 (October-December 1972): 113-38.

18. These were regarded as important means of party identification. For example, the AD division of 1962 resulted in both the resultant groups' claiming the traditional white tarjeta and party symbol from the CSE. After a legal tangle proved unresolvable, the CSE eliminated the color and symbol for 1963, promising to award it to the group that ran strongest in those elections. Details appear in Acción Democrática, La batalla por el nombre y símbolos de Acción Democrática.

19. Details were set forth in Consejo Supremo Electoral, Instrucciones para las mesas electorales.

20. For an account that centers on the CSE investigation and decision, see SIC 36, no. 357 (July-August 1973): 330-31.

21. An invaluable reference work containing many of the documents and official reports is Las 10,000 máquinas de votar y el escándolo de las comisiones.

22. El Nacional, 28 November 1973, p. 11.

23. República de Venezuela, Ley orgánica del sufragio.

24. Different scholars have presented a variety of regional divisions, none of which are fully satisfactory. The schema described here follows that of Myers in his Democratic Campaigning in Venezuela, pp. 28-30. For a slightly different version employed by Martz for 1958 and 1963 elections, see his Acción Democrática, pp. 353-55. We believe that the Myers division had become more appropriate by the time of the 1968 elections.

25. The eventual reduction of inscribed voters by some 250,000 reflected the deletion of names on a host of grounds: false identification papers, minors, people who had died, recent entry into obligatory military service, and multiple inscriptions.

26. We were able to include all of our 1,521 respondents in the scales as follows:

Respondent Attitude	Score	Frequency	Percent
Very favorable	1	602	39.6
Favorable	2	467	30.7
Moderately favorable	3	331	21.8
Unfavorable	4	94	6.2
Very unfavorable	5	27	1.8

Coefficient of reproducibility = 0.93
Coefficient of scalibility = 0.71

27. We will have considerably more to say on the subject in our second volume; at present we will be reporting those results that are immediately relevant to the main topic of this volume, democratic campaigning.

28. As utilized in his Responsible Electorate (Cambridge, Mass.: Harvard University Press, 1966).

29. The field work of this pre-test was conducted for us by DATOS during late June and early July. Feedback from the results of the pre-test was extremely useful in the development of the definitive instrument.

30. The phrasing of the probe was altered in one important respect. In our summer pre-test we asked our respondents "Who can solve this (most important national) problem?" During our fall interviewing this had become "Whom do you think ought to have the greatest responsibility in the solution of that (most important national) problem?"

31. A few of the more familiar are Lucian W. Pye, Samuel P. Huntington, and Gabriel A. Almond.

32. For a revealing study of decision-making involving Caracas's urban renewal, see David J. Myers, Toma de decisiones sobre la renovación urbana en El Conde (Caracas: Ediciones IESA, 1974).

33. Our occasional comparisons of such data for Venezuela and the United States are employedas convenient reference points for North American readers. Obviously, we neither believe nor imply that Venezuela should follow U.S. paths in development rather than those consistent with her own heritage and tradition.

CHAPTER III

1. "Herrera Campins versus Beaujon," Bohemia 538 (16-22 July 1973): 4-7.

2. For a later manifestation, El Nacional's regular Miraflores reporter, Jésus Lossada Rondón, wrote that the visits to the president by Secretary General Beaujón were lacking in warmth, and that

Beaujon entered and departed unaccompanied. The contrast with the next secretary general was striking; presidential secretary Luis A. Macahdo cordially escorted him in and out, and the enthusiasm within Miraflores was evident.

3. Former leader of a radical student faction within the JRC, Vivas Terán had at one point been suspended from his position by Caldera and the party leadership. Having moderated his avowed position little, Vivas had found it possible to join the Caldera administration, thereby improving his legitimacy in the eyes of senior party leaders.

4. This was confirmed in several interviews with party members in a position to know. For one of several published versions, see "Herrera Campins versus Beaujon."

5. It is quite true that there was officially no herrerista candidate and that Vivas was backed by the JRC. As a practical matter, however, it was clear that the JRC strongly preferred Herrera to other possibilities as the nominee for 1973.

6. As one small measure, on the opening day of the convention in March the morning edition of El Nacional alone carried over seven full pages of advertisements for the four candidates--a total of over 21,000 bolivares in costs.

7. COPEI regulations dictate that in any such party contests, a majority vote is necessary for victory. If a second ballot is required, all but the two leading vote-getters from the first round will be eliminated.

8. The president maintained a careful neutrality in his public statements. There can be no serious question, however, that he was firmly committed to the nomination of his lifelong colleague and associate.

9. Herrera Campins later told the press that family obligations had prevented his attendance of the Fernández proclamation. Herrerista anger over its perception of intervention in favor of the nominee certainly included the aspirant himself.

10. For stories incorporating both the COPEI press release and the words of Dagoberto González, see El Nacional, 19 April 1972, D-1.

11. The best English equivalent would be "The Bag Man."

12. For a recent republication of the letter, see Resumen 2, no. 10 (13 January 1974): 62-63.

13. Perhaps the only other letter that bore as profound political implications was the alleged message of Rómulo Betancourt to party leaders in 1967 concerning the internal AD disputes. In that case, Betancourt was to steadfastly deny authorship.

14. This was drawn largely through Angel Zerpa Mirabel in the CTV, and Américo Chacón in the rival CUTV.

15. Larrazábal was largely inactive in party affairs, spending much of the period as Venezuelan ambassador to Canada.

16. Semana 267 (31 May-6 June 1973): 8, 11-13.

17. Ibid. For an interview with Jorge Dáger concerning the pact, see Semana 268 (7-13 June 1973): 15.

18. El Nacional, 12 July 1973, D-1.

19. After the extraordinary physical and mental demands of the 1959-64 years, Betancourt was in need of extended travel and rest. Moreover, his presence in Venezuela would have nourished inevitable political charges that he was running the Leoni government through his old colleague. Thus he departed for Europe and the United States, not to return until 1968 in support of the Barrios campaign.

20. During Martz's brief visit in May and June of 1972, virtually every conversation related to Betancourt's intentions, his health, his appearance, his attitude, his likely decision, etc.

21. The complete text appeared in all newspapers the following day—22 July 1972.

22. There were many factors in Betancourt's thinking, including the following: exemplifying to fellow Venezuelans his opposition to continuism and personalism in politics; belief in the importance of passing political leadership to others, both nationally and within the party; the benefits of new guidance and leadership; concern for his own place in Venezuelan history; and the general conviction that his own most important and constructive legacy to party and country would be graceful withdrawal and semiretirement from politics. These were among points noted in our interview with Rómulo Betancourt, 9 August 1973.

23. For biographical details, see ch. 7.

24. Ex-president Raúl Leoni was not a factor in these party matters, having recently entered the hospital with an illness culminating in his July 1972 death.

25. Interview with Carlos Andrés Pérez, 16 July 1973.

26. While David Morales Bello had also aspired to the secretary generalship, the competition with Lepage was not **damaging**; the former was to become an important figure in the Pérez campaign, as described later. Perhaps the most heated contest was the repacement of Cristóbal Hernández by Héctor Alonso López as youth secretary. The move was strongly opposed by the AD Youth Bureau itself, but Pérez insisted upon the change.

27. The PRN signed an accord with the AD on 24 February 1973 and participated in registering the Perez candidacy with the CSE on 1 June 1973. The Congreso del Trabajo officially announced its support the following day.

28. Interviews with mepista leaders in August and September

of 1973 elicited the general opinion that the fervor of Villalba's profession of support at the Congress had for a time dissipated their skepticism over his acceptance of a candidacy other than his own. It should be noted that conversations with Paz himself found the Nueva Fuerza candidate careful not to attack or criticize Villalba; he maintained this same posture when queried by the press about URD actions.

29. Semana 228 (10-16 August 1972): 5-6.

30. The former group included such veteran urredistas as Humberto Bartoli, Enrique Betancourt y Galíndez, Omar Rumbos, Francisco Faraco, and Tenorio Sifontes; the latter was headed by Leonardo Montiel Ortega.

31. William García Insausti, "Jóvito Villalba: 'He Fracasado Buscando la Unidad por Arriba,'" Bohemia 541 (6-12 August 1973):38.

32. For biographical details see ch. 7.

33. For Rangel's views toward the activities and elements within the left prior to his candidacy, see Jesús Sanoja Hernández, "Rangel: un José Gregorio que puede ganar el cielo pero no las elecciones," Summa 3, no. 77 (10-25 October 1973): 2-6.

34. "Los empresarios alarmados," Bohemia 536 (2-8 July 1973): 7.

35. President Caldera announced the suspension of the political disqualification of the MIR on 29 March 1973.

36. In its early years, Sáez Mérida and Martín had favored the guerrilla path to revolutionary power, while the nonviolent strategy was advocated by Jorge Dáger and Gumersindo Rodríguez. The former had soon left the MIR to organize the FDP in support of Wolfgang Larrazabal; the latter had returned to AD and by 1973 was a leading economic spokesman for the AD.

37. For a discussion of stresses between the two parties, see "MIR-MAS: Socialismo 'duro' vs. socialismo 'primaveral,'" Semana 287 (18-24 October 1973): 12-13.

38. The leading exponent of this thesis was the ever-polemical iconoclast of the left, Domingo Alberto Rangel, whose writings are cited elsewhere. For a statement of those who advocated this electoral position for 1973, see Juan Luna, Voto nulo.

39. For a more detailed account, see the mirista weekly Al margen 27 (30 June-6 July 1973), especially pp. 10-11.

40. As was sometimes overlooked, there was no certainty that Pérez Jiménez desired another term. Even more important, there was the question whether he would opt to relinquish his life of luxurious pleasure in Madrid for the rigors, not to mention physical perils, of public appearances in Venezuela. The eventual constitutional disqualification provided him a convenient excuse for not returning and for claiming that COPEI and the AD had gone

contrary to the public will in its fear of his return and an
alleged wave of national acclamation.

41. Among the most eloquent and incisive proponents of this
view was AD Senator Enrique Tejera París; he expressed his views to
us in an interview on 6 September 1973.

42. Such were the divisions and shifting loyalties within the
sector that it was difficult to cite a specific figure that would
not soon change.

43. It was widely believed that Llovera Páez provided the
military brains of the regime. He did not possess Pérez Jiménez's
canny telluric shrewdness of men and their foibles, nor his
colleague's desire for absolute power. Llovera, instead, was
content to retain his position of eminence while enjoying the finer
pleasures of life.

44. Something of a political chameleon, Verde Rojas had once
belonged to the URD. He had followed Alirio Ugarte Pelayo out of
the party following disciplinary action imposed by Jóvito Villalba
and was aiding Ugarte in founding the MDI when the latter committed
suicide. He had then committed the MDI to Caldera in 1968 before
casting his lot elsewhere. With the literal translation of his
surnames "Green Red," he was referred to by fellow congressmen and
news reporters as Diputado Semáforo ("Deputy Semaphore" or "Deputy
Traffic Light").

45. See ch. 7 for fuller biographical discussion.

46. A well-informed account of the struggle within the FND
appears as ". . . Y ahora le toca al FND," Bohemia 534 (18-24 June
1973): 4-6.

47. The primary juridical bases for the decision were two:
first, the Corte Supremo de Justicia had sentenced Pérez Jiménez to
four years' imprisonment for crimes committed while serving as
president; second, the constitutional amendment established a
condition of eligibility that Pérez Jiménez therefore failed to
meet. There were additional points that dealt with legalistic
details. All CSE members except the representatives of the URD and
MEP voted in favor of the disqualification. The latter two
criticized what they viewed as retroactive application of the
amendment. For the URD, this action was later cited as not only
its opposition to the "status," but as a basis for justifying
possible perezjimenista sympathy towards the Villalba candidacy.

48. We have not forgotten the final two; they will appear
shortly.

49. A good summary of the confused picture was "El camporismo:
un fracaso," Bohemia 541 (6-12 August 1973): 4-7.

50. It would be neither unkind nor inaccurate to note that
Doña Flor had remained in the background throughout her husband's
career, had devoted herself to family matters, and had never shown
either interest or vocation for politics. She had been virtually

unknown to the public during her husband's decade in power, in contrast to later presidential wives.

51. El Nacional, 1 September 1973, D-18.

52. For an interview discussing his thinking at that juncture, see William García Insausti, "Salas Castillo: un candidato táctico," Bohemia 545 (3-9 September 1973): 36-38.

53. El Nacional, 16 September 1973, C-5.

54. Ibid., 16 October 1973, D-1.

55. "El 'Sancocho' Pérez Jiménez," Bohemia 554 (5-11 November 1973): 4-7.

56. El Nacional, 22 November 1973, C-13.

CHAPTER IV

1. This point was often made, including a 4 July 1973 interview with Eduardo Fernández. At that time confidence was expressed that the difficulty was being solved. Events were to prove otherwise, however.

2. For a detailed discussion of established party organs, see Rivera Oviedo, Los social cristianos en Venezuela. However, as Rivera remarked in an interview on 11 July 1973, the formal structure does not explain fully the dynamics of the situation, especially in terms of campaign activity.

3. The venerable Pedro del Corral served as party president for many years in a largely honorary role. During his illness in 1973, Godofredo González served as acting party president.

4. In addition to the MPJ, a splinter group of perezjimenistas led by Abdelkader Márquez, COPEI had to cope with the demands of the Movimiento Alirista (composed of the widow and friends of Alirio Ugarte Pelayo), the Movimiento de los Independientes Progresistas (headed by former URD leader Luis Hernández Solís), and some 200 local, state, or national committees of independents, often known by such acronyms as MONTRI and MUTRAL.

5. Its members were Godofredo González, J. N. Pérez Díaz, Eduardo Fernández, José Rodríguez Sáez, Juan José Rachadell, Oswaldo Alvarez Paz, and María de Guzmán.

6. As a result of decisions on this plancha, the former COPEI governor of Bolívar, its state secretary general, and the party's ranking labor leader in the state all resigned from the party in protest and sat out the campaign.

7. Publicity over such disputes was particularly distasteful to COPEI, traditionally a party that hid its internal problems from sight. As Hugo Briceño Salas had told interviewers during a television program, "our family affairs are not discussed outside the home." See "Herrera Campins versus Beaujon," Bohemia 536 (16-22 July 1973): 4-7.

8. Jesús Bernardoni, who had led COPEI's list of deputies from Zulia, was placed second for the Senate behind Arístides Beaujon in Falcón. His best hope of returning to congress was dependent upon a Fernández victory and the entry of Beaujon into the new administration, which would then have left the Senate seat vacant for Bernardoni to occupy.

9. Interview with Oswaldo Alvarez Paz on 16 September 1973. For a press account, see El Nacional (Caracas), 17 September 1973, D-1.

10. Thus the zones included the Andean, Eastern, Capital, Center, Center-West, etc.

11. For description and justification of the system by Secretary of Organization Adolfo Melchert, see El Nacional (Caracas), 27 August 1973, D-11.

12. Operations were already underway when Martz visited Boleita in June of 1972, well in advance of the nomination of opposition presidential candidates.

13. The authors found that permission to visit and enter the Santa Ana building was literally more difficult to arrange than an interview with President Caldera in Miraflores.

14. GAMA was an acronym for Ganador con Mayoría ("Winner with [a congressional] Majority").

15. By this time denying a polarization of the vote between Fernández and Pérez, COPEI reasoned that dispersion of the anti-Fernández vote assured that a total in the neighborhood of 36 percent would suffice to win the election.

16. See ch. 8 for discussion of the CSE performance in this regard, as well as that of COPEI and others once the balloting had been completed.

17. El Nacional (Caracas), 27 August 1973.

18. Interview with Octavio Lepage, 8 July 1973.

19. Such were the problems of the planchas for many of the parties that the CSE was forced to extend the deadline for inscription by a week. As the tugging and hauling took place in respective party headquarters, a telling remark was attributed to Juan Herrera, a veteran adeco labor leader from the Federation of Construction Workers: "I was second [for deputy], but with all the pushing and shoving I'm now fourth, and if I don't watch out I'll end up as a substitute for councilman." Momento 896 (16 September 1973): 28. In the end, Herrera was fourth on the list of deputies from Lara and returned to Congress in 1974.

20. It might be noted that while accompanying the Pérez campaign to Nueva Esparta in July of 1973--before completion of the plancha process--we noted that it was Salazar Meneses who most actively traveled with the candidate and dealt with local leaders on arrangements. González Navarro, though present, was largely in the background.

21. For further information see J.M. Domínguez Chacín, "A propósito de Carlos Andrés--El movimiento de independientes pro elección de Carlos Andrés Pérez como candidato presidencial," Summa 75 (7-21 September 1973): 27.

22. Interview with Luis Piñerúa Ordaz, 14 August 1973.

23. Activists were not paid for two reasons: the necessity of allocating party funds to other campaign needs, and the belief that the necessary commitment and conviction of the activistas would be diluted were they to receive pay. Of course, AD leaders at both the national and regional leadership received salaries from the party.

24. The AD explained informally that the designated term mosca or "fly" could also be characterized as a bulls-eye, with the center of the target representing victory on election day.

25. For the official announcement of Operación Mosca, see El Nacional (Caracas), 16 September 1973, D-1.

26. Acción Democrática, Comité Ejecutivo Nacional, Secretaría de Organización, Operación Mosca; instructivo para representantes de Acción Democrática ante las mesas electorales 1973 (Caracas: Acción Democrática, 1973). When this private document was discovered by the press, the Prologue also charged COPEI with having committed electoral fraud in 1968 at the mesa level. A brief but angry flurry inevitably resulted, with copeyanos unsuccessfully demanding that the AD retract its imputation of 1968 fraud.

27. Antonio Leidenz, "Operación Mosca--con los ojos abiertos," El Nacional, 19 October 1973, A-4.

28. Two of the unsung aides who played significant roles in the campaign were Teo Camargo and Ildemagno Flores. The former had served as Pérez's private secretary for fifteen years and was close to the candidate and his family. Flores, at twenty-four a leader of the adeco youth wing, traveled constantly with Pérez throughout the long months of campaigning.

29. As was reported nearly a decade earlier, the AD saw the payment of dues largely as a symbolic act encouraging a sense of participation and commitment. See Martz, Acción Democrática, pp. 215-16.

30. Public curiosity was aroused in August of 1973 when the party raffled off private belongings of various of its more eminent figures. Among the articles were a pipe of Betancourt, a pair of Pérez's shoes, and Diego Arria's walking stick.

31. The alleged involvement of "Toñito" Prieto in the voting machine scandal was an important factor in his political decline.

32. An influential leader of both the teachers' federation and of AD for many years, Mercedes Fermín had been strongly influenced by a lifetime of loyalty to Prieto in leaving the AD in 1967. Disenchanted by the mepista move to the left after 1968, and especially by the alliance with the PCV, she announced her

withdrawal from politics in September 1973. The action was precipitated by the withdrawal of MEP support in Congress for educational reform legislation, which Fermín had been shepherding toward probable adoption along the lines advocated for years by Prieto. For her resignation statement, see El Nacional, 4 September 1973, D-1. Contrary to rumor, she did not seriously consider rejoining AD, although retaining admiration for Rómulo Betancourt.

33. For a report on the ninth Plenum of the PVC Central Committee, see Semana 273 (12-18 July 1973): 8-9.

34. Headed by Guillermo Muñoz, the Comisión included Adelso González, Demetrio Boersner, Salom Mesa, Siuberto Martínez, Oscar Carvallo, and Héctor Atilio Pujol.

35. His concern was symbolized by the establishment of Nueva Fuerza offices in major cities, separate from those of the MEP. Similarly, in Caracas Paz's campaign offices were located on the second floor of the La Perla building, two blocks' distance from the MEP party headquarters.

36. Interview with José Herrera Oropeza, 23 August 1973.

37. In a limited number of cases the MEP and PCV had agreed upon a single slate for municipal councilmen. At least from the standpoint of the PCV, this was encouraging. Interview with Radamés Larrazábal, 14 September 1973.

38. Interview with Siuberto Martínez, 1 September 1973.

39. The membership of the CEN numbered nine: Pompeyo Márquez, Teodoro Petkoff, Freddy Muñoz, Antonio Urbina, Juvencio Pulgar, Jacobo Borges, Luis Bayardo Sardi, Jesús Valedón and Anselmo Natale.

40. Although a miniscule group, the CUR included several important figures on the left, including Luis Miquelena, Héctor Malavé Mata, and José Marcano. The first was of particular consequence, having joined with Rangel and José Herrera Oropeza as leaders of the URD left wing a decade earlier. Moreover, Miquelena and Rangel had retained a close friendship.

41. Among these microparties and groups were the Movimiento Prensa Libre (MPL), Unión de Mujeres Socialistas (UMS), Comité de Independientes por el Socialismo (CIPES), Organización de Revolucionarios (OR), Vox Marxista, and Vanguardia Socialista.

42. The MIR tarjeta showed a single profile of Rangel, with "José Vicente" and "MIR" also appearing. That of the MAS featured two clenched fists, five outlines of Rangel in a standing pose, plus an inset showing the candidate's face. Background colors for the two cards differed.

43. El Nacional, 24 November 1973, C-6.

44. Ibid., 27 November 1973, D-18.

45. A good example was observed by Martz in a September visit with Rangel to Bolívar state. Germán Lairet for the MAS and Rigoberto Lanz for the MIR worked together, seemingly in harmony

and without difficulty. Some of the masista and mirista youth cadres were less cooperative with one another, however, going so far as to dispute positions of their sound trucks in Rangel caravans.

46. For an interesting treatment based on an interview with Juvencio Pulgar, see Raúl Fojas P., "Así hacemos la campaña de José Vicente Rangel," Summa 3 (10–25 October 1973): 14–16.

CHAPTER V

1. In addition to ch. 1, see David J. Myers, Democratic Campaigning in Venezuela, pp. 136–48.

2. A typical illustration is the editorial by Campaign Coordinator Oswaldo Alvarez Paz, "Están derrotados!" El Nacional, 23 August 1973, A–4. Charging the AD with a bragging and sectarian attitude which contributed to their failures in providing a democratic opposition, he described them as defeated, facing final and inevitable liquidation.

3. He was often described as Señor Pérez, in contrast to Doctor Fernández.

4. For a full account of the 10 August rally, see El Nacional, 15 August 1973, D–3.

5. Eduardo Fernández, "Tiene la palabra," Summa 73 (30 July–15 August 1973): 29.

6. El Nacional, 24 October 1973, D–1.

7. Ibid., 23 September 1973, D–1. Final touches were also added to Lorenzo Fernández's Program of Government, prior to its forthcoming release.

8. A representative excerpting of questions and answers at the Pro-Venezuela meeting appeared in Momento 900 (14 October 1973): 28–31.

9. Partido Social Cristiano COPEI, Directrices para una acción de gobierno, p. 3.

10. El Nacional, 22 October 1973, C–7.

11. In 1967 and 1968 Rafael Caldera had employed to great advantage the holding of countless morning coffees with small groups of women. His intended successor, for whatever reason, did not repeat the tactic.

12. Lorenzo Fernández, "Yo pido la palabra," Summa 73 (30 July–15 August 1973): 20–22.

13. A key person for COPEI was Antonio Daza Medina, secretary of the National Coordinating Committee for Relations with Independents. Godofredo González was also significantly involved as president of the party's Comisión Nacional Coordinadora de Independientes (CONACIL).

14. A typical example is found in El Nacional, 10 August 1973, D-13, 14, and 15. Three full pages of advertising list dozens of regional and local committees of independents; the main headline on D-13 proclaimed that "never has a candidate received so much backing from great independent majorities."

15. For example, in March of 1973 at a meeting of the Directorio Nacional, Pedro Pablo Aguilar reported a clear polarization between the Fernández and Pérez candidacies. He gave COPEI a marked advantage in urban areas, with the oriente the only region of relative weakness. See Semana 259 (29 March-4 April 1973): 17.

16. El Nacional, 11 August 1973, D-1.

17. Alfredo Tarre Murzi (Sanín) had lived an opportunistic career politically, most recently having served as Caldera's minister of labor and then as director of INCIBA. His columns include "Palco de Sombra" in El Nacional and "Política para Variar" in Momento. He also wrote frequently in the weekly Semana, which he directed in highly partisan fashion since early 1973, when he left the administration. Also see further discussion in ch. 7.

18. El Universal, 6 August 1973.

19. This paid series of "news" items appeared Tuesdays in Ultimas Noticias, Thursdays in El Universal, and Sundays in El Nacional. Similar adeco "pages" are discussed in ch. 7.

20. El Nacional, 31 October 1973, D-1.

21. Oswaldo Alvarez Paz, "En la recta final," ibid., 6 October 1973, A-4.

22. Ibid., 2 November 1973, D-1.

23. Jorge Dáger, "Elecciones y dinero," ibid., 10 September 1973, A-4.

24. Venezuelan attitudes toward Colombians, generally somewhat acerbic, have worsened in Andean border regions during recent years. The presence and employment of Colombians seeking better pay and working conditions--much of it illegal--has tended to exacerbate sentiment. Although the question of Pérez's birthplace may have hurt elsewhere, it is believed to have boomeranged against COPEI in the Andes, and especially in Pérez's home state of Táchira.

25. Among the more widely disseminated was a poster bearing the photograph of a mutilated body, with the caption accusing Pérez of culpability and predicting "more political assassinations" should he be elected president.

26. At a copeyano "Feria Navideña" to enliven the 1972 Christmas holidays, slanderous anti-Pérez "documents" and exhibits were on display, a few of a frankly scatalogical nature. These were removed in the wake of adeco protests.

27. "Con Lorenzo a la conquista del futuro ya!", Programa de gobierno, p. 8.

28. Among his considerations of the theme in pre-presidential writings, see especially Rafael Caldera, El bloque latinoamericano, and also La idea de justicia social internacional. A useful collection of articles and essays is found in Rafael Caldera, Justicia social internacional y nacionalismo latinoamericano.

29. The Betancourt Doctrine, followed by the adeco governments of 1959-69, had revived and updated earlier hemispheric theories such as the Tovar Doctrine in the defense of democratic principles, and called for nonrecognition of unconstitutional regimes.

30. For an early discussion of the anticipated electoral centrality of Zulia, see "El Zulia después del mitín," Bohemia 499 (20-26 October 1972): 4-7.

31. This was confirmed in our conversations with numerous party leaders, including the AD candidate himself.

32. This phrase, uttered by Betancourt during the time of the mepista division, might be translated as "an adeco is an adeco until he dies" or, less literally, "once an adeco, always an adeco."

33. Betancourt had commented during the 1968 campaign with assurance that, although that election might be lost, the party would come back stronger than ever, winning an impressive triumph in 1973.

34. Dubuc had withdrawn from party activities in 1968 and devoted his attention to private affairs in his home state of Trujillo; Ciliberto, for some years a virtual independent, had been a supporter of Barrios in 1968; González Navarro, who had gone with the prietistas in 1968, had recently defected to form his own Congreso de Trabajo, after failing to win the presidential candidacy of the MEP; Quijada, who had first gone with ARS in 1962 and then backed the candidacy of Arturo Uslar Pietri the following year, returned to the AD asking "to serve as a soldier where I didn't know how to serve as a general."

35. As noted elsewhere, the PRN's Manzo González and García Mackle were incorporated on AD planchas and thus were returned to congress for 1974-79. The same proved true of González Navarro, Pedro Torres, and Pedro Brito of the Congreso del Trabajo. Within one month of 1973 elections, the PRN was in virtual dissolution with its members effectively rejoining AD, while labor leaders were planning a conference to unify the country's several major organizations, a move strongly backed by González Navarro.

36. An historian and man of letters, Velásquez had served as secretary of the presidency curing much of Betancourt's term. He was discussed as a possible coalition candidate for president in 1963, and five years later was a prime pre-candidate for the URD-FDP-FND alliance, which ultimately selected Burelli Rivas. Velásquez had then served as minister of communications during the early portion of the Caldera administration.

37. El Nacional, 14 October 1973, D-1.

38. It should be noted that Pérez rarely made reference to individuals in his speeches, and then only indirectly. The same, of course, was true of Fernández and of most other presidential candidates; it did not necessarily suggest a gentle or uncritical speech.

39. Dated 6 September 1973, the letter was released to the press the following day.

40. Although acceptable in some polities, such a practice was clearly in violation of Venezuelan electoral codes and practices. After widespread dissemination of this poster at one point, most were withdrawn from circulation, although the authors occasionally saw a sample in the interior of the country some months later.

41. El Nacional, 9 September 1973, D-1.

42. A good sample of his style and tone is found in a collection of earlier articles and columns, published in 1963 under the title Los días y la política.

43. Gonzalo Barrios, "La campaña electoral de COPEI o los riesgos de lo excesivo," El Nacional, 11 August 1973, A-4.

44. El Universal, 15 August 1973, 1ff.

45. Gonzalo Barrios, "La legitimidad y sus compatibilidades," El Nacional, 20 October 1973, A-4.

46. Octavio Lepage, "Tribuna abierta--el presidente en campaña," Momento 890 (5 August 1973): 32.

47. On 2 August at his 199th press conference, President Caldera firmly rejected adeco criticisms. His tours and press statements were a continuing effort at "constant dialogue, not for electoral purposes, but ...as an expression of [my] concept of government...." See El Nacional, 3 August 1973, D-1.

48. Octavio Lepage, "El Presidente no rectifica," El Nacional, 8 August 1973, A-4.

49. Octavio Lepage, "Tribuna abierta--no hay que votar a ciegas," Momento 907 (2 December 1973): 32.

50. Prior to his more public activities, opponents alleged that Betancourt was disillusioned with both the AD and its candidate. When he became more visible, critics predictably interpreted this as a sign that the Pérez candidacy was sinking.

51. The speech was reported in the press on 14 September. A full text was published by the AD in a one-page advertisement the following month; see El Nacional, 12 October 1973. The address was also a significant statement in calling for campaign responsibility from all participants. As seen in ch. 8, both Caldera and Betancourt, despite their own partisan interests in the electoral verdict, were eloquent in their advocacy of democratic institutions. Betancourt's 13 September speech was viewed by partisans as an admonition to COPEI not to overstep accepted boundaries in the

campaign. A more balanced judgment, however, shows these declarations as forthright advice directed to all political participants, not excluding those of his own party.

52. Characteristic was the treatment in the highly partial pages of Semana 277 (16–22 August 1973). Its lead story, entitled "Lepage: Una confesión de derrota," assured the reader that the AD was panicking, Lepage was agitated by the tension of impending defeat, and even that Villalba was likely to run second to Fernández in December. The magazine's anecdotal political gossip column included several cutting remarks about the secretary general, allegedly voiced by Luis B. Prieto and also by Rómulo Betancourt.

It was upon the occasion of Lepage's statement concerning a possible accord that the secretary general predicted a percentage of votes for Pérez which proved precisely accurate in December.

53. El Nacional, 11 August 1973, D–2.

54. Ibid., D–1.

55. Toward the conclusion of the campaign, several prominent adecos commented privately, without attribution, that they hoped for a margin of well over 100,000 votes. Should the result be closer, they were apprehensive of the possibilities. There were few who seriously doubted the president's integrity in such a circumstance, but the campaign strategists for COPEI were largely seen as suspect. The very existence of COPEI's elaborate plans to issue bulletins from its Boleita operation were questioned as being unnecessary unless conspiratorial plans were afoot.

56. Octavio Lepage, "Los copeyanos son así," El Nacional, 14 November 1973, A–4.

57. Semana 270 (21–28 June 1973): 6.

58. The authors heard this metaphor and assorted variations during travels with the Nueva Fuerza candidate.

59. Oscar Carvallo G., "Tiene la palabra," Summa 3, no. 76 (26 September–10 October 1973): 28.

60. Full discussion of the electoral impact of Salvador Allende's overthrow appears in ch. 8.

61. As an anecdotal aside, the Paz editorial herein paraphrased had been written and delivered to the offices of El Nacional shortly before the violent ouster of Allende and his dramatic suicide. Martz was at breakfast with Paz and his entourage in the Caracas airport, preparatory to a campaign trip to Zulia and Trujillo, when the candidate reread his column and received verbal reports on the latest news from Santiago. He remarked that, after considering the withholding of his article, he had revised it slightly so that events in Chile might not render it meaningless.

62. Jesús Angel Paz Galarraga, "Emplazamiento a la Democracia Cristiana," El Nacional, 13 September 1973, A–4.

63. Jesús Angel Paz Galarraga, "Ratificación de compromisos," ibid., 29 November 1973, A-4.

64. Among the best sources for a presentation and exposition of the Nueva Fuerza program were the erudite if partisan columns written regularly by Luis B. Prieto and appearing in El Nacional, Panorama of Maracaibo, and occasionally in Momento's "Tribuna abierta."

65. Luis B. Prieto, "Elecciones y propaganda," El Nacional, 9 October 1973, A-4.

66. Semana 270 (21-28 June 1973): 6-7.

67. Interview with Guillermo Pantín, El Nacional, 2 July 1973, D-1.

68. Ibid.

69. A seven-day swing through the oriente was followed by a huge rally in Maracaibo, with the campaign then concluding at the traditional closing in Caracas's El Silencio.

70. See "El Indio limpia la casa...y ruedan las cabezas," Bohemia 516 (12-18 February 1973): 4-7.

71. This general picture was sketched in our 16 August 1973 interview with Jesús Angel Paz Galarraga. It was further elaborated, without significant alteration, by other Nueva Fuerza leaders; Paz also reiterated its features in conversations with the authors during later campaign trips.

72. For a knowledgeable account, see "Consigna del PCV: Destruir a Rangel," Bohemia 540 (30 July-5 August 1973): 47.

73. It should of course be recalled that the PCV, historically weak at the grass roots, had been further crippled by the debilitating 1971 division that resulted in the MAS.

74. 2001, 27 November 1973, p. 3.

75. It was not coincidental that he gave no additional speeches during Paz's trip through the oriente. Prieto also administered a sharp rebuke, first from the podium in his own speech, and later in a private tongue-lashing.

76. Interview with Rafael Poleo in Bohemia 515 (5-11 February 1973): 6.

77. José Vicente Rangel, "Tribuna abierta--una campaña y una respuesta," Momento 902 (28 October 1973): 32.

78. He made this clear to Martz on several occasions while being accompanied on campaign trips to the interior.

79. José Vicente Rangel, "Las dos caras de la moneda," Semana 273 (12-18 July 1973): 48.

80. From the text of Rangel's statement, released in Barquisimeto on 3 October 1973.

81. Teodoro Petkoff, Razón y pasión del socialismo, p. 328.

82. See ch. 8 for a fuller account.

83. The initial denunciation by the MAS was released to the press on 10 September 1973.

84. Interview with Rafael Poleo in Bohemia 515 (5-11 February 1973): 6.

85. El Nacional, 18 October 1973, D-1.

86. Americo Martín, "No buscamos competir con el MAS," Semana 272 (5-11 July 1973): 12.

87. José Reynaga, "Un día con José Vicente," Bohemia 539 (23-29 July 1973): 37-38.

88. El Universal, 8 October 1973, 3.

89. The scheme was outlined to us by José Vicente Rangel in an interview during a September campaign trip to Bolívar and Anzoátegui.

90. For aficionados of crowd sizes and students of the Venezuelan left, the authors can attest to the larger and more responsive turnout for Rangel in El Silencio. On the other hand, Paz drew inordinately larger attendance in the final Maracaibo meetings.

91. El Universal, 8 July 1973, 18.

92. El Nacional, 7 July 1973, C-16.

93. Ibid., 31 July, 1973, D-1.

94. Ibid., 14 August 1973, D-1.

95. Press conference in Valencia, 29 July 1973.

96. Press conference in Maturin, 7 July 1973.

CHAPTER VI

1. As cited in Jorrín and Martz, Latin-American Political Thought and Ideology, p. 3.

2. A more extensive examination and analysis, including detailed attention to the historical evolution of party thought and doctrine, will appear subsequently.

3. As footnoted in ch. 1, ongoing investigation by Naudy Suárez Figueroa is bringing to light important documentation of the infancy of Venezuelan Christian Democracy. Especially note his lengthy introduction in the edited volume Por los legítimos ideales.

4. For a synthesis of Christian Democratic thought, see Jorrín and Martz, Latin-American Political Thought and Ideology, ch. 13. Also see Williams, Latin-American Christian Democratic Parties.

5. A hopeful view of progressive, modernizing forces is presented in Edward J. Williams, "Latin-American Catholicism and Political Integration," Comparative Political Studies 2, no. 3 (October 1969): 327-49.

6. For the 57-page text, appearing in the smallest print, see COPEI, Programa de gobierno, 1969-1974.

7. Not all shared this view, of course. In August of 1968 Ramón Díaz, a noted Caracas lawyer, attacked COPEI's program as fascist-inspired, intended ultimately to establish a corporate state in Venezuela. For details see Myers, Democratic Campaigning in Venezuela, p. 144.

8. Among the best-known was perennial presidential aspirant Germán Borregales. For a lengthy exposition of his views, see Borregales, Copei, hoy, una negación.

9. A forthright statement of his views is Edecio La Riva Araujo, Los fusiles de la paz. For a more recent declaration reflecting his assessment of the 1973 elections see the interview with la Riva in Resumen 2, no. 10 (13 January 1974): 44-48.

10. A convenient summary of this intellectual current in Latin America is Pensamiento Comunitario. Included is a chapter by one of COPEI's finest minds, Abdón Vivas Terán, "La estructura macroeconómica de la sociedad comunitaria," pp. 141-56.

11. In addition to the many writings of Rafael Caldera cited elsewhere, standard Venezuelan sources include Cárdenas, El combate político; José Barbeito, Introducción al pensamiento socialcristiano; and Rivera Oviedo, Los socialcristianos en Venezuela.

12. Fernández's appearance before Fedecámaras was at the twenty-ninth assembly of the organization in Barquisimeto, where a number of presidential candidates spoke. The most convenient and detailed source, which we are using, is the special newspaper supplement appearing in October of 1973: Fedecámaras, Diálogo con los candidatos a la presidencia de la república. Referred to hereafter as Diálogo, it printed Fernández's words on pp. 14-20.

The appearance before Pro-Venezuela was reported extensively, if not verbatim, in the press and news media. Our sources include Momento and Semana in addition to the dailies.

The official program, entitled Directrices para una acción de gobierno, was unavailable when Fernández presented a summary of its contents. Only in late November did it circulate, most commonly as a 16-page supplement in the newspapers. It will be cited as Directrices.

El Nacional directed a set of thirty questions to all of the candidates late in the campaign, publishing them in full on a daily basis. For those of the copeyano candidate, see El Nacional, 18 November 1973, D-1 and D-2.

13. Diálogo, p. 14.

14. Directrices, p. 3.

15. Ibid.

16. "En Pro-Venezuela: Lorenzo ganó el reto," Momento 900 (14 October 1973): 31.

17. Directrices, p. 5.

18. Ibid.

19. Ibid.

20. Ibid.

21. Ibid., p. 6.

22. Diálogo, p. 15.

23. Directrices, p. 6.

24. "En Pro-Venezuela: Lorenzo ganó el reto," Momento 900 (14 October 1973): 29.

25. From speech delivered in Tucupido, Guárico, 30 October 1973.

26. For a representative expression of dismay at Fernández's pronouncements, see Pablo Liendo Coll, "Lorenzo contra Caldera?" El Nacional, 8 October 1973, A-4.

27. The previous COPEI campaign programs, though prepared with much care and study by party experts and technicians, were then reviewed with assiduous care by Rafael Caldera. His attention bore not only on the substance and content, but the very style and editing of the document. In 1973, the document was drafted by a team of copeyanos under the direction of Haydeé Castillo, an economist and formerly Caldera's minister of development. The candidate gave it much less attention than had Caldera in earlier years.

28. Diálogo, p. 16.

29. Directrices, p. 8.

30. Diálogo, p. 16.

31. Directrices, p. 8.

32. Diálogo, p. 15.

33. Directrices, p. 7.

34. Ibid., p. 10.

35. "En Pro-Venezuela: Lorenzo ganó el reto," Momento 900 (14 October 1973): 31.

36. Directrices, p. 11.

37. Luis Rojas Vásquez, "Lorenzo Fernández," El Nacional, 18 November 1973, D-2.

38. El País, 15 February 1944, p. 11.

39. For emergent adeco thought during the PDN years (1937-41), see lengthy excerpts in Troconis Guerrero, La cuestión agraria en la historia nacional, pp. 42-51.

40. Luis Ruiz Pineda, Venezuela bajo el signo del terror, el libro negro de la dictadura, p. 25.

41. Six individual theses were incorporated into a single volume as Acción Democrática: doctrina y programa (Caracas: Editorial "Antonio Pinto Salinas," 1962).

42. For a convenient summary of party doctrine on the eve of the campaign, which confirms a broad consistency over the years, see Manuel Vicente Magallanes, 4 partidos nacionales, pp. 14-21.

43. Ibid., p. 12.

44. Pérez's acceptance speech, delivered on 12 September 1972, was subsequently published as Carlos Andres Pérez, Mensaje como candidato de Acción Democrática a la presidencia de la República, hereafter referred to as Mensaje. Lengthy excerpts later appeared under Pérez's name with the title "Yo pido la palabra" in Summa 75 (7-21 September 1973): 51-56.

The appearance before Fedecámaras, at the twenty-ninth assembly meeting in Barquisimeto, which took place on 11 May 1973, is reported verbatim in Diálogo, as footnoted for Lorenzo Fernández, on pp. 34-39.

The candidate's statement celebrating the party's thirty-second birthday in September 1973 was published in full in several papers. See "Mensaje de Carlos Andrés" in El Nacional, 16 September 1973, subsequently cited as "Mensaje Aniversario."

The official platform is Acción de gobierno, released and distributed simultaneously with the candidate's official presentation of his program at Barquisimeto on 17 November 1973.

Finally, the response to El Nacional's thirty questions was published there on 19 November 1973, D-1 and D-2.

45. Mensaje, p. 3.

46. Ibid., p. 13.

47. Ibid., p. 14.

48. Ibid., p. 17.

49. Ibid., p. 25.

50. Ibid., p. 29.

51. Pérez, "Mensaje aniversario."

52. Acción de gobierno, p. 5.

53. Diálogo, p. 37.

54. Acción de gobierno, p. 32.

55. Ibid., pp. 30-31.

56. Ibid., pp. 53-54.

57. José Hernán Briceño, "Carlos Andrés Pérez," El Nacional, 19 November 1973, D-2.

58. Acción de gobierno, p. 54.

59. Diálogo, p. 38.

60. Highly resistant to brief characterization, this section of the platform requires a close reading for those interested in the topic. See Acción de gobierno, pp. 41-51.

61. Mensaje, pp. 5-7.

62. Acción de gobierno, p. 9.

63. Diálogo, p. 38.

64. Ibid., p. 39.

65. "Carlos Andrés Pérez," El Nacional, 19 November, 1973, D-1.

66. Acción de gobierno, p. 24.

67. Ibid., p. 76.

68. Plinio Apuleyo Mendoza, "Carlos Andrés, el enérgico," Bohemia 552 (22-28 October 1973): 86.

69. Acción de gobierno, p. 75.

70. Apuleyo Mendoza, "Carlos Andrés," p. 86.

71. Ibid., p. 85.

72. It should be noted that Pérez was explicit on this point throughout his campaign, before both rural and urban audiences. Martz heard him reiterate, literally dozens of times, that priorities would go to the countryside--feeder roads in the interior rather than super highways, agricultural credits instead of a new opera house in Caracas, and so forth.

73. El Nacional, 6 December 1973, D-1.

74. Interview with Martz, 22 July 1973.

75. Diálogo, p. 37.

76. Movimiento Electoral del Pueblo, Tesis política del MEP, explained party ideology.
For the coalition program, see Nueva Fuerza, Programa de gobierno.

77. MEP, Tesis política, p. 71.

78. Ibid., p. 72.

79. Ibid., pp. 72-73. Emphases in the original.

80. Ibid., p. 75.

81. Ibid., p. 69.

82. Ibid.

83. Ibid., pp. 70-71.

84. The Nueva Fuerza Programa de gobierno has already been cited; a convenient source for the summary appears by Paz Galarraga as "Yo pido la palabra," Summa 3 (26 September-10 October 1973): 12-14. For further comments by the candidate, see Luis Buitrago Segura, "Paz Galarraga," El Nacional, 20 November 1973, D-1 and D-2.

85. Programa, p. 6.

86. "Yo pido la palabra," Summa, p. 12.

87. Ibid., p. 13.

88. "Paz Galarraga," El Nacional, 20 November 1973, D-2.

89. Ibid., D-1.

90. Programa de gobierno, p. 7.

91. "Yo pido la palabra," Summa, p. 14.

92. For a pro-MAS discussion, see Alejandro Tarquín, "La Nueva Fuerza y el MAS; Dos programas, dos perspectivas, algunas semejanzas," Summa 3, no. 79 (26 November-21 December 1973): 18-19.

93. Pompeyo Márquez, "Prólogo a la tercera edición," in Teodoro Petkoff, ¿Socialismo para Venezuela?, p. 21.

94. Teodoro Petkoff, Checoeslovaquia.

95. This is a basic work for an understanding of the Venezuelan left. Another useful work, also authored by a masista, is Freddy Muñoz, Revolución sin dogma.

96. For orthodox communist criticisms of those who left the PCV and founded the MAS, see Radamés Larrazábal, Socialismo bobo o socialismo para Venezuela; also Pedro Ortega Díaz and Antonio García Ponce, Sobre las tesis antisoviéticas y antiproletarias del camarada Teodoro Petkoff.

97. Petkoff, ¿Socialismo para Venezuela?, p. 160. Emphases in the original.

98. Ibid., p. 163. Emphases in the original.

99. Parliamentary speeches, documents, and magazine articles concerning the disappearance and death of Alberto Lovera provide the content for José Vicente Rangel, Expediente negro. A later collection of speeches and articles, produced during the campaign, is extremely useful in analyzing Rangel's political beliefs. See José Vicente Rangel, Tiempo de verdades.

100. "La candidatura de José Vicente Rangel," Momento 885 (1 July 1973): 36.

101. Movimiento al Socialismo, Programa del MAS. For reports on the candidate's appearance at the Forum of Pro-Venezuela, see the press for the two days following his 16 October speech.

102. The work of a team of advisers was coordinated by Freddy

Muñoz. Others especially important in its elaboration included Márquez, Petkoff, Armando Córdova, José Agustín Silva Michelena, Alfredo Chacón, and Joaquín Marta Sosa.

103. *Programa del* MAS.

104. Rangel, *Tiempo de verdades*, p. 225.

105. *Programa del* MAS.

106. *Ibid.*

107. *Ibid.* Emphasis in the original.

108. Among the first group were Eugenio Mendoza, Gustavo Vollmer, Oscar Machado Zuloaga, and other such noted names as Boulton, Neuman, Delfino, Branger, and Tamayo. The second included Phelps, Conde Jahn, and Guillermo Machado Morales (brother of communist leaders Gustavo and Eduardo Machado), and the third such figures as Andrés Germán Otero and Arturo Sosa.

109. Rangel at the Forum of Pro-Venezuela on 16 October 1973, as quoted by José Gerbasi in *El Nacional*, 21 October 1973, D-4.

110. In addition to the Gerbasi commentary, see *Semana* 288 (25 October-1 November 1973): 8.

111. *Programa del* MAS.

112. Rangel, *Tiempo de verdades*, pp. 293-94.

113. While officially announced on 28 November 1973, the outlines of the program had been appearing in newspaper advertisements for some weeks previously, as well as in campaign literature being distributed as early as October. For the brief document, see URD, *Levántate pueblo.*

114. Euro Fuenmayor, "Jóvito Villalba," *El Nacional*, 21 November 1973, D-1 and D-2.

115. Pedro Tinoco, *El estado eficaz.* Another useful source is provided by his remarks to Fedecámaras. For the text, see the previously cited *Diálogo*, pp. 44-46.

116. *El Nacional*, 31 July 1973, D-1.

117. Ronald Nava, "Dice Tinoco: Pérez Jiménez fue el primer desarrollista," *Bohemia* 542 (13-19 August 1973): 36.

118. For a detailed discussion see Pt. II of his *El estado eficaz*, pp. 39-80.

119. See Pt. IV of *ibid.*, pp. 105-33.

120. *Ibid.*, p. 6.

121. Ricardo Azpúrua Ayala, "Desarrollismo e ideología," *Summa* 3, no. 78 (8-22 November 1973): 9.

122. *Diálogo*, p. 44.

123. *Ibid.*, p. 45.

124. For a somewhat rambling but enlightening interview that includes favorable references to Marcos Pérez Jiménez and his rule, see "Café de redacción con Pedro R. Tinoco," Summa 3, no. 78 (8-22 November 1973): 48-56.

125. The "Decálogo de la vergüenza" appeared in numerous large newspaper advertisements, such as "Mensaje de Marcos Pérez Jiménez a la nación," El Nacional, 16 July 1973, C-10 and C-11.

126. Ibid., C-10.

127. Among the more useful sources that might be consulted would be, for Pedro Segnini La Cruz, pp. 40-42 of Fedecámaras's Diálogo, and the interview by Guillermo Campos, "Segnini La Cruz," El Nacional, 24 November 1973, D-1 and D-2; for Martín García Villasmil, pp. 28-32 of Diálogo, plus the interview by Anselmo Reyes, "García Villasmil," El Nacional, 26 November 1973, D-1 and D-2.

128. See pp. 6-12 of Fedecámaras's Diálogo, and the interview by Guillermo Campos, "Burelli Rivas," El Nacional, 25 November 1973, D-1 and D-2. Another useful interview is that of Ronald Nava, "Miguel Angel Burelli Rivas: 'Este es un país de damnificados,'" Bohemia 546 (10-16 September 1973): 35-38.

CHAPTER VII

1. The bulk of our data on campaign impact and effect is examined more fully in the final chapters. Our interest here is in citing a few findings broadly relevant to more general aspects of images and political communications.

2. As to the press, more than three dozen newspapers appear daily, with those published in Caracas enjoying nationwide circulation. El Nacional, with a circulation of over 100,000, is among the most prestigious in the hemisphere. Generally independent politically, its editorial pages in 1973 remained open to a wide spectrum of political leaders, many of whom write for it on a regular basis. El Universal, founded in 1909 (circulation around 75,000), tends to be somewhat conservative in cast, appealing especially to members of the business community. The Capriles family publications include Ultimas Noticias, which claims a circulation of over 130,000 and is popular in the barrios; the afternoon El Mundo, daily begun in 1958; and Crítica of Maracaibo, that city's second leading paper. The Capriles chain also includes a number of weekly and monthly magazines as well, most notably Elite and Venezuela Gráfica. The controversial political bargain between Caldera and Capriles was noted in ch. 1. By the 1970s a rival empire, directed by the De Armas family, was publishing both Meridiano and 2001. The former, a tabloid, enjoyed the highest circulation in Venezuela, exceeding 150,000 copies daily; the latter grew rapidly following its establishment in mid-1973. Both made garish use of color photographs and headlines to enliven their

makeup. The weekly magazines Bohemia, Variedades, and Vanidades
were among other De Armas publications. In Maracaibo, the most
important daily remained Panorama.

News magazines have assumed growing importance, and although
in volume their readership cannot rival that of newspapers, their
political influence is substantial. Those stressing photo stories
and extensive pictorial layouts include Elite, Momento, and Bohemia;
greater attention to news coverage and political interpretation
comes from Semana, Summa, and Resumen. Significantly, political
partisanship is generally more pronounced than with the newspapers.
Elite invariably follows the preferences of the Capriles, which
despite the break with Caldera and COPEI was more unsympathetic
during the 1973 campaign to the AD, not to mention the left.
Momento, which in the last decade contained long and informed
interpretive pieces, inexplicably dropped much of its political
reportage in recent years. Its partisan preferences long reflected
those of its politically active owner and director, Carlos Ramírez
MacGregor. An admirer of Rómulo Betancourt who had been elected to
congress as an independent on AD lists, he later changed favorites.
He backed Burelli Rivas in 1968 and was elected on the Frente de la
Victoria legislative slates. In 1973 his preference for Fernández
brought him inclusion and later election on copeyano lists. In
March 1974 he sold Momento and left to found another magazine. The
De Armas chain acquired Momento and placed the eighteen-year-old
magazine under the direction of Andrés de Armas Silva, youngest son
of the family head. Ramírez's choice of Lorenzo Fernández in the
1973 competition resulted in moderate but obvious partisanship,
with so-called news stories highly biased in favor of COPEI.

Bohemia, fundamentally independent prior to the campaign, had
also been noted for the accuracy of its interpretive "Informe
Político," but this declined in quality following the dismissal of
news director and 2001 editor Rafael Poleo in mid-year, and a
gentler line was taken toward COPEI. It was widely believed that
the rift between the owners and Poleo resulted from his pro-adeco
views; some maintained that COPEI had exerted pressure on the
publishers. In any event, Bohemia's political reporting visibly
declined in quality after Poleo's dismissal. Semana, established
in 1967 and following a format suggestive of its contractual
agreement with Newsweek, prints signed columns by a wide range of
spokesmen. Its early independence swiftly disappeared in 1973 when
Alfredo Tarre Murzi (the columnist "Sanín") assumed its direction,
leading to abysmal reporting and extreme partisanship on behalf of
COPEI. A political chameleon whose preferences had made fortuitous
shifts through the years, Tarre Murzi had served in the Caldera
government as an "independent" before moving to Semana. For a
highly critical questioning of "Sanín's" journalistic integrity,
see "El poder, ¿para qué?", Resumen 2, no. 10 (13 January 1974):
14. Also see n. 17, ch. 5.

Summa, more inclined to interpretive essays than the others and
appearing every other week, pursues an iconoclastic view from the
left. Summa's series of issues that featured a given candidate and
his program every two weeks during the final months of the campaign

were of considerable merit. The reader had to bear in mind, of
course, the leftist perspective from which the stories were written.
Resumen, initiated by Jorge Olavarría shortly before election day
in 1973, gave the heaviest coverage of all to Venezuelan news.
Olavarría, originally a supporter of Arturo Uslar Pietri, had
organized the PL, which in 1968 backed the Caldera candidacy. He
had been elected to congress on COPEI planchas and for a time
served as ambassador to Great Britain. Olavarría was also the
son-in-law of Eleazar López Contreras. The first issues were
tough-minded and independent. Interpretations of the campaign,
which excoriated the copeyano campaign managers in particular and
the oficialista wing of the party in general, raised the possibility
that Resumen might become anti-COPEI. In February 1974 Olavarría
denied anti-COPEI views on the interview program "Buenos Días" and
published the transcript. It appears in Resumen 2, no. 17 (3 March
1974): 38-42.

Television and radio both held inordinate importance for the
campaign. By the decade of the 1970s 90 percent of the population
lived in areas reached by television, with an estimated 50 percent
of households owning television and over 80 percent with radio.
Three commercial television channels beam their programming through
local outlets in virtually all major population centers, while the
government channel also reaches throughout the country. Radio
stations are seemingly omnipresent and cover the population even
more completely than does television. The dissemination of
encapsulated news briefs is achieved most effectively and swiftly
by radio, although the nightly reports on television provide less
superficial information for those who watch. With expense
particularly high for paid political messages on television, the
less affluent candidacies were largely deprived of this form of
communication. However, a host of interview programs regularly
invited representatives of all political forces, and this provided
at least some visibility on this medium. Partisanship on radio
and television, then, existed more through the function of
candidates' financial resources than through actual content of
programming. With the news magazines, pro-COPEI and anti-AD
sentiment was dominant, in most cases strongly biasing alleged
"news" stories. Daily newspapers were far more balanced, despite
charges of partisanship voiced by both copeyanos and adecos. The
left received somewhat less effective treatment, with news stories
sometimes buried on inside pages or headed by small headlines.
Although the MAS, PCV, and MIR all had their own organs, the
readership was small.

The campaigners had extensive and varied media available to
them, and the climate was characterized by noteworthy freedom of
expression. The large advantage of the two establishment parties
lay not in legal inequities, nor even primarily in political
partisanship on the part of management and staff of the media
outlets; it was a matter of economic resources. Notwithstanding
the great importance of financing, moreover, the shaping of media
campaigns and of candidate images was heavily dependent upon the
aspirant himself. In examining the communications phase of the

campaign, therefore, we will need to focus on the candidate, his political leadership, and his personal style in campaigning. This provides the necessary understanding preparatory to an examination of his public image as shaped and presented to the public. Moreover, our survey data will provide further evidence as to the relative effectiveness of respective candidates, although the bulk of this will be introduced in the concluding chapter of this study. The result will provide insight into both presentational and participatory techniques, with their relative efficacy judged within the context of the Venezuelan environment.

3. A prominent colleague during the early years of the movement, Lara Peña clashed over the presidential choice preceding the 1945 golpe de estado, advocating support for López Contreras. A born polemicist whose writings appeared under the pen name "Pejolape," he stayed out of COPEI. In 1973 he remained a conservative critic of the party and of Rafael Caldera.

4. It was sometimes claimed that Fernández and Pérez had been fellow members of the Betancourt cabinet. Actually, Lorenzo Fernández had resigned as minister of development effective 9 October 1961, to be succeeded by copeyanos Godofredo González and then Hugo Pérez La Salvia. Carlos Andrés Pérez followed Luis Augusto Dubuc as minister of interior relations on 12 March 1962. Pérez resigned in July 1963 to resume party duties in the AD.

5. The break from campaign rigors also permitted him to visit and be photographed with an array of dignitaries ranging from Marshall Tito and Nikolai Podgorny to Pope Paul VI and leaders of West German Christian Democracy.

6. Harvey Rosenhouse, "Por su simple nombre," Visión 41, no. 20 (20 October 1973): 24-F.

7. The green was, of course, the traditional copeyano color.

8. El pueblo unido, 15 July 1973. For a partisan but informative account by the candidate's private secretary, see Carlos Parada-Quintero, Diario de un jefe en campaña.

9. We were unable to confirm or refute common rumors--some of them heard shortly after Caldera's inauguration in 1969--that Fernández had suffered more than one heart attack in earlier years. It is at least possible that the measured campaign schedule of the candidate was owing to matters of health and stamina. There is little doubt that Fernández aged visibly during the long campaign; photographs comfirm this impression.

10. Reports circulated in Caracas that the candidate had been spirited out of the country for a recuperative visit to a Caribbean island. There was no substantiating evidence, but the nature of the report testified to attitudes and opinions concerning Fernández's health and public activity.

11. Published in the Caracas press on 12 August 1973.

12. The first appeared Tuesdays at 10:30 P.M. on Radio

Caracas; the second Wednesdays at 11 P.M. on CVTV; and the third
Friday at 12:15 P.M. on Venevisión.

13. "COPEI DICE" appeared each Tuesday in Ultimas Noticias;
Thursday in El Universal; and Sunday in El Nacional.

14. For a text published by COPEI, see El debate Caldera-
Uslar Pietri.

15. See accounts in the Caracas press on both 27 and 28
September 1968.

16. That such a debate might be damaging to Fernández had
been suggested months earlier. See "Los candidatos y sus planes
para el 73," Bohemia 510 (1-7 January 1973): 4-7.

17. Interview in Daily Journal, 17 September 1973, p. 1.

18. Martz was told that only after some disagreement was it
decided to proceed with the series of advertisements, of which
Pérez himself approved.

19. For one of the first of these advertisements, see El
Nacional, 2 October 1973, D-13.

20. Oswaldo Alvarez Paz, "En la recta final," ibid., 6 October
1973, A-4.

21. "En Pro-Venezuela: Lorenzo ganó el reto," Momento 900
(14 October 1973): 28-29.

22. A remark we first heard from members of the Nueva Fuerza
offered the sly correction to Lorenzo, un amigo del presidente
(Lorenzo, a friend of the President).

23. In this burst of activity for the Social Christian, he
was in La Victoria on 28 November; Barquisimeto the thirtieth;
Mérida the first; Valera and Acarigua the second; Cumaná the third;
Maracaibo the fourth; and Caracas the fifth. On 6 December, the
final day of campaign activity according to law, Fernández limited
himself to a fifteen-minute appearance before party faithful in
Caracas's Plaza Venezuela.

24. Leonardo Ruiz Pineda, one of the most talented party
leaders of his generation, was assassinated by agents of the
dictatorship while serving as clandestine secretary general in 1952.
The relationship between Ruiz Pineda and Pérez had been important
during the early years of Perez's political career. Some of Ruiz
Pineda's speeches and related materials were published posthumously
in Leonardo Ruiz Pineda, Ventanas al mundo. Also see the
commentaries and eulogies in Leonardo Ruiz Pineda.

25. For an excellent biographical descriptior of Pérez's
youth and early political career, see Plinio Apuleyo Mendoza,
"Carlos Andrés--el enérgico," Bohemia 552 (22-28 October 1973):
80-89.

26. AD campaign literature occasionally distributed excerpts
of Rafael Caldera's warm praise for the work of Pérez as minister

of interior relations at a dinner on 1 July 1963, shortly after Pérez's resignation. Caldera said that "few have given so much of themselves, of their time, of their energies to this struggle, for which the country honestly must recognize him." For full statement see El Nacional, 2 July 1963.

27.   Apuleyo Mendoza, "Carlos Andrés," p. 87.

28.   Bernardo Viera, one of the leading communications advisers, created this slogan.

29.   The verb caminar in Spanish also has a connotation of movement, which enriched the meaning and import of the phrase.

30.   The authors shared the general view that Ese hombre sí camina was easily the catchiest and most pleasing of the campaign; Martz would have to add that, however, having heard it dozens of times during travels with Pérez, enough was finally enough. For a post-election interview with Chelique Sarabia, see Marianela de la Cruz, "La publicidad tiene una sola misión: decir la verdad bien dicha," Resumen 2, no. 9 (6 January 1974): 20-21.

31.   For a hostile if provocative discussion of political image-building, see José Enrique Bravo, "Carlos Andrés; una candidatura en venta," Summa 3, no. 75 (7-21 September 1973): 10-11. The author described Pérez as a product whose image required: dynamic body exercises; healthy teeth which must be shown often; an absence of tobacco and liquor; youth and movement; an expression of serenity to suggest maturity; and avoidance of stridency in speech.

32.   As the candidate splashed ahead through the swirling agua negra ("black water") and a bedraggled entourage unenthusiastically followed, an exuberant resident shouted to a presumably copeyano friend that Lorenzo wouldn't be campaigning through the elements in such conditions. The response was a silent scowl. Leaving Santa Rosalía later in the afternoon, Pérez spoke to Martz at length about the problems and possible solutions, clearly distressed by what would have been a common occurrence to those living in the site.

33.   The first was shown Mondays at noon on Venevisión; the second Tuesdays at 10:30 P.M. on CVTV; and the third Friday at 10:30 P.M. on Radio Caracas Televisión.

34.   White's experience included the managing of Barry Goldwater's 1964 presidential campaign; Napolitan had worked for Hubert Humphrey, and the Squiers had been employed by Edmund Muskie in 1972. For a revealing picture of the profession, see Joseph Napolitan, The Election Game and How to Win It (Garden City: Doubleday and Company, 1972).

35.   Jules Witcover, "Venezuelan Candidates Hire U.S. Image-Builder," Washington Post, 22 September 1973.

36.   El Nacional, 27 September 1973, D-1.

37.   "Página de Acción Democrática" appeared each Wednesday in Ultimas Noticias, Thursday in El Meridiano, and Sunday in El Nacional.

38.   A report of the first such breakfast is found in El Nacional, 4 October 1973, D-1.

39.   Similar endorsements of public figures were employed by other candidates, notably Lorenzo Fernández. One of the more striking newspaper advertisements appeared in a full-page spread on 27 November. A large headline proclaimed "My vote is for Carlos Andrés," followed by several lines of endorsement; beneath was a large photograph of Pérez with Venezuela's famed shortstop Luis Aparicio.

40.   Estimates ran as high as one-half million for both rallies. Such a figure is certainly too high, although the physical locales were such as to render systematic evaluation impossible. If pressed for a figure, the authors would opt for 300,000 each.

41.   By law, all campaign activity came to an end at midnight on Thursday the sixth. Friday and Saturday were free from campaigning, in anticipation of the vote on Sunday 9 December.

42.   As with the other parties, the AD attempted to budget its funds in order to make its major effort at the end. Some 20 percent of the AD's publicity funds were withheld for the last month of the campaign.

43.   Such phrases of the ex-president induce despair for the translator. What he meant in this case, of course, was simply to state somewhat colloquially that his activities would be other than those of the traditional political rally and speech.

44.   El Nacional, 10 November 1973, D-1.

45.   One former member of the CEN reported having suggested the name of "Gregorio"--Paz's code name during clandestine times-- as new national secretary general, to which there was swift assent from Rómulo Betancourt and other members.

46.   Critics of Paz have often contended that he had quietly encouraged Raúl Ramos Giménez and other arsistas in their incipient insurgency, then withheld his support at the critical juncture and conveniently eliminated them from the AD. Pacistas have retorted that he was completely loyal to the party and that there is no substantiation for such allegations of manipulation.

47.   See our forthcoming volume for further discussion.

48.   A sympathetic biographical sketch which concentrates on the internal disputes of AD is Jesús Sanoja Hernández, "Paz...un hombre de guerra en la política," Summa 3, no. 76 (26 September-10 October 1973): 2-6. In the same issue of the magazine, which was largely devoted to the Paz candidacy, also see José León Contreras, "Paz Galarraga: el candidato incógnito," p. 23.

49. Faulty communications between Caracas and the interior concerning arrival times of the candidate, vocal disagreement over the order of speakers at a meeting, noise and distractions on the podium while the candidate was speaking, these and similar problems would presumably not have been permitted when Paz had the resources of the AD at his beck and call. The authors were frequently surprised by the unfailing patience and even temper of the nominee in the face of sometimes distressing if not inexcusable errors of omission and commission.

50. Other examples can of course be cited; this one is remembered vividly, however, as the result of Martz's observation of a September trip which began in the first state and concluded in the second.

51. Perhaps needless to say, a virtually unanimous show of hands would result.

52. The symbol of the perezjimenista CCN was an Indian with feathers. Paz joked with his audiences that "el indio Paz" was not plumed; when accompanied by Prieto, he would often refer to the prietista symbol of the ear.

53. Thus during a brief radio interview in Trujillo in September Doña Victoria was quite nervous, although performing in fine fashion. By the end of campaign she was fully at ease. In fact, while her husband concluded his final tour in Caracas on 4 December, she flew on for additional campaigning of her own in the Andes.

54. For example, in August Prieto campaigned for two days in the interior, returning at night to Caracas. Up the next morning at 6 A.M., he drove to Portuguesa to join Paz, arriving at 11 A.M. Following outdoor meetings in Píritu and Turén, as well as barrio visits under a wilting sun, his car left for Caracas in a driving thunderstorm. Arriving at his home after 1 A.M., Prieto was at his office by mid-morning for a mepista meeting.

55. Among the best reviews of Rangel's career, especially during the 1958-64 years, is Jesús Sanoja Hernández, "Rangel: un José Gregorio que puede ganar el cielo pero no las elecciones," Summa 3, no. 77 (10-25 October 1973): 2-6.

56. Magallanes, Los partidos políticos en la evolución histórica venezolana, p. 519.

57. A collection of speeches, writings, and documents from this period were published as Rangel, Expediente negro.

58. The virtual retirement of Raúl Ramos Giménez and the dispersal of other leaders decimated the organization. Supporting Carlos Andrés Pérez as the PRN candidate in 1973, such remaining leaders as José Manzo González and Miguel García Mackle returned to Congress as the result of inclusion on adeco legislative slates.

59. A medical doctor in Caracas at the turn of the century, Hernández had been virtually canonized--indeed, the Venezuelan

Church has been seeking his recognition from the Vatican for several years. His birthplace in Isnotú, Trujillo, has become a veritable shrine, and images of Hernández hang from the visers of taxis and windows of ranchitos in many parts of Venezuela.

60. A tongue-in-cheek version of critics was to show a similar picture of Rangel from the back, revealing the candidate to be hiding a submachine gun behind him.

61. Chelique Sarabia, author and composer of the Pérez songs, spoke enthusiastically of the creativity of Rangel propaganda (Resumen 2, no. 9 [6 January 1974]: 21).

62. A popular Rangel practice was to autograph small cards with his picture on one side and campaign propaganda on the other. Martz remembers a visit by the candidate to a hospital in Ciudad Bolívar; as word of his presence spread, Rangel was surrounded by patients, nurses, administrators, doctors, and cleaning personnel-- predominantly female. Nearly a half-hour of autograph signing was necessary before he could move beyond the reception area and visit the hospital facilities fully.

63. At larger meetings, protest songs and music were often provided by the young "Grupo Ahora," prominently featuring appropriate revolutionary compositions by Theodorakis.

64. Baloyra observed Villalba twice during the campaign and Martz once. On each occasion he was accompanied by a very small entourage and was received with limited interest or enthusiasm. It should be said that Villalba proceeded doggedly in the face of the discouraging response.

65. For a measure of anti-Tinoco sentiment by the left, hear the excoriation of Jesús Sanoja Hernández in his "El subdesarrollismo político no quiere jugar banco," Summa 3, no. 78 (8-22 November 1973): 5: "Tinoco has the skill of the bourgeoisie, the cynicism of the Goths, the money of the oligarchs, the affronteries of the conservatives, the desires of the anti-communists, the machiavellianism of the rightists...."

CHAPTER VIII

1. For example, the 1962 division reached deeply into the ranks of the peasant movement, whose president, Ramón Quijada, had accompanied the arsistas out of the AD. In the struggle that followed, President Betancourt and officials of the Instituto Agrario Nacional traveled the interior extensively, delivering titles of land to peasants through the agrarian reform program. See Martz, Acción Democrática, pp. 282-86. Also see Powell, Political Mobilization of the Venezuelan Peasant, pp. 194-96.

2. El Nacional, 3 August 1973, A-1 and D-1.

3. Antonio Léidenz, the adeco president of the Changer of Deputies, had sent Caldera a telegram in July charging an attempt

to discredit Congress as obstructionist. Octavio Lepage reiterated the contention; noting the expenditures approved for the administration, he termed as false the copeyano claims that Congress had sabotaged the policies of the government. Caldera denied the charges and declared that a confrontation between the legislature and executive was not beneficial to the nation. Especially in later campaign speeches and statements, copeyano leaders commonly argued that it was congressional opposition--and especially that of AD--that had been responsible for any policy failures on the part of the government.

4. Complex and mutually calculating parliamentary maneuvering between COPEI and AD during this period goes beyond the scope of our work. Suffice it to say that leaders on both sides left no effort undone in seeking electoral advantage as well as gaining the upper hand in the Carmen de Valera affair.

5. El Nacional, 19 August 1973, D-1.

6. Text of the Pérez letter appeared in the Caracas press on 7 September 1973.

7. Text of the Caldera conference appeared in the Caracas press on 7 September 1973.

8. Gonzalo Barrios, "Otra reforma del Estado?" El Nacional, 8 September 1973, A-4.

9. Text as printed in the Caracas press on 9 September 1973.

10. El Nacional, 9 September 1973, D-1.

11. El Universal, 10 September 1973, p. 1.

12. Martz saw copies of the posters in Portuguesa, Yaracuy, Sucre, and Guárico during the final four months of the campaign. It should be noted, however, that these were essentially individual and isolated cases; there is great practical difficulty in removing all examples of a given piece of propaganda in mid-campaign after having distributed thousands of copies nationally.

13. El Nacional, 20 October 1973, D-1.

14. Ibid.

15. Ibid., 7 October 1973, D-1.

16. Barrios interview with Guillermo Pantín, ibid., 9 October 1973, D-1.

17. Ibid., 10 October 1973, D-1.

18. Ibid., 12 October 1973, D-1.

19. Ibid., 11 October 1973, D-1.

20. The Nueva Fuerza was strongly convinced of official sabotage during campaign trips. On at least one occasion--traveling with Paz from the mainland to Nueva Esparta in early December--the authors saw a series of re-routed plane flights and power failures

that were suggestive of official disruptions.   The Paz entourage was convinced of government complicity.

It should also be added that such episodes were not new to the "dirty tricks" department in Venezuelan campaigns.   To cite but one instance, Martz recalls the loss of power and lights at a Caldera rally in San Fernando de Apure in 1968 which, as Caldera aide Eduardo Fernández charged, was highly suggestive of government sabotage—in that case, the AD government.

21.   It is not known if there were "re-dedications," but toward the close of the campaign the government press office unblushingly described presidential activities including "pre-inaugurations."

22.   El Nacional, 15 October 1973, D-1.

23.   Conferencia Episcopal Venezolana, Iglesia y política.

24.   Ibid., pp. 6-7.

25.   Ibid., p. 3.

26.   Among these were Cristianos por el Socialismo, Cristianos por la Liberación, Equipos Docentes para la Liberación, the Movimiento Estudiantil Revolucionario, and others.

27.   "Díos los une y la política...," Bohemia 544 (27 August-2 September 1973): 5-8.

28.   "Polémica—Iglesia y política," Semana 277 (9-15 August 1973): 7.

29.   The document was prepared by Gerhard Cartay, Gustavo Martens, and Ramón Aveledo.

30.   "Documento político de la Juventud Revolucionaria Copeyana," El Nacional, 9 August 1973, D-5.

31.   Ibid.

32.   Ibid., 12 September 1973.

33.   Paz Galarraga had learned of antisocialist advertising plans when an eminent newspaper editor called him privately.   The Nueva Fuerza candidate apparently helped prevent the initiation of the antisocialist campaign at that time by promising to respond with an avowedly antibusiness, anti-Fedecámaras campaign should it become necessary.

34.   José Vicente Rangel, "Tribuna Abierta—una campaña y una respuesta," Momento 902 (28 October 1973): 32.

35.   El Nacional, 6 November 1973, D-1.

36.   This sample appeared in ibid., 30 October 1973, C-10.

37.   "Chile repercute en la política venezolana," Bohemia 548 (24-30 September 1973): 8.

38.   Rangel speech delivered Thursday, 13 September, in Rubio, Táchira.

39. Rangel made this point repeatedly during a campaign trip to Bolívar and Anzoátegui on which Martz accompanied him later in September.

40. As quoted in "Chile repercute...."

41. Jesús Angel Paz Galarraga, "Emplazamiento a la Democracia Cristiana," El Nacional, 13 September 1973, A-4.

42. In a campaign trip to Maracaibo and Trujillo later that week, Paz characteristically handled the issue with urbane aplomb. Members of his entourage and local leaders made little effort to hide their concern, however.

43. There was some speculation that it might lead to further collaboration between the MAS and the Nueva Fuerza, but campaigning had gone much too far for that to be a realistic possibility.

44. El Nacional, 14 September 1973, D-2.

45. As quoted in "Chile repercute...."

46. Ibid.

47. Dated 15 September 1973, the full communiqué reached the pages of the national press the following day.

48. El Nacional, 19 September 1973, D-1.

49. El Universal, 23 September 1973, 18.

50. Ibid., 5 October 1973, 1.

51. Figures are based on information from both public and private sources. The most useful and public sources during the campaign were published in Bohemia 558 (3-9 December 1973): 24-25. We have received estimates for specific items—such as a newspaper page, and a minute on television—which provide further support. Of those to whom we have suggested the total expenditures suggested here, the most common response is the opinion that our figures are too low. At the least, what is presented gives a general idea of the expense of the 1973 campaign in Venezuela.

52. Without data from the rival parties, there is no way to make more than a highly impressionistic comparative judgment. The authors feel that the relative expenditures of COPEI and AD were not significantly different, although COPEI was aided by the advertising of the government as well.

53. One month before elections Pedro Segnini La Cruz, an experienced and knowledgeable politician, estimated that the two would spend some 32 million bolívares each. This, he specified, did not include afiches, theater commercials, travel expenses, the cost of meetings, or similar expenses. Both parties naturally denied the charges—Eduardo Fernández for COPEI and Gonzalo Barrios for the AD.

54. Resumen claimed that COPEI spent 84,224,701 bolívares in the last thirty days of the campaign (see "Una derrota pagada con barras de oro," Resumen 1, no. 7 23 December 1973 : 29-30). The magazine had earlier concluded that COPEI and AD would spend a total

of 313,877,000 bolívares each. Although the estimate seems quite
high and Resumen was sharply critical of the Fernández campaign,
there is little question that expenditures increased markedly in
the closing weeks of the campaign.

55. El Nacional, 15 November 1973, C-3.

56. These poll results appeared in "El fiasco de las encuestas
electorales," Semana 42 (21 December 1968-3 January 1969): 5-7.

57. As noted elsewhere, our own survey was carried out with
the cooperation and collaboration of DATOS, with whom we enjoyed a
contractual agreement. It should therefore be noted here that the
following information is a matter of public record, and that we
have divulged no confidences of the organization. Our account is
drawn from a Bohemia report and from a press interview with DATOS
Director General A. F. Templeton. For further details see "La
verdad sobre las encuestas electorales," Bohemia 518 (26 February-
4 March 1973): 4-7; and Luis Buitrago Segura, "Como operan los
profesionales del pronóstico," El Nacional, 27 September 1973, D-1.
     Briefly, DATOS was founded in 1954 by Luis Beltrán González
and was initially a subsidiary of Publicidad CORPA. In 1967, DATOS
employees themselves purchased the firm under the leadership of
A. F. Templeton, Edmundo Sade, Neréo Fabro, and Parkinson Nigel.
DATOS's political polling in 1969 took on regular and systematic
soundings under contract to CORPA subsidiary VOVICA (Voz y Visión
de Venezuela, C.A.). Both a monthly and half-year poll became
regularized, with the monthly "pulso" based on surveys in
Venezuela's seven leading cities: Caracas, Maracaibo, Barquisimeto,
San Cristóbal, Maracay, Valencia, and Barcelona-Puerto La Cruz.
The fuller, twice-yearly poll samples throughout the nation drew on
some 2500 respondents. Results of these polls are customarily
presented as sizable volumes that not only record the findings but
provide accompanying analysis. A small number of clients receive
the findings, and DATOS maintains tight security over the results.
As Director General Templeton has noted, however, once the reports
are submitted to subscribers, there is nothing to prohibit them
from using or distributing the information as they see fit.

58. "La verdad sobre las encuestas electorales."

59. "Empate en diciembre," Bohemia 542 (13-19 August 1973):
4-7.

60. Lucas Benacerraf, "Radiografía de las Encuestas
electorales," Momento 899 (7 October 1973): 28-30.

61. The decision to release the Gaither data was not lightly
taken, for the AD was concerned over the reaction and possible
COPEI counterattack. It was the candidate himself who made the
decision to publicize the returns, despite opposition by a majority
of AD's Comité Ejecutivo Nacional.

62. El Nacional, 28 October 1973, D-1.

63. A day after the television commercials began to appear, a
cabinet-level copeyano told Martz privately that, after initial

anger, he had concluded that the AD had made a serious misjudgment, especially in filming and recording Gaither for television, poor Spanish and all.

To the AD, this had seemed preferable and more believable than a statement by a member of the party. Perhaps a more effective means would have been shots of Dr. Gaither and his charts, but with a Venezuelan voice narrating the findings.

64. El Nacional, 31 October 1973, A-1 and D-1.

65. Ibid., D-1

66. Ibid., 3 November 1973, C-9.

67. The Junta in Libertador Department ordered cessation of the AD message on the grounds that Article 155 of the Suffrage Law prohibited the use of a person's name without authorization. The AD representative disputed this interpretation, arguing that the voice of Aguilar was presented as recorded, and that he had not issued a denial.

68. El Nacional, 1 November 1973, D-1.

69. Following Pérez's release of DATOS figures, newsmen beat a path to the office of Director General Templeton for confirmation. Neither Templeton nor others were available, nor were officials of Voz y Visión or CORPA. Following further inquiry, the press wrote on 1 November that the cited DATOS figures for the May 1973 poll were correct, and that those for the September-October six-month report were still being processed. See ibid.

70. Ibid., 2 November 1973, D-1.

71. Ibid., 3 November 1973, D-1.

72. The AD had its counterparts of Matt Reese in Napolitan, the Squiers, and White, of course. It similarly employed North Americans in producing a television documentary on its candidate.

73. El Nacional, 3 November 1973, D-1.

74. Ibid.

75. Ibid.

76. 2001, 3 November 1973, 1.

77. El Nacional, 31 November 1973, D-1.

78. As it happened, Martz was in Maracaibo for what had been scheduled as a two-day campaign visit by Pérez. Thus he attended the press conference at the Hotel del Lago as well as private conversations prior to the candidate's return to Caracas the same day; his notes provide the source for this account of Pérez's press statements.

79. El Nacional, 4 November 1973, D-1.

80. Ibid.

81. Ibid., D-5.

82. Ibid., A-12 and 13.

83. Ibid., D-19.

84. Ibid., 5 November 1973, D-14.

85. Ibid., 6 November 1973, B-8 and 9.

86. Ibid., 11 November 1973, A-13.

87. Gonzalo Barrios, "El Watergate de Maracaibo," ibid., 10 November 1973, A-4.

88. For example, see ibid., 7 November 1973, C-9.

89. Oswaldo Alvarez Paz, "Un debate interesante," ibid., 15 November 1973, A-4.

90. Ibid., 9 November 1973, D-1.

91. The Gaither-Maracaibo events at least helped produce one of the more imaginative and lighter touches to the propaganda battle. In an advertisement that was rejected by several publications, the AD announced the holding of a contest, with the reader asked to indicate "the next infamy of COPEI." Choices included: accusing the AD candidate of being born in Tokyo; discovery in a Maracaibo shop of the 100,000 homes per year the government had promised, but which had been hoarded by the AD to prevent delivery; and a birth certificate showing that adviser Matt Reese was actually Venezuelan-born. Prizes for the winner would include: a drawing of the nonexistent 100,000 homes; a prefabricated poll of Pedro Pablo Aguilar; a reproduction to scale of the "maletín" used by COPEI to bribe convention delegates; and so forth. The advertisement closed by advising the reader "to answer copeyano infamy with a smile and punish it with the vote on December 9th." See Bohemia 556 (19-25 November 1973): 25.

92. El Nacional, 4 November 1973, A-1.

93. Octavio Lepage noted in an aside that limitation on numbers of political commercials would please boxing and baseball fans, who could enjoy sports broadcasts "without the irritating interference of the incessant cuñas in favor of the candidate of COPEI." Ibid., 5 November 1973, D-1.

94. Ibid., 13 November 1973, A-1.

95. Luis Rojas Vásquez, "El CSE limitó utilización de la prensa, la radio y la TV por partidos políticos," ibid., 16 November 1973.

96. The two with the greatest activity and festivity were the traditional Plaza Venezuela for COPEI, and Plaza Altamira for the AD.

97. El Nacional, 21 November 1973, A-1 and C-13.

98. The national parties have been cited elsewhere, including the final page of ch. 3. For the record, the ten regional parties were: Nuevo Ideal Nacional (NIN) in twelve states; Alianza

Revolucionaria Patriótica (ARPA) in twelve states; Democracia
Popular (DP) in seven states; Alcina in six states; Frente
Independiente Popular (FIPO) in the Federal District; others in one
state only were Acción Nacional Progresista (ANAPRO), Bloque
Independiente Nacionalista (BIN), Movimiento Independiente Apureño
(MIA), Movimiento Libertador (ML), and Unión del Pueblo Venezolano
(UPV). The four groups organized at district or municipal levels
only were: Agrupación Electoral Independiente (AEI), Movimiento
Pro Desarrollo de la Comunidad, Acción Revolucionaria Vencedora
Independiente (ARVI), and the Unión de Revolucionarias
Independientes (URI).

99. Our appreciation to several CSE members for providing a
variety of information and materials, especially Dra. Marieli
Marrero and Ing. Rosa Aguilera. For a review of the mechanical
apparatus employed by the CSE, see William García Insausti, "El
sí de las computadores," Bohemia 558 (3-9 December 1973): 30-31.

100. El Nacional, 7 December 1973, D-7, D-24.

101. Ibid., C-19.

102. Most cases fell into four categories: (1) a voter with
proof of registration who had been placed in the wrong voting
district (he should go to the municipal electoral board where he
had originally registered, to request reassignment); (2) a voter
without the comprobante but assigned to the wrong voting district
(same procedure as above); (3) a voter not on the registration list
who has his comprobante (with his cédula of identification and other
documents, he could be assigned a voting place by the municipal
board); and (4) the voter not on the registration list and without
his comprobante, but who claimed to have registered (at the
municipal board a check with the regional CSE would be processed,
checking duplicate registration copies in the archives). There
were also isolated cases that did not fall neatly into any of these
groupings.

103. El Nacional, 8 December 1973, D-1ff.

104. Interest in the returns diverted further attention from
the maladroit CSE performance. Once the dust had settled fully,
however, there was wide agreement that major reforms were in order.
For a critical view that sets forth many areas of difficulty, see
Resumen 1, no. 6 (16 December 1973): 42-44.

105. The headline of Monday's El Nacional put it accurately if
modestly: "Venezuela voted in exemplary fashion despite all
obstacles."

CHAPTER IX

1. The authors found that by noon Monday the streets of
Caracas were filled with talk about the adeco victory; certainty
over Pérez's election seemed universal.

2. El Nacional, 11 December 1973, D-1.

3. CSE Bulletin No. 6, which appeared on the front page of all morning dailies Tuesday, 11 December.

4. CSE Bulletin No. 10, which appeared on the front page of all morning dailies Wednesday, 12 December.

5. El Universal, 13 December 1973, IV-1.

6. Ibid., I-1.

7. El Nacional, 13 December 1973, D-1.

8. Ibid., 14 December 1973, D-1 and D-5.

9. Ibid., D-1.

10. Among the guests was Lorenzo Fernández, making his first and only public appearance until his March departure for a recuperative trip to Europe. Edgar Sanabria had served briefly as provisional president in late 1958 upon Admiral Larrazábal's resignation to campaign for the constitutional presidency.

11. These figures, used as the official basis for the CSE proclamation of the president-elect, were an updated and corrected version of those earlier announced in CSE Bulletin No. 17 (see table 15), which had first been termed "final."

12. Although Gallegos had won 74.4 percent in December 1947, he had lost two Andean states--Mérida and Táchira--to COPEI and the thirty-one-year-old Rafael Caldera. For a discussion of the three 1945-48 elections and their outcomes, see Martz, Acción Democrática, pp. 66-69 and 73-77.

13. Ironically, this proportion of the vote was consistent with pre-electoral estimates by party técnicos; however, COPEI's scenario had never considered that an even higher proportion might go to the AD. Several interpretations of this electoral polarization are plausible. These and other aspects of the vote in 1973 will receive careful quantitative consideration in our second volume.

14. We are using the votes for Barrios and Prieto on their respective AD and MEP tarjetas, but excluding those they received from various small parties. This provides a more accurate reading on the nature of the 1968 partisanship; it also produces, of course, slightly different totals than recorded elsewhere in citing the Barrios and Prieto vote in 1968.

15. Most of the key figures were accessible for interviews with the authors: among those who shared their views were Carlos Andrés Pérez, Octavio Lepage, David Morales Bello, and Diago Arria for AD; Jésus Angel Paz Galarraga, and Luis B. Prieto for the Nueva Fuerza; and José Vicente Rangel for the MAS/MIR campaign. Lorenzo Fernández was unavailable to all interviewers after election day, until his March departure on a European trip; the willingness of other COPEI campaign leaders was minimal. We were able, however, to meet with President Caldera shortly before

completion of his term in office. Moreover, as cited in the
footnotes, there were extensive analyses published in many of the
leading Venezuelan news magazines.

16. Carlos E. Aguilera A., "COPEI: la derrota y el futuro,"
Bohemia 563 (7-13 January 1974): 20.

17. Ibid.

18. Ibid., p. 21.

19. Carlos E. Aguilera A., "COPEI se defiende," Bohemia 566
(28 January-3 February 1974): 25.

20. Ibid., p. 24.

21. Ibid., p. 25.

22. Perhaps no copeyano had labored more diligently, or with
greater dedication, than Rafael Salvatierra. A full-page photograph
accompanying the Bohemia interview, showing him with head in hands
in seeming dejection, provoked comment among political cognoscenti.
More a campaign technician than leader, Salvatierra was soon
relegated, at least temporarily, to minor party duties.

23. "Los 28 años de COPEI: Entrevista con Edecio la Riva,"
Resumen 10 (13 January 1974): 44-48.

24. Interview with Anselmo Reyes in El Nacional, 11 January
1974, D-14.

25. Interview with José Emilio Castellanos in ibid., 18
December 1973, D-1.

26. Jorge Olavarría, "Conversación con Luis Herrera Campins,"
Resumen 10 (13 January 1974): 56. Also see Herrera's statement in
William García Insausti, "Analizar primero...y después utilizar
las cuatro C: constancia, corazón, cooperación y coraje para
reconquistar el poder...," Bohemia 561 (24-30 December 1973): 22-25.

27. Jorge Olavarría, "Conversación con el Presidente del
Congreso Nacional...José Antonio Pérez Díaz," Resumen 10 (13 January
1974): 78.

28. Among lengthy newspaper and newsmagazine treatments, see
the reports in Bohemia (18-24 February 1974) and Resumen (24
February 1974). Martz was also shown a mimeographed summary of the
Aguilar report, although he was not permitted to retain a copy.
These sources provide the information for our account.

29. José Rodríguez Iturbe, et al., Polarización y bipartidismo
en las elecciones de 1973.

30. Ibid., p. 106.

31. El Nacional, 13 January 1974.

32. During the weeks of speculation preceding the naming of
the new cabinet, there were persistent reports that Morales Bello
was a prime contender for a major appointment. When he was not

named, opponents suggested that the outspoken lawyer and jurist had fallen into disfavor. However, there was no evidence to show that he was no longer trusted by Pérez. Moreover, his involvement in party matters held the potential of strengthening his 1978 presidential possibilities.

In the case of Lepage, there was at no point the slightest indication that he might leave the secretary general's post to join the administration. This, of course, left him in an excellent position concerning a possible presidential nomination five years hence. Only a year later did he become Pérez's minister of interior relations.

33. José María R. Vernal, "Octavio Lepage: el líder sereno," Bohemia 561 (24-30 December 1973): 18.

34. Ibid., p. 20.

35. "El país exige al próximo gobierno una acción imaginativa y audaz," interview with Octavio Lepage, Resumen 8 (30 December 1973): 16.

36. Vernal, "Octavio Lepage."

37. Ibid., p. 21.

38. Resumen 8 (30 December 1973): 17.

39. Edith Marín, "Un candidato para ganar," interview with David Morales Bello, Bohemia 568 (11-17 February 1974): 49.

40. He also singled out relatively unsung members of the machinery, notably including Roberto Agostini (tours and travel arrangements), David Coirán in the Executive Secretariat, and public opinion expert Héctor Silva. For a retrospective view from Silva, see El Nacional, 18 December 1973, D-12.

41. "AD: Iquierda Democrática, Conversación con David Morales Bello," Bohemia 567 (4-10 February 1974): 22.

42. Ibid., p. 23.

43. Ibid., p. 25.

44. Donata Andreutti, "Los perdedores analizan su derrota," Summa 80 (special number, 1974): 29.

45. Ibid., p. 30.

46. Demetrio Boersner, "El proceso electoral de 1973 y las perspectivas de la izquierda," in Alexis Márquez Rodríguez, ed., La izquierda venezolana y las elecciones del 73 (Caracas: Síntesis Dosmil, 1974), p. 167.

47. Ibid., p. 172.

48. Miguel Acosta Saignes, "Futuro de luchas en un país neocolonial," in ibid., pp. 239-94.

49. Before mid-1974, the PCV had yet again divided, with the García Ponce brothers and Eduardo Machado leading their followers out of what remained of the original party to create the Vanguardia

Comunista. This added yet another tier to the complicated array of leftist organizations which rendered so difficult any meaningful unity in the foreseeable future.

50. Andreutti, "Los perdedores," pp. 30-31.

51. Pompeyo Márquez, Socialismo en tiempo presente, p. 246.

52. Ibid., pp. 241-42.

53. Manuel Caballero, "1973--el fin del comienzo?" in La izquierda venezolana, pp. 79-121.

54. Américo Martín, "1973--victoria o derrota?" in ibid., pp. 123-62.

55. Guillermo Campos, "Wolfgang recomienda tomar el revés electoral como punto de referencia para emprender una política distinta," El Nacional, 15 December 1973, D-1.

56. Andreutti, "Los perdedores," p. 31.

57. Guillermo Campos, "Análisis de Burelli Rivas; El electo electorado produjo un presidente con mayoría y corrigió la proliferación de partidos políticos," El Nacional, 13 December 1973, D-17.

58. With Pérez's agreement, Burelli was soon appointed by the Caldera government as director and coordinator of the heavily attended international Conference of the Seas in Caracas. Upon its conclusion in August 1974, he was named Venezuelan ambassador to the United States.

59. Copeyano failure to face reality remained evident in the post-election exaltation of Lorenzo Fernández by his private secretary, Parada-Quintero, Diario de un jefe en campaña.

60. As noted earlier, Martz personally witnessed the calm with which Paz received news of Salvador Allende's overthrow, despite the obvious negative implications for his candidacy. Both Martz and Baloyra were with Paz as he received news of Eduardo Machado's damaging interview with 2001 concerning a PCV preference for Fernández over Pérez. Although members of the candidate's entourage on both occasions were both angered and depressed at the news, Paz was characteristically unflappable; that is not to say that he was not fully conscious of the potential impact for his candidacy.

CHAPTER X

1. Thorough discussion of our sample, as well as an evaluation of the validity and reliability of our measuring instrument, appears in our introduction to Vol. II.

2. The zero-order (Pearson) correlation coefficient between voting intention in 1973 and choice of the best campaign was 0.7225. This result is based on only 905 cases, excluding the "undecideds,"

"don't knows," and "would not say" for each question. Thus the exclusion of the more apathetic and nonpartisan voters does not produce a one-to-one correspondence between the two. Yet voting intention in 1973 and choice of the best campaign were conceptualized as "dependent variables" in our analytical model, and we do not anticipate the utilization of one to explain the other in our future inquiry.

On the other hand, tentative further exploration of the causes of choice of the best campaign suggests that party identification is the best predictor we could find; the Pearson (multiple) correlation was 0.69781, and the inclusion of three additional variables--sympthy for Pérez, identity of the candidate whom the respondent met during the campaign, and selection of the party that would govern the country best during the next five years-- brought the proportion of total explained variance to about 60 percent. This is merely to illustrate the soundness of our basic assumptions regarding the open-endedness of campaigning and campaign impact.

3. We are indebted to Dr. Andrew F. Templeton of DATOS, and to the clients for whom he conducted these surveys, for permission to present the findings here.

4. Anticipating the need to measure polarization, we asked our VENEVOTE respondents in October which party they would vote for if choosing the AD and COPEI. The pattern was as follows: COPEI, 38.1 percent; AD, 36.0 percent; neither, 18.4 percent; and refused to say, 2.8 percent. The difference between COPEI and AD cancels out with sampling error, but two additional facts are more interesting. First, polarization had increased to almost 75 percent in terms of our figures. Second, we found that concern about the economic situation of the country during the next five years was the most relevant source of polarization. This factor alone accounts for 60 percent of the variation of our measure of polarization.

5. The other data that are relevant at this point concern popular sympathies for the different parties. Below, we have annotated the main sympathy scores (and their standard deviations) for the main political parties. A maximum of 5 (for great sympathy) and a minimum of 1 (for no sympathy) were possible.

Parties	Means	Standard Deviations	N
AD	2.290	1.575	1,495
COPEI	2.522	1.593	1,500
FDP	1.416	0.902	1,484
MAS	1.700	1.190	1,481
MEP	1.480	0.984	1,489
PCV	1.311	0.801	1,481
CCN	1.532	1.078	1,489

The scores suggest that COPEI and MEP could not possibly have picked less popular parties as their coalition partners. Averaging the score of the two coalitions--a procedure that could be vulnerable to criticism and is solely intended for illustrative purposes here--we derive scores of 1.969 for COPEI-FDP and 1.396 for MEP-PCV. Comparison of the original party scores with the coalition scores clearly shows who won and who lost in each of these arrangements.

6. A set of VENEVOTE results is particularly relevant here. It involves the distribution of responses to the following question: "There is also much talk...that people are on the Right, the Center, or the Left. What is your position in Venezuelan politics, are you on the left, the center, or the right?"

left	20.5%	would not say	.2%
center	22.0	does not know	10.8
right	30.6		
nowhere	15.9%		

Surely, a leftist campaign could be waged, but would have entailed certain risks that had to be pondered very carefully during its planning stages, and confronted very forcefully during its execution.

7. Concerning economic system preference, respondents were asked "There is much talk today about economic systems. People speak of capitalism, socialism, and communism. Which of these economic systems do you like most?"

communism	28	1.8%	none	455	29.9%
socialism	615	40.4	would not say	17	1.1
capitalism	324	21.3	does not know	82	5.4

8. The previous passage on campaign impact during the final weeks of the contest illustrates the point vividly. Given the major commitments of DATOS to Venezuelan clients for November sampling of opinion, it was impossible to conduct our own survey later than we did. Of course, many of our concerns--notably those to be reported in Vol. II--were unrelated to such precision of timing.

9. To be presented in Vol. II.

BIBLIOGRAPHY

General Works

Alexander, Robert J. Latin American Political Parties. New York:
  Frederick A. Praeger, 1973.
Ames, Barry. "Bases of Support for Mexico's Dominant Party."
  American Political Science Review 64, no. 1 (March 1970): 153-
  67.
Antonio, W. V., and Richard Suter. "Elecciones preliminares en un
  municipio mexicano: nuevas tendencias en la lucha de México
  hacia la democracia." Revista Mexicana de Sociología 29,
  (January-March 1967): 93-108.
Ayres, Robert L. "Political History, Institutional Structure, and
  Prospects for Socialism in Chile." Comparative Politics 5, no.
  4 (July 1973): 497-523.
Blanksten, George I. "The Politics of Latin America." In Gabriel
  Almond and James S. Coleman, eds., The Politics of the
  Developing Areas. Princeton: Princeton University Press, 1960.
Bryce, James. The American Commonwealth. Toronto: Copp Clark,
  1893.
Campos, Judith Talbot, and John F. McCamant. Cleavage Shift in
  Colombia. Beverly Hills: Sage Publications, 1972.
Cornelius, Wayne A., Jr. "Urbanization as an Agent of Latin
  American Political Instability." American Political Science
  Review 63, no. 3 (September 1969): 833-58.
Davis, Harold E. Latin American Thought: A Historical Introduction.
  Baton Rouge: Louisiana State University Press, 1972.
Dennis, Jack. "Support for the Institution of Elections by the
  Mass Public." American Political Science Review 64, no. 3
  (September 1970): 819-35.
Dunn, Delmer D. Financing Presidential Campaigns. Washington:
  The Brookings Institution, 1972.
Duverger, Maurice. Political Parties; Their Organization and
  Activity in the Modern State. Translated by Barbara and Robert
  North. New York: Wiley, 1963.

English, Burt H. Liberación Nacional in Costa Rica: The Development of a Political Party in a Traditional Society. Gainesville: University of Florida Press, 1971.

Fitzgibbon, Russell H. "The Party Potpourri in Latin America." Western Political Quarterly 10, no. 1 (March 1957): 3-22.

Francis, Michael J. The Allende Victory: An Analysis of the 1970 Chilean Presidential Election. Tucson: University of Arizona Press, 1973.

Furlong, William L. "Peruvian and Northern Mexican Municipalities: A Comparative Analysis of Two Political Subsystems." Comparative Political Studies 5, no. 1 (April 1972): 59-83.

Gil, Federico G. The Political System of Chile. Boston: Houghton-Mifflin, 1966.

_____, and Charles J. Parrish. The Chilean Presidential Election of September 4, 1964: An Analysis. Washington: Institute for the Comparative Study of Political Systems, 1965.

Gott, Richard. Guerrilla Movements in Latin America. Garden City: Doubleday, 1970.

Hansen, Roger D. The Politics of Mexican Development. Baltimore: Johns Hopkins University Press, 1971.

Heard, George Alexander. The Costs of Democracy. Chapel Hill: University of North Carolina Press, 1960.

Hilliker, Grant. The Politics of Reform in Peru: The Aprista and Other Mass Parties of Latin America. Baltimore: Johns Hopkins Press, 1971.

Horowitz, Irving Louis. "Electoral Politics, Urbanization, and Social Development in Latin America." In Glenn H. Beyer, ed., The Urban Explosion in Latin America: A Continent in Process of Modernization. Ithaca: Cornell University Press, 1967.

Johnson, Kenneth F. The Guatemalan Election of March 6, 1966. Washington: Institute for the Comparative Study of Political Systems, 1967.

_____. Mexican Democracy: A Critical View. Boston: Allyn and Bacon, 1971.

Jorrín, Miguel, and John D. Martz. Latin American Political Thought and Ideology. Chapel Hill: University of North Carolina Press, 1970.

Kantor, Harry. The Costa Rican Election of 1953: A Case Study. Latin American Monographs No. 5. Gainesville: University of Florida Press, 1958.

_____. The Ideology and Program of the Peruvian Aprista Movement. Berkeley: University of California Press, 1953.

Kaufman, Clifford. "Urbanization, Material Satisfaction, and Mass Political Involvement: The Poor in Mexico City." Comparative Political Studies 4, no. 3 (October 1971): 295-321.

Key, V. O. "Secular Realignment and the Party System." Journal of Politics 21, no. 2 (May 1959): 198-210.

_____. "A Theory of Critical Elections." Journal of Politics 17, no. 1 (February 1955): 3-18.

LaPalombara, Joseph, and Myron Weiner, eds. Political Parties and Political Development. Princeton: Princeton University Press, 1966.

Lipset, Seymour Martin, and Stein Rokkan, eds. Party Systems and
     Voter Alignments: Cross National Perspectives. New York: Free
     Press, 1967.
Martz, John D. "Costa Rican Electoral Trends, 1953-1966." Western
     Political Quarterly 20, no. 4 (December 1967): 88-99.
     _____. "Democratic Political Campaigning in Latin America:
     A Typological Approach to Cross-Cultural Research." Journal of
     Politics 33, no. 2 (May 1971): 370-99.
     _____. "Dilemmas in the Study of Latin American Political
     Parties." Journal of Politics 26, no. 3 (August 1964): 509-32.
     _____. "Political Science and Latin American Studies:
     Discipline in Search of a Region." Latin American Research
     Review 6, no. 1 (Spring 1971): 73-99.
McDonald, Ronald H. "Apportionment and Party Politics in Santiago,
     Chile." Midwest Journal of Political Science 13, no. 3 (August
     1969): 455-71.
     _____. Party Systems and Elections in Latin America. Chicago:
     Markham, 1971.
Mill, John Stuart. Considerations on Representative Government.
     New York: Harper, 1862.
Milnor, Andrew J. Elections and Political Stability. Boston:
     Little, Brown, 1969.
Neumann, Sigmund, ed. Modern Political Parties. Chicago:
     University of Chicago Press, 1956.
O'Donnell, Guillermo. Modernization and Bureaucratic
     Authoritarianism: Studies in South American Politics. Berkeley:
     Institute of International Studies, 1973.
Portes, Alejandro. "Leftist Radicalism in Chile: A Test of Three
     Hypotheses." Comparative Politics 20, no. 2 (June 1970): 251-
     75.
Powell, Sandra. "Political Change in the Chilean Electorate, 1952-
     1964." Western Political Quarterly 23, no. 2 (June 1970): 374-
     84.
     _____. "Political Participation in the Barriadas."
     Comparative Political Studies 2, no. 2 (July 1969): 195-216.
Prothro, James W., and Patricio Chaparro. "Public Opinion and the
     Movement of Chilean Government to the Left, 1952-1972." Journal
     of Politics 36, no. 1 (February 1974): 2-44.
Rae, Douglas W. The Political Consequences of Electoral Laws. Rev.
     ed. New Haven: Yale University Press, 1971.
Rose, Richard, ed. Electoral Behavior. New York: Free Press,
     1974.
     _____. Influencing Voters: A Study of Campaign Rationality.
     London: Faber and Faber, 1967.
Ross, Stanley, ed. Latin America in Transition: Problems in
     Training and Research. Albany: State University of New York
     Press, 1970.
Sartori, Giovanni. "European Political Parties: The Case of
     Polarized Pluralism." Political Parties and Political
     Development, edited by LaPalombara and Weiner. Princeton:
     Princeton University Press, 1966.

Scott, Robert E. Mexican Government in Transition. Urbana:
  University of Illinois Press, 1959.
Schmitt, Karl. "Congressional Campaigning in Mexico." Journal of
  Inter-American Studies 11, no. 1 (January 1969): 93-111.
Schwartzenberg, Roger-Gérard. La campagne presidentielle de 1965.
  Paris: Presses Universitaires de France, 1967.
Sinding, Steven H. "The Evolution of Chilean Voting Patterns: A
  Reexamination of Some Old Assumptions." Journal of Politics 34,
  no. 3 (August 1972): 774-97.
Soares, Glaucio, and Robert L. Hamblin. "Socio-Economic Variables
  Voting for the Radical Left: Chile 1952." American Political
  Science Review 61, no. 4 (December 1967): 1053-66.
Taylor, Philip B., Jr. Government and Politics in Uruguay. New
  Orleans: Tulane Studies in Political Change, 1960.
Valenzuela, Arturo. "The Scope of the Chilean Party System."
  Comparative Politics 4, no. 1 (March 1972): 179-99.
von Sauer, Franz A. The Alienated "Loyal" Opposition: Mexico's
  Partido Acción Nacional. Albuquerque: University of New Mexico
  Press, 1974.
Wagley, Charles, ed. Social Science Research on Latin America.
  New York: Columbia University Press, 1964.
Williams, Edward J. Latin American Christian Democratic Parties.
  Knoxville: University of Tennessee Press, 1967.
Yochelson, John. "What Price Political Stability? The 1966
  Presidential Campaign in Costa Rica." Public and International
  Affairs 5, no. 1 (Spring 1967): 270-307.

CONCERNING VENEZUELA

Acción Democrática. Acción de gobierno. Caracas: n.p., 1973.
_____. Acción Democrática: Doctrina y programa. Caracas:
  Editorial Antonio Pinto Salinas, 1962.
_____. La batalla por el nombre y símbolos de Acción
  Democrática. Caracas: Publicaciones de la Secretaría Nacional
  de Propaganda, 1963.
_____. Comité Ejecutivo Nacional, Secretaría de Organización.
  Operación Mosca; Instructivo para representantes de Acción
  Democrática ante las mesas electorales 1973. Caracas: Acción
  Democrática, 1973.
Acedo de Sucre, María de Lourdes, and Carmen Margarita Nones
  Mendoza. La generación venezolana de 1928: Estudio de una élite
  política. Caracas: Ediciones Ariel, 1967.
Albornoz, Orlando. Desarrollo político en Venezuela. Caracas:
  Universidad Central de Venezuela, Consejo de Desarrollo
  Científico y Humanístico, 1974.
Alexander, Robert J. The Communist Party of Venezuela. Stanford:
  Hoover Institution Press, 1969.
_____. The Venezuelan Democratic Revolution: A Profile of
  the Regime of Rómulo Betancourt. New Brunswick, N.J.: Rutgers
  University Press, 1964.

Ameringer, Charles D. The Democratic Left in Exile: The
Antidictatorial Struggle in the Caribbean, 1945-1959. Coral
Gables, Fla.: University of Miami Press, 1974.
Arnove, Robert F. Student Alienation: A Venezuelan Study. New
York: Praeger, 1971.
Barbeito, José. Introducción al pensamiento socialcristiano.
Caracas: COPEI Secretaría de Formación Política, 1965.
Barrios, Gonzalo. Los días y la política. Caracas: Editorial A
Arte, 1963.
Betancourt, Rómulo. Hacia América Latina democrática e integrada.
2nd ed. Caracas: Editorial Senderos, 1967.
_____. Posición y doctrina. Caracas: Editorial Cordillera,
1959.
_____. Venezuela, política y petróleo. 2nd ed. Caracas:
Editorial Senderos, 1967.
Blank, David Eugene. Politics in Venezuela. Boston: Little,
Brown, 1973.
Bonilla, Frank. The Failure of Elites. Cambridge: MIT Press,
1970.
_____, and José A. Silva Michelena, eds. A Strategy for
Research on Social Policy. Cambridge: MIT Press, 1967.
Bonomo, Santiago Alejandro. Sociología electoral en Venezuela:
Un estudio sobre Caracas. Buenos Aires: Editorial Paidos, 1973.
Borregales, Germán. Copei, hoy, una negación. Caracas: Ediciones
Garrido, 1968.
Bunimov-Parra, Boris. Introducción a la sociología electoral
venezolana. Caracas: Editorial Arte, 1968.
Burggraaff, Winfield J. The Venezuelan Armed Forces in Politics,
1935-1959. Columbia: University of Missouri Press, 1972.
Caldera, Rafael. El bloque latinoamericano. Santiago: Editorial
del Pacífico, 1961.
_____. Especificidad de la democracia cristiana. Barcelona:
Editorial Nova Terra, 1973.
_____. Justicia social internacional y nacionalismo
latinoamericano. Madrid: Seminarios y Ediciones, A.S., 1973.
_____. La idea de justicia social internacional. Caracas:
Editorial Sucre, 1962.
_____. Moldes para la fragua. Buenos Aires: Librería "El
Ateneo" Editorial, 1962.
Cannon, Mark W., R. Scott Fosler, and Robert Witherspoon. Urban
Government for Valencia, Venezuela. New York: Praeger, 1973.
Cárdenas, Rodolfo José. El combate político; Sólo para líderes
nuevos. Caracas: Editorial Doña Barbara, 1966.
Carpio Castillo, Rubén. Acción Democrática, 1941-1971: Bosquejo
histórico de un partido. Caracas: Ediciones República, 1971.
Claudio, Iván. Breve historia de URD. Caracas: n.p., 1968.
Conferencia Episcopal Venezolana. Iglesia y política. Caracas:
Ediciones spev, 1973.
Consejo Supremo Electoral. Cómputos definitivos especificados por
circunscripciones electorales. 8 vols. Caracas: Consejo
Supremo Electoral, 1968.

_____. Instrucciones para las mesas electorales. Caracas: Consejo Supremo Electoral, 1968.

_____. Resultado final del registro electoral. Mimeographed. Caracas, 1968.

COPEI [Partido Social Cristiano COPEI]. Diagnóstico económico de Venezuela. Caracas: Partido Social Cristiano COPEI, 1968.

_____. Directrices para una acción de gobierno. Caracas: n.p., 1973.

_____. El debate Caldera-Uslar Pietri. Caracas: n.p., 1963.

_____. El pueblo unido. Caracas: n.p., 1973.

_____. Programa de gobierno, 1969-1974. Caracas: COPEI, 1968.

Díaz Rangel, Eleazar. Cómo se dividió el P.C.V. Caracas: Editorial Domingo Fuentes, 1971.

Escovar Salom, Ramón. Evolución política de Venezuela. Caracas: Monte Avila Editores, 1972.

Fedecámaras. Diálogo con los candidatos a la presidencia de la república. Caracas: Fedecámaras, 1973.

Feo Calcaño, Guillermo. Democracia vs. dictadura. Caracas: n.p., 1963.

Fernández, Lorenzo. Programa de gobierno. Caracas: n.p., 1973.

Franco Quijano, Juan Francisco. Sistemática electoral. Caracas: n.p., 1968.

Fuenmayor, Juan Bautista. 1928-1948: Veinte años de política. Madrid: Editorial Mediterráneo, 1968.

Gallegos Ortiz, Rafael. La historia política de Venezuela: De Cipriano Castro a Pérez Jiménez. Caracas: Imprenta Universitaria, 1960.

Gilmore, Robert L. Caudillism and Militarism in Venezuela, 1810-1910. Athens: Ohio University Press, 1964.

Harding, Timothy F., and Saul Landau. "Terrorism, Guerrilla Warfare and the Democratic Left in Venezuela." Studies on the Left 4, no. 4 (Fall 1964): 118-28.

Herrera Oropeza, José. América Latina: Proceso hacia el socialismo. 2nd ed. Caracas: Fondo Editorial Salvador de la Plaza, 1973.

Jackson, D. Bruce. Castro, the Kremlin, and Communism in Latin America. Baltimore: Johns Hopkins University Press, 1969.

Kolb, Glen L. Democracy and Dictatorship in Venezuela, 1945-1958. New London: Connecticut College, 1974.

La Riva Araujo, Edecio. Los fusiles de la paz. Caracas: Tipografía Remar, 1968.

Larrazábal, Radamés. Socialismo bobo o socialismo para Venezuela. Caracas: Editorial Cantaclaro, 1970.

Los 10,000 máquinas de votar y el escándolo de las comisiones. Caracas: Ediciones Centauro, 1973.

Levine, Daniel H. Conflict and Political Change in Venezuela. Princeton: Princeton University Press, 1973.

Lieuwen, Edwin. Petroleum in Venezuela: A History. Berkeley: University of California Press, 1954. 2nd ed. New York: Russell and Russell, 1964.

_____. Venezuela. London: Oxford University Press, 1961.
Lindenbert, Klaus. "Zur Krise der revolutionären Linken in
Lateinamerika: Das Beispiel Venezuela." Viertel Jahres
Berichte 33 (September 1968): 281-309.
Liscano, Juan. "Aspectos de la vida social y política de Venezuela."
150 años de vida republicana (1811-1961). Caracas: Ediciones
de la Presidencia de la República, 1963.
Lott, Leo B. "The 1952 Venezuela Elections: A Lesson for 1957."
Western Political Quarterly 10, no. 3 (September 1957): 451-58.
_____. Venezuela and Paraguay: Political Modernity and
Tradition in Conflict. New York: Holt, Rinehart and Winston,
1972.
Luna, Juan. Voto nulo: Una línea electoral revolucionaria.
Caracas: Editorial Proceso, 1973.
Luzardo, Rodolfo. Notas histórico-económicas 1928-1963. Caracas:
Editorial Sucre, 1963.
Magallanes, Manuel Vicente. 4 partidos nacionales. Caracas:
DIANA, 1973.
_____. Los partidos políticos en la evolución histórica
venezolana. Caracas: Editorial Mediterráneo, 1973.
_____. Partidos políticos venezolanos (ensayos). Caracas:
Tipografía Vargas, 1960.
Márquez, Pompeyo. Socialismo en tiempo presente. Caracas:
Ediciones Centauro, 1973.
Márquez Rodríguez, Alexis, ed. La izquierda venezolana y las
elecciones del 73 (un análisis político y polémico). Caracas:
Síntesis Dosmil, 1974.
Martz, John D. Acción Democrática: Evolution of a Modern Political
Party in Venezuela. Princeton: Princeton University Press,
1966.
_____. "Venezuela's Generation of '28': The Genesis of
Political Democracy." Journal of Inter-American Studies 6, no.
1 (January 1964): 17-33.
_____, and Peter B. Harkins. "Urban Electoral Behavior in
Latin America: The Case of Metropolitan Caracas, 1958-1968."
Comparative Politics 5, no. 3 (July 1973): 523-49.
Medina Angarita, Isaías. Cuatro años de democracia. Caracas:
Pensamiento Vivo, C.A., 1963.
Movimiento al Socialismo. Programa del MAS. Caracas: n.p., 1973.
Movimiento Electoral del Pueblo. Tesis política del MEP:
Liberación nacional y democracia socialista. Multilith.
Caracas, 1970.
Muñoz, Freddy. Revolución sin dogma. 2nd ed. Caracas: Ediciones
Alcino, S.A., 1971.
Myers, David J. Democratic Campaigning in Venezuela: Caldera's
Victory. Caracas: Fundación La Salle, 1973.
Njaim, Humberto, et al. El sistema político venezolano. Caracas:
UCV, 1975.
Nueva Fuerza. Programa de gobierno: Frente nacionalista popular.
Caracas: Editora El Nacional, 1972.
Ojeda, Fabricio. Hacia el poder revolucionario. Havana: Guairas,
1967.

Ortega Díaz, Pedro, and Antonio García Ponce. <u>Sobre las tesis</u>
<u>antisoviéticas</u> y <u>antiproletarias del camarada</u> Teodoro <u>Petckoff.</u>
Caracas: Ediciones Cantaclaro, 1970.
Parada-Quintero, Carlos. <u>Diario de un jefe en campaña.</u> Caracas:
Tipografía Principios, 1974.
Peattie, Lisa Redfield. <u>The View from the Barrio.</u> Ann Arbor:
University of Michigan Press, 1968.
<u>Pensamiento comunitario.</u> Caracas: Ediciones CIESLA, 1973.
Pérez, Carlos Andrés. <u>Acción Democrática en la oposición</u>
<u>(reflexiones para dirigentes y militantes).</u> Caracas: n.p.,
1969.
_____. <u>Mensaje como candidato de Acción Democrática a la</u>
<u>presidencia de la República.</u> Caracas: Ediciones del Comité
Ejecutivo Nacional de Acción Democrática, 1972.
_____. <u>Mensaje de Carlos Andrés.</u> Caracas: n.p., 1973.
Pérez Alfonzo, Juan Pablo. <u>Petróleo: Jugo de la tierra.</u> Caracas:
Ediciones del Arte, 1961.
_____. <u>Petróleo y dependencia.</u> Caracas: Síntesis Dosmil,
1971.
_____. <u>Política petrolera.</u> Caracas: Imprenta Nacional, 1962.
_____. <u>Venezuela y su petróleo: Lineamientos de una política.</u>
Caracas: Imprenta Nacional, 1960.
Pérez Jiménez, Marcos. <u>Decálogo de la vergüenza.</u> Caracas: n.p.,
1973.
Petkoff, Teodoro. <u>Checoeslovaquia: El socialismo como problema.</u>
Caracas: Editorial Fuentes, 1969.
_____. <u>Razón y pasión del socialismo (el tema socialista en</u>
<u>Venezuela).</u> Caracas: Ediciones Centaura, 1973.
_____. <u>¿Socialismo para Venezuela?</u> 3rd ed. Caracas:
Editorial Fuentes, 1972.
Powell, John Duncan. <u>Political Mobilization of the Venezuelan</u>
<u>Peasant.</u> Cambridge, Mass.: Harvard University Press, 1971.
Prieto Figueroa, Luis Beltrán. <u>De una educación de castas a una</u>
<u>educación de masas.</u> Havana: Editorial Lex, 1951.
_____. <u>La política y los hombres.</u> Caracas: Grafarte C.A.,
1968.
_____. <u>Sufragio y democracia.</u> Caracas: Ediciones del
Congreso de la República, 1971.
Rangel, Domingo Alberto. <u>Los andinos en el poder.</u> Mérida:
Talleres Gráficos Universitarios, 1966.
_____. <u>Los mercaderes del voto: Estudio de un sistema.</u>
Valencia: Vadell Hermanos, 1973.
_____. <u>La oligarquía del dinero.</u> 3rd ed. Caracas: Editorial
Fuentes, 1972.
Rangel, José Vicente. <u>Expediente negro.</u> 3rd. ed. Caracas:
Editorial Fuentes, 1972.
_____. <u>Tiempo de verdades.</u> Caracas: Ediciones Centauro, 1973.
Ray, Talton F. <u>The Politics of the Barrios of Venezuela.</u> Berkeley
and Los Angeles: University of California Press, 1969.
República de Venezuela. <u>Compilación legislativa de Venezuela, 1946.</u>
Caracas: Imprenta Nacional, 1947.

_____. Estatuto para la elección de representantes a la
Asamblea Nacional Constituyente y garantías ciudadanas, acordadas
por el Gobierno Revolucionario. Caracas: Imprenta Nacional,
1946.
_____. Ley orgánica del sufragio (Gaceta oficial no. 1435).
Caracas: Distribuidora Paz Pérez C.A., 1973.
_____. Congreso de la República. Ley de reforma parcial de
la ley orgánica del sufragio: Ley orgánica del sufragio.
Caracas: Imprenta Nacional, 1973.
_____. Ministerio de Defensa. La agresión a Mansalva.
Caracas: n.p., 1963.
Rivas Rivas, José, ed. Las tres divisiones de Acción Democrática.
Caracas: Pensamiento Vivo C.A., 1968.
Rivera Oviedo, José Elías. Los social cristianos en Venezuela.
Caracas: Impresos Hermar, 1970.
Rodríguez Iturbe, José; Carmen G. de Cuahonte; Gustavo Tarre
Briceño; and Adolfo Melchert F. Polarización y bipartidismo en
las elecciones de 1973. Caracas: Editorial Arte, 1974.
Rojas, Juan Bautista. Los adecos (sus contrarios, renegados y
conversos). Caracas: Editorial Fuentes, 1973.
Romero Martínez, Vinicio. Lo bueno y lo malo durante el gobierno
de Caldera. Caracas: n.p., 1974.
Rourke, Thomas. Gómez: Tyrant of the Andes. New York: Morrow,
1941.
Ruiz Pineda, Leonardo. Leonardo Ruiz Pineda: Guerrillero de la
libertad. Caracas: Ediciones Centauro, 1973.
_____. Venezuela bajo el signo del terror, el libro negro de
la dictadura. Santiago: Publicaciones Valmore Rodríguez,
Talleres Gráficos Astudillo, 1953.
_____. Ventanas al mundo. Caracas: Editorial Arte, 1961.
Silva Michelena, José A. The Illusion of Democracy in Dependent
Nations. Cambridge, Mass.: MIT Press, 1971.
Suárez Figueroa, Naudy, ed. Por los legítimos ideales del
estudiante venezolano. Caracas: Ediciones Nueva Política, 1973.
Taylor, Philip B., Jr. The Venezuelan Golpe de Estado of 1958:
The Fall of Marcos Pérez Jiménez. Washington: Institute for
the Comparative Study of Political Systems, 1968.
Tinoco, Pedro. El estado eficaz. Caracas: Italgráfica, 1973.
Torres Molina, Bhilla. Alirio. Caracas: CROMOTIP, 1968.
Troconis Guerrero, Luis. La cuestión agraria en la historia
nacional. Caracas: Editorial Arte, 1962.
Tugwell, Franklin. The Politics of Oil in Venezuela. Stanford:
Stanford University Press, 1975.
Unión Republicana Democrática. Levántate pueblo: Jóvito
presidente. Caracas: Publicaciones de la Dirección Nacional
de la Juventud Urredista, 1973.

NEWSPAPERS

Crítica (Maracaibo)
El Mundo (Caracas)

El Nacional (Caracas)
El Universal (Caracas)
Panorama (Maracaibo)
2001 (Caracas)
Ultimas Noticias (Caracas)

MAGAZINES AND PERIODICALS

Al Margen (Caracas)
Bohemia (Caracas)
Elite (Caracas)
Momento (Caracas)
Nueva Política (Caracas)
Pueblo Unido (Caracas)
Punta (Caracas)
Resumen (Caracas)
Semana (Caracas)
SIC (Caracas)
Summa (Caracas)
Visión (México, D.F.)

INDEX